Under the Fifth Sun

A California Legacy Book

Santa Clara University and Heyday Books are pleased to publish the California Legacy series, vibrant and relevant writings drawn from California's past and present.

Santa Clara University—founded in 1851 on the site of the eighth of California's original 21 missions—is the oldest institution of higher learning in the state. A Jesuit institution, it is particularly aware of its contribution to California's cultural heritage and its responsibility to preserve and celebrate that heritage.

Heyday Books, founded in 1974, specializes in critically acclaimed books on California literature, history, natural history, and ethnic studies.

Books in the California Legacy series appear as anthologies, single author collections, reprints of important books, and original works. Taken together, these volumes bring readers a new perspective on California's cultural life, a perspective that honors diversity and finds great pleasure in the eloquence of human expression.

SERIES EDITOR: Terry Beers
PUBLISHER: Malcolm Margolin
ADVISORY COMMITTEE: Stephen Becker, William Deverell, Charles Faulhaber, David Fine, Steven Gilbar, Dana Gioia, Ron Hansen, Gerald Haslam, Robert Hass, Jack Hicks, Timothy Hodson, James Houston, Jeanne Wakatsuki Houston, Maxine Hong Kingston, Frank LaPena, Ursula K. Le Guin, Jeff Lustig, Tillie Olsen, Ishmael Reed, Alan Rosenus, Robert Senkewicz, Gary Snyder, Kevin Starr, Richard Walker, Alice Waters, Jennifer Watts, Al Young.

Thanks to the English Department at Santa Clara University and to Regis McKenna for their support of the California Legacy series.

UNDER THE FIFTH SUN

LATINO LITERATURE FROM CALIFORNIA

EDITED BY RICK HEIDE

FOREWORD BY JUAN VELASCO

Santa Clara University, Santa Clara, California • *Heyday Books, Berkeley, California*

**NATIONAL
ENDOWMENT
FOR THE ARTS**

This project is supported in part by an award from the National Endowment for the Arts and from The James Irvine Foundation.

Library of Congress Cataloging-in-Publication Data

Under the fifth sun : Latino literature from California / edited by Rick Heide ; introduction by Juan Velasco.
    p. cm. — (A California legacy book)
Includes index.
  ISBN 1-890771-59-7 (alk. paper)
  1. American literature—California. 2. American literature—Hispanic American authors. 3. Hispanic Americans—Literary collections. 4. California—Literary collections. I. Title: Under the 5th sun. II. Heide, Rick, 1943– III. Series.
  PS571.C2 U545 2002
  810.8'08680794—dc21

                      2002014979

Cover Art: Sal Garcia, "California Muse," collage, 7.5" x 9.75" (2002)
Cover/Interior Design: Rebecca LeGates
Printing and Binding: Banta Book Group, Eden Prairie, MN

Orders, inquiries, and correspondence should be addressed to:
    Heyday Books
    P. O. Box 9145, Berkeley, CA 94709
    (510) 549-3564, Fax (510) 549-1889
    www.heydaybooks.com

Printed in the United States of America

10 9 8 7 6 5 4 3 2 1

For *mi familia.* To my beautiful Debbie, *el amor de mi vida,*
without whose sacrifices and support this "labor of love"
would not have been possible, and to our *hijas maravillosas:*
Cedra, Rachel, and Heather.

Contents

POP CULTURE

IDENTITY

WORKING

POLITICS

VIOLENCE

COMMUNITY

LOVE & FAMILY

My Road to the Fifth Sun

JUAN VELASCO

As I REMEMBER IT NOW, the road to the Fifth Sun, my road, started fifteen years ago. That's when I arrived in Los Angeles from my native Spain, infused with images of California from Raymond Chandler's novels, scenes from Hollywood, and of course, my new—burning—interest, Latino literature.

What was it exactly—whose novel or poetry or essay—that drew me across the ocean to this new continent to learn a new language and start a new life? A few names I knew: Luis Valdez, Pat Mora, Gary Soto...In the work of these writers I found a tradition of intermixing, of cultural hybridity that goes back to the birth of Spanish culture and the Spanish language itself, a language of colonization derived from the conquest by Rome of the Iberian peninsula two thousand years ago. In that conquest—never completed, still in flux—Celtic, Iberian, and Basque peoples were overrun by a new order. Moors, Jews, Rom (Gypsies), and other unassimilated groups would later add to the multicultural nature of Spanish society, sometimes fighting, sometimes co-existing peacefully. Journeying to the New World, the Spanish intermixed with Aztecs, Mayas, Incas, Arawaks, and others. These centuries of experience produced tragedy, beauty, and insight. As cultures collided and interacted, people used the power of storytelling, the power of myth, to understand each other better, to bridge, to criticize, to daydream, and to excoriate. Who, then, is better equipped to deal with America, with California and its themes of conquest, cultural domination, and multicultural coexistence, than those who come from Spanish-speaking worlds?

California's very name originated in the imagination of a storyteller: in *Las sergas de Esplandián,* a popular Spanish novel published in the early 1500s, Garcí Rodríguez Ordoñez de Montalvo describes a terrestrial paradise inhabited by black Amazons, an island ruled by a certain

Calafia, queen of "California." Early tales of California, whether told by the Spanish or Native Americans, Latinos or Euro-Americans, dwelled also in the mythic realm. In the 1880s, for example, the philosopher Josiah Royce imagined California not just as a political or economic or geographic entity but as a sort of island, a community of expectation, a "community of hope." And today's writers—the scientists of myth-making—continue to diagram the hopes, the dreams, and the nightmares of California's people. Reading *Under the Fifth Sun,* you may gain an understanding of the sometimes surprising roads that myths take, the ways cultures move from one place to another, the ways in which the past illuminates our everyday understanding of the future.

As anthologies of Latino literature proliferate, Latinos and non-Latinos alike can appreciate the breadth and history of a literary tradition once limited to a few specialists; but the unique significance of this particular anthology is that it illuminates the way the tradition has evolved here on the West Coast, presenting California Latino literature as a complex net of diverse experience created over time by history and culture.

Luis Leal, one of the founders of Latino literary criticism, has concluded that the history of Chicano literature should include "everything written before 1848 (published and in manuscript form), as it rightfully forms part of the Chicano cultural inheritance."* While offering a rich array of works by such legends of Chicano literature as alurista, Luis Valdez, and Cherríe L. Moraga, *Under the Fifth Sun* also includes selections that recall the very early Spanish and Latin American presence in California that Leal refers to. But Chicano literature is only *la punta del iceberg.* The fullness of range of Latino literature is one of the best-kept secrets in the United States; Salvadorans, Chileans, Guatemalans, Cubans, Puerto Ricans, Mexicans, and others are building on the earlier Hispanic tradition to create a literary culture that can stand alongside any European or Latin American literary achievement.

The wave of Latina writers of the 1980s is represented here, and so are the works of new young writers like Michele Serros and María Amparo Escandón—women's writings that intend, as literary critic María Herrera-Sobek describes it, "to formulate, to conceptualize, to

---

*Luis Leal, *Chicano Literary History: Origin and Development* (Julian Samora Research Institute, Michigan State University, June 1896).

freeze in a moment of poetic intensity a new vision, a new perspective."* And carefully chosen texts by Carlos Fuentes, Pablo Neruda, and Octavio Paz provide us with a wonderful view of Latin American interactions with California. In all, more than a hundred writers appear here, each using language in a uniquely evocative way. The cumulative effect is powerful: a wealth of art, a diversity of voices, an explosion of truth and myth.

The myths of California have evolved—from Calafia to the gold rush to the Silicon Valley's version of the American dream—but their evocative power hasn't changed. "California is an archetype of Royce's great community of hope," my friend Wills said to me years ago with an ambiguous wink. (From this retired Spanish professor who lived here all his life, I learned a lot about this new place).

Richard Rodriguez, another Californian, paraphrases Royce, asserting that maybe "some epic opportunity had been given California—the chance to reconcile the culture of the Catholic south and the Protestant north. California had the chance to heal the sixteenth-century tear of Europe." But Rodriguez adds, "The opportunity was lost. The Catholic—the Mexican—impulse was pushed back."†

I remember going to East Los Angeles for the first time and finding Mexico and Latin America there. I discovered a city divided by an east-west line, a postmodern city with a hidden past: East Los Angeles, the home of Latino culture, has always been a reminder of the past; the west side, full of optimistic enterprise as capital moves through the veins of the entertainment industry, provides California with the alluring dream of endless expansion into the future. As distant as these lifestyles seem—two conceptions of history moving away from each other in opposite directions—both the past and the future of California converge as the language of myths reemerges.

As California convokes Latino culture in its many forms (Salvadoran, Chicano, Argentinian, Guatemalan, Mexican, Spanish, and Zapotec, to name a few), I think of another myth: the Fifth Sun. According to diverse indigenous American traditions, the world has been

---

*María Herrera-Sobek, ed., *Beyond Stereotypes: The Critical Analysis of Chicana Literature* (New York: Bilingual Press, 1985).

†Richard Rodriguez, *Days of Obligation: An Argument with my Mexican Father* (New York; Viking, 1992).

destroyed and recreated several times. We live in a new era—the era of the Fifth Sun. This sun's emergence coincides with arrival at the promised land, a balance between day and night, a union between heaven and earth. Resurrected by the activists and intellectuals of the 1960s, the concept of the Fifth Sun embraces the rebirth of the conquered people, a new era of peace and social justice, a gathering of cultures in search of a better future in modern-day America. Latinos have not, as Rodriguez feared, been pushed back; they are more vital than ever to the cultural and economic life of California, and every year increasingly so.

And as California brings together Latino writing from all over the world, I realize now that it was the intermixing and reemergence of these traditions that attracted me to this place. No one ever mentioned this to me about the pursuit of academic achievements: the seeds of change take root first in our minds, then in our hearts. My first glimpse of California was through books, but California and its literature have transformed my life; I have learned to filter reality through the history of California and its Latino literature. Looking back, I realize that I have also become more American; my interest in Latino literature has opened my eyes to the cultures of California and the United States as a whole. And in California, in the United States, I have also rediscovered Spain and Latin America. A nomad in search of a dream, I have tried to find a sense of peace—who I am—journeying from Spain to Mexico and California. Oddly enough, my journey resembles the many pasts and vistas of California's history, its diversity of traditions, the hope that brought so many people together in pursuit of a dream of prosperity.

In California, writers have discovered a place of their own. *Under the Fifth Sun* assembles the many stories created by the writers of this "island," the many roads that myths take, the many ways cultures interact and travel, create fruitful unions or cause irremediable damage to each other. Not only a rich literary heritage, but our past, the truth of who we are, awaits us quietly in our common Californian history. I hope that this book will offer to Latino and non-Latino readers (to all of us) the possibility of a *reencuentro,* a re-encounter with our rich history, a real understanding of who we are and who we aspire to be, a vision of the interconnectedness of our past and our new possibilities.

"California breathes at the crossroads of Europe, Latin America, Asia, Native American culture, and all the other cultures of the United States," my friend Wills said to me years ago. I tried to imagine what he meant then. I think now of the Fifth Sun, of the use of myths to envision a space where, perhaps, multiple cultures will come together, a place of mutual learning, of social justice and change. Maybe Wills was right. This could be the place, after all. Perhaps even, finally, a home. (Coming to California may be the only significant attempt I have made to connect to a place in my entire adult life.) It is a very special home, a home built by the myths of Native Americans and Spanish explorers, a place rescued by the stories dreamed by Latino poets, travelers, and writers. California, under the Fifth Sun, could be the place where we can finally pay homage to the efforts of our collective imagination, to the survival of dreams, and to our collective search for peace and well-being under the radiant sky.

Acknowledgments

I MUST THANK MY PARENTS, Bob and Elisabeth, for taking a leap of faith and moving our family from California to Santiago, Chile, when I was young. Living there for two years and also getting to see a bit of Mexico, Panama, Peru, Ecuador, and Colombia led to a lifetime interest in Latin America.

I owe a great debt to teachers and professors, including Father Marcos McGrath (later Archbishop of Panama) in Chile, Father Ray Decker at Oakland's Bishop O'Dowd High School, and the late Jack Page at Oakland's Merritt College. At the University of California, Berkeley, Dr. Woodrow Borah educated me about Mexico and challenged me to improve. In the bilingual education program at California State University, Hayward, the Chicano Dr. Hermínio Rios, the Cubana American Dr. Dana Martin-Newman, and the Chicana Dr. Carmen Canales taught me much about the challenges facing California Latinos. The remarkable Institute of Latin American Studies (ILAS) in London attracts students from almost every country in Latin America, providing a wonderful atmosphere. Dr. Colin Lewis of Wales, at the London School of Economics, and Dr. Eduardo Posada-Carbo of Colombia, at London University, conducted rigorous, intellectually stimulating seminars for the ILAS.

This book is a joint effort of Heyday Books and Santa Clara University. My new friends and colleagues at Santa Clara, Juan Velasco, Terry Beers, and Francisco Jiménez, have been enthusiastic and helpful supporters of the book. At Heyday, longtime friends Rina Margolin and Jeannine Gendar and a newer colleague, Lisa K. Manwill, have done much to improve this anthology. Special thanks go to Rebecca LeGates for beautiful design and painstaking layout. Kirsten Silva-Gruesz of the University of California, Santa Cruz, and Francisco X. Alarcón of the University of California, Davis, were among the many others whose suggestions and advice were a great help.

Librarians have a noble calling. I am grateful to librarians all over the state of California, as well as in New York and London, who helped me in my "diggings."

Four people deserve special mention. My lifelong best friend, the late Jim Bunker, always encouraged me, particularly in the early stages of this project. He and his wife, Gail, have been active together in progressive causes ever since they met at Santa Clara University in the early 1960s. He would be happy to know of the university's role in this project.

The great Argentine historian Dr. Tulio Halperín Donghi imbued me with his love of Latin American history back in the 1970s, when I was an undergraduate. The author of the best-selling history of Latin America *in* Latin America (*Historia contemporanea de America Latina*) and a brilliant scholar, he was kind enough to be my advisor and mentor at the University of California. I have long regretted that, due to financial reasons, I was unable to finish my graduate studies with him.

Dr. James Dunkerley is the director of the ILAS in London, a scholar whose interests are truly pan-American—and beyond. He is the author of many excellent books and articles, and his recent *Americana,* which pictures the Americas around 1850, is a work of genius. He made me, the oldest student in my graduating class and the only one from the United States, feel welcome.

I have known Malcolm Margolin, publisher of Heyday Books, for over twenty years. He epitomizes the best in publishing. He has helped Californians enjoy a sense of their history, literature, literary history, natural environment, and the lives of the people of many ethnicities who have enriched the state. Perhaps as much as any living non-Indian person in California, he has helped give a voice to the descendants of the state's earliest people—the Native Californians. Malcolm is a remarkable man and a treasured friend.

Last, thanks to the Latino and Latina authors who created this literature that illuminates California so well. Immersing myself in their writings has been a great pleasure for me. For a long time, the "majority" culture made it difficult for them to be noticed. Thankfully for this wonderful group of persistent and talented writers, their time has come.

Rick Heide

Introduction

MANY PEOPLE IMAGINE that the history of the United States began when English explorers made contact with native people along the Atlantic Coast in the early 1600s. Besides overlooking centuries of occupation by even the most recent Native American peoples, this perspective ignores the much earlier arrival of Spanish explorers. Ponce de León was exploring Florida from 1513 to 1521. In the West, the Alarcón squadron of the great Coronado land expedition was on the east bank of the Colorado River in 1540. And ships captained by Juan Rodríguez Cabrillo landed in what we now know as San Diego in 1542. It was here that the Spanish met the first of the many native Californians they would meet on their nine-month expedition. The *encuentro* had begun.

Lashed by storms and all the other hardships of life at sea, and having seen their captain die of gangrene after breaking his leg, Cabrillo's men returned to their home port of Navidad in Mexico nearly a year after setting out. They had found Alta California to be remote and dangerous, with no known gold deposits. For the next two hundred and twenty-seven years, Spanish ships visited from time to time, but the Spanish empire, which had acquired more new territory in one generation than Rome conquered in five centuries,★ did not attempt to colonize Alta California until 1769.

Among those who walked hundreds of miles up the Baja California peninsula in that fateful year was Father Junípero Serra. With his founding of Mission San Diego de Alcalá in 1769 and Mission San Carlos Borromeo in 1770, the seeds were sown for Spanish dominance from the southern California coast as far north as Sonoma, where San Francisco Solano, the last Alta California mission, was founded in 1823. For a short period the missions thrived, coming close to being the self-sufficient centers of supply that Spain had envisioned. Historian Jo Mora cites statistics showing that in 1834 the twenty-one missions possessed

---

★Samuel Eliot Morison, Henry Steele Commager, and William E. Leuchtenberg, *The Growth of the American Republic* (New York: Oxford University Press, 1980).

396,000 cattle, 321,500 goats, sheep, and pigs, and 61,600 horses.★ The first cowboys, or vaqueros, in what is now the United States were Spanish riders who came up from Mexico in the 1700s. California Indians soon joined the ranks of these vaqueros, starting a long tradition of expertise that continues to this day. But the fleeting success of the mission system came at great cost to the native population: between 1769 and 1848, the California Indian population is estimated to have declined by two-thirds as a result of disease, hunger, and violent conflict.

By the time the Mexican government secularized the missions in 1833, ongoing conflicts between the clergy, the military, and the government had led to a slow, steady decline in mission productivity, worsened by Indian rebellions. Mission lands were divided into huge private grants, and soon the ranchos began to dominate life in Alta California. Two events in rapid succession ended this era abruptly, almost before it had started. First, there was the 1847–48 war between Mexico and the United States, generally known in English as the Mexican War but usually known in Spanish by the more descriptive phrase *la invasión norteamericana*. With General Winfield Scott's forces occupying Mexico City, the Mexican government was forced to surrender half its territory— basically, the entire southwestern portion of what is now the United States—in the Treaty of Guadalupe Hidalgo. Then the 1848 discovery of gold in California started the largest mass migration in U.S. history. From 1849 to 1854, the gold rush brought three hundred thousand people to the state, more than tripling the total population in five years.

The huge influx of gold-seekers overwhelmed California's fragile institutions. The large ranchos were taken away from their Californio owners through intimidation, biased laws, and other quasi-legal means. Mob rule and racist violence often went unpunished. So began a new era for Californios, Mexicans, and other Latinos remaining in the state— an era of ongoing political and economic repression.

As early as the 1850s, agriculture began to overtake gold mining as California's leading industry. As Ernesto Galarza astutely noted: "The Treaty of Guadalupe Hidalgo…left the toilers on one side of the border, the capital and the best land on the other. This mistake migration undertook to correct."†

★Joseph Jacinto (Jo) Mora, *Californios: The Saga of the Hard-Riding Vaqueros, America's First Cowboys* (Garden City, N.Y.: Doubleday, 1949).

†Ernesto Galarza, *Merchants of Labor: The Mexican Bracero Story* (Santa Barbara, Calif.: McNally & Loftin, 1964).

That correction has gone on for over a century and a half. Mechanization of agriculture, seizure of the ranchos, and immigrant labor have made large-scale, Anglo-owned agribusiness a reality; without a steady immigrant population, California would never have become the leading agricultural state in the nation.

The International Workers of the World made fitful attempts to organize farmworkers in the early 1900s, and other unions had tried to organize in the fields in the 1930s and beyond, but success was limited and fleeting. In the early 1960s, however, a new wave of union organizers were working among Mexican and Filipino farmworkers in the agricultural heartland. The emergence of the United Farm Workers (UFW), led by two charismatic, principled, and untiring leaders, César Chávez and Dolores Huerta, galvanized Mexican Americans. Its effect in cities and on campuses was perhaps almost as great as in the fields. UFW labor actions and boycotts attracted not only farmworkers but people from across the social spectrum. Not only farm labor issues but institutional racism, inequality in education, and the Vietnam War (in which Latinos fought and died in numbers out of all proportion to their share of the population) were among the major issues that awakened many California Latinos to political activism in the late 1960s and 1970s. "Chicano," "la raza," "Aztlán," and other proud terms made their way into common use as Chicano studies departments proliferated on California's university campuses. At this time, Chicano and Chicana writers, whose work forms and informs so much of this anthology, began to emerge, often with urgent political messages.

Protests against the U.S. role in Latin American wars and dictatorships arose in the 1970s and 1980s. In the 1990s, many Latinos fought against anti-immigration, anti-bilingual, and anti–affirmative action measures. Today, only a few years after Governor Pete Wilson backed the anti-immigrant Proposition 187, which was aimed largely at Latinos, both Democrats and Republicans are avidly courting Latino voters, and a Latino gubernatorial candidate, Peter Miguel Camejo, represents the Green Party. Among the state's political leaders are Antonio Villaraigosa, who in the late 1990s became speaker of the California Assembly, and Cruz Bustamante, who in 1998 was elected lieutenant governor—the first Latino elected to statewide office in California since the 1800s.

Some of California's Latinos and Latinas have only recently arrived, but many have roots in California going back several generations, some all the way back to the 1700s and early 1800s. "The Anglo hegemony was only an intermittent phase in California's arc of identity, extending from the arrival of the Spanish," historian and State Librarian Kevin Starr points out. "The Hispanic nature of California has been there all along, and it was temporarily swamped between the 1880s and the 1960s, but that was an aberration."★ These comments were made in conjunction with the announcement that non-Hispanic whites, at 47.6 percent, no longer comprise a majority in California: Latinos ("Hispanics of any race," according to U.S. census terminology) now make up just under a third (32.4 percent) of the population. But numbers are only a part of the picture. At one time overlooked and underappreciated, the Latino element of California culture is coming to the foreground. For over a century after California became a state, Latino authors found it very difficult to be published here, but fortunately for us, a few writers persevered and overcame daunting odds to help start what would become a Latino literary boom. Many of those pioneering writers continue to make important contributions, younger writers continue the trend, and the future is bright—Latino literature in California has never been healthier. This anthology could have easily filled three volumes. Sometimes painful decisions were necessary, and the diversity of voices, approaches, and styles led to many small dilemmas. For example, readers will find that non-English words are sometimes italicized and sometimes in roman type; there are sound arguments for either approach, and we found it best to reproduce each author's work as it was originally written or published.

All in all, this anthology is a good sampling of some of the best writing in the Americas about a truly fascinating place. Whether it leads you to seek out other works by California's Latino and Latina authors or whether you pick it up to become reacquainted with writers whose work you have treasured, you will be richly rewarded.

★Starr was quoted by Todd S. Purdum in "California Census Confirms Whites Are in Minority," *New York Times,* March 30, 2001.

ARRIVING

✳ Five Thousand Years

Jaime de Angulo

1925

Jaime de Angulo was born in 1887 in Paris to Spanish parents and came to the United States in 1905. A noted bohemian wanderer, he moved between the United States and South and Central America before finding a job in California as a genetic researcher at Stanford University, having recently completed medical school at Johns Hopkins University. Ever restless and curious, he left Stanford for the Alturas plateau, Big Sur, and the University of California, Berkeley, where he studied Native American culture and language under anthropologists Alfred Kroeber and Paul Radin. "Five Thousand Years" was written in response to the destruction in the early 1920s of an ancient Indian shell mound.

ON THE SHORE OF THE BAY, across from San Francisco, where the Saklan once lived and hunted and fished and dug clams and sat around their campfires, they are digging away one of the big shell mounds with a steam shovel.

An acre of shells twenty feet deep.

It is close to the railroad tracks. Trains rumble by. Factory whistles blow. Chimney stacks all around. Valuable land. The steam shovel crunches into the shell mound.

Across the bay, Tamalpais, always beautiful. Other tribes of the Miwok had their campfires in those hills.

Sometimes, the steam shovel crunches into a skeleton, to the delight of the anthropologists who come here every day to watch for discoveries. You don't often get such an opportunity. They recover every valuable bit from the tons of rubbish. Some little balls of stone with a hole drilled through—what were the thoughts of the woman who wore them as a necklace? What was she like? Young sturdy mother stirring the acorn mush, or withered, half-blind old witch muttering by the fire? And this broken fishhook of soapstone. Perhaps a young boy, with his ears yet unpierced, threw it away crossly; he had sat so long by the fire, evening after evening, grinding it into shape. Or perhaps it was a full-fledged hunter, accustomed to the hardships, who lost it.

Spearheads, bone awls, an obsidian knife traded from the north—on the whole, not much. There was not much of a culture in the Neolithic Age.

An acre of campfire refuse twenty feet deep.

They say it represents five thousand years.

Five thousand years without any advance in material culture. Five thousand years of living on the shores of the bay, always the same—hunting, digging for clams, reciting the old tales around the campfires: the tale of Yayali the Giant; the tale of how "He Who Walks Alone" made the world and Coyote helped him; the tale of how the fire was stolen from the people who had it.

It was Lizard who first saw the smoke, and he said, "Smoking below, smoking below, smoking below, smoking below. My grandmother starts a fire to cook acorns. It is very lonely." And they sent Flute-player, the Mouse, to get the fire. He took with him four flutes. He put the people to sleep with his music and he stole their fire. He filled his flutes with coals and brought them back to his people.

And another time they stole the Sun. It was Coyote who stole the Sun. He discovered the Sun on one of these trips. He wondered how he could get it. He changed himself into a broken stick and lay down on the path. The chief came along. He took the stick home for his fire. He was getting sleepy. He kept poking the stick back into the fire. Always, it jumped out. When the chief fell asleep, the stick changed back into Coyote. He ran away with the Sun and brought him back to his own people in the dark land.

They sit around the fire telling the old stories. They hunt and gather acorns. They dig for roots. They sit in the sun for hours, chipping flint knives. They wander in lonely places and talk to the spirits. For five thousand years, the same; they watch the Sun in the daytime and the Moon at night. They call them by the same name. For five thousand years, the same; they sit around the fire, they look into the fire, wondering, dreaming.

In fifty years they have all gone.

The trains rumble by. Eastbound trains. Through the desert where the warlike Mohave roved. Up through higher lands to the mesas of the Southwest; through the country of the wild Apache, of the taciturn Navajo; through the land where the Pueblo live in their villages.

They dance in the pueblos. Elaborate dances. The acme of ritual. In the kivas, underground, the secret societies perform their long rites. The Sun beats fiercely in this droughty land. We must raise Corn or starve. The land is frozen hard. O Sun, Father, beat hard upon the land. Warm our Mother. We dance upon the Earth. We dance hard to the beat of the drum. We wave the sacred Corn. Scatter the pollen. Come down, Rain. Rainmaker, hear us. Fire for the Sun. Water for the Earth. We offer food to our parents. Breed, O Sun, O Earth. Breed the world for your children.

Taos, the highest of the pueblos, sleeping at the foot of a mountain. Taos proudly secret. Wake up in the pueblo, make ready for the vernal equinox. Our Father is waking up out of his long sleep. Make ready, men and women. The whole people will move up to the mountain for three days. The summer people and the winter people. They will sing all night till their voices crack. It is now time for the winter people to hand the Sun over to the summer people. They will take care of him now.

They dance sullenly in the pueblos, for the whites are watching.

The whites have forbidden the dances.

The whites understand nothing. They think the Sun is just a shining plate. They are cold and cruel. They kill everything they can. They think only with their heads. They have lost their hearts. That is why all the animals are hiding in the mountains. It is because they don't like the smell of the whites.

The Sun and the Moon and the Stars and the Earth are working for us. You can't pay them with money. Only with your heart. That's what we Indians do. We do it for ourselves, and for the whole world, and for you, too. Why do you want to stop us?

For five thousand years they looked into the fire. Then they knew.

The trains rumble by with fire in their engines. The factories whir incessantly with fire in their engines. The white men run about, crazy. They have lost something.

The Symbol is dead, like a shiny plate. Knowledge is like life. It must forever die to be reborn.

♛ Antepasados/Ancestors

Nina Serrano

1980

Nina Serrano was born in 1934 in New York City. A founding member of the activist group Pocho Che Collective (later the San Francisco Mission Poets) and Third World Communications, she helped publish a literary review, several poetry books, and one of the first English language anthologies by women of color, *Third World Women* (1972). She has also worked as a filmmaker and radio producer, and was a founding member of the Mission Cultural Center for Latino Arts in San Francisco. She currently lives in Oakland, where she is a storyteller in schools and community and senior centers.

We are one
because America is one continent
tied by the slender curves
of Panama.
We are one people
tied by the buried bones of antepasados
the buried bones of ancestors.
      from Asia to America
      from Africa to America
      from Europe to America
Back to the first mothers and the first fathers
back to the first gardens of flowers and fruits,
where vegetables grew wild.
The soft thick grasses cushioned their bodies
when they lay down to love.
Warm water gurgled up from the earth

and spilled down into clear pools.
Feathers waved their heads
and floated across their bodies
as they strutted in the afternoon.

But then the snake of greed
grew like a weed
planted the seed
that made one person think that to fill their need
or to succeed
they had to use someone else's labor
for their own profit.
Wars came. Animals died.
Women and cattle became property,
Slaves were chained, put to work,
endless work
that finally built factories and smog,
rich parts of town and poor
built on the buried bones of antepasados
the buried bones of ancestors.
Shake the bones
hear their ghostly moans.
We learn from our past
to build our future.

from

♛ Boyhood Days

Ygnacio Villegas (edited by Albert Shumate)

c. 1850

Ygnacio Villegas was born in 1840 in Baja California and in
1848 moved with his parents to Monterey, where the family
had a cattle ranch. *Boyhood Days* (1895) is his memoir about
growing up in Monterey and Rancho San Felipe, a small
community about thirty miles south of San Jose, where he
experienced the excitement and violence of the gold rush.
Villegas died in 1914.

WHEN MY FAMILY MOVED TO SAN FELIPE IN 1849, the country was
teeming with game of all kinds, including deer, elk, bear, wolves, mink,
antelope, and small fowl by the millions. It was the ideal country for
the sportsman and hunter. The Kentucky rifle was the favorite with
the hunters.

Hudson's Bay trappers and many other outfits were covering the
country after mink, beaver, and otter, and later hunters came down to
kill elk and deer for the hides and meat. I have seen pack trains of forty
horses camp at San Felipe, loaded with jerked venison to be taken to the
mines. The hides of the elk and deer were shipped to San Francisco,
where they sold for fifty cents each. Later, market hunters of quail and
ducks sent out thousands of pounds each year. When I first went to
Soledad, when it was the end of the Southern Pacific line, I have known
hunters to ship out four thousand quail in a year, besides hundreds of
deer, to the San Francisco market. They never shot individual quail, but
only shot flocks, getting sometimes as many as thirty quail a shot. Traps
also were used to get hundreds for market.

The otter and beaver skins were obtained mostly from the larger
rivers. Otter skins, even in 1849, brought as high as fifty dollars each, and

beaver skins five dollars. These were sold to Boston traders, who came to Monterey and exchanged guns, knives, food, and clothes for them. These boats would then take the skins to China, where they were exchanged for tea and silk. The latter two commodities were then taken back to Boston and sold at enormous profit.

Elk and deer were everywhere. However, there were places where enormous bands ranged, such as the marshes around Castroville and midway between San Jose and Gilroy. I have heard the young men from Monterey once rodeoed a herd of elk near the treacherous ground called the Tembladeras, located between Castroville and Salinas, and drove the elk into the bog with such speed that the animals could not select their footing, with the result that they killed a hundred or more when they sank into the mire.

Many of the elks had a sixty-inch spread, and for years there was a set of horns at the first stage station out of Gilroy that measured three yards, according to the hostlers, but I never measured to see if they were telling the truth.

The grizzly bear and cinnamon bear were most plentiful, with few black bear. The grizzlies were ferocious animals, and some weighed close to a ton. They were frequently eight feet in height. These animals killed many hogs, horses, sheep, and cattle. They could grab a pig and run away with it like a coyote does with a rabbit. The trappers claimed that the foxy old grizzlies would get out in the meadows and lie on their backs, with their feet in the air, and cattle or other animals would get very curious, and when they got close enough, up would jump Mr. Grizzly and grab one for his dinner.

I had two harrowing experiences with grizzlies. I met one on the high bank of a creek near San Felipe. He was digging into the bark of a dead tree, and I did not see him until I was so close that I could have touched him. For a minute he was as frightened as I, but he started after me, so I leaped out over the bank some thirty feet, landing in the sand below. I expected any minute to see his huge claws enfold me, so I looked around, and there he was, still on the bank, looking angrily at me.

Another time I was returning from Monterey, and was crossing the Salinas plains near what is now Blanco. My horse became mired in the quicksand, and while I was trying to get him out, he got away from me, so I started on foot to San Felipe, some thirty miles away. I was follow-ing the trail through the dry mustard when I spotted two huge grizzlies in front of me, some one hundred yards away. They started after me, and as I had no gun, I started to run, but after a few steps it occurred to me that they would catch me easily, so I tried the old Indian trick of setting fire to the grass. The bears were almost upon me when they saw the smoke and blaze, so they quickly turned and ran. It was only a minute before the fire was a raging furnace, crackling like gunfire. I ran as fast as I could to the river and climbed a tall cottonwood tree. I was there six or seven hours and saw hundreds of deer, bears, wolves, and other wild animals seeking refuge along the river. The fire frightened them as badly as the bears had me.

The fire burned for several days, extending as far south as the present town of Soledad.

There were many antelope on the Salinas plains, and I saw them as late as 1872. They were beautiful, graceful animals as they bounded over the ground. At first they were very tame, and one could get close to them, but after the immigrant trains came trooping up to the Salinas Valley, and they were being constantly shot at and chased by horsemen, they became very shy.

As for small game, they were countless. I have seen young mallard ducks by the thousands in the small lagoons around Salinas. The mallards and teal seemed to prefer that section to nest. The mallards made their nests at a considerable distance from the water, and I have often seen the mother mallard go marching down a trail with her young brood. The young mallard, just before it could fly, made the best meal of any game I ever tasted. Where the water was shallow they were easily caught, and we frequently caught a mess to take home.

Doves and wild pigeons were also plentiful. I have seen so many doves in the wild mustard on the Salinas plains that when they got between you and the sun they darkened the ground. The doves built their nests everywhere, and I have seen as many as twelve nests on one branch of a sycamore tree.

However, the ruthless slaughter of the early days killed off most of the game of all kinds, so that the present generation has to be content with little or nothing.

from

♜ Diario de un viaje a California

Vicente Pérez Rosales (translated and edited by Edwin A. Beilharz and Carlos U. López)

1849

Vicente Pérez Rosales was born in 1807 in Santiago, Chile. As a young man he studied in France and worked odd jobs (including as a distiller, a cooper, and a tobacco and cattle smuggler) before sailing to California for the gold rush. In 1878 he published a memoir based on his California travels that was later released in an edited version as *Recuerdos del pasado* (1882). Upon returning to his homeland, Rosales was sent to Europe to promote immigration to Chile, and he later served his country as a member of the Chilean senate. He died in 1886. The following excerpt is from the original diary of his travels.

FEBRUARY 18, 1849

It is four o'clock. The opening called the Golden Gate is in sight. We are entering it now. It is an emotional experience. How beautiful and how impressive this coast is. All its hills are covered with trees, and you can see cattle on the slopes.

We are at last in California. The bay of San Francisco is without doubt the greatest in the whole Pacific Ocean, and the loveliest in the world next to Rio de Janeiro. Its entrance, the Golden Gate, is like a throat two miles wide and three leagues long, adorned with cliffs and small islands that do not interfere with either entering or leaving. The tides alternate with mathematical regularity.[...]

A boat headed for us. To understand how we felt as we waited for it, you would have to have been there to see our strained expressions.

Our very souls were quivering with hope and fear. We thought the boat had come from shore, but it was only the captain of the ship *Anamakin,* wanting news from Chile. Believe it or not, this gentleman's arrival was upsetting to us. We had all run up to him with the same question in mind, no matter how differently we would have put it. The vitally important question was this: "Is there gold here as they say?" But, strange to say, we all backed away toward the other rail before we could hear the answer. We wanted to prolong the uncertainty; no matter how painful, it was better than a disappointment. We turned quickly enough, though, when one of the questioners, unable to contain himself, ran toward us yelling, "It is all true! There is a lot of gold! A whole lot of gold!" As you can imagine, these words were enough to draw our souls back into our bodies. Once the wave of emotion passed, we gathered in a happy circle.[…]

[After two months of mining on the American River, Pérez Rosales returns to San Francisco.] How different San Francisco was from what it had been when I left it to go into the interior. Instead of an "Araucanian" village with foundations marked off here and there on which buildings were to rise, now those buildings were finished and others were under rapid construction. The tents, huts, and windbreaks of old were now lined up beside streets in the suburbs. But, by the look of things, all these suburbs too would soon be built over and become part of a beautiful town. Building lots were already being laid out and measured in feet there, and prices had gone out of sight!

What a mistake we had made in not acquiring land in the towns at prices that would almost have made them gifts. It was depressing to me now to see how much they had increased in value in so short a time! Here I want to say something, without meaning to offend anyone: the men who made fortunes in California were gentlemen who lacked the hardihood to go prospecting for gold all out, scorning hunger, weariness, and danger. It was those who acquired valuable building sites either by just taking them or buying them at low prices; or those men who happened, without meaning to do so, to bring merchandise into the area to sell. Such men found themselves wealthy overnight.

The bay was full of ships, all of them abandoned. Their passengers and crews had swelled the town's population to thirty thousand souls; and, whether permanent residents or transients, their activity was so great that the city seemed to change and expand as if by enchantment. Long piers, supported on redwood piles, were being constructed or were being further extended at the end of every street that ran down to the beach. These carried the street out over the tidal flat and provided road-ways and foundations for additional buildings. At one place a lack of ready materials for piers had been solved by piling boxes and sacks of earth across the muddy beach; at other locations, so as not to lose time, piers had been improvised by grounding ships side by side at the ends of streets and laying beams up to them; and there, too, shops and offices were built.

One of the first to transform his ship into a home ashore was a young Chilean, Wenceslao Urbistondo. He had taken advantage of an unusually high tide to beach his deserted and useless bark at the end of the last street to the north of town; then he had laid his masts and spars to form a bridge across the mud so he could get back and forth.

The sidewalks along the streets were made with bales of jerky, because it was the cheapest and most readily available material. The bales were pushed down into the mud along the front of the buildings so one could get around without sinking into mud up to the knees.

Business was at the mercy of the shifting tides in that city. Sometimes the high water invaded everything, reducing the value of the highest quality merchandise; at other times it left everything high and dry. The most provident merchant was not safe from the ruinous effects an unexpected high or low tide might produce. One man might get rich with no idea how it happened. Another would be ruined despite precautions of the most meticulous sort. I remember, for example, that because there was a shortage of housing in San Francisco, they asked that prefabricated houses be brought from Chile. When these arrived, houses were so plentiful in San Francisco that those who had ordered the houses had to pay to get them landed and then had to pay someone to accept them. I am witness and victim of what I am describing.

Nobody, however, was discouraged. Even the lowest-priced items could be given scarcity value by arranging for convenient fires. We saw such fires break out all over town day after day, posing the danger of a general conflagration.

In this theater, where the most uproarious international fair that memory records was in process, no actor played the role his lot would have assigned him in his native country. Masters were transformed into servants; a lawyer might be a freight agent; a doctor, a stevedore; sailors found themselves digging excavations; and philosophers, having abandoned the realm of the abstract, were working with the most concrete materials. I have seen, without surprise and with the just pride of a Chilean, a soft and effeminate dandy from Santiago, with the same gold vest chain he wore at dances in our capital city still hanging from the buttonhole of a sweaty wool shirt, standing in water up to his waist and carrying the baggage of a tarred and brawny sailor with a smile on his face; and then, after having got paid for that job, offering his services to some other oaf.

The most ostentatious signs had been hung up everywhere. A wooden barracks bore the name "Hotel Frémont." One man had a sign that said "So-and-so, Physician and Surgeon" painted on the flap of his tent, though he had never been more than a grave digger. An insurance salesman from Valparaíso had a hut that bore two signs: "So-and-so, Attorney at Law" and "So-and-so and Company, General Insurance Brokers." An arbor made of poles called itself "French Hotel"; it belonged to an old Santiago barber. This sort of thing was done by Chileans of prominent families—few of which were not represented by family members in California.[...]

It is not surprising that lawsuits and appeals [were] often decided with pistol or dagger. The relations between Chileans and Americans were anything but cordial. When General Persifer Smith sent a decree from Panamá to the effect that, after that date, no foreigner was to be allowed to exploit gold mines in California, that decree brought to a head all the hostility shown to peaceful and defenseless Chileans.

Merchants and traders were alarmed by this, and the authorities proposed to the aliens that they become full United States citizens; they were to be charged only ten dollars, a small sum for such an imposing title. But this safe-conduct was only halfway effective: it worked only where it was accepted. In other places it was treated as a joke. A little later on, the provisional government in San José made a ruling that an alien could work the mines on payment of twenty dollars a month in advance. A receipt would serve as sufficient authorization for the right to work. But how many clashes there were that arose from that agreement between collectors and contributors.

The ill will of the Yankee rabble against the sons of other nations, and especially Chileans, was rising by that time. They offered a simple and conclusive argument: Chileans were descended from Spaniards; Spaniards were of Moorish ancestry; therefore a Chilean was at the best something like a Hottentot, or, to put it more gently, something like the humbled but dangerous Californio. They could not stomach the fearlessness of the Chilean, who might be submissive in his own country but did not behave that way abroad. A Chilean would face up to a loaded pistol at his chest if he had his hand on the haft of his knife. For his part, the Chilean detested the Yankee and constantly referred to him as a coward. This mutual bad feeling explains the bloody hostilities and atrocities we witnessed every day in this land of gold and hope.

It was not long in San Francisco until an organized group of bandits appeared, called the Hounds. They were vagrants, gamblers, or drunks, drawn together in a fellowship of crime; and they had as their motto, "We can get away with it." Fear and hatred spread in advance of their appearance, and they deliberately generated these feelings by their provocations. Everywhere they went they established their control by quarrelsomeness and violence.

They did not always "get away with it," though. One morning when they were passing by a little point of land to the north of town where a sort of Little Chile had grown up, separated from the center of the city, these vicious Hounds decided to give it a savage going over. Because in California time is money, these merciless ruffians in large numbers charged the Chileans there with pistols and clubs. You can imagine the shouting and uproar this brutal and unprovoked attack brought on. The Chileans rallied and counterattacked by hurling stones. One respectable Chilean gentleman, not being able to escape through the front of his tent because it was jammed with a threatening band of Hounds, brought one of them down with a pistol shot as he came toward him and then, slashing with his dagger the cloth of his tent, managed to escape through that improvised exit and join his friends in safety.

Brannan, ex-Mormon owner of the unforgettable Daice-maynana, informed by some Chileans of what was happening in Little Chile, climbed up on top of his own house in just indignation and shouted in a loud voice for the people to come. Then in a short but forceful speech he declared it was time to make an example of those who had perpetrated such unheard-of atrocities against the sons of a friendly country, a country that had day after day supplied the city of San Francisco with its best flour, as well as the most skillful arms in the world when it came to making adobe bricks! "I propose," he said, "that to take care of this once and for all, the Chileans of good will, led by citizens of the United States, go at once to the scene and arrest these disturbers of the peace!" A general "Hurrah!" was raised, and the almost instantaneous appearance of the defenders of order at [that] point put an end to the savagery that could have brought on the most terrible consequences.

Eighteen of the bandits were dragged from hideouts by force and were incarcerated on board the flagship of the Yankee American squadron, and with this, peace returned to the new Babylon.

Three days later, while I was busily preparing to go and rejoin our company, I read with alarm in a San Francisco paper this ominous news: "North American blood shed by infamous Chileans in the placers! Citizens, be on your guard!"

By the following day the report had taken on unimaginable proportions, and by evening it was being said not only that the Chileans had been expelled violently from the banks of the San Joaquín River, but that the same band of vigilantes, seeking vengeance and plunder, was moving in upon the Chileans working the tributaries of the American River!

You can imagine my state of mind in such a fearful situation. What should I do? An acquaintance gave me a very exaggerated account of the most savage atrocities that had just been inflicted on Chileans near Sutter's mill. I confess my sin of credulity. I should have known better than to believe him. I knew the distance between Sutter's mill and San Francisco, and that it was impossible for news to have covered that distance so quickly even if it flew in. It was the fact that my brothers were in the midst of the situation then that nearly drove me crazy. My brothers, my poor brothers all alone there, and I without the means to join them in their hour of peril. Without thinking, with nothing but my weapons, with no hope except for revenge, I paid two hundred pesos for a passage by boat to the beaches of Sacramento. Without listening to the voice of prudence—or not wishing to listen to it—I dedicated myself to a violent destiny.

Where was I going? What was I going to do? I had no idea. The one thing I remember is that anything seemed more feasible, anything far easier, than to return to Chile without my brothers.

We pressed on day and night without rest. We arrived at Sacramento. I jumped into the water without waiting for the ship to land, and, with my heart full of anguish, I ran all the way to the residence of Señor Gillespie.

Imagine my surprise. God had not abandoned me. My brothers had arrived in Sacramento the day before. They were destitute, having been robbed of all they had; but they were safe. They had agreed with Gillespie that they should join me in San Francisco as soon as possible. To meet them, to see them, count them, and feel my anxieties drain away was all a great experience. You would have to have been in my position to know what it was like. Desperation, hate, and the desire for vengeance, all had given my sick body a strength and vigor that, in this moment of great happiness, I could feel ebbing away.

Once we were together again, recounting our experiences to one another in a makeshift tent made of sarapes, our good spirits returned.

We could see all that happened to us had been only an ugly and ridiculous nightmare. We were all safe and sound; no one was missing. What more could we want? The Yankees had not needed much force to drive us Chileans from Sutter's mill.

True, they had robbed us of everything we had; but in California that did not amount to much.

Our friends were all gone, so on that same night we organized ourselves into a committee to decide what we should do from then on. No one thought we should go back to Chile. Instead we were unanimous in feeling we should make an effort to reverse our luck, trying various plans of operation until we found one that succeeded.

Mining was not the only occupation California offered at that time to men willing to work. If prospecting was closed to foreigners, commerce was eminently within reach.

from

✸ Los Chilenos en California

Ramón Gil Navarro (translated and edited by Edwin A. Beilharz and Carlos U. López)

1853

Ramón Gil Navarro (d. 1883) was born in Argentina, later settled in Chile, and in 1849 sailed for gold-rush California, where his superior English-speaking skills earned him a job as an interpreter in the state court system. When he returned to Chile in the 1850s, he became a journalist and published a series of articles about his experiences in California, from which the following selection is taken.

ON DECEMBER 10 [1849] BEGAN THE CHAIN OF EVENTS that culminated in the tragic affair at Calaveras. A group of Chileans had found a gulch full of gold on the banks of the river; naturally it was called Chile Gulch. They were joined by others who brought supplies for a year, bought at very high prices and at great sacrifice. Each group built a house to winter in. It was hard work, but they had to do it because the weather was turning cold. It was at that point that they were told to leave the area within ten days.[…]

[When they refused, altercations ensued. A self-appointed judge and jury, after scaring off the actual judge, put the Chileans on trial for rebellion against the legal government of the United States.]

On the night of December 31, at ten o'clock, the trial ended and the following sentence was pronounced:

José del Carmen Terán, Damián Urzúa, and Francisco Cárdenas are to suffer the extreme penalty. The three named individuals are to be taken at ten o'clock the following morning to Mokelumne Hill, taken to the top, and thrown down the cliff toward the river.

Mokelumne Hill is one of the highest in the California mining area. The cliff to which the sentence referred is more than six hundred feet high, rising from inaccessible rocks. There the condemned men were to be flung from the top down the whole face of the cliff, bound hand and foot. It would truly take more than the disposition of a cannibal to devise a method of execution more cruel, and to enjoy its most gruesome details. Terán and the other two listened to their sentence being translated with stoicism. Terán wanted to make some reply, but the interpreter refused to relay his words.

Ignacio Yáñez and two companions were sentenced to receive thirty lashes, to have their heads shaved ignominiously, and then finally to have their ears cut off, to their agony and eternal disgrace. No such penalty has ever been imposed in any part of the modern world—even among the Chinese, who are notoriously cruel in the treatment of prisoners. I have before me a book, *The Mysteries of the Inquisition,* that contains one thousand or more engravings of different tortures imposed by that tribunal; and whether they are real or imaginary, I do not find in any of them the sort of torture inflicted on the wretched Chileans by the bandits of Calaveras. From four to six of the other boys were sentenced to be tied to the branches of a tree, given fifty lashes, and have their heads shaved.

Both those sentenced to lose their ears and the ones sentenced to be whipped asked, as a favor, that they be shot instead of being made to undergo a punishment applicable to robbers and criminals of a different sort. But this petition was refused. The Yankees wanted to torture and humiliate the Chileans more than they did to kill them. All of these penalties were more deserved by those who imposed them than they were by their innocent victims. The Americans wanted the mutilated Chileans to serve as a horrendous warning to all their compatriots in California, and to have the threat of such punishment carried all the way back to their mother country. The Yankees intended, when they harshly sentenced our young men to be whipped, to make them suffer shame (in addition to pain), as honorable young men would on seeing themselves subjected to such punishment as was usually applied only to the basest of criminals. The Americans' studied hatred and insatiable desire for vengeance made them determined to outrage the dignity and gentlemanly feelings that they themselves lacked, but which their captives had, and thus subject their victims to mental as well as physical suffering. Such was the condition of the Chileans in captivity on the night of December 31.[…]

The arrival of the Americans from Mokelumne [who had objected to the judicial proceedings] stirred up a genuine storm at [Judge] Coller's camp. If they did not succeed in saving the lives of the Chileans, at least they got the sentence passed on Terán and his comrades changed into something less cruel and barbarous. In defending the rights of the Chileans they almost came to blows. Their attitude did influence some members of the jury. "Four Eyes," for example, let Maturano live, in a show of generosity and gratitude for kindnesses he said he had been shown himself when he was a prisoner at Stockton. No one else, though, was let off and no change was made except that in the mode of execution; all else went on as planned.

The first thing they did was to administer the whippings. They lashed the Chileans with all the ferocity of savages with victims to torture. Our young men pleaded vainly to be shot rather than dishonored; the Yankees were indifferent or pretended they did not understand. One fourth of them were absolute sadists. After the victim was in position they applied the lash without caring whether they cut the flesh or shattered the skull of the poor devil. One by one the Chileans had their hands tied up to an overhanging branch so that their feet barely touched the ground, and then they were whipped so that blood spurted from their lungs. […]

Thus did the Americans greet the New Year, in a presentation that even they themselves would have to admit was half-tragic, half-comic. Men would have to be both wild beasts and cowards to have staged such a farcical trial and followed it by such merciless sadism. "Listen to the brave fellows," they shouted when, in the midst of the torture the Chileans were suffering, one of them let a cry of pain escape his lips. After the whippings, carried out to the very letter, Ignacio Yáñez was to undergo the third penalty, that of losing his ears; to be followed in turn by his two fellow sufferers—after they had been whipped and had their heads shaved. I still shudder, remembering the screams of those poor men as they were so barbarously mutilated. An American armed with a huge knife came to carry out the sentence. The condemned men begged on their knees as a last supreme favor that they be shot, but pleading was useless with those bandits and they did not even bother to listen. Three or four of them held the first victim and the executioner cut off his ears. The cutting was followed by a cry of pain such as one might hear in the last agony of a martyr. The ear with a part of the cheek was in the hand of the executioner who, after a moment, threw it aside and went after the other ear with the coldest insensitivity. A sea of blood inundated the face and clothing of the poor fellow, giving him a look more horrible than you can imagine. The horror of losing the second ear was not so great because the victim had fainted. But what must have been the torture and terror of those who were waiting their turn as they watched the monstrous act!

It is not possible to dwell on the account of those exquisite cruelties by the Americans. The fate that awaited Terán and his friends was even worse because they had to undergo many tortures before death, and all without the comforts of religion; religion which alone can make such sufferings bearable, and help a man rise above martyrdom and any physical or moral evils. One of the Chileans who was to die with Terán had his son with him, a boy of eight or ten; but the sobbing pleas of the innocent boy could not soften or inspire pity for his father in such men as they were. Just one glimpse of that scene of sorrow between a son and his father should have affected the most barbarous and pitiless of executioners. What would become of the boy, left an orphan among such men? Who would be a father to him, direct him away from a life of infamy and crime, when he had been exposed to the perverse example of those men and watched his own father die? This thought must have tortured the last hour of the poor father. Nevertheless the son had to be present at the execution of his own father.

The three condemned men were brought out to an open space with fifty armed riflemen standing around. The Chileans were to be shot but the firing squad had not been picked. All of them were to demonstrate their marksmanship with the chests of the Chileans as targets. It was as though the Americans intended to spare no suffering whatsoever to their victims until they were dead. The spot picked for the execution was a mile, more or less, from the house of the judge, and the prisoners were made to walk there after all the torment they had been put through during the last twelve days. Terán spoke briefly to the others during the march to encourage them; he never lost his calm, even when one of his comrades collapsed; he bent over and helped him up before anyone else could do so. Oddly the prisoners were not bound, probably so they could get through the difficult places they had to cross. Three or four of those who had been whipped had to witness the execution of their comrades so they could report on it to other Chileans in all its details.

When the execution site was reached, Terán in his own name and in that of his comrades offered money if they were let go, and promised to leave Calaveras and even California and go back to his own country. The Yankees did not believe he had any money after having been robbed twice and put no faith in his offer. The boy's father in turn said he would give thirty ounces of gold that he had if they would let him take his son out of California. The Yankees asked him whether he had that much gold. He answered, yes; he had it in a secret pocket that had escaped the searching. The Americans took it, then told him he could not be let go but they would give the gold to his son. The poor boy no more got the gold than he was ever to see his father again—except in the next world.

Terán was infuriated at seeing what was happening and said in a low voice to his companions, "Give me a knife and, by God, if I have to die I will kill three or four of those devils and die fighting." No one answered him. The other Chileans were afraid the Yankees might have heard him and would take some special vengeance on all of them because of his attitude. Terán repeated his request two or three times. He felt that even they were abandoning him. But what could they do? What he wanted was impossible; no one had any weapons. When the Americans came to tie him, Terán turned to them and said, "Give me a dagger and then you can kill me any way you choose." Some were annoyed, other paid no heed, and all went on with their work. Terán, seeing he was going to die, then asked for a pencil and paper so he could write a few words to his family. One of the Yankees dug a piece of paper out of his pack and gave it to him along with a pencil. Terán wrote on both sides of the sheet, and the Yankee promised to give the letter to the other Chileans when they were released. I am afraid the letter no more reached his family than the gold did the boy. No one knew what he had written, but his friends said he had wanted to leave his property to his brother, and earlier had told them he would like to make his will.

Finally Terán, Damián Urzúa, and Francisco Cárdenas were tied to oak trees. It is sad to write this; they had wanted to go back to their country and see their native soil, their families, and friends once more, but they had only a few minutes of life left. Death was to be their whole future. The most pathetic thing of all was the death of the boy's father. He embraced his son with tears and many words of tenderness and sorrow. But not even this most hallowed and solemn grief affected the Yankees. They separated the two and began the execution. They shot from a distance of fifty feet, not all at once but one after another. This intensified the suspense because some bullets struck and others missed, and firing successively that way only strung out the agony. But I will not prolong the harrowing of the sensibilities of their parents and fellow countrymen by dwelling upon the details of their suffering. Let me only add that the Chileans who had to bury the men found fifteen bullet holes in Terán and about the same number in the other two.

The Chilean workers were held for several weeks and made to cook for the Americans. The orphaned boy they kept permanently as a slave. The whipped and mutilated Chileans were free to leave but for several days not one of them could move.

These tragic events took place three years ago. [Judge] Coller is today a rich and respected American citizen and holds the legitimate title of a judge in Double Springs. [Jury member] Nickleson, or "Four Eyes," is a licensed doctor of medicine in Marysville. The area where it happened is populated today by farming families from New Orleans. A traveler who goes past the camp at Mokelumne toward Melones will find the ruins of the Chilean buildings in Chile Gulch on the Calaveras. A mile farther on he will see three crosses that the pious survivors erected in the names of their fallen countrymen. There is an inscription: "Say the Our Father and a Hail Mary for the souls of the Chileans who were killed here on January 1, 1850." There is no other memorial, and in years to come, when the crosses have crumbled away, these men will exist only in legend. [There is a bronze plaque at Chile Gulch today.]

✺ Life, Trial, and Death of Aurelio Pompa

anonymous (translated by Margaret P. Redfield)

c. 1910

"Life, Trial, and Death of Aurelio Pompa" is an example of the time-honored corrido tradition of Mexican music. This ballad form has been traced to medieval Andalusian music brought to the Americas by the Spanish, as well as to Nahuatl and other native epic poetry traditions from before the arrival of Europeans.

I am going to tell you the sad story
of a Mexican who emigrated out there—
Aurelio Pompa, so he was called,
our countryman who died there.

Back in Caborca, which is in Sonora,
the humble village where he was born,
"Come on, mother," he said one day,
"over there are no revolutions."

"Goodbye, friends, goodbye, Maria,"
he said to his sweetheart very sadly,
"I promise you that I will return soon,
so we can get married, God willing."

"Goodbye, Aurelio," said the girl,
and she went sobbing to pray.
Look after him, Virgin Mary,
I feel a foreboding he won't return.

The priest and his friends
along with his sweetheart went to talk
and to beg poor Aurelio
not to leave his native village.

All this advice was useless
and so were the pleas of his mother,
"Let's go, mother, that's where the dollar is,
and I swear I'll earn a lot of them."

Four years ago in the month of May
the two of them went to California
and, unhappily, on that very same date
there he died in prison.

A carpenter who was very strong,
very cruelly struck the poor young man,
and Aurelio Pompa swore he'd avenge
those blows he had received.

Filled with rage, he told his mother,
and the poor old woman advised him,
"*por Dios,* forget it, dear son,"
and Aurelio, good man, forgave him.

But one afternoon, when he was working
with three friends at the railroad station,
the carpenter came by, mocking at him
and managed to provoke poor Pompa.

His three friends advised him
to leave him alone and go his way,
and then the carpenter, with a hammer,
very insultingly threatened him.

Then Pompa, seeing the danger,
fired in self-defense
with a revolver and face to face,
like a man, he killed him.

The case came to court, the jury arrived,
and the Yankee people sentenced him.
"The death penalty," they all demanded,
and the lawyer did not object.

Twenty thousand signatures of compatriots
asked the governor for his pardon,
the entire press requested it too
and even Obregón sent a message.

But all proved useless; the societies,
all united, asked his pardon;
his mother, half-dead already
went too to see the governor.

"Farewell, friends, farewell, my village.
Dear mother, cry no more,
tell *la raza* not to come here,
for here they will suffer; there is no mercy."

The jailer asked him:
"Are you Spanish?" And he answered,
"I am a Mexican and proud of it,
although they deny me a pardon."

This is the story of our countryman
who four years ago arrived,
and, unhappily, on that same date
died an unfortunate death in prison.

from

✹ Across the Wire

Luis Alberto Urrea

1993

Luis Alberto Urrea was born in 1955 in Tijuana and moved
to San Diego when he was three years old. He has published
three volumes of poetry, one novel, and four autobiographical nonfiction works, including *Nobody's Son: Notes from an
American Life* (1998), which won an American Book Award,
and *Across the Wire: Life and Hard Times on the Mexican Border*
(1993), which was named a *New York Times* Notable Book of
the Year. Urrea has taught writing workshops at universities
in California, Louisiana, and Massachusetts, and he is currently a professor at the University of Illinois, Chicago. His
latest book, *Six Kinds of Sky: A Collection of Short Fiction,* was
published in 2002, and selections from his works in progress
and many of his illustrations can be accessed through the
website http://www.luisurrea.com.

WHEN I WAS YOUNGER, I WENT TO WAR. The Mexican border was the
battlefield. There are many Mexicos; there are also many Mexican borders,
any one of which could fill its own book. I, and the people with me, fought
on a specific front. We sustained injuries and witnessed deaths. There were
machine guns pointed at us, knives, pistols, clubs, even skyrockets. I caught
a street-gang member trying to stuff a lit cherry bomb into our gas tank.
On the same night, a drunk mariachi opened fire on the missionaries
through the wall of his house.

We drove five beat-up vans. We were armed with water, medicine,
shampoo, food, clothes, milk, and doughnuts. At the end of a day, like
returning veterans from other battles, we carried secrets in our hearts

that kept some of us awake at night, gave others dreams and fits of crying. Our faith sustained us—if not in God or "good," then in our work.

Others of us had no room for or interest in such drama, and came away unscathed—and unmoved. Some of us sank into the mindless joy of fundamentalism, some of us drank, some of us married impoverished Mexicans. Most of us took it personally. Poverty *is* personal: it smells and it shocks and it invades your space. You come home dirty when you get too close to the poor. Sometimes you bring back vermin: they hide in your hair, in your underpants, in your intestines. These unpleasant possibilities are a given. They are the price you occasionally have to pay.

In Tijuana and environs, we met the many ambassadors of poverty: lice, scabies, tapeworm, pinworm, ringworm, fleas, crab lice. We met diphtheria, meningitis, typhoid, polio, *turista* (diarrhea), tuberculosis, hepatitis, VD, impetigo, measles, chronic hernia, malaria, whooping cough. We met madness and "demon possession."

These were the products of dirt and disregard—bad things afflicting good people. Their world was far from our world. Still, it would take you only about twenty minutes to get there from the center of San Diego.

For me, the worst part was the lack of a specific enemy. We were fighting a nebulous, all-pervasive *It*. Call it hunger. Call it despair. Call it the Devil, the System, Capitalism, the Cycle of Poverty, the Fruits of the Mexican Malaise. It was a seemingly endless circle of disasters. Long after I'd left, the wheel kept on grinding.

At night, the Border Patrol helicopters swoop and churn in the air all along the line. You can sit in the Mexican hills and watch them herd humans on the dusty slopes across the valley. They look like science fiction crafts, their hard-focused lights raking the ground as they fly.

Borderlands locals are so jaded by the sight of nightly people-hunting that it doesn't even register in their minds. But take a stranger to the border, and she will *see* the spectacle: monstrous Dodge trucks speeding into and out of the landscape; uniformed men patrolling with flashlights, guns, and dogs; spotlights; running figures; lines of people hurried onto buses by armed guards; and the endless clatter of the helicopters with their harsh white beams. A Dutch woman once told me it seemed altogether "un-American."

But the Mexicans keep on coming—and the Guatemalans, the Salvadorans, the Panamanians, the Colombians. The seven-mile stretch of Interstate 5 nearest the Mexican border is, at times, so congested with Latin American pedestrians that it resembles a town square.

They stick to the center island. Running down the length of the island is a cement wall. If the "illegals" (currently, "undocumented workers"; formerly, "wetbacks") are walking north and a Border Patrol vehicle happens along, they simply hop over the wall and trot south. The officer will have to drive up to the 805 interchange, or Dairy Mart Road, swing over the overpasses, then drive south. Depending on where this pursuit begins, his detour could entail five to ten miles of driving. When the officer finally reaches the group, they hop over the wall and trot north. Furthermore, because freeway arrests would endanger traffic, the Border Patrol has effectively thrown up its hands in surrender.

It seems jolly on the page. But imagine poverty, violence, natural disasters, or political fear driving you away from everything you know. Imagine how bad things get to make you leave behind your family, your friends, your lovers; your home, as humble as it might be; your church, say. Let's take it further—you've said good-bye to the grave-yard, the dog, the goat, the mountains where you first hunted, your grade school, your state, your favorite spot on the river where you fished and took time to think.

Then you come hundreds—or thousands—of miles across territory utterly unknown to you. (Chances are, you have never traveled farther than a hundred miles in your life.) You have walked, run, hidden in the backs of trucks, spent part of your precious money on bus fare. There is no AAA or Travelers Aid Society available to you. Various features of your journey north might include police corruption; violence in the forms of beatings, rape, murder, torture, road accidents; theft; incarceration. Additionally, you might experience loneliness, fear, exhaustion, sorrow, cold, heat, diarrhea, thirst, hunger. There is no medical attention available to you. There isn't even Kotex.

Weeks or months later, you arrive in Tijuana. Along with other immigrants, you gravitate to the bad parts of town because there is nowhere for you to go in the glittery sections where the gringos flock. You stay in a run-down little hotel in the red-light district, or behind the bus terminal. Or you find your way to the garbage dumps, where you throw together a small cardboard nest and claim a few feet of dirt for yourself. The garbage pickers working this dump might allow you to squat, or they might come and rob you or burn you out for breaking some local rule you cannot possibly know beforehand. Sometimes the dump is controlled by a syndicate, and goon squads might come to you within a day. They want money, and if you can't pay, you must leave or suffer the consequences.

In town, you face endless victimization if you aren't streetwise. The police come after you, street thugs come after you, petty criminals come after you; strangers try your door at night as you sleep. Many shady men offer to guide you across the border, and each one wants all your money now, and promises to meet you at a prearranged spot. Some of your fellow travelers end their journeys right here—relieved of their savings and left to wait on a dark corner until they realize they are going nowhere.

If you are not Mexican, and can't pass as *tijuanense,* a local, the tough guys find you out. Salvadorans and Guatemalans are routinely beaten up and robbed. Sometimes they are disfigured. Indians— Chinantecas, Mixtecas, Guasaves, Zapotecas, Mayas—are insulted and pushed around; often they are lucky—they are merely ignored. They use this to their advantage. Often they don't dream of crossing into the United States: a Mexican tribal person would never be able to blend in, and they know it. To them, the garbage dumps and street vending and begging in Tijuana are a vast improvement over their former lives. As Doña Paula, a Chinanteca friend of mine who lives at the Tijuana garbage dump, told me, "This is the garbage dump. Take all you need. There's plenty here for *everyone!*"

If you are a woman, the men come after you. You lock yourself in your room, and when you must leave it to use the pestilential public bathroom at the end of your floor, you hurry, and you check every corner. Sometimes the lights are out in the toilet room. Sometimes men listen at the door. They call you "good-looking" and "bitch" and *"mamacita,"* and they make kissing sounds at you when you pass.

You're in the worst part of town, but you can comfort yourself— at least there are no death squads here. There are no torturers here, or bandit land barons riding into your house. This is the last barrier, you think, between you and the United States—*los Yunaites Estaites.*

You still face police corruption, violence, jail. You now also have a wide variety of new options available to you: drugs, prostitution, white slavery, crime. Tijuana is not easy on newcomers. It is a city that has always thrived on taking advantage of a sucker. And the innocent are the ultimate suckers in the Borderlands.

If you have saved up enough money, you go to one of the coyotes (people smugglers) who guide travelers through the violent canyons immediately north of the border. Lately, these men are also called *polleros,* or "chicken wranglers." Some of them are straight, some are land pirates. Negotiations are tense and strange: *polleros* speak a Spanish you don't quite understand—like the word *polleros*. Linguists call the new border-speak "Spanglish," but in Tijuana, Spanglish is mixed with slang and *pochismos* (the polyglot, hip talk of Mexicans infected with *gringoismo*: the *cholos* in Mexico, or Chicanos on the American side).

Suddenly, the word for "yes," *sí*, can be *simón* or *siról*. "No" is *chale*. "Bike" *(bicicleta)* is *baica*. "Wife" *(esposa)* is *waifa*. "The police" *(la policía)* are *la chota*. "Women" are *rucas* or *morras*. You don't know what they're talking about.

You pay them all your money—sometimes it's your family's life-long savings. Five hundred dollars should do it. *"Orale,"* the dude tells you, which means "right on." You must wait in Colonia Libertad, the most notorious barrio in town, ironically named "Liberty."

The scene here is baffling. Music blares from radios. Jolly women at smoky taco stands cook food for the journeys, sell jugs of water. You can see the Border Patrol agents cruising the other side of the fence; they trade insults with the locals.

When the appointed hour comes, you join a group of *pollos* (chickens) who scuttle along behind the coyote. You crawl under the wires, or, if you go a mile east, you might be amazed to find that the famous American Border Fence simply stops. To enter the United States, you merely step around the end of it. And you follow your guide into the canyons. You might be startled to find groups of individuals crossing the line without coyotes leading them at all. You might wonder how they have mastered the canyons, and you might begin to regret the loss of your money.

If you have your daughters or mothers or wives with you—or if you are a woman—you become watchful and tense, because rape and gang rape are so common in this darkness as to be utterly unremarkable. If you have any valuables left after your various negotiations, you try to find a sly place to hide them in case you meet *pandilleros* (gang members) or *rateros* (thieves: rat-men). But, really, where can you put anything? Thousands have come before you, and the hiding places are pathetically obvious to robbers: in shoulder bags or clothing rolls, pinned inside clothes, hidden in underwear, inserted in body orifices.

If the coyote does not turn on you suddenly with a gun and take everything from you himself, you might still be attacked by the *rateros*. If the *rateros* don't get you, there are roving zombies that you can smell from fifty yards downwind—these are the junkies who hunt in shambling packs. If the junkies somehow miss you, there are the *pandilleros*—gangbangers from either side of the border who are looking for some bloody fun. They adore "taking off" illegals because it's the perfect crime: there is no way they can ever be caught. They are Tijuana *cholos,* or Chicano *vatos,* or Anglo head bangers.

Their sense of fun relies heavily on violence. Gang beatings are their preferred sport, though rape in all its forms is common, as always. Often the coyote will turn tail and run at the first sight of *pandilleros.* What's another load of desperate chickens to him? He's just making a living, taking care of business.

If he doesn't run, there is a good chance he will be the first to be assaulted. The most basic punishment these young toughs mete out is a good beating, but they might kill him in front of the *pollos* if they feel the immigrants need a lesson in obedience. For good measure, these *boys*—they are mostly boys, aged twelve to nineteen, bored with Super Nintendo and MTV—beat people and slash people and thrash the women they have just finished raping.

Their most memorable tactic is to hamstring the coyote or anyone who dares speak out against them. This entails slicing the muscles in the victim's legs and leaving him to flop around in the dirt, crippled. If you are in a group of *pollos* that happens to be visited by these furies, you are learning border etiquette.

Now, say you are lucky enough to evade all these dangers on your journey. Hazards still await you and your family. You might meet white racists, complimenting themselves with the tag "Aryans"; they "patrol" the scrub in combat gear, carrying radios, high-powered flashlights, rifles, and bats. Rattlesnakes hide in bushes—you didn't count on that complication. Scorpions, tarantulas, black widows. And, of course, there is the Border Patrol *(la migra).*

They come over the hills on motorcycles, on horses, in huge Dodge Ramcharger four-wheel drives. They yell, wear frightening goggles, have guns. Sometimes they are surprisingly decent; sometimes they are too tired or too bored to put much effort into dealing with you. They collect you in a large group of fellow *pollos,* and a guard (a Mexican Border Patrol agent!) jokes with your group in Spanish. Some cry, some sulk, most laugh. Mexicans hate to be rude. You don't know what to think—some of your fellow travelers take their arrest with aplomb. Sometimes the officers know their names. But you have been told repeatedly that the Border Patrol sometimes beats or kills people. Everyone talks about the Mexican girl molested inside its building.

The Border Patrol puts you into trucks that take you to buses that take you to compounds that load you onto other buses that transport you back to Tijuana and put you out. Your coyote isn't bothered in the least. Some of the regulars who were with you go across and get brought back a couple of times a night. But for you, things are different. You have been brought back with no place to sleep. You have already spent all your money. You might have been robbed, so you have only your clothes—maybe not all of them. The robbers may have taken your shoes. You might be bloodied from a beating by *pandilleros,* or an "accident" in the Immigration and Naturalization Service compound. You can't get proper medical attention. You can't eat, or afford to feed your family. Some of your compatriots have been separated from their wives or their children. Now their loved ones are in the hands of strangers, in the vast and unknown United States. The Salvadorans are put on planes and flown back to the waiting arms of the military. As you walk through the cyclone fence, back into Tijuana, the locals taunt you and laugh at your misfortune.

If you were killed, you have nothing to worry about.

Now what?

Perhaps you'll join one of the other groups that break through the Tortilla Curtain every night. The roadrunners. They amass at dusk along the cement canal that separates the United States from Mexico. This wide alley is supposedly the Tijuana River, but it's usually dry, or running with sewage that Tijuana pumps toward the U.S. with great gusto.

As soon as everybody feels like it—there are no coyotes needed here—you join the groups passing through the gaping holes in the fence. Houses and alleys and cantinas back up against it, and in some spots, people have driven stolen cars into the poles to provide a wider passage. You rush across the canal and up the opposite slope, timing your dash between passing *migra* trucks and the overflights of helicopters. Following the others, you begin your jog toward the freeway. Here, there are mostly just Border Patrol officers to outrun—not that hard if you're in good shape. There are still some white-supremacist types bobbling around, but the cops will get them if they do anything serious. No, here the problem is the many lanes of I-5.

You stand at the edge of the road and wonder how you're going to cut across five lanes of traffic going sixty miles an hour. Then, there is the problem of the next five lanes. The freeway itself is constructed to run parallel to the border, then swing north. Its underpasses and storm-drain pipes offer another subterranean world, but you don't know about them. All you know is you have to get across at some point, and get far from the hunters who would take you back.

If you hang around the shoulder of I-5 long enough, you will find that many of your companions don't make it. So many have been killed and injured that the gringos have put up warning signs to motorists to watch for running people. The orange signs show a man, a woman, and a child charging across. Some gringos are so crazy with hate for you that they speed up or aim for you as you run.

The vague blood of over a hundred slain runners shadows the concrete.

On either side of the border, clustered near the gates, there are dapper-looking men, dressed in nice cowboy clothes, and they speak without looking anyone in the eye. They are saying, "Los Angeles. San Bernardino. San Francisco."

They have a going concern: business is good.

Once you've gotten across the line, there will always be the question of *Where do I go now?* "Illegal aliens" have to eat, sleep, find work. Once across, you must begin another journey.

Not everyone has the energy to go on. Even faith—in Jesus, the Virgin Mary, or the Streets of Gold—breaks down sooner or later. Many of these immigrants founder at the border. There is a sad swirl of humanity in Tijuana. Outsiders eddy there who have simply run out of strength. If North America does not want them, Tijuana wants them even less. They become the outcasts of an outcast region. We could all see them if we looked hard enough: they sell chewing gum. Their children sing in traffic. In bars downtown, the women will show us a breast for a quarter. They wash our windshields at every stoplight. But mostly, they are invisible. To see them, we have to climb up the little canyons all around the city, where the cardboard shacks and mud and smoke look like a lost triptych by Hieronymus Bosch. We have to wade into the garbage dumps and the orphanages, sit in the little churches and the hospitals, or go out into the back country, where they raise their goats and bake red bricks and try to live decent lives.

They are not welcome in Tijuana. And, for the most part, Tijuana itself is not welcome in the Motherland. Tijuana is Mexico's cast-off child. She brings in money and gringos, but nobody would dare claim her. As a Mexican diplomat once confided to me, "We both know Tijuana is not Mexico. The border is nowhere. It's a no-man's-land."

from

♨ Paula

Isabel Allende (translated by Margaret Sayers Peden)

1994

Isabel Allende was born in 1942 in Lima, Peru, and grew up in Chile. Following the 1973 coup and assassination of president Salvador Allende (her uncle), she moved to Venezuela, where she wrote her early novels, including *The House of the Spirits* (1982), which has been translated into twenty-seven languages and made into a major motion picture in the United States. She now lives in Marin County, California. Her work also includes a short-story collection, several stories and plays for children, a narrative cookbook, and a memoir, excerpted below, which was written to and named for her daughter as she lay in a coma before her death in 1992.

I, LIKE THOUSANDS OF OTHER CHILEANS, have often asked myself whether I did the right thing in leaving my country during the dictatorship, whether I had the right to uproot my children and drag my husband to an uncertain future in a strange country, or whether it would have been better to stay where we were, trying to pass unnoticed—these are questions that cannot be answered. Events developed inexorably, as in Greek tragedies; disaster lay before my eyes, but I could not avoid taking the steps that led to it.[...]

It was a priest who showed me the safest routes to political asylum. Some of the people I helped leap over a wall ended up in France, Germany, Canada, and the Scandinavian countries, all of which accepted hundreds of Chilean refugees. Once I had started down that road, it was impossible to turn back, because one case led to another and then another...and there I was, committed to various underground activities, hiding or transporting people, passing on for publication in Germany information others had obtained about the tortured or disappeared, and taping interviews with victims in order to establish a record of everything that happened in Chile, a task more than one journalist took on in those days. I could not suspect then that eight years later I would use that material to write two novels. At first I had no sense of the danger, and moved about in broad daylight, in the hubbub of the center of Santiago, in the warm summer and golden autumn. It was not until the middle of 1974 that I truly recognized the risks involved. I knew so little about the workings of terror that I was slow to perceive the warning signs: nothing indicated that a parallel world existed in the shadows, a cruel dimension of reality. I felt invulnerable. My motivations were not heroic, not in the least, merely compassion for such desperate people and, I have to admit it, the irresistible attraction of adventure. During moments of greatest danger I remembered the advice Tío Ramón gave me the night of my first party: *Remember that all the others are more afraid than you.*

In those uncertain times, people revealed their true faces. The most contentious political leaders were the first to subside into silence or to flee the country; in contrast, other people who had lived quiet, unassuming lives exhibited extraordinary valor. I had one good friend who was an out-of-work psychologist who earned his living as a photographer on our magazine, a gentle and somewhat naive man with whom we shared family Sundays with the children and whom I had never heard utter a word about politics. I called him Francisco, although that was not his name, and nine years later he served as model for the protagonist of *Of Love and Shadows*. He had contacts with religious groups because his brother was a worker priest and, through him, he learned of the atrocities committed throughout the country; more than once he put himself in danger to help others. During secret walks on San Cristobal Hill, where we believed no one could hear us, he used to pass on the news to me. Sometimes I worked with him, and other times I acted alone. I had devised a rather unimaginative system for the first meeting, generally the only meeting, with the person I was to help: we would agree on a time, I would drive very slowly around the Plaza Italia in my unmistakable vehicle until I picked up a quick signal, then slow down just long enough for someone to jump into the car. I never knew the names or stories behind those pale countenances and shaking hands, because our instructions were to exchange a minimum of words. I would be left with a kiss on the cheek and whispered thanks, and never know anything more of that person. It was more difficult when there were children. I know of one baby that, to get past the guard at the gate and be reunited with its parents, was smuggled into an embassy drugged with a sedative and hidden in the bottom of a basket of lettuce.

Michael knew about my activities and never objected, even when it came to hiding someone in the house. Serenely, he warned me of the dangers, somewhat amazed that so many assignments fell into my hands while he rarely knew anything that was going on. I don't know, I suppose my being a journalist had something to do with it; I was out in the streets talking to people, while he was always in the company of executives, the caste that benefited most from the dictatorship. I showed up one day at the restaurant where Michael always lunched with his associates in the construction company, to point out to them that they spent enough money on a single meal to feed twenty children for a month in the kitchen run by the priests, and then suggested that once a week they eat a sandwich in their office and give me the money they saved. My words were met with a stony silence, even the waiter stood frozen with his tray in his hand, and all eyes turned toward Michael; I expect they were wondering what kind of man this was who was unable to control his insolent wife. The president of the company removed his eyeglasses, slowly cleaned them with his napkin, and then wrote me a check for ten times the amount I had asked. Michael did not eat with them again and with that gesture made his position clear. It was difficult for him, brought up as he was by strict and noble ideals, to believe the horror stories I told him or to conceive that we could all die, including our children, if any of the poor wretches who passed through our lives was arrested and confessed under torture to having been beneath our roof. We heard the most bloodcurdling rumors, but through some mysterious mechanism of the brain, which at times refuses to see the obvious, we dismissed them as exaggerations—until it was no longer possible to deny them. At night we would wake up sweating because a car had stopped outside during curfew, or because the telephone rang and no one was there, but the next morning the sun would rise, the children and the dog would crawl into our bed, we would get up and make coffee, and life would start all over again, as if everything were normal. Months went by before the evidence was irrefutable and we were paralyzed by fear. How could everything change so suddenly and so completely? How could reality be so distorted? We were all accomplices, the entire society was mad. The devil in the mirror....Sometimes, when I was alone in some secret place on the hill with time to think, I again saw the black waters of the mirrors of my childhood where Satan peered out at night, and as I leaned toward the glass, I realized, with horror, that the Evil One had my face. I was not unsullied, no one was: a monster crouched in each of us, every one of us had a dark and fiendish side. Given the conditions, could I torture and kill? Let us say, for example, that someone harmed my children.... What cruelty would I be capable of in that situation? The demons had escaped from the mirrors and were running loose through the world.

By the end of next year, when the country was completely subjugated, a system of pure capitalism was initiated; because it favored only the executive class and workers lost all their rights, it had to be imposed by force. It did not follow the law of supply and demand, as the young ideologues of the Right claimed, because the work force was repressed and at the mercy of their employers. The social benefits people had obtained decades before were terminated, the right to hold meetings or strike was abolished, and labor leaders disappeared or were murdered with impunity. Businesses, caught up in a mad course of inhuman competition, demanded maximum productivity from their workers for minimum compensation. There were so many unemployed lining up at factory doors to find work that labor was available at near slave wages. No one dared protest, because in the best of circumstances a man could lose his job, but worse, he could be accused of being a Communist or a subversive and wind up in a cell tortured by the political police. An apparent economic miracle was created at great social cost; never before had Chile witnessed such a shameless exhibition of wealth, nor so many people living in extreme poverty. As an administrator, Michael had to dismiss hundreds of workers; he called them to his office by list to tell them that beginning the next day they were not to report to work, and to explain to them that in accord with the new rules they had lost their severance pay. He knew that each of those men had family, and that it would be impossible for them to find another job; this dismissal was tantamount to an irrevocable sentence of misery. He started coming home demoralized and dejected; after a few months his shoulders sagged and his hair turned gray. One day he called a meeting of his associates to tell them that the situation was becoming obscene, that his foremen were earning the equivalent of three liters of milk per day. With laughter, they replied, "What matter? Those people don't drink milk, anyway." By that time, I had lost my position on both magazines and was taping my program in a studio under the surveillance of a guard with a machine gun. Censorship was not all that affected my work; I became aware that it was to the liking of the dictatorship that a member of the Allende family had a light comedy program on television—what better proof of normality in the nation? I resigned. I felt I was being watched, fear kept me awake nights, and I broke out in hives that I scratched till they bled. Many of my friends were leaving the country; some disappeared and were never mentioned again, as if they had never existed. One afternoon, an artist friend I hadn't seen in months visited me; once we were alone, he took off his shirt to show me scars that were not completely healed: his torturers had carved an "A" for Allende on his back. From Argentina, my mother implored me to be cautious and not do anything to provoke trouble. I could not forget the prophecies of María Teresa Juárez, the seer, and feared that, just as with the bloodbath she had foreseen, her prediction for me of immobility or paralysis might also come true. Didn't that in fact mean years in prison? I began to contemplate the possibility of leaving Chile, but did not dare speak of it aloud because it seemed that putting the thought into words could set in motion the gears of an irreversible mechanism of death and destruction. I went often to walk the paths on San Cristóbal where I had played so many years ago on family picnics; I hid among the trees and screamed, with pain like a spear piercing my breast. Sometimes I packed food and a bottle of wine in a basket and went there with Francisco, who, using his knowledge of psychology, tried vainly to help me. Only with him could I talk about my clandestine activities, my fears, my unconfessable desire to escape. "You're crazy," he would tell me. "Anything is better than exile. How can you leave your home, your friends, your country?"

My children and Granny were the first to notice my state of mind. Paula, who was then a wise little girl of eleven, and Nicolás, who was three years younger, understood that all about them fear and poverty were spreading like a river overrunning its banks. They became silent and cautious. They had learned that the husband of one of their school-teachers, a sculptor who before the coup had made a bust of Salvador Allende, had been arrested by three unidentified men who suddenly burst into his studio and hauled him away. No one knew where he was, and his wife didn't dare mention her trouble for fear of losing her job—we were still in the period when everyone thought that if someone disappeared, surely he was guilty. I don't know how my children learned of it, but that night they told me. They had gone to see their teacher, who lived a few blocks from our house, and found her bundled in shawls and sitting in the dark because she couldn't pay the electric bill or buy paraffin for the stoves. Her salary barely fed her three children, and she had had to take them out of school. "We want to give them our bicycles because they don't have money to take the bus," Paula informed me. They did and, from that day, Paula's mysterious activities increased; now she not only hid her grandmother's bottles and took gifts to her friends in the old people's home nearby, she also stowed jars of preserves and packages of rice in her book bag for her teacher. Months later, when the sculptor returned home after surviving torture and prison, he created a Christ on the Cross in iron and bronze and gave it to our children. Ever since, it has hung beside Nicolás's bed.

My children never repeated what we talked about in the family, or mentioned the strangers who sometimes passed through the house. Nicolás began to wet his bed at night; he would wake up, humiliated, and come to my room with his head hanging and hug me, shivering. We should have given him more affection than ever, but Michael was depressed by the problems with his workers and I was running from one job to another, visiting the poor neighborhoods, and hiding people, all with my nerves rubbed raw. I don't think either of us provided the children the security or consolation they needed. In the meantime, Granny was being torn apart by opposing forces; on one side, her husband was boasting about the feats of the dictatorship and, on the other, we were telling her stories of repression. Her uneasiness turned into panic as her small world was threatened by hurricane-force winds. "Be careful," she would say from time to time, not sure herself what she meant, because her mind refused to accept the dangers her grandmotherly heart could sense. Granny's entire existence revolved around those two grandchildren. "Lies, it's all a pack of lies made up by the Soviets to run down Chile," my father-in-law told her any time she mentioned the terrible rumors contaminating the atmosphere. Just like my children, she learned not to voice her doubts and to avoid comments that might attract misfortune.[...]

By midyear of 1975, repression had been refined to perfection, and I fell victim to my own terror. I was afraid to use the telephone, I censored letters to my mother in case they were opened at the post office, and was careful about what I said even in the bosom of the family. Friends who had contact with the military had warned me that my name was on the blacklists, and soon after we received two death threats by telephone. I was aware that there were people who took pleasure from spreading panic, and perhaps I should not have listened to those anonymous voices, but [...] I didn't feel safe. One April afternoon, Michael and the children and I went to the airport to say good-bye to friends who, like so many others, had opted to leave. They had learned that Australia was offering land to new immigrants and had decided to test their luck as farmers. We were watching the departing plane when a woman who was a total stranger to me came up and asked, wasn't I the person on television? She insisted I go with her because she had something to tell me in private. Without giving me time to react, she pulled me into the restroom and once we were alone removed an envelope from her purse and handed it to me.

"Deliver this, it's a matter of life and death. I have to leave on the next plane; my contact didn't appear and I can't wait any longer," she said. She made me repeat the address twice, to be sure I had memorized it, and then ran away.

"Who was that?" Michael asked when he saw me come out of the restroom.

"I don't have any idea. She asked me to deliver this; she said it's very important."

"What is it? Why did you take it? It could be a trap..."

All those questions, and others that occurred to us later, resulted in very little sleep that night. We didn't want to open the envelope because it was better not to know its contents, we were afraid to take it to the address the woman had given me, and neither could we bring ourselves to destroy it. During that long night I think that Michael realized that I didn't seek out problems, they found me. We could see finally how twisted reality had become when a request as simple as delivering a letter could cost us our lives, and when the subject of torture and death was now a part of our everyday conversation, something fully accepted. At dawn the next morning, we spread a map of the world on the dining-room table to look for somewhere we might go. By then, half the population of Latin America was living under military dictatorships; using the pretext of combating communism, the armed forces of several countries had been transformed into mercenaries for the privileged class and instruments of repression for the poor. In the next decade, military governments waged all-out war against their own peoples; millions of persons died, disappeared, and were exiled; never before on our continent had such a vast movement of human masses poured across borders. That morning, we discovered that there were very few democracies left in which to seek refuge, and that several of those—like Mexico, Costa Rica, and Colombia—were no longer issuing visas for Chileans because too many had emigrated there in the last year and a half. As soon as the curfew was lifted, we left the children with Granny, gave instructions in case we did not return, and went to deliver the envelope to the indicated address. We rang the bell of an old house in the middle of town; a man dressed in blue jeans came to the door and, with great relief, we saw that he was wearing a clerical collar. We recognized his Belgian accent because we had lived in that country.

After fleeing Argentina, Tío Ramón and my mother found themselves with nowhere to go, and for months had to accept the hospitality of friends in foreign countries, unable to unpack their suitcases once and for all in a place of their own. About this time, my mother recalled the Venezuelan she had met in the geriatric clinic in Romania; following a hunch, she looked for the card she had kept all those years and called her friend in Caracas to tell him briefly what had happened. "Come on here, my dear, there's room for everyone," was Valentín Hernández's immediate response. That gave Michael and me the idea that we might move to Venezuela; from what we knew, it was a green and generous country where we could count on one friend and stay a while until the situation in Chile improved. We began to make plans: we would have to rent the house, sell the furniture, and find new jobs, but we rushed everything through in less than a week. That Wednesday, the children came home from school in abject terror; two strangers had cornered them in the street and then, after threatening them, gave them a message for me: "Tell that bitch your mother that her days are numbered."

The next day I flew to Venezuela, alone. I did not know I would never see my grandfather again. I went through the formalities at the airport with Memé's relics clutched to my chest. The biscuit tin contained the remnants of a crown of wax orange blossoms, a pair of child-size kid gloves the color of time, and a well-thumbed prayer book with mother-of-pearl covers. I also took with me a plastic bag with a handful of dirt from our garden, with the idea of planting forget-me-nots in another land. The official who checked my passport saw the frequent Argentine entrance and exit stamps and my newspaper pass and, as I assume he did not find my name on his list, let me leave. The plane climbed through a feather bed of clouds, and minutes later we crossed the snow-covered heights of the Andes. Those white peaks thrusting through winter clouds were the last image I had of my country. "I'll be back, I'll be back," I repeated like a prayer.

 Exiles

Juan Felipe Herrera

1985

Juan Felipe Herrera was born in Fowler, California, and
traveled the state as a child with his migrant farmworker
parents. In addition to authoring several memoirs and
numerous poetry collections, Herrera has written many
award-winning children's and young-adult books, including
CrashBoomLove: A Novel in Verse (1999), which won an
Americas Award. His most recent book is *Notebooks of a
Chile Verde Smuggler* (2002). He is currently the chairman of
the Chicano and Latin American studies department at
California State University in Fresno, where he lives with
his wife, Margarita Luna Robles.

> *and I heard an unending scream piercing nature.*
> *—from the diary of Edvard Munch, 1892*

At the greyhound bus stations, at airports, at silent wharfs
the bodies exit the crafts. Women, men, children; cast out
from the new paradise.

They are not there in the homeland, in Argentina, not there
in Santiago, Chile; never there no more in Montevideo, Uruguay
and they are not here

in *America*

They are in exile: a slow scream across a yellow bridge
the jaws stretched, widening, the eyes multiplied into blood
orbits, torn, whirling, spilling between two slopes; the sea, black,

swallowing all prayers, shadeless. Only tall faceless figures
of pain flutter across the bridge. They pace in charred suits,
the hands lift, point and ache and fly at sunset as cold dark
birds. They will hover over the dead ones: a family shattered
by military, buried by hunger, asleep now with the eyes burning
echoes calling *Joaquín, María, Andrea, Joaquín, Joaquín, Andrea,*

en exilio

From here we see them, we the ones from here, not there or across,
only here, without the bridge, without the arms as blue liquid
quenching the secret thirst of unmarked graves, without
our flesh journeying refuge or pilgrimage; not passengers
on imaginary ships sailing between reef and sky, we that die
here awake on Harrison Street, on Excelsior Avenue clutching
the tenderness of chrome radios, whispering to the saints
in supermarkets, motionless in the chasms of playgrounds,
searching at 9 a.m. from our third-floor cells, bowing mute,
shoving the curtains with trembling speckled brown hands. Alone,
we look out to the wires, the summer, to the newspapers wound
in knots as matches for tenements. We that look out from
our miniature vestibules, peering out from our old clothes,
the father's well-sewn plaid shirt pocket, an old woman's
oversized wool sweater peering out from the makeshift kitchen.
We peer out to the streets, to the parades, we the ones from here
not there or across, from here, only here. Where is our exile?
Who has taken it?

from

✴ In Search of Bernabé

Graciela Limón

1993

Graciela Limón was born and raised in Los Angeles. She taught Chicano studies at Loyola Marymount University for thirty-five years and was chair of the department until her retirement in 2001. She is the author of five novels, the most recent being *Erased Faces* (2001). While in El Salvador as part of a delegation investigating the assassination of Jesuit priests in 1989, Limón gathered inspiration for her first novel, *In Search of Bernabé* (1993), which was a Critic's Choice for the *New York Times Book Review* and won a 1994 American Book Award and the University of California Irvine Award for Chicano Literature. Although the story is fictional, *In Search of Bernabé* begins with the very real massacre that occurred in San Salvador in 1980 at the funeral of the assassinated Archbishop Oscar Arnulfo Romero. In the following excerpt, Luz Delcano continues her search for her son, Bernabé, who has been missing since the incident.

AFTER THE MASSACRE, LUZ DELCANO SCOURED THE STREETS of San Salvador for two months looking for her son Bernabé, but every lead given by acquaintances and even strangers turned up empty. In her search, she found that the city was under a pall of terror and confusion because a new wave of killings was hitting the streets. Some foreigners and even some of Luz's acquaintances were disappearing. Bodies, mutilated beyond recognition, were being discovered daily.

Many of Luz's friends, leaving everything behind, were flocking to bus stations with no other aim than to escape El Salvador. The majority of them were heading up to Mexico, and some as far as the United

States. Young men were leaving jobs and families because rumors spread from street to street telling of youths being kidnapped at gunpoint by patrols, then being forced into the army.

These events, as well as her futile search for her son, bewildered and frightened Luz. She felt dragged and torn by forces beyond her control, for she could not believe that Bernabé might be dead, or even that he had been pressed into the army. Yet she didn't have a clue as to his whereabouts. Those around her began to convince her that her son must have fled the city along with the other young men, and that more than likely he had headed north. But where to the north? Her friends shrugged their shoulders and rolled their eyes when Luz asked this question.

As weeks slipped by and Bernabé's whereabouts remained unknown, Luz's intense desire to find her son finally overshadowed her apprehensions. Putting aside her emotions she decided to join the others in their northbound trek, blindly hoping that her son had done the same thing. Uncertain of where her road would ultimately end, she purchased a bus ticket for Mexico City knowing that she would not be alone since others were following the same course. Luz figured that once she got to that city, she would determine her next step.[…]

Luz and [her friend] Arturo arrived at the Tijuana bus terminal [...] exhausted and bloated from sitting in their cramped seat. As soon as they stepped out of the bus, they were approached by a woman who asked them if they wanted to cross the border that night. Without waiting for an answer, she told them she could be their guide. The price was five hundred American dollars apiece.

Luz stared at the woman for a few moments, caught off guard by the suddenness of what was happening. More than her words, it was the woman's appearance that held Luz's attention. She was about thirty-five. Old enough, Luz figured, to have experience in her business. The woman was tall and slender, yet her body conveyed a muscular strength that gave Luz the impression that she would be able to lead them across the border.

The coyota returned Luz's gaze, evidently allowing time for the older woman to make up her mind. She took a step closer to Luz, who squinted as she concentrated on the woman's face. Luz regarded her dark skin and high forehead, and the deeply set eyes that steadily returned her questioning stare. With a glance, she took in the coyota's faded levis and plaid shirt under a shabby sweatshirt, and her eyes widened when she saw the woman's scratched, muddy cowboy boots. She had seen only men wear such shoes.

Luz again looked into the woman's eyes. She was tough, and Luz knew that she had to drive a hard bargain. She began to cry. "¡Señora, por favor! Have a heart! How can you charge so much? We're poor people who have come a long way. Where do you think we can find so many dólares? All we have is one hundred dollars to cover the two of us. Please! For the love of your mamacita!"

The woman crossed her arms over her chest and laughed out loud as she looked into Luz's eyes. She spoke firmly. "Señora, I'm not in the habit of eating fairy tales for dinner. You've been in Mexico City for a long time. I have eyes, don't I? I can tell that you're not starving. Both of you have eaten a lot of enchiladas and tacos. Just look at those nalgas!"

She gave Luz a quick, hard smack on her behind. Then, ignoring the older woman's look of outrage, the coyota continued to speak rapidly. "Look Señora. Just to show you that I have feelings, I'll consider guiding the both of you at the reduced rate of seven hundred dollars. Half now; the rest when I get you to Los Angeles. Take it or leave it!"

Luz knew that she was facing her match. She answered with one word. "Bueno."

The coyota led them to a man who was standing nearby. He was wearing a long overcoat, inappropriate for the sultry weather in Tijuana. The coat had a purpose though, for it concealed deep inner pockets which were filled with money. The coyota pulled Luz nearer to the man, then whispered into her ear, "This man will change your pesos into American dollars. A good rate, I guarantee."

When Arturo began to move closer, the coyota turned on him. "You stay over there!"

Arturo obeyed.

Even though she felt distrust, Luz decided that she and Arturo had no alternative. However, she needed to speak with him, so she pulled him to the side. "Hijo, we're taking a big chance. We can be robbed, even killed. Remember the stories we've been hearing since we left home. But what can we do? We need someone to help us get across, so what does it matter if it's this one, or someone else? What do you say?"

Arturo agreed with her. "Let's try to make it to the other side. The sooner the better. I think you made a good bargain. We have the money, don't we?"

"With a little left over for when we get to Los Angeles."

Before they returned to where the others were waiting, she turned to a wall. She didn't want anyone to see what she was doing. Luz withdrew the amount of pesos she estimated she could exchange for a little more than seven hundred American dollars. She walked over to the money vendor, and no sooner had the man placed the green bills on her palm than she heard the coyota's sharp voice. "Three hundred and fifty dollars, por favor!"

She signaled Luz and Arturo to follow her to a waiting car. They went as far as Mesa Otay, the last stretch of land between Mexico and California. There, the coyota instructed them to wait until it got dark. Finally, when Luz could barely see her hand in front of her, the woman gave the signal. "¡Vámonos!"

They walked together under the cover of darkness. As Luz and Arturo trekked behind the woman, they sensed that they were not alone, that other people were also following. Suddenly someone issued a warning, "¡La migra! ¡Cuidado!" The coyota turned with unexpected speed, and murmured one word, "¡Abajo!"

All three fell to the ground, clinging to it, melting into it, hoping that it would split open so that they could crawl into its safety. Unexpectedly, a light flashed on. Like a giant eye, it seemed to be coming from somewhere in the sky, slowly scanning the terrain. No one moved. All that could be heard were the crickets and the dry grass rasping in the mild breeze. The light had not detected the bodies crouched behind bushes and rocks. It flashed out as suddenly as it had gone on.

"¡Vámonos!" The coyota was again on her feet and moving. They continued in the dark for hours over rough, rocky terrain. The coyota was surefooted but Luz and Arturo bumped into rocks and tripped over gopher holes. Luz had not rested or eaten since she had gotten off the bus. She was fatigued but she pushed herself, fearing she would be left behind if she stopped. Arturo was exhausted too, but he knew that he still had reserves of energy, enough for himself and for Luz.

Dawn was breaking as they ascended a hill. Upon reaching the summit, they were struck with awe at the sight that spread beneath their feet. Their heavy breathing stopped abruptly as their eyes glowed in disbelief. Below, even though diffused by dawn's advancing light, was an illuminated sea of streets and buildings. A blur of neon formed a mass of light and color, edged by a highway that was a ribbon of liquid silver. Luz and Arturo wondered if fatigue had caused their eyes to trick them, because as far as they could see there was brilliance, limited only in the distance by a vast ocean. To their left, they saw the lights of San Diego unfolding beneath them, and their hearts stopped when they realized that farther north, where their eyes could not see, was their destination.

Without thinking, Luz and Arturo threw their arms around one another and wept.

The lights of San Diego receded behind them. The coyota had guided Luz and Arturo over an inland trail, taking them past the U.S. Immigration station at San Onofre, and then down to connect with the highway. A man in a car was waiting for them a few yards beyond Las Pulgas Road on California Interstate 5.

The driver got out of the car as they approached, extending a rough hand first to Luz and then to Arturo. "Me llamo Ordaz."

Ordaz turned to the coyota and spoke in English. His words were casual, as if he had seen her only hours before. "You're late. I was beginning to worry."

"The old bag slowed me down."

The coyota spoke to the man in English, knowing that her clients were unable to understand her. Then she switched to Spanish to introduce herself to Luz and Arturo. "Me llamo Petra Traslaviña. I was born back in San Ysidro on a dairy farm. I speak English and Spanish."

There was little talk among them beyond this first encounter. The four piled into a battered Pontiac station wagon, and with Ordaz at the wheel, they headed north. The woman pulled out a pack of Mexican cigarettes, smoking one after the other, until Ordaz started to cough. He opened the window complaining, "Por favor, Petra, you wanna choke us to death?"

"Shut up!" she retorted rapidly, slurring the English *sh*.

The phrase engraved itself in Luz's memory. She liked the sound of it. She liked its effect even more, since she noticed that Ordaz was silenced by the magical phrase. Inwardly, Luz practiced her first English words, repeating them over and over again under her breath.

Luz and Arturo were quiet during the trip mainly because they were frightened by the speed at which Ordaz was driving. As she looked out over the coyota's shoulder, Luz knew that she didn't like what she was feeling and hearing. She even disliked the smell of the air, and she felt especially threatened by the early morning fog. When the headlights of oncoming cars broke the grayness, her eyes squinted with pain.

The hours seemed endless, and they were relieved when Ordaz finally steered the Pontiac off the freeway and onto the streets of Los Angeles. Like children, Luz and Arturo looked around, craning their necks, curiously peering through the windows and seeing that people waited for their turn to step onto the street. Luz thought it was silly the way those people moved in groups. No one ran out onto the street, leaping, jumping, dodging cars as happened in Mexico City and back home. Right away, she missed the vendors peddling wares and the stands with food and drink.

Suddenly, Luz was struck by the thought that she didn't know where the coyota was taking them. As if reading Luz's mind, the woman asked, "Do you have a place you want me to take you to?"

Rattled by the question, Luz responded timidly. "No. We didn't have time to think."

"I thought so. It's the same with all of you."

The coyota was quiet for a while before she whispered to Ordaz, who shook his head in response. They engaged in a heated exchange of words in English, the driver obviously disagreeing with what the coyota was proposing. Finally, seeming to have nothing more to say, Ordaz shrugged his shoulders, apparently accepting defeat. The coyota turned to her passengers.

"Vieja, I know of a place where you two can find a roof and a meal until you find work. But..." She was hesitating. "¡Mierda!...just don't tell them I brought you. They don't like me because I charge you people money."

What she said next was muttered and garbled. Luz and Arturo did not understand her so they kept quiet, feeling slightly uneasy and confused. By this time Ordaz was on Cahuenga Boulevard in Hollywood. He turned up a short street, and pulled into the parking lot of Saint Turibius Church, where the battered wagon spurted, then came to a stand-still.

"Hasta aquí. You've arrived."

The coyota was looking directly at Luz, who thought she detected a warning sign in the woman's eyes. "It was easy this time, Señora. Remember, don't get caught by la migra, because it might not be so good the next time around. But if that happens, you know that you can find me at the station in Tijuana."

Again, the coyota seemed to be fumbling for words. Then she said, "Just don't get any funny ideas hanging around these people. I mean, they love to call themselves voluntarios, and they'll do anything for nothing. Yo no soy así. I'll charge you money all over again, believe me!"

The coyota seemed embarrassed. Stiffly, she shifted in her seat, pointing at a two-story, Spanish-style house next to the church.

"See that house?"

Luz nodded.

"Bueno. Just walk up to the front door, knock, and tell them who you are, and where you're from. They'll be good to you. But, as I already told you, don't mention me."

She turned to Arturo. "Take care of yourself, muchacho. I've known a few like you who have gotten themselves killed out there."

With her chin, she pointed toward the street. When Arturo opened his mouth to speak, the coyota cut him off curtly. "My three hundred and fifty dollars, por favor."

She stretched out her hand in Luz's direction without realizing that her words about other young men who resembled Arturo had had an impact on Luz. "Petra, have you by any chance met my son? His name is Bernabé and he looks like this young man."

The coyota looked into Luz's eyes. When she spoke her voice was almost soft. "They all look like Arturo, madre. They all have the same fever in their eyes. How could I possibly know your son from all the rest?"

Luz's heart shuddered when the coyota called her madre. Something told her that the woman did know Bernabé. This thought filled her with new hope, and she gladly reached into her purse. She put the money into the coyota's hand, saying, "Hasta pronto. I hope, Petra, that our paths will cross again sooner or later."

Luz and Arturo were handed the small bundles they had brought with them from Mexico City. As they stepped out of the car, the engine cranked on, backfiring loudly. When it disappeared into the flow of traffic, both realized that even though only three days had passed since they had left Mexico, they had crossed over into a world unknown to them. They were aware that they were facing days and months, perhaps even years, filled with dangers neither of them could imagine.

Feeling apprehensive, they were silent as they approached the large house that their guide had pointed out. They didn't know that the building had been a convent and that it was now a refuge run by priests and other volunteers. Neither realized that they were entering a sanctuary for the displaced and for those without documents or jobs. When they were shown in, Luz and Arturo were surprised at how warmly they were received. No one asked any questions. Afterwards, they were given food to eat and a place to sleep.

from

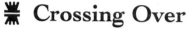 # Crossing Over

Rubén Martínez

2001

Rubén Martínez was born in Los Angeles to immigrants from Mexico and El Salvador. A poet, essayist, playwright, musician, record producer, teacher, performance artist, and Emmy Award–winning journalist, he makes his living traveling throughout the United States and Mexico, writing and reporting about his experiences on the road and the lives of people he meets. The following excerpt is from his most recent book, *Crossing Over: A Mexican Family on the Migrant Trail* (2001).

I AM IN THE BADLANDS OF SOUTHERN CALIFORNIA, en route to an appointment with the dead. I'm headed to Temecula, a growing city on the edge of Riverside County. It is arid country here, the westernmost point of the vast desert that spreads from the California beach all the way to the Gulf Coast of Texas.

For the American migrants who rode the wagon trains westward, California was once the "other side," just as it is today for the migrants heading north. Up from the fine yellow dust of these hills rise imported laurels, palms, sycamores, avocados, willows, oleander, eucalyptus. There are even apple and citrus orchards. But now and again, the old desert, a reminder of Mexican, or even Indian, California, appears in the form of an ancient, lonely stand of nopal cactus.

I take the exit at Rancho California Road. Temecula is picturesque, with its Western wagon-wheel decor. The elite live in the hills above town, in huge, recently built homes of the faux California mission variety: red tile roofs, beige stucco, wrought iron. There are rose gardens and the occasional artificial pond gracing the spacious yards. One of the local realty agents is called Sunshine Properties.

I head west along a winding two-lane that climbs into the Santa Rosa Mountains, a range that runs southward and eventually crosses the international line. The Santa Rosas are beautiful and bizarre: gently rolling hills of green give way suddenly to boulder-strewn peaks and chasms. On the Mexican side, the landscape is precipitous—and infamous. There, a stretch of Mexico Federal Highway 2 known as La Rumorosa (The Whispering One, for the haunted winds that blow through the canyons) has been the site of hundreds of fatal wrecks over the decades.

My destination is the intersection of Calle Capistrano and Avenida Del Oro. The names are, of course, Spanish—appropriated by the whites to romance their idyll with a dash of old California. The street signs are rendered in faux rustic, engraved wood. Most of the whites who live here now were once migrants themselves, belonging to subsequent waves of American wanderers—the Depression-era and postwar generations that pulled up stakes in the Midwest and on the East Coast to spend their lives in balmy paradise. This land was a final destination for them, the consummation of their California dream. You don't leave paradise once you've found it.

But for the Mexican migrants, Temecula is a stopover, not a final destination. Sure, there are Mexican gardeners tending to the rose bushes, cleaning the swimming pools, washing and folding the clothes, cooking the meals; brown women sing lullabies in Spanish to white babies. But the Mexicans are here for just as long as they have to be. They are mostly young and don't think of retiring, not only because they have no money to do so but also because they can't imagine themselves old yet. Most of the Mexicans in Temecula are literally just passing through, crammed into pickup trucks and vans driven by the coyotes. Temecula is just another of the hundred places they will blow through en route to St. Louis, Los Angeles, Houston, New York, Chicago, Decatur. But even these are not final destinations. The migrants will follow trails determined by America's labor economy: they will keep moving, from one coast to another, from picking the fields to working in hotels and restaurants, from cities to heartland towns.

Temecula was long a quiet town. But to the retirees' dismay, it is now a staging area for the battle of the border, in which two armies face off, usually under cover of darkness. It is a battle in which, occasionally, blood is spilled, though usually only on one side.

I turn right at Avenida Del Oro and pick up speed on a steep downhill grade. The road begins a long curve between hills dotted with rural mansions and avocado orchards. At the bottom of the gully, at the intersection with Calle Capistrano, I stop the car. The sun has fallen behind the hills to the west but still illuminates the higher terrain with a lush, classic California gold. Silvery plumes from the irrigation sprinklers are over the fields.

This is where it happened. Where Benjamín, Jaime, and Salvador Chávez and five others, all of them undocumented Mexican migrants, "illegals," died crammed in a truck that sped along this rural road four and a half years ago.

I clamber down into the drainage ditch below the road. Yellow dirt and sickly weeds. I find a screen from the window of the truck's camper shell and a blue piece of plastic from the shell itself, about a foot long and six inches wide. And another piece of black plastic: a fragment of the truck's running board. I pick up and examine a faded, crumpled tube of Colgate toothpaste, its ingredients listed in Spanish. There is an equally faded and torn McDonald's medium-size Coca-Cola cup.

Above the ditch, an anonymous artisan has built a small altar by taking the trunk of a California oak, slicing it in half, and carving out seven small crosses that he has filled in with light blue paint. (There should be eight crosses; the artisan was apparently unaware of the last victim's death in a nearby hospital several days after the accident.) It is a simple, beautiful monument.

I walk a ways up the hill, the bed of dead avocado leaves crunching underfoot. There is very little traffic and it is quiet, except for the leaves of the avocados rustling in the warm wind and, suddenly and eerily, the voices of men. Men speaking in Spanish. It sounds like they are nearby, but it takes me a while to spot them, high on a hill south of me. They are Mexican farmworkers, chatting casually as they pick avocados. They are a good half mile away, but the wind has brought their voices very close. These men traveled the same road that Benjamín and his brothers did. They are farmworkers now. Benjamín, Salvador, and Jaime Chávez are not. This is where their road ended.

It is five o'clock in the morning on Saturday, April 6, 1996. Two weeks before Easter, two more weeks of Lent before the Passion. The sun will soon break over the Temecula Valley. The moon is a little less than half full, dipping low into the southwestern sky. The stars have dimmed with the approach of the sun. Only the planet Jupiter is visible, and it is just about to fall into the leaves of a stand of avocados on the south side of Avenida Del Oro. It is a clear and dry morning, and although it is early spring, the temperature is already seventy degrees; it will reach into the nineties at midday.

Avenida Del Oro is an east–west rural two-lane road of pitch black asphalt and a bright solid yellow dividing line that runs for several hundred feet across the intersection with Calle Capistrano. Here, Avenida Del Oro falls into a steep gully along a long, sharp curve, the kind that creeps up on you and causes you to instinctively hit the brakes as you come to the bend. Calle Capistrano is a smaller road that runs north toward a few residences and orchards. The point at which the two streets join is precisely the bend in Avenida Del Oro's curve.

Deck lights glow amber from a ranch house high up on a hill to the east. There is no breeze. Occasionally there is the sound of an avocado falling, at first slithering through the branches, then hitting the thick bed of dry dead leaves below with a loud, brittle crash.

At 5:15 the eastern sky is pale yellow. Shades of dusty pink rise into blue greens and finally into deep blue at the zenith and in the west. A 1989 GMC truck, blue with silver trim, equipped with a camper shell of darkly tinted windows, speeds westward down Avenida Del Oro. Twenty-seven people are inside, twenty-five of them in the camper and two in the front seat. All are undocumented Mexican migrants.

The reason the coyote is on this isolated rural road is the inauguration of the U.S. Border Patrol interdiction effort known as Operation Gatekeeper. In 1994, a massive new steel wall was built along several miles of the border running east from the beach at Tijuana. After the Border Patrol claimed success with Operation Gatekeeper, it followed with similar measures in Nogales, Arizona (Operation Safeguard); El Paso, Texas (Operation Hold the Line); and McAllen, Texas (Operation Rio Grande). Consequently, the Mexican coyotes, not to be outdone by gringo technology, have chosen more circuitous routes through rugged terrain eastward. These new routes are extremely dangerous. Dozens of migrants have died of exposure in the torrid heat and bitter cold of the Colorado Desert since 1994. There are hundreds of such crossings between the beaches of Southern California and the Gulf Coast of Texas, and the cat-and-mouse game between the coyotes and the Border Patrol is never-ending.

A Border Patrol truck spots the GMC several miles south of the intersection of Avenida Del Oro and Calle Capistrano. What the BP agents see is a vehicle clearly overloaded, its fenders practically scraping the tires. From this point on, there are differing versions as to what occurred. The BP maintains that their personnel followed the vehicle at a discreet distance, with its emergency lights off. Lawyers representing the victims say that the BP wrecklessly and needlessly endangered the lives of the migrants by engaging in a high-speed pursuit.

For most of the hour-long ride up from the border, Benjamín, Jaime, and Salvador Chávez and their compatriots in the camper shell see nothing, not even one another's faces, because very little of the approaching dawn's light penetrates the camper's tinted windows.

When the coyote notices the BP truck in his side mirrors (he couldn't have seen much in the rearview mirror, given the dark glass and the twenty-five bodies piled like a cord of wood in the back), he speeds up, the tires screeching on the curves.

Inside the camper, panic rules. Those closest to the small window that looks in on the cab of the truck pound on it and scream at the coyote to stop. Several survivors recall that Benjamín Chávez shouted the loudest, a deep-throated yell. But it is to no avail. The coyote has been drinking. He has been snorting coke. He is hunched over the steering wheel, oblivious to everything but the BP truck behind him and the dark, winding road ahead.

Increasingly desperate, the migrants pop the camper's rear window open. They throw their small travel bags, their water bottles, and even a tire jack in the direction of the BP vehicle, but these fall harmlessly by the side of the road. They make dramatic hand gestures at the agents, imploring them to give up the pursuit, not because they want to avoid apprehension but because they want their driver to slow down. They are in fear for their lives.

The Chávez brothers, crunched against one another in the truck bed, see very little even when the rear window is opened. They are deep inside the camper, hemmed in by twenty-three other bodies. They only feel the lurching of the truck and hear the men's groans as they are slammed about on the curves.

The GMC hurtles down Avenida Del Oro at close to seventy miles an hour. About three hundred feet from Calle Capistrano, the coyote realizes he can't negotiate the curve and slams on the brakes. The realization comes too late.

There is a long skid, and the truck spins 180 degrees.

Then there is silence for a split second, as the truck flies off the road and turns over in the air.

And now a thousand sounds at once: the crumpling, the breaking, the crushing, and the snapping of glass, metal, plastic, bone. The truck comes down roof first in the ditch. Most of the bodies inside the camper shell spill out. Not all are completely ejected. Several are crushed underneath the mangled chassis of the truck. A cloud of dust rises from the impact.

The sun crests the horizon in the east now. It is possible that one of the last things some of the migrants saw, for just a fraction of a second, was the yellow glow on the horizon. Or maybe some of them saw the dust from the crash hanging in the air and heard the silence of the desert return as the groans of the dying faded.

Benjamín, Jaime, and Salvador were crushed under the truck. They had departed their home in Cherán, an Indian town in the highlands of Michoacán, a few days earlier and were on their way to Watsonville, California, to their usual stint of seasonal work picking strawberries in the fertile hills east of Santa Cruz. The accident made headlines in the United States for the enormity of the tragedy (eight people killed, nineteen injured, many critically) and because just a few days earlier another incident involving Mexican migrants had attracted attention. A videotape reminiscent of the Rodney King footage had aired on the evening news showing Riverside sheriff's deputies beating unarmed Mexican migrants, none of them visibly resisting, by the side of a Southern California freeway at rush hour.

Over the last decade, the numbers of casualties at the U.S.-Mexico line have begun to look like the tallies from a low-intensity conflict in a corner of the developing world. A University of Houston study counted some three thousand deaths in the last half of the 1990s, a conservative figure. Many bodies, the researcher concluded, will never be found. The bones of these migrants are hidden in the sludge at the bottom of the Rio Grande and scattered across the open desert.

And yet the migrants continue to cross, because ideals of paradise die hard, especially for Mexicans, who for several decades have regarded the Rio Grande as a river of life more than of death, notwithstanding accidents like the one at Temecula. They continue to cross despite the tragedies and despite Operation Gatekeeper because the odds remain in their favor. To truly "hold the line," as American politicians say, the United States would have to spend hundreds of billions of dollars—currently it is spending some four billion a year—to either build the Great Wall of America or amass all along the line, like at the border between North and South Korea or at the old divide between East and

West Berlin, thousands of troops and all manner of physical obstacle, weaponry, and technology. Despite continuing anti-immigrant sentiment in the United States, there are no credible proposals to do so at this time. After all the rhetoric, the line is still more an idea than a reality. Most of the border between the United States and Mexico is represented not by Operation Gatekeeper's twelve-foot-tall steel barriers but by barbed-wire fences often little more than a few feet high. In hundreds of places, the wire has been cut. You can stand on the line through most of California, Arizona, New Mexico, and Texas and hop from one side to the other, screaming at the top of your lungs, and no one will see you, except perhaps a desert tortoise or a real coyote.

Wetbacks

Beverly Silva

1983

Beverly Silva was born in Los Angeles and is a longtime resident of San Jose, where she teaches English as a second language to adults. Her poetry has appeared in many journals and magazines, she co-edited the anthology *Nosotros: Latina Literature Today* (1986), and she is the author of *The Cat and Other Stories* (1986) and *The Second St. Poems* (1983).

used to cross the river
& sometimes their backs got wet.
They wanted to enter the promised land
make a few dollars at minimum wage or less
then split back to their families.
Nada más
y no problemas.
        Only there's a fence
between Baja and California, U.S.A.
climb the fence
drop down to the highway below
& run for the woods.
        Only it's not done that way.
You need a good coyote to bring you across
know when the guard changes
give you a bed for the night
a plate of frijoles before departure
cross the checkpoint with papers intact
& deliver you up to L.A.
$300 for services rendered.
Then you can make a few American dollars

split back to the family
y no problemas.
Only the family writes,
los niños necesitan ropa
el papá está enfermo
no hay mucha comida
& if otro hermano could make American dollars
to send home...
Only it takes much saving for the coyote
to bring the brother across.
Then waiting in an L.A. cantina
an empty car arrives,
the brother's in a Tijuana jail
& the coyote's very sorry
but a no-good hombre,
immigration man,
give him the double cross.
¡Y chingada!
You know how these things are.
¡Así es la vida!
The family writes again,
the brother is sick,
many bruises from los policías.
Necesita un mejor coyote.
& It takes much money
for a better coyote.
Eighteen-year-old wetback
only looking for a job
washing dishes for American dollars.
Nada más
y no problemas.

BETWEEN CULTURES

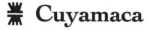 # Cuyamaca

Gloria Anzaldúa

1987

Gloria Anzaldúa was born in 1942 in the Rio Grande valley
in Texas and spent her childhood working in the fields on
the U.S./Mexico border with her immigrant parents. A noted
feminist and lesbian activist, she has authored and edited
bilingual poetry, fiction, and nonfiction for adults and children, and has taught courses in feminism, Chicano studies,
and creative writing at universities in Texas, Vermont, and
California. She has won numerous writing awards, including
an American Book Award for co-editing (with Cherríe L.
Moraga) *This Bridge Called My Back* (1981). The following
poem is from *Borderlands/La Frontera* (1987), in which
Anzaldúa combines poetry, memoir, and historical analysis
in several dialects of Spanish and English. It was chosen as
one of the 38 Best Books of 1987 by the *Literary Journal*.

for Beth Brant and Chrystos

"This tribe is the most numerous and the most restless,
stubborn, haughty, warlike and hostile toward us...."
—Don Pedro Fages, 1787

Driving down the canyon
on a road gouged out of the side of the mountain
red red earth and exposed roots
sticking out like amputated fingers.
145 acres for sale

the Indians safely locked up in reservations
or urban ghettos.

Driving around the mountain
inside the car
fighting for silence.
Houses stick out like pimples
on the face of the mountain.

At the skirt of the mountain ranges
I met a woman from a nearly extinct tribe,
the Kumeyaay.
Her name was Til'pu,
meaning Roadrunner.
By a stream amidst the gushing water
under the olive woolly head of the mountain
I met her.

Under the encina tree I sat.
She emerged out of the smooth amber flesh
of the manzanita,
in sandals of woven yucca,
skin polished bronze by the sun
she appeared
with a tattoo on her arm
pricked by cactus thorns
ground charcoal rubbed on the wound.

There's a forest fire in the Cuyamaca Peaks,
a sign: 4 Parcels For Sale,
the Indians locked up in reservations
and Til'pu behind glass in the museum.

from

✸ The Lariat

Jaime de Angulo

1974

Jaime de Angulo was known as an eccentric and outspoken scholar in several academic fields, but he also turned his formal education to more artistic ends, writing creative works like *Indian Tales, Indians in Overalls, Jaime in Taos,* and *How the World Was Made,* all published after his death in 1950. The following excerpt is from his novel *The Lariat* (1974), a work inspired by the California diaries of early Spanish missionaries and shaped by de Angulo's unique sense of history. Another selection by de Angulo, "Five Thousand Years," also appears in this collection.

WHO WAS FRAY LUIS?

We do not really know. He had come from Old Spain, so much is clear. He may perhaps have been that second son of the Don Aniceto mentioned in a family record of the parish of Haro, and whose name was so curiously omitted by the scribe's oversight. The record reads:

> …The second son of Don Aniceto, after a turbulent youth, was touched by the grace of God and entered holy orders. He took the habit of San Francis, and was sent to the Americas, to the missions of Alta California. Recognizing his indomitable energy, his superiors turned the adventurous spirit of the man to the greater glory of God, and thus it was that he traveled from one mission to another along the coast of the Pacific Ocean, entering the wild hills covered with forests to preach the Holy Doctrine to the savage

Indians of the woods. Until the Devil, Father of all Malice, alarmed at his success, counseled their priests to kill him, and he was crowned with the glory of the martyrs. The third son of Don Aniceto, Don Jaime, studied in Salamanca...

But even if his name had not been so strangely omitted, we would still remain in doubt as to his identity, for like many friars of that time he was known only by his nom de religion: Fray Luis. Fray Luis he remains for us, may God rest his passionate soul!

Fray Luis came to Monterey in California, in the days of the Indians. He came to save their pagan souls, but as we shall see, he used the powers of sorcery, once, and lost his own.

We may find some excuse for his sin in the violence of the passion of a man surrendered to God, in his agony as the day drew near when he would be forced to witness the profanation, the rape of his own soul. For, was not that Indian girl part and parcel of his soul? He himself had redeemed her. He himself had instructed her in the true faith. He himself had poured the waters of baptism over her lovely head.... The water had trickled down her throat, and a drop ran between her breasts. They were full and goat-shaped, like most Indians', and he associated them vaguely in his mind with the aroma of chocolate scented with vanilla.

And now he must perform another sacrament, bind her to the object of her carnal desire, a handsome half-breed, a half-savage, a youth in whose eyes lurked the gleam of untamed passions. He must deliver his dove into such claws! It would have been better indeed to leave her a pagan....To find one's soul revealed only to be forced to prostitute it, and in the very name of God's sacred ministry!

Let us be charitable and realize the enormous temptation for such a mind in its agony to clutch at a straw and turn for help to the very monsters he had come to destroy. The monsters helped him. They gave him their power. He used it. Then, in the terror of his repentance, he betrayed his new masters, he went back to his own God. But the monsters had hold of him by a rope. The monsters had hold of one end, and the other was girt around his loins. An unbreakable rope, a vaquero's riata, a monk's cord...

Struggle, struggle, Fray Luis! the monsters are pulling, pulling, dragging you down...Ah! It is useless, Fray Luis. You gave them your soul. Down you go.

Who was Fray Luis? Who he was appears best from his own curious diary:

> ...Wednesday, Feast of San Fernando, Confessor and
> Martyr. I arrived here last night, at this Mission of San
> Carlos Borromeo del Carmelo, and very tired. Fray
> Bernardo is superior of this mission which is a very thriv-
> ing one having been the pet of Fray Junípero, may his soul
> rest in heaven. And it surely must, for he earned it, as does
> anyone who comes here from the south by following the
> coast. A more villainous country I have never seen. There
> are neither roads nor trails. I would have done better to
> come roundabout by the valley and Mission Soledad, but I
> tried to take a short-cut and came directly along the coast
> through the country of those wild Esselen Indians whom I
> hope so much to convert. But it was an infernal trip and
> my donkey agrees with me. I shall not be able to ride him
> for a week. And yet I walked a great deal of the time dur-
> ing the last four days, so much so that I wore out a new
> pair of sandals and the bottom of my cassock is in shreds.
> Usually during my journeys into the rough country I wrap
> it around my waist, it is so much easier to walk or ride, and
> I don't think that our father San Francis was dreaming of
> American missions, we do enough penance in this wilder-
> ness, but this time it was worse penance yet, lacerating my
> bare legs with the thorns of the trail. I must either wrap my
> legs with strips of buckskin like some of these Indians or
> wear leather trousers like the vaqueros. That will shock that
> old maid of Fray Bernardo and he will send a long epistle
> to Mexico. Fussy old mollycoddle, trotting from one ware-
> house to another, he prays the mass of Saint Tallow, Saint
> Wool, and Saint Corn. May he be granted as many days of
> indulgence as all the heads of cattle he has made the con-
> verts raise for the Church. That is enough in any case to
> send him straight to heaven, for the old eunuch knows not
> temptation and his only sins are those of old women...
> grumbling and avariciousness. Well, each one serves God
> according to his own talent, I tame wild horses and he
> makes them work. I wear out my sandals and tear my cassock
> and risk an arrow in the seat thereof or a more vital spot to
> bring the effulgent fight of the true faith to these lost sheep
> sunk in the dark labyrinth of superstitious slavery. "Come,

my brothers, the life is not in your trees and in your rocks, it is in Our Father, He who made us and all, the only God. See Him behind the tree, under the rock, all beauty, incandescent and terrible, lovely in the image of His Son. Come and adore the true God." But evidently I should amend it thus: "Come and work for Fray Bernardo of the Tallow." Fray Tallow! I will wrap my cassock around my waist, if I please, and wear boots and spurs, beautiful silver spurs, and a wide sombrero to save my tonsure from the sun, I'll tie a bright silk around my neck, I'll mount a wild stallion, I'll turn in the saddle and thumb my nose at you, I'll ride to the hills.…Father in Heaven, Jesus, Saint Fernando, Angel of my guard, come and save me! Chase this devil away! Scourge me, beat me! Oh, my God, why must thou always tempt me? Have pity! Has it not been enough?…

Fray Luis must have spent a night of remorse, for the next day he writes in a more chastened mood:

I spent the morning with Fray Bernardo, making the rounds of the mission. We had to visit everything, the tallow works, the piles of hides, the granaries, the tile works, and the adobería. The good padre is very proud of it all, of the good order, of the prosperousness, of the apparent contentment of the Indians. They are working in their usual lazy way, and they smiled when we passed. Their eyes followed Fray Bernardo and I could see that they were fond of him. Well, he gives them plenty of atole, and he does not whip them much. This noon I tasted the pozole myself, and I found a lot of meat scraps in it, much more than we ever put in at San Antonio or at San Juan Capistrano or any of the other missions where I have stayed. No wonder the Indians here are so fat. And I didn't notice any of the sullen looks of San Antonio, nothing but that shadow of gentle sadness over their eyes. They all have it, these Indians, when they are away from their rancherías. Fray Bernardo talked and talked in his tight Catalonian accent. I think he comes from Mallorca or another one of the Balearic Islands. Anyway he is the most active old man I ever saw. Quite an administrator and very pious. But oh! so garrulous and such a child in some ways. For instance, he took me this afternoon to see the magnificent beach which is not far from the mission. Well, there, just on the other side of the rocks, there was an Indian girl bathing and all naked. What a scolding she got from Fray Tallow! "…Didn't that hussy know that it was strictly against the rules? She would get the lash for that! Shameless wench, why didn't she go back among the gentiles?…" all of this in mixed Rumsen and Catalan. The poor little one was standing before us, with tears in her eyes, very much distressed at all the violence, but quite plainly not understanding a word of what he said. I questioned her in the language of Mission San Antonio where she came from. She said she belonged to a ranchería of Esselen, back in the hills near the coast between here and San Antonio, that she had only been here a week, that she did not understand the language of the Rumsen Indians, nor the language of the white men, why was this man so angry, was he a powerful sorcerer, and would I please ask him not to give her the evil eye. When I interpreted all this, Fray Bernardo tore his hair. "What? Another language yet? Misericordious Father in Heaven, how many languages are there in this California? I have been here all these years and I never heard of Helens before. And now who is going to instruct this poor wild girl?" I assured him that I would, since I knew the Sextapay language and this girl seemed to understand it. At this he was very much relieved, and we went home, he to his account books and I to my worries. I am worried. I think that innocently I put an evil thought into that girl's heart. I need not have explained to her the cause of Brother Tallow's wrath. I should have invented some excuse. But my wits were asleep because I was struggling with the work of translation. At first she didn't understand. She looked at me incredulously. Then she seemed to comprehend, and she began to laugh, but she suddenly checked herself, and slowly the blush of shame crept all over her dark skin. And I who had been innocent of any thought up to this moment, felt myself blushing by contagion. Seeing this, the girl turned and fled toward the rocks where she had left her sarape.[…]

At the Mission of the Carmel, Fray Luis was catechizing his especial neophyte, that girl who had run away from the Esselen tribe. He had other neophytes also to instruct, men and women from the Rumsen tribe, mostly people from the Carmel Valley and from the rancherías along the lower part of the Salinas River, but he was especially interested in the Esselen girl because she was the only Esselen at the mission. It was the first time that anyone from that wild tribe had been persuaded to leave the mountains and come to the mission. In fact she had come of her own free will. She had appeared there, one morning, foot-sore and hungry, and very shy, just a few days before Fray Luis arrived. She was of course a godsend for that friar whose very ambition was precisely to bring the light of the true God to the wild Esselen. And so he spent more of his time learning the Esselen language from her than teaching her the catechism.

He wrote in that curious diary of his:

> Dia de Sta. Gertrudis, Virgin, and a most beautiful day, too, with an amethyst tint spread over the valley. I called this to the attention of Fray Bernardo. "Yes, yes," quoth he, "very beautiful, very beautiful, and just think, my dear Fray Luis, just think of how much grain could be raised here and exported if only the home government were not so short-sighted in its policy!"…and he went on to explain a lot of things which I did not understand. That Catalan has a head on his shoulders! I also asked my little wild beauty what they call that color in her language. She said there was no name for it, but it made her think of the inside of an abalone shell. I asked why. "Because it isn't real," she answered. She says things like that, all the time, that make me restless. And then when I try to teach her the catechism I find her stupid. Strange little animal! But anyway she is a good teacher when it comes to language. Only, what a devil of a language! You say everything upside down. It reminds me more of the Sextapay of San Antonio than of the Rumsen of these parts. As soon as I know enough of it I am going down into that country. I am burning to convert these poor wild Esselen. Something is drawing me to that place. I have been dreaming of it, several times, curious dreams, almost nightmares. I must go there. I did not come here to get fat and lazy. As soon as I know enough of the language I will go. God will help me…and if He has

reserved me for the fate of the martyrs, blessed be His will, say I. What more do I crave than to expiate my sins? What could be sweeter than to forget?…I must make a friend of that young vaquero. He may be able to help me. They say that his father and he are the only white men living down there, and that they are on good terms with the Indians. The young fellow was here again last night. I must say I don't like him, and I don't know why. There is something subtly insolent in his bearing. It's not his manners. He is boorish enough, but so is everybody in this country. For the matter of that, he is not half as boorish as the people of the presidio, the commander of the garrison included, and they have not the excuse of having been raised like an animal of the wilds.…Fray Luis! remember that you are no longer in Salamanca, this cassock is not a cappa, remember above all that this crucifix is not the hilt of your sword. Ah! my sword, my lovely, my pretty where are you? Is it a sin to remember you, and your lithe body, my mistress, my very myself? Is it a sin? Is it not enough to stand with patience and humility this fellow's searching gaze? And how well he rides! I believe that is what I am jealous of. What a figure he would make in the streets of Sevilla!…Bah! This is an edifying diary I keep. Shame on you, Fray Luis, pray, Fray Luis, you unworthy monk, take your breviary and pray, I'll discipline you, I'll make you forget, I'll scourge you, the lash for you, the lash for the devil in you.…

I don't know how many strokes I gave my poor back, enough anyway to bring the blood…but I feel better, I will sleep peacefully tonight. Saint Gertrudis, you noble virgin, I offer my pain to you. I offer it for this poor Indian girl, take her under your protection.…Nine o'clock! To bed, to bed, three hours only before matins and the shaking hand of Fray Tallow on my shoulder. How I do hate to hear his Catalan rasp from under my dreams, "Come come, Fray Luis, up with you, it's almost a quarter past midnight. Come, come, to the chapel, don't be so lazy"…well, to bed!

Look at these two men at matins, in the echoing empty church, just these two, on either side of the nave, each one with a candle to his book, throwing back and forth the versicle and the response, the two voices alternating in sonorous cadence, monotonously for an hour, while outside the constellations swing around the pole toward the chilly dawn. Ah! the wonderful technique in all ritual, this losing of one's own self into the magma of a cosmic rhythm, the dissolving of the individual and his pain, and his sorrow, and all that effort to hold the self together. To stamp a chant around a drum under the moon, or to swing a psalm in the gloom of the nave, two techniques for two cultures, but the same psychological problem, at bottom, and after all very much the same treatment.... Therein lies the beauty of prayer in common. And therefore it was a wise monastic rule that held these two friars to what may seem an almost meaningless, an unnecessary formality. Two monks holding matins by themselves, just exactly as if they had been a whole congregation. It makes one think of those white men who live alone in the tropics and dress every evening for supper. Two monks, two white monks, isolated in their mission, on the outskirts of a not even very civilized colony, and surrounded by more than a hundred so-called converts, and several thousand not far outside the mission adobe walls, in all the rancherías, practicing actively all the rites of magic and sorcery, these two white monks they had need, indeed, to hold on tight to all the forms and formalities of their own culture...one of these two especially.

✹ we've played cowboys

alurista

1971

alurista was born Alberto Baltazar Urista in 1947 in Mexico City and came to the United States at age thirteen. His university education in religion, sociology, social welfare, and psychology is evident in his work as a teacher, performance artist, activist, editor, publisher, scholar, and critic. His activism in and around San Diego includes co-founding the Movimiento Estudiantil Chicano de Aztlán (MEChA), the Brown Berets, Chicano Park, the Centro Cultural de la Raza, the Chicano Free Clinic, and the Chicano studies department at San Diego State University. He has written many volumes of poetry, including *Et Tu...Raza?* (1997), which won an American Book Award, and his latest book, *As Our Barrio Turns...Who the Yoke B On?* (2000), which won an award from the Latino Literary Hall of Fame.

We've played cowboys
        not knowing
nuestros charros
        and their countenance
con trajes de gala
        silver embroidery
on black wool
        Zapata rode in white
campesino white
        and Villa in brown
y nuestros charros
        parade of sculptured gods

on horses
        —of flowing manes
proud
        erect
they galloped
and we've played cowboys
        —as opposed to indians
when ancestors of mis charros abuelos
indios fueron
        de la meseta central
and of the humid jungles of Yucatán
        nuestros MAYAS
if we must
        cowboys play
—con bigotes
        y ojos negros

✹ My Grandmother Would Rock Quietly and Hum

Leonard Adame

1975

Leonard Adame has spent his entire life in Fresno, where he was part of the school of poets studying with Philip Levine. His poems appeared regularly in the *American Poetry Review*, and he is one of the authors featured in *Entrance: 4 Chicano Poets* (1975) with Luis Omar Salinas, Gary Soto, and Ernesto Trejo.

in her house
she would rock quietly and hum
until her swelled hands
calmed

in summer
she wore thick stockings
sweaters
and gray braids

mornings,
sunlight barely lit
the kitchen.
flour tortillas
were rolled quietly;
the papas
crackling in hot lard
wakened me,
and where

there were shadows
it was not cold

with bread soaked
in café,
she sat and talked
of girlhood—
of things strange to me:
        Mexico
        epidemics
        relatives shot
        her father's hopes
        of this country,
        and how they sank
        with cement dust
        to his insides

now,
at the old house,
there are
worn spots by the stove
where she shuffled,
and Mexico
hangs in her
fading calendar pictures…

✳ Doña Toña of Nineteenth Street

Luis "Louie the Foot" González

1976

Luis "Louie the Foot" González co-founded the Royal
Chicano Air Force (originally the Rebel Chicano Art
Front), a Sacramento-based arts collective established in
1969 to promote civil rights and labor rights. His poster art
reflects the satiric tone the RCAF became known for, but
the following story provides a more subtle view of what
happens when cultures collide.

HER NAME WAS DOÑA TOÑA and I can't help but remember the fear I
had of the old lady. Maybe it was the way all the younger kids talked
about her:

"Ya, man. I saw her out one night and she was pulling some weeds
near the railroad tracks and her cat was meowing away like it was ready
to fight that big black dog and, man, she looked just like a witch, like
the Llorona trying to dig up her children."

"Martin's tellin' everybody that she was dancin' aroun' real slow
and singin' some witch songs in her backyard when it was dark and
everybody was asleep."

Doña Toña was always walking somewhere…anywhere…even
when she had no particular place to go. When she walked, it was as
though she were making a great effort because her right leg was kind of
funny. It dragged a little and it made her look as if her foot were made
of solid metal.

Her face was the color of lightly creamed coffee. The wrinkles
around her forehead and eyes were like the rings of a very old tree. They
gave her age as being somewhere around seventy-five years old, but as I
was to discover later, she was really eighty-nine. Even though her eyes
attracted much attention, they always gave way to her mouth. Most of

the people that I had observed looking at her directed their gaze at her mouth. Doña Toña had only one tooth to her name and it was the strangest tooth I had ever seen. It was exceptionally long and it stuck out from her upper gum at a forty-five degree angle. What made it even stranger was that it was also twisted. She at one time probably had an overabundance of teeth, until they began to push against each other, twisting themselves, until she had only one last tooth left. It was the toughest of them all, the king of the hill, "el mero chingón."

Doña Toña was born in 1885 in one of the innumerable little towns of México. The Mexican Revolution of 1910 drove her from her little-town home when she was twenty-seven years old. She escaped the mass bloodshed of the Revolution by crossing the border into the United States and living in countless towns from Los Angeles to Sacramento, where she became the most familiar sight in Barrio Cinco. She was one of the barrio's landmarks; when you saw her, you knew that you were in the barrio. She had been there longer than anyone else and yet no one, except perhaps her daughter María, knew very much about her. Some people said that was the way she wanted it. But as far as I could see, she didn't show signs of wanting to be alone.

Whenever Doña Toña caught someone watching her during one of her never-ending strolls, she would stop walking and look at that person head-on. No one could keep staring at her once she had started to stare back. There was something in Doña Toña's stare that could make anybody feel like a child. Her crow-black eyes could hypnotize almost anybody. She could have probably put an owl to sleep with her stare.

Doña Toña was Little Feo's grandmother. She lived with her daughter, María, who was Little Feo's mother. All of Little Feo's ten years of life had passed without the outward lovingness that grandmothers are supposed to show. But the reason for it was Little Feo's own choice.

Whenever Little Feo, who was smaller, thinner, and darker than the rest of the barrio ten-year-olds, was running around with us (Danny, Fat Charlie, Bighead, Joe Nuts, and a few other guys that lived close by) nobody would say anything about his "abuelita." Before, whenever anybody used to make fun of her or use her for the punch line of a joke, Little Feo would get very quiet; his fists would begin to tighten and his face would turn a darker shade as all the blood rushed to his brain. One time when Fat Charlie said something like "What's black and flies at night? Why…it's Feo's granny," Little Feo pounced on him faster than I had ever seen anybody pounce on someone before. Fat Charlie kicked the hell out of Little Feo, but he never cracked another joke like that again, at least not about Doña Toña.

Doña Toña was not taken very seriously by very many people until someone in the barrio got sick. Visits to Doctor Herida when someone got sick were common even though few people liked to go to him, because he would just look at the patient and then scribble something on a prescription form and tell the sick one to take it next door to McAnaw's Pharmacy to have it filled. Herida and the pharmacist had a racket going. When the medicine Herida prescribed didn't have the desired effect, the word was sent out in the barrio that Doña Toña was needed somewhere. Sometimes it was at the Osorio house where Jaime was having trouble breathing, or the Canaguas place where what's-her-name was gaining a lot of weight. Regardless of the illness, Doña Toña would always show up, even if she had to drag herself across the barrio to get to where she was needed; and, many times, that's exactly what she did. Once at the place of need, she did whatever it was she had to and then she left, asking nothing of anyone. Usually, within a short time of her visit—hours (if the illness were a natural one) or a day or two (if it were supernatural)—the patient would show signs of improvement.

Doña Toña was never bothered about not receiving any credit for her efforts.

"You see, comadre, I tol' you the 'medicina' would estar' to work."

"Andale, didn't I tell you that Doctor Herida knew what he was doing."

"I don't know what that stupid old lady thought she was going to accomplish by doing all the hocus-pocus with those useless herbs and plants of hers. Everybody knows that an old witch's magic is no match for a doctor's medicine. That crazy old WITCH."

And that's how it was. Doña Toña didn't seem to mind that they called on her to help them and, after she had done what she could, they proceeded to bad-mouth her. That's the way it was and she didn't seem to mind.

I remember, perhaps best of all, the time my mother got sick. She was very pale and her whole body was sore. She went to see Doctor Herida and all he did was ask her what was wrong and, without even examining her, he prescribed something that she bought at McAnaw's. When all the little blue pills were gone, the soreness of her bones and the paleness of her skin remained. Not wanting to go back to Herida's, my mother asked me to go get Doña Toña. I would have never gone to get the old lady, but I had never before seen my mother so sick. So I went.

On the way to Little Feo's house, which was only three blocks from my own, I saw Doña Toña walking towards me. When she was close enough to hear me, I began to speak but she cut me off, saying that she knew my mother was sick and had asked for her. I got a little scared because there was no way that she could have known that my mother had asked for her, yet she knew. My head was bombarded with thoughts that perhaps she might be a witch after all. I had the urge to run away from her but I didn't. I began to think that if she were a witch, why was she always helping people? Witches were bad people. And Doña Toña wasn't. It was at this point that my fear of her disappeared and in its place sprouted an intense curiosity.

Doña Toña and I reached my house and we climbed the ten steps that led to the front door. I opened the door and waited for her to step in first, but she motioned with her hand for me to lead the way.

Doña Toña looked like a little moving shadow as we walked through the narrow hallway that ended at my mother's room. Her leg dragged across the old faded linoleum floor, making a dull scraping sound. I reached the room and opened the door. My mother was half-asleep on the bed as Doña Toña entered. I walked in after her because I wanted to see what kind of magic she was going to have to perform in order to save my mother; but as soon as Doña Toña began taking some candles from her sack, my mother looked at me and told me to go outside to play with the other kids.

I left the room but had no intentions of going outside to play. My mother's bedroom was next to the bathroom and there was a door that connected both of them. The bathroom could be locked only from the inside, so my mother usually left it unlocked in case some unexpected emergency came up. I went into the bathroom and, without turning on the light, looked through the crack of the slightly open door.

My mother was sprawled on the bed, face down. Her nightgown was open, exposing her shoulder blades and back. Doña Toña melted the bottoms of two candles and then placed one between the shoulder blades and the other at the base of the spine. Doña Toña began to pray as she pinched the area around the candles. Her movements were almost imperceptible.

The candlelight made her old brown hands shine and her eyes looked like little moons. Doña Toña's voice got louder as her hands moved faster across my mother's back. The words she prayed were indecipherable even with the increase in volume. The scene reminded me of a priest praying in Latin during Mass, asking God to save us from damnation while no one knew what he was saying. The wax from the candles slid down onto my mother's back and shoulder blades, forming what looked like roots. It looked as though there were two trees of wax growing out of her back.

About a half an hour went by before the candles had burned themselves into oblivion, spreading wax all over my mother's back. Doña Toña stopped praying and scraped the wax away. She reached into the sack and pulled out a little baby food jar half-filled with something that resembled lard. She scooped some of the stuff out with her hand and rubbed it over the areas that had been covered by the wax. Next, she took from the sack a coffee can filled with an herb that looked like oregano. She sprinkled the herb over the lardlike substance and began rubbing it into the skin.

When she was almost finished, Doña Toña looked around the room and stared straight into the dark opening of the bathroom. I felt that she knew I was behind the door but I stayed there anyway. She turned back to face my mother, bent down, and whispered something in her ear.

Doña Toña picked up all her paraphernalia and returned it to its place in the sack. As she started to leave, she headed for the bathroom door. The heart in my chest almost exploded before I heard my mother's voice tell Doña Toña that she was leaving through the wrong door.

I hurried from the bathroom and ran through the other rooms in the house so that I could catch Doña Toña to show her the way out. I reached her as she was closing the door to my mother's room and led her to the front of the house. As she was making her way down the stairs I heard her mumble something about "learning the secrets"; then she looked up at me and smiled. I couldn't help but smile back because her face looked like a brown jack-o'-lantern with only one strange tooth carved into it. Doña Toña turned to walk down the remaining four stairs. I was going to ask her what she had said, but by the time I had the words formed in my mind, she had reached the street and was on her way home.

I went back inside the house and looked in on my mother. She was asleep. I knew that she was going to be all right and that it was not going to be because the "medicina" was beginning to work or because Doctor Herida knew what he was doing.

from

✖ The Labyrinth of Solitude

Octavio Paz (translated by Lysander Kemp)

1961

Octavio Paz was born in 1914 in Mexico City, of Spanish and Indian ancestry. A protegé of Pablo Neruda, Paz was a poet and political activist who also worked as a journalist, diplomat, soldier, publisher, professor, and magazine editor, and he founded several influential literary reviews. Before his death in 1998, he had published more than forty books of poetry, fiction, and essays and won numerous prestigious awards, including the 1982 Neustadt Prize, the 1981 Cervantes Prize, and the 1990 Nobel Prize in Literature.

WHEN I ARRIVED IN THE UNITED STATES I lived for a while in Los Angeles, a city inhabited by over a million persons of Mexican origin. At first sight, the visitor is surprised not only by the purity of the sky and the ugliness of the dispersed and ostentatious buildings, but also by the city's vaguely Mexican atmosphere, which cannot be captured in words or concepts. This Mexicanism—delight in decorations, carelessness and pomp, negligence, passion and reserve—floats in the air. I say "floats" because it never mixes or unites with the other world, the North American world based on precision and efficiency. It floats, without offering any opposition; it hovers, blown here and there by the wind, sometimes breaking up like a cloud, sometimes standing erect like a rising skyrocket. It creeps, it wrinkles, it expands and contracts; it sleeps or dreams; it is ragged but beautiful. It floats, never quite existing, never quite vanishing.

Something of the same sort characterizes the Mexicans you see in the streets. They have lived in the city for many years wearing the same clothes and speaking the same language as the other inhabitants, and they feel ashamed of their origin; yet no one would mistake them for authentic North Americans. I refuse to believe that physical features are as important as is commonly thought. What distinguishes them, I think, is their furtive, restless air: they act like persons who are wearing disguises, who are afraid of a stranger's look because it could strip them and leave them stark naked. When you talk with them, you observe that their sensibilities are like a pendulum, but a pendulum that has lost its reason and swings violently and erratically back and forth. This spiritual condition, or lack of a spirit, has given birth to a type known as the pachuco. The pachucos are youths, for the most part of Mexican origin, who form gangs in southern cities; they can be identified by their language and behavior as well as by the clothing they affect. They are instinctive rebels, and North American racism has vented its wrath on them more than once. But the pachucos do not attempt to vindicate their race or the nationality of their forebears. Their attitude reveals an obstinate, almost fanatical will-to-be, but this will affirms nothing specific except their determination—it is an ambiguous one, as we will see—not to be like those around them. The pachuco does not want to become a Mexican again; at the same time he does not want to blend into the life of North America. His whole being is sheer negative impulse, a tangle of contradictions, an enigma. Even his very name is enigmatic: pachuco, a word of uncertain derivation, saying nothing and saying everything. It is a strange word with no definite meaning; or, to be more exact, it is charged like all popular creations with a diversity of meanings. Whether we like it or not, these persons are Mexicans, are one of the extremes at which the Mexican can arrive.

Since the pachuco cannot adapt himself to a civilization which, for its part, rejects him, he finds no answer to the hostility surrounding him except this angry affirmation of his personality. Other groups react differently. The Negroes, for example, oppressed by racial intolerance, try to "pass" as whites and thus enter society. They want to be like other people. The Mexicans have suffered a less violent rejection, but instead of attempting a problematical adjustment to society, the pachuco actually flaunts his differences. The purpose of his grotesque dandyism and anarchic behavior is not so much to point out the injustice and incapacity of a society that has failed to assimilate him as it is to demonstrate his personal will to remain different.

It is not important to examine the causes of this conflict, and even less so to ask whether or not it has a solution. There are minorities in many parts of the world who do not enjoy the same opportunities as the rest of the population. The important thing is this stubborn desire to be different, this anguished tension with which the lone Mexican—an orphan lacking both protectors and positive values—displays his differences. The pachuco has lost his whole inheritance: language, religion, customs, beliefs. He is left with only a body and a soul with which to confront the elements, defenseless against the stares of everyone. His disguise is a protection, but it also differentiates and isolates him: it both hides him and points him out.

His deliberately aesthetic clothing, whose significance is too obvious to require discussion, should not be mistaken for the outfit of a special group or sect. *Pachuquismo* is an open society, and this in a country full of cults and tribal costumes, all intended to satisfy the middle-class North American's desire to share in something more vital and solid than the abstract morality of the American Way of Life. The clothing of the pachuco is not a uniform or a ritual attire. It is simply a fashion, and like all fashions it is based on novelty—the mother of death, as Leopardi said—and imitation.

Its novelty consists in its exaggeration. The pachuco carries fashion to its ultimate consequences and turns it into something aesthetic. One of the principles that rules in North American fashions is that clothing must be comfortable, and the pachuco, by changing ordinary apparel into art, makes it "impractical." Hence it negates the very principles of the model that inspired it. Hence its aggressiveness.

This rebelliousness is only an empty gesture, because it is an exaggeration of the models against which he is trying to rebel, rather than a return to the dress of his forebears or the creation of a new style of his own. Eccentrics usually emphasize their decision to break away from society—either to form new and more tightly closed groups or to assert their individuality—through their way of dressing. In the case of the pachuco there is an obvious ambiguity: his clothing spotlights and isolates him, but at the same time it pays homage to the society he is attempting to deny.

This duality is also expressed in another, perhaps profounder way: the pachuco is an impassive and sinister clown whose purpose is to cause terror instead of laughter. His sadistic attitude is allied with a desire for self-abasement which in my opinion constitutes the very foundation of his character: he knows that it is dangerous to stand out and that his behavior irritates society, but nevertheless he seeks and attracts persecution and scandal. It is the only way he can establish a more vital relationship with the society he is antagonizing. As a victim, he can occupy a place in the world that previously had ignored him; as a delinquent, he can become one of its wicked heroes.

I believe that the North American's irritation results from his seeing the pachuco as a mythological figure and therefore, in effect, a danger. His dangerousness lies in his singularity. Everyone agrees in finding something hybrid about him, something disturbing and fascinating. He is surrounded by an aura of ambivalent notions: his singularity seems to be nourished by powers that are alternately evil and beneficent. Some people credit him with unusual erotic prowess; others consider him perverted but still aggressive. He is a symbol of love and joy or of horror and loathing, an embodiment of liberty, of disorder, of the forbidden. He is someone who ought to be destroyed. He is also someone with whom any contact must be made in secret, in the darkness.

The pachuco is impassive and contemptuous, allowing all these contradictory impressions to accumulate around him until finally, with a certain painful satisfaction, he sees them explode into a tavern fight or a raid by the police or a riot. And then, in suffering persecution, he becomes his true self, his supremely naked self, as a pariah, a man who belongs nowhere. The circle that began with provocation has completed itself and he is ready now for redemption, for his entrance into the society that rejected him. He has been its sin and its scandal, but now that he is a victim it recognizes him at last for what he really is: its product, its son. At last he has found new parents.

The pachuco tries to enter North American society in secret and daring ways, but he impedes his own efforts. Having been cut off from his traditional culture, he asserts himself for a moment as a solitary and challenging figure. He denies both the society from which he originated and that of North America. When he thrusts himself outward, it is not to unite with what surrounds him but rather to defy it. This is a suicidal gesture, because the pachuco does not affirm or defend anything except his exasperated will-not-to-be. He is not divulging his most intimate feelings: he is revealing an ulcer, exhibiting a wound. A wound that is also a grotesque, capricious, barbaric adornment. A wound that laughs at itself and decks itself out for the hunt. The pachuco is the prey of society, but instead of hiding he adorns himself to attract the hunter's attention. Persecution redeems him and breaks his solitude: his salvation depends on his becoming part of the very society he appears to deny. Solitude and sin, communion and health become synonymous terms.

✦ Recipe: Chorizo con Huevo Made in the Microwave

Barbara Brinson Curiel

1989

Barbara Brinson Curiel was born in 1956 in San Francisco. A poet, literary critic, translator, and professor, she is the author of several poetry collections and her work has appeared in anthologies in the United States, Mexico, and Europe. She has taught creative writing, English, ethnic studies, and women's studies, and she is currently a professor at Humboldt State University.

I won't lie,
It's not the same.

When you taste it
memories of abuelita
feeding wood into the stove
will dim.

You won't smell the black crisp
of tortillas
bubbling on cast iron.
Microwaved,
they are pale and limp as avena—
haven't a shadow of smoke.

There's no eggy lace
to scrape from the pan.
No splatters of grease
on the back of the stove.

Everything is clean:
vaporized
dripless.

It's not the same.

If your mother saw you
she'd raise an eyebrow—
the same one she arched
when, at eight,
you turned down sopa de fideo
for peanut butter and jelly at lunch.

You can turn away
from that eyebrow,
but there's no escaping the snarl
grandma will dish out
from her photo on the mantle.

It's the same hard stare
you closed your eyes to
on the day you brought
that microwave home.

Ni modo, pues.

Get out a plastic dish.
Cook the chorizo on high for 4 minutes.
Crack the eggs.
Fold them in.
Microwave 2 minutes.
Stir.
Microwave 2 minutes.
Serve.

Eat your chorizo con huevo
with pale tortillas.
Remember grandma eating,
craving chorizo cooked
over an outdoor stove
in a Tucson summer.

Busing

Rubén Medina

1986

Rubén Medina is the author of two poetry collections,
including *Amor de Lejos...Fool's Love* (1986), in which the
following poem appears. He is currently a professor at the
University of Wisconsin–Madison specializing in Mexican
and Chicano literature and culture, with a focus on writers,
intellectual history, film, and immigration to the United
States. He is the director of the university's Chicano studies
program and has sponsored a community service internship
program in Mexico.

On this bus / brother / it is prohibited to eat
argue / look into eyes / laugh like you mean it.

Prohibited are radios / disorderly feet
the smells of distant relatives / touching
the furthest person.

It is prohibited to sit next to the driver / cry
interrupt dreams / wipe your snot
strike / and save up *Excuse me*'s.

It is prohibited to board with birds / open the window
smoke / embrace one another / dress up like Father Monday.

Definitely / brother / this bus
doesn't go by our house.

from

♜ The Road to Tamazunchale

Ron Arias

1975

Ron Arias (b. 1941) is best known as a print journalist, having worked for major publications and wire services including the *New York Times,* the *Christian Science Monitor,* and the Associated Press. He is currently a *People* magazine correspondent in his home town of Los Angeles. Arias is the author of two nonfiction books, a forthcoming memoir titled *Moving Target,* and one novel, excerpted below, which was nominated for a National Book Award. *The Road to Tamazunchale* (1987) tells the story of an elderly man's vacillating reality—from Pizarro's army in Peru in the 1500s to contemporary Los Angeles—as he faces his imminent death.

IN THE MORNING AFTER CARMELA LEFT, he began searching his room for a cape. This time he would go prepared for the cold. A doublet and woolen stockings would be nice, too, if he had the right sizes and colors. But a cape would fit anyone, cover any color.

Nothing. He looked in closets, drawers, boxes, Carmela's giant armario, the attic, the linen cabinet, everywhere, in every room. Giving up in the house, he went into the backyard and waded through the weeds beneath the cherimoya and avocado trees. In the lopsided storage shed he found his wife's hatbox, filled with moth-eaten clothes. Fausto fished past the underwear and pulled out the fragile, pink cape she used to wear on cold nights. He tied the silk tassels under his chin and left the shed. Of course the fit was perfect, and although the cloth was wrinkled and only hung down to his ribs, there was still a bit of sheen left.

For a while Fausto postured in the sunlight next to the trash cans, then marched around the old, headless incinerator. While looking up through the muzzle of smog, he stepped on a hoe, and the handle banged his forehead. "Eva," he apologized, "I need your cape. I'll put it back when I'm done."

Taking the hoe by its rusty head, he entered the house with his staff and announced he was ready. He wasn't sure where he was going, either to the river or to the mountains. Maybe the Lincoln Heights bus.

Cape flapping, Fausto reached the bus stop on Riverside Drive and sat on the bench next to two young women wearing shorts and halter tops. They stopped chewing their gum and openly examined the odd figure with the hoe. Out of the corner of his good eye Fausto could see the slender legs, shaved up to the knees. Why wear clothes, his wife would have said.

He nodded to the women and made a clicking sound with his tongue.

"Something bothering you?" the one with dyed-blond hair asked.

"You're very beautiful."

The women looked at each other for a moment and silently seemed to agree he was harmless. The darker of the two turned. "You always that fast?"

"I only say what I see," Fausto said confidently. He smoothed the wrinkles in his cape and leaned on the hoe.

"Okay, who's the prettiest, her or me?"

"Both of you are."

"Come on, one of us has got to be prettier."

"All women are beautiful," Fausto lied.

The blonde blew a large, blue bubble, then sucked it in.

"That's a cop-out," the other said, looking serious. "Now who's prettier, me or her?"

"She is," Fausto said.

"I knew it, I knew it! It's 'cause she's blonde, right?"

The two waited for an answer. "Well?" the darker one said. "Tell us, here comes the bus."

"Because you, my dear," Fausto said, rising from the bench, "can't blow a bubble."

The bus pulled alongside the curb and the door folded open with a creak. Fausto stepped aside. The blonde hopped up, but the other woman held his arm. "Hey, what does that got to do with it?" He turned, blocking her way.

"Nothing."

"Then why'd you say it?"

"You gonna talk all day?" the driver called down.

"Well, why'd you say it?"

"Let's go, mister, let the lady by."

"Because I knew she would get madder if I said you were prettier."

"Oh..."

"And you are."

"Goddamit! I'm closing the door. You want on or not?"

"Hey, leave the old man alone," a goateed teenager shouted from the rear seat.

"Shut up, you!"

Fausto followed the young woman up the steps and dropped two coins in the meter box.

"Watch your stuff," the driver said. "I got my eye on you."

Fausto walked toward the rear, winking to the two women and passing several others who stared at him the way they would at a disease. The goatee waved and gave him the thumbs-up sign. "Good try," he said as Fausto sat down. "But I'll tell you what's wrong."

"What?"

The boy slid over to Fausto's side and tugged at the cape. "This."

"My cape?"

"Yeah, it don't look too cool. I mean it's not the thing to wear when you're trying to score."

"Score?"

"The chick, man." The boy cocked his head and pointed with his nose. "They don't dig capes no more. That went out two years ago."

Fausto inspected his know-it-all neighbor. The kid was dressed all in black. His hair, combed straight back without a part, reeked of brilliantine, and the cuffs of his long, creased shirtsleeves were turned under one fold. Inquisitive eyes, bony, triangular face. An apprentice wizard.

"Thank you for the advice," Fausto said earnestly, "but I'll keep my cape on."

"Maybe change the color?"

"No."

The boy leaned over and with his middle finger snapped the creases of his starched trousers. For a while he seemed to lose interest and stared down the aisle. The bus grated into low gear and started up the incline that led to the bridge over the river. Fausto pulled the cord with the hoe.

"Hey, I get off here too."

Fausto refused the boy's help, explaining his staff would do.

"Man," the wizard said, "I thought you was a gardener."

The two left the bus, and Fausto walked to the bridge railing and squinted at the jumble of rocks and tumbleweeds. The boy spit over the edge and counted. He spit again, waited, then turned and clapped his hands. "I know a better place."

"Better?" Fausto said, surprised.

"Yeah, it's for one-timers only. See, if you jump here, all you do is break a leg or something."

"Who said I'm going to jump?"

"Okay, you're not gonna jump."

"And what if I was? Were you going to help me?"

"Psychology, ese, psychology. See, I'd show you this other place, and nobody'd want to jump from there."

"What's your name?"

"Mario."

"Mario qué?"

"Don't be so nosy. Just Mario."

"All right, Mario. You can help me."

"Hey, I was only playing, ese."

"Help me look for some water. There's got to be some water down there."

"Sure.... You had me going for a second. But you ain't gonna find no water. It's summer, remember?"

"So there's no river?"

"That's right...unless you wanna call that a river."

Mario studied the dejected face. "How 'bout something to drink? That'll help you."

"I don't drink."

"Come on. Nothing strong. The liquor store's right over there."

Mario led Fausto to the end of the bridge, across the parking lot to the store. A flabby faced man behind the counter casually looked up at the tall, skinny boy in black and his short, decrepit friend.

"Wait here," Mario said, and he sauntered over the cracked linoleum. Fausto stood in the doorway, nervously tamping his hoe on the rubber mat. The entrance bell kept ringing.

"Tell your buddy to stop that," the fat man said. "What's he think, he's in a church or something?"

"He's sick," Mario said, frowning hard. "Give us a quart…"

"Some ID first."

"For a quart of milk? Come on…"

"It's in the cooler, get it yourself. And tell your friend to stop that shit. It hurts my ears."

Mario motioned Fausto off the mat and went to the cooler. Returning to the counter, he bent over the fat man's racing page and whispered that Fausto was dying. "Doctor says a few more days, and that's it. No more vida for my dad."

"Poor guy. Does he know?"

"Yeah, that's why he's acting so funny."

Fausto had stopped tamping his hoe; his cape fluttered timidly under the air-conditioning vent.

"Look at those eyes…the yellow skin. That's a sure sign."

"Of what?"

"Cholera."

"What's that?" the fat man said, squeezing his fingers in one hand.

"Hey, he needs his fix of milk. Doctor says that's all that keeps him alive. How much I owe you?"

"Is what he's got catchy?"

"Yeah."

"What'd you bring him in here for? You guys get out!"

"Take it easy. Let me pay you first." Mario fumbled in his shirt pocket, then searched his other pockets. "I got it somewhere…just a minute." As he laid the contents of his wallet on the counter, the fat man stepped back.

At that moment Fausto heard the faint, high-pitched strains of a flute. He dropped his hoe and began to shuffle in circles, uttering raspy, whistling noises.

"See what I mean?" Mario said. "Sooner than I thought."

"Take it! Go on, get him out of here before he drops."

"Thank you," Mario said, gathering up his wallet pictures. "God will pay you back."

"Get him out!"

Mario hung an arm over Fausto's shoulder, and the two walked out. In the parking lot the dance continued. "Hey, you can stop now. We got the milk." Mario opened the carton spout. "Here, have some.

The vato's still watching us from the window.…Come on, drink some, or he's gonna be after us."

Fausto put the spout to his lips. "Too cold," he said, handing it back.

"Pretend you're drinking."

"Why?"

"'Cause you're supposed to be sick."

"I am."

"Let's get outta here, he's comin' to the door."

They crossed the street, passed through an empty Standard station and stopped behind the telephone booth. The hard cover of the Yellow Pages dangled from a chain next to a Coke bottle with cigarette stubs floating on the bottom. Mario checked the coin-return slot with his finger, shrugged, and caught up with Fausto. The old man was returning to the liquor store, still whistling and pounding his hoe.

"I can't drink this stuff," Mario said. "You want it?"

"Give it to him," Fausto said and pointed along the asphalt cracks toward the restrooms. The sleeper had curled himself against the wall, using the telephone book as a pillow. Mario walked over, knelt, and picked up the brown paper bag, twisted at the top. "Empty." He tapped the grizzled head. "Hey, you, want some milk?"

The man opened one glaucous eye, peeked in the carton, shook his head and turned over in another position.

Mario pushed in the spout and sat down next to the wino. The shade felt good and he wiped a finger around the inside of his buttoned-up shirt collar. Fausto remained on his feet, listening intently. The freeway traffic seemed to have swallowed the flute.

"Where you going now?" Mario asked.

"I'm not sure."

"You know, we make a good team. I didn't think you'd do it. Man, you should've seen the pendejo's face! He was so scared we could've copped anything in the store." Mario patted the wino's sockless ankle. "We should've got something for him."

"Sssssh," Fausto wheezed and turned in time to see a herd of alpacas trot around the street corner.

"What's that?" Mario said, jumping up.

Fausto hurried to the sidewalk. "Vente, don't be afraid," he told Mario, then stepped off the curb into the mass of bobbing, furry heads. The shepherd, lagging behind, seemed confused by the traffic lights and horns. At the intersection leading to the freeway on-ramp, the frightened alpacas blocked a row of funeral cars, headlights on. Fausto, shouting and waving his hoe, stumbled up the ramp and tried to turn the herd from disaster. Mario ran after him, catching a glimpse of the motorcycle escort racing to the head of the funeral procession.

"Hey, ese!" Mario yelled. "Forget the sheep."

At the bottom of the ramp, the bewildered shepherd shrank from the screeching tires as the officer forced his bike past the rumps of the strange, skittish animals.

Mario, milk carton tucked to his ribs, made a hopeless gesture with his free hand. The officer had left his bike and was running toward Fausto. But as he left the herd, the officer slipped on some dung. Mario lost no time. Leaping over the ice plant alongside the pavement, he reached the motorcycle, uncapped the tank and poured in the milk. By the time he finished, the officer was stiff-arming Fausto down the ramp. The alpacas had abruptly shifted and were being led by the shepherd around the curve and onto the overpass.

"Take it easy on him," Mario shouted. "He's sick."

"He's sick all right...taking them sheep on the freeway."

"Alpacas," Fausto corrected, glancing at the herd trotting across the bridge.

"I don't care what they are....You too, kid."

"Hey, I didn't do nothin'."

"My ass. You were helping him. Both of you, get in that car." The officer, still wiping his hands from the fall, spoke to the driver of the hearse. They argued and the driver gestured to the other cars. Finally the officer returned to the prisoners and ordered them in.

"You ain't gettin' me in no hearst," Mario said.

"Shut up."

Mario whispered in Fausto's ear. The driver and another man with "Forest Lawn" embroidered on his coat pocket had opened the rear door. The driver made a crazy-sign gesture to the next car in line and pointed to the officer.

"You first," the officer told Fausto. The giant's face was flushed pink, except for the whitish pock scars, which gave him the look of a madman. Mario helped Fausto up and pushed in the hoe next to the casket.

"What's that?" the officer asked.

"My staff."

"Let me have it."

"No."

"Goddammit!" and the officer jerked it away from Fausto. It hit the gutter with a clang. "Now you, come here." Mario backed away from the giant's arm. "I said come here!"

"No way..."

The driver and his assistant nonchalantly leaned against the hearse door and watched the boy in black duck between the cars, zigzagging to the end. A woman screamed at the sight of the revolver, the wino next to the restrooms sat up, and two boys in car-club jackets yelled, "Pig!" The officer jammed the revolver into his holster and sprinted back to his motorcycle. Blocks away, Mario waved good-bye and disappeared into the Elysian High recess crowd.

The motorcycle sputtered twice, then coasted to the end of the ramp.

"Milk," the hearse driver said, casually walking over.

"Milk?"

"Yeah, he put milk in your tank."

"You think that's funny?"

"Me? No..."

"Well, tell your people we're taking a ride."

"Wait a minute! You can't use the hearse to go chasing some kid."

"No, dumb-dumb, we're taking the old man in. I'll get the kid on the radio."

"You can't. He pulled some wires."

The officer dug a fist into his hip and marched around to the rear of the hearse. "Tell everybody to get back in their cars. Excitement's over." Hopping up, he poked through the wreaths covering the casket. "All right, where is he?"

The Forest Lawn men glanced inside. "Beats me," the driver said. "Must have run away."

"Jesus! And you guys just stood around and watched?"

"I think he went over there," the assistant said.

"No, I think he's hiding behind that tree," the driver said.

"Aw, hell," the officer muttered, "you go on without me."

"You sure? We can always call off the funeral."

"Go on..."

The caravan moved by, and the giant lowered himself to the curb. Raising his eyes to the hills above the freeway, he saw the alpacas disappear into the ridge of spindly pine trees. He cleared his throat loudly, gurgled, and spit on the hoe.

At Forest Lawn the grave diggers had already opened their lunch pails when the late arrival appeared. The casket was pulled out, lifted by the aluminum handrails and swung around. One of the pallbearers, smaller and older than the others, seemed to falter.

"Gentlemen," the driver said, "easy does it."

"But it's heavy. Are they always this heavy?"

"Please, gentlemen. Let's not have a disaster."

The crowd moved toward the burial hole. A carpet of paper grass had been thrown over a patch of dirt just in front of a row of fold-up chairs. The casket was placed on the platform, and when everyone was seated or standing behind the chairs, the minister began. Fortunately he was behind schedule. He read quickly, skipping over words and finishing in a mumbled monotone. Ashes to ashes, dust to dust.

Fausto squirmed. He was nauseous and somewhat cramped by his companion. Bracing himself on the man's cold forehead, he pushed up on the casket lid, blinked at the sudden light, and sat up. He smiled weakly to his audience, then slowly climbed out and walked away.

"Oh my God!"

"Is that John?"

"Do something…"

"Gentlemen, please!"

"Jesus!"

"John, is that you?"

"Oh my God!"

"Gentlemen, please, the deceased is still in the casket…"

"Jesus!"

"John! Come back…"

from

✹ Days of Obligation

Richard Rodriguez

1992

Richard Rodriguez was born in 1944 in San Francisco and grew up in Sacramento. Known for his controversial reporting style, he has written for major publications including the *New York Times,* the *Wall Street Journal,* and *Time* magazine, winning several major journalism awards for his work. He is currently an editor at Pacific New Service and a contributing editor for *Harper's Magazine, U.S. News & World Report,* and the *Los Angeles Times.* He is the author of three nonfiction books: *Hunger of Memory: The Education of Richard Rodriguez* (1982); *Brown: The Last Discovery of America* (2002); and *Days of Obligation: An Argument with My Mexican Father* (1992), which was a finalist for the Pulitzer Prize.

I AM ON MY KNEES, MY MOUTH OVER THE MOUTH of the toilet, waiting to heave. It comes up with a bark. All the badly pronounced Spanish words I have forced myself to sound during the day, bits and pieces of Mexico spew from my mouth, warm, half-understood, nostalgic reds and greens dangle from long strands of saliva.

I am crying from my mouth in Mexico City.

Yesterday, the nausea began. Driving through Michoacán with a television crew, I was looking for a village I had never seen. The production assistant fed a Bobby Brown tape into the car stereo.

We had been on the road since breakfast. I was looking for the kind of village my parents would have known as children, the kind they left behind.

The producer was impatient—"What about that one?"—indicating with the disinterested jerk of his head yet another church spire, yet another configuration of tile roofs in the distance.

The British Broadcasting Corporation has hired me to serve as the "presenter" for a television documentary on the United States and Mexico. A man who spent so many years with his back turned to Mexico. Now I am to introduce Mexico to a European audience.

For the last several years, I have told friends that I was writing a book about California and Mexico. That was not saying enough. I've been writing a book about comedy and tragedy. In my mind, in my life, Mexico plays the tragic part; California plays the role of America's wild child.

Or was I writing a book about competing theologies?

Josiah Royce, another Californian, another writer, became a famous Harvard professor. Royce wrote about California with disappointment, from the distance of New England. Royce believed that some epic opportunity had been given California—the chance to reconcile the culture of the Catholic south and the Protestant north. California had the chance to heal the sixteenth-century tear of Europe. But the opportunity was lost. The Catholic—the Mexican—impulse was pushed back, vanquished by comedy; a Protestant conquest.

I use the word "comedy" here as the Greeks used it, with utmost seriousness, to suggest a world where youth is not a fruitless metaphor; where it is possible to start anew; where it is possible to escape the rivalries of the Capulets and the McCoys; where young women can disprove the adages of grandmothers.

The comedy of California was constructed on a Protestant faith in individualism. Whereas Mexico knew tragedy.

My Mexican father, as his father before him, believed that old men know more than young men; that life will break your heart; that death finally is the vantage point from which a life must be seen.

I think now that Mexico has been the happier place for being a country of tragedy. Tragic cultures serve up better food than optimistic cultures; tragic cultures have sweeter children, more opulent funerals. In tragic cultures, one does not bear the solitary burden of optimism. California is such a sad place, really—a state where children run away from parents, a state of pale beer, and young old women, and divorced husbands living alone in condos. But at a time when Californians are driven to despair by the relentless optimism of their state, I can only marvel at the comic achievement of the place, California's defiance of history, the defiance of ancestors.

Something hopeful was created in California through the century of its Protestant settlement. People believed that in California they could begin new lives. New generations of immigrants continue to arrive in California, not a few of them from Mexico, hoping to cash in on comedy.

It is still possible in California to change your name, change your sex, get a divorce, become a movie star. My Mexican parents live in a California house with four telephones, three televisions, and several empty bedrooms.

How could California ever reconcile comedy and tragedy? How could there not have been a divorce between Mexico and California in the nineteenth century?

The youth of my life was defined by Protestant optimism. Now that I am middle-aged, I incline more toward the Mexican point of view, though some part of me continues to resist the cynical conclusions of Mexico.

Which leaves me with at least a literary problem to start with: How shall I present the argument between comedy and tragedy, this tension that describes my life? Shall I start with the boy's chapter, then move toward more "mature" tragic conclusions? But that would underplay the boy's wisdom. The middle-aged man would simply lord over the matter.

No, I will present this life in reverse. After all, the journey my parents took from Mexico to America was a journey from an ancient culture to a youthful one—backward in time. In their path I similarly move, if only to honor their passage to California, and because I believe the best resolution to the debate between comedy and tragedy is irresolution, since both sides can claim wisdom.

Yesterday, around noontime, I recognized it. We were driving along the two-lane Mexican highway and there it was—just off to the right, past a grove of eucalyptus—the village of childhood imagining.

The production assistant radioed the other cars in our caravan to follow. We turned down a muddy road.

The village was constructed around a central square. Passage toward the center was narrow; just room enough for a van filled with our television equipment to pass. Most of the doors of the village were open. We saw few people about, those few more curious than friendly, more Indian than mestizo.

This is perfect, I kept saying from the back seat, perfect.

I could imagine my father as a boy, dreaming of running away from just such a village. I could see my mother's paradise—she of the sausage curls, the lampshade dress.

Ahead I spied a church on the south side of the square. There was a crumbling fountain. Also a crowd of women in dark shawls. Market day? All the better.

The church bell was tolling. I don't wear a watch. It must be noon.

And then I saw the reason for the crowd in the plaza—a tiny coffin was being lifted from the bed of a truck. At the same moment, people at the edge of the crowd turned toward our noisy procession.

Bobby Brown panted Unh-oh-ahhhhhhhh from our rolled-down windows.

A village idiot—a cripple—hobbled toward us, his face contorted into what was either a grin or a grimace, his finger pressed against his lips.

Silencio. Silencio.

"Turn off the music," the producer shouted.

The production assistant radioed the rest of the convoy: Back up, back up.

There was no room to turn.

The van, the two cars shifted into reverse. Then my stomach began to churn.

My vision of the Mexican village—yellow doors, wet gutters, children with preternaturally large eyes—floated backward. The crowd of mourners in the village square became smaller and smaller and smaller.[...]

When I was a boy it was still possible for Mexican farmworkers in California to commute between the past and the future.

The past returned every October. The white sky clarified to blue and fog opened white fissures in the landscape.

After the tomatoes and the melons and the grapes had been picked, it was time for Mexicans to load up their cars and head back into Mexico for the winter.

The schoolteacher said aloud to my mother what a shame it was the Mexicans did that—took their children out of school.

Like wandering Jews, Mexicans had no true home but the tabernacle of memory.

The schoolteacher was scandalized by what she took as the Mexicans' disregard of their children's future. The children failed their tests. They made no friends. What did it matter? Come November, they would be gone to some bright world that smelled like the cafeteria on Thursdays—Bean Days. Next spring they would be enrolled in some other school, in some other Valley town.

The schoolroom myth of America described an ocean—immigrants leaving behind several time zones and all the names for things.

Mexican American memory described proximity. There are large Mexican American populations in Seattle and Chicago and Kansas City, but the majority of Mexican Americans live, where most have always lived, in the southwestern United States, one or two hours from Mexico, which is within the possibility of recourse to Mexico or within the sound of her voice.

My father knew men in Sacramento who had walked up from Mexico.

There is confluence of earth. The cut of the land or its fold, the bleaching sky, the swath of the wind, the length of shadows—all these suggested Mexico. Mitigated was the sense of dislocation otherwise familiar to immigrant experience.

By November the fog would thicken, the roads would be dangerous. Better to be off by late October. Families in old trucks and cars headed south down two-lane highways, past browning fields. Rolls of toilet paper streaming from rolled-down windows. After submitting themselves to the vegetable cycle of California for a season, these Mexicans were free. They were Mexicans! And what better thing to be?

HAIIII-EEE. HAI. HAI. HAI.

There is confluence of history.

Cities, rivers, mountains retain Spanish names. California was once Mexico.

The fog closes in, condenses, and drips day and night from the bare limbs of trees. And my mother looks out the kitchen window and cannot see the neighbor's house.

Amnesia fixes the American regard of the past. I remember a graduate student at Columbia University during the Vietnam years; she might have been an ingenue out of Henry James. "After Vietnam, I'll never again believe that America is the good and pure country I once thought it to be," the young woman said.

Whereas Mexican Americans have paid a price for the clarity of their past.

Consider my father: when he decided to apply for American citizenship, my father told no one, none of his friends, those men with whom he had come to this country looking for work. American citizenship would have seemed a betrayal of Mexico, a sin against memory. One afternoon, like a man with something to hide, my father slipped away. He went downtown to the Federal Building in Sacramento and disappeared into America.

Now memory takes her revenge on the son.[...]

Mexico, mad mother. She still does not know what to make of our leaving. For most of this century Mexico has seen her children flee the house of memory. During the Revolution ten percent of the population picked up and moved to the United States; in the decades following the Revolution, Mexico has watched many more of her children cast their lots with the future; head north for work, for wages; north for life. Bad enough that so many left; worse that so many left her for the gringo.

America wanted cheap labor. American contractors reached down into Mexico for men to build America. Sons followed fathers north. It became a rite of passage for the poor Mexican male.

I will send for you or I will come home rich.

I would see them downtown on Sundays—men my age drunk in Plaza Park. I was still a boy at sixteen, but I was an American. At sixteen, I wrote a gossip column, "The Watchful Eye," for my school paper.

Or they would come into town on Monday nights for the wrestling matches or on Tuesday nights for boxing. They worked on ranches over in Yolo County. They were men with time on their hands. They were men without women. They were Mexicans without Mexico.

On Saturdays, Mexican men flooded the Western Union office, where they sent money—money turned into humming wire and then turned back into money—all the way down into Mexico. America was a monastery. America was a vow of poverty. They kept themselves poor for Mexico.

Fidel, the janitor at church, lived over the garage at the rectory. Fidel spoke Spanish and was Mexican. He had a wife down there, people said; some said he had grown children. But too many years had passed and he didn't go back. Fidel had to do for himself. Fidel had a clean piece of linoleum on the floor; he had an iron bed; he had a table and a chair; he had a frying pan and a knife and a fork and a spoon. Everything else Fidel sent back to Mexico. Sometimes, on summer nights, I would see his head through the bars of the little window over the garage of the rectory.

My parents left Mexico in the twenties: she as a girl with her family; he as a young man, alone. To tell different stories. Two Mexicos. At some celebration—we went to so many when I was a boy—a man in the crowd filled his lungs with American air to crow over all, ¡VIVA MEXICO! Everyone cheered. My parents cheered. The band played louder. Why VIVA MEXICO? The country that had betrayed them? The country that had forced them to live elsewhere?

I remember standing in the doorway of my parents' empty bedroom.

Mexico was memory—not mine. Mexico was mysteriously both he and she, like this, like my parents' bed. And over my parents' bed floated the Virgin of Guadalupe in a dime-store frame. In its most potent guise, Mexico was a mother like this queen. Her lips curved like a little boat. *Tú. Tú.* The suspirate vowel. *Tú.* The ruby pendant. The lemon tree. The song of the dove. Breathed through the nose, perched on the lips.

Two voices, two pronouns were given me as a child, like good and bad angels, like sweet and sour milks, like rank and clement weathers; one yielding, one austere.

In the sixteenth century, Spain bequeathed to Mexico two forms of address, two versions of "you": in Mexico there is *tú* and there is *usted*.

In Sacramento, California, everything outside our house was English, was "you"—hey you. My dog was you. My parents were you. The nuns were you. My best friend, my worst enemy was you. God was You.

Whereas the architecture of Mexico is the hardened shell of a Spanish distinction.

Treeless, open plazas abate at walls; walls yield to refreshment, to interior courtyards, to shuttered afternoons.

At the heart there is *tú*—the intimate voice—the familiar room in a world full of rooms. *Tú* is the condition, not so much of knowing, as of being known; of being recognized. *Tú* belongs within the family. *Tú* is spoken to children and dogs, to priests; among lovers and drunken friends; to servants; to statues; to the high court of heaven; to God Himself.

The shaded arcade yields once more to the plaza, to traffic and the light of day. *Usted,* the formal, the bloodless, the ornamental you, is spoken to the eyes of strangers. By servants to masters. *Usted* shows deference to propriety, to authority, to history. *Usted* is open to interpretation; therefore it is subject to corruption, a province of politicians. *Usted* is the language outside Eden.[...]

I went to a village in the state of Michoacán, on the far side of Lake Chapala.

A dusty road leads past eucalyptus, past the cemetery, to the village. For most of the year the village is empty—nearly. There are a few old people, quite a few hungry dogs. The sun comes up; the sun goes down. Most of the villagers have left Mexico for the United States. January 23 is the feast day of the patron saint of the village, when the saint is accustomed to being rocked upon his hillock of velvet through the streets. On that day, the villagers—and lately the children of villagers—return. They come in caravans. Most come from Austin, Texas; from Hollister, California; and from Stockton, California. For a week every year, the village comes alive, a Mexican Brigadoon. Doors are unlocked. Shutters are opened. Floors are swept. Music is played. Beer is drunk. Expressed fragments of memory flow outward like cigarette smoke to tumble the dust of the dead.

Every night is carnival. Men who work at canneries or factories in California parade down the village street in black suits. Women who are waitresses in California put on high heels and evening gowns. The promenade under the Mexican stars becomes a celebration of American desire.

At the end of the week, the tabernacle of memory is dismantled, distributed among the villagers in their vans, and carried out of Mexico.

Returning

Elías Miguel Muñoz (translated by Elías Miguel Muñoz and Karen Christian)

1989

Elías Miguel Muñoz was born in 1954 in Cuba and came to California when he was seven years old. The author of several textbooks and a series of novellas for students learning Spanish as a foreign language, Muñoz has also written a bilingual collection of poetry and two novels in English, the first of which, *Crazy Love* (1989), he adapted into an off-Broadway musical called *L.A. Scene.*

While in the barrio no one spoke
of leaving or of telegrams.
And we all dreamed about apples
and mint-flavored chewing gum.
Remember?

The rice and black beans
no longer satisfied us.
Without the eternal summer,
without dirt streets and sugarcane
we would no longer have dark skin.
The lines would end,
and so would the *quimbumbia,*
the *yuca,*
and the mud puddles.

So we could sing, later,
to a different beat.
So we could forget your

conga player's outfit.
So we could chew away
until we had no teeth.
So we could speak of the things
we lost,
things we never had.
So that later,
under the northern skies,
we could begin to dream
about returning.

from

✸ The Multicultural Paradigm

Guillermo Gómez-Peña

1989

Guillermo Gómez-Peña (b. 1955) grew up in Mexico City
and came to the United States in 1978. His work often
addresses current issues in politics, ethnicity, and nationality,
using poetry, journalism, criticism, cultural theory, performance art, installations, and video and audio recordings. In
addition to his involvement with the community art troupe
La Pocha Nostra, he has been a contributor to radio programs, arts collectives, newspapers, magazines, and journals
in the United States and Mexico. His long list of honors
includes a place on the *Utne Reader's* 1995 List of 100
Visionaries, an American Book Award for *The New World
Border* (1997), and a 2000 Cineaste Lifetime Achievement
Award from the Taos film festival. He has published five
books containing scripts from some of his larger projects.
The following excerpt is taken from the first of these,
Warrior for Gringostroika (1993).

THE PARADIGM SHIFT

It's 1989 in this troubled continent accidentally called America. A
major paradigm shift is taking place in front of our eyes. The East
Coast/West Coast cultural axis is being replaced by a North/South one.
The need for U.S. culture to come to terms with the Latino-American
"cultural other" has become a national debate. Everywhere I go, I meet
people seriously interested in our ideas and cultural models. The art,
film, and literary worlds are finally looking South.

To look South means to remember; to recapture one's historical
self. For the United States, this historical self extends from the early

Native American cultures to the most recent immigration from Laos or Guatemala.

It's 1989 in this troubled country mistakenly called America. The current Latino and Asian immigration to the United States is the direct result of international conflicts between the so-called First and Third worlds. The colonized cultures are sliding into the space of the colonizer, and in doing so, they are redefining its borders and its culture. (A similar phenomenon is occurring in Europe with African immigration.)

The First and Third worlds have mutually penetrated one another. The two Americas are totally intertwined. The complex demographic, social, and linguistic processes that are transforming this country into a member of the "Second World" (or perhaps the "Fourth World"?) are being reflected in the art and thought produced by Latinos, African Americans, Asians, Native Americans, and Anglo-Europeans. Unlike the images on TV or in commercial cinema depicting a monocultural middle-class world existing outside of international crisis, contemporary U.S. society is fundamentally multiracial, multilingual, and socially polarized. So is its art.

Whenever and wherever two or more cultures meet—peacefully or violently—there is a border experience.

In order to describe the trans-, inter-, and multicultural processes that are at the core of our contemporary border experience as Latino artists in the United States, we need to find a new terminology, a new iconography, and a new set of categories and definitions. We need to rebaptize the world in our own terms. The language of postmodernism is ethnocentric and insufficient. And so is the existing language of cultural institutions and funding agencies. Terms like Hispanic, Latino, ethnic, minority, marginal, alternative, and Third World, among others, are inaccurate and loaded with ideological implications. They create false categories and neocolonial hierarchies. In the absence of a more enlightened terminology, we have no choice but to utilize them with extreme care.

My artistic sensibility as a deterritorialized Mexican/American artist living a permanent border experience cannot be explained solely by accepted historical notions of the twentieth-century Western vanguard (from dada to techno-performance). I am as Western and American as Laurie Anderson or Terry Allen. Yet my primary traditions are Chicano and Latin American art, literature, and political thought. We must realize that the West has been redefined. The South and the East are already in the West. And being American today means participating in the drafting of a new cultural topography.

Let's get it straight: America is a continent, not a country. Latin America encompasses more than half of America. Quechuas, Mixtecos,

Yaquis, and Iroquois are American (not U.S. citizens). Chicano, Nuyorrican, Cajun, Afro-Caribbean, and Quebecois cultures are American as well. Mexicans and Canadians are also North Americans. Newly arrived Vietnamese and Laotians will soon become Americans. U.S. Anglo-European culture is but a mere component of a much larger cultural complex in constant metamorphosis.

This pluralistic America within the United States can be found, among other places, in the "Indian reservations" and the Chicano barrios of the Southwest, the African American neighborhoods of Washington, Chicago, or Detroit, or the multiracial neighborhoods of Manhattan, San Francisco, Los Angeles, or Miami. This sui generis America is no longer part of the First World. It still has no name or configuration, but as artists and cultural leaders, we have the responsibility to reflect it.

Despite the great cultural mirage sponsored by the people in power, everywhere we look we find pluralism, crisis, and nonsynchronicity. The so-called dominant culture is no longer dominant. Dominant culture is a meta-reality that only exists in the virtual space of the mainstream media and in the ideologically and aesthetically controlled spaces of the monocultural institutions.

Today, if there is a dominant culture, it is border culture. And those who still haven't crossed a border will do it very soon. All Americans (from the vast continent America) were, are, or will be border-crossers. "All Mexicans," says Tomas Ybarra-Frausto, a Chicano theoretician in New York, "are potential Chicanos." As you read this text, you are crossing a border yourself.

✷ Underground Mariachi

Lucha Corpi (translated by Catherine Rodríguez-Nieto)

1980

Lucha Corpi was born in 1945 in Veracruz, Mexico, and moved to California at age nineteen. She has written five volumes of poetry in Spanish and four novels in English, one of which, *Eulogy for a Brown Angel* (1992), received the PEN Oakland Josephine Miles Award and the Multicultural Publishers' Exchange award for best fiction. Her series of detective novels features a Chicana feminist who solves murders involving the Latino civil rights movement. She has worked as coordinator of the Chicano Studies Library at UC Berkeley, as a college instructor, and as founder and president of Aztlán Cultural and Centro Chicano de Escritores, and she currently teaches English as a second language through the Oakland public school system.

The barrel-belly guitar
awkwardly
hangs from the wall
its twelve strings mute;
the violin observes it
attentively
from the dresser
its delicate notes
hanging on silence;
and the horn, mouth down
over the table
sighs deafened.

There are no musicians
there are no singers

la migra picked them up
and sent them to their land
(because they say that California
is no longer ours).

An old man in the park
listened to my story
with a glitter in his eyes
"Hijita," he said,
"they will be back
hands open and ready
arms stretched
across the Rio Grand
and we may have our first
underground mariachi band
Ah, the sweet music
of the revolution!"

POP CULTURE

from

♜ Las sergas de Esplandián

Garcí Rodríguez Ordóñez de Montalvo
(translated by Edward Everett Hale)

c. 1510

Garcí Rodriguez Ordóñez de Montalvo is often credited
with inventing the name "California," which he gave to a
fictional Caribbean island with an "infinite host of wild
beasts, such as never were seen in any other part of the
world" in his tremendously popular novel *Las sergas de
Esplandián,* published about 1510. Edward Everett Hale, the
translator of the following excerpt, proposed in an 1864
Atlantic Monthly article that the explorer Hernán Cortés was
probably familiar with the popular novel and chose the
name of Montalvo's island for the Baja California peninsula,
which was believed to be an island when he landed there.

KNOW, THEN, THAT ON THE RIGHT HAND OF THE INDIES, there is an island
called California, very close to the site of the Terrestrial Paradise, and it
was peopled by black women, without any man among them, for they
lived in the fashion of Amazons. They were of strong and hardy bodies,
of ardent courage and great force. Their island was the strongest in all
the world, with its steep cliffs and rocky shores. Their arms were all of
gold, and so was the harness of the wild beasts which they tamed and
rode. For, in the whole island, there was no metal but gold. They lived
in caves wrought out of the rock with much labor. They had many ships
with which they sailed out to other countries to obtain booty.

In this island, called California, there were many griffins, on
account of the great ruggedness of the country, and its infinite host of
wild beasts, such as never were seen in any other part of the world. And

when these griffins were yet small, the women went out with traps to take them. They covered themselves over with very thick hides, and when they had caught the little griffins they took them to their caves, and brought them up there. And being themselves quite a match for the griffins, they fed them with the men whom they took prisoners, and with the boys to whom they gave birth, and brought them up with such arts that they got much good from them, and no harm. Every man who landed on the island was immediately devoured by these griffins; and although they had had enough, none the less would they seize them, and carry them high up in the air in their flight; and when they were tired of carrying them, would let them fall anywhere as soon as they died. Now, at the time when those great men of the Pagans sailed with their great fleets, as the history has told you, there reigned in this island of California a Queen [Calafia], very large in person, the most beautiful of all of them, of blooming years, and in her thoughts desirous of achieving great things, strong of limb, and of great courage, more than any of those who had filled her throne before her.

from

✷ The Adventures of Don Chipote or When Parrots Breast-Feed

Daniel Venegas (translated by Ethriam Cash Brammer)

1928

Daniel Venegas made his living in the 1920s as publisher, writer, editor, and cartoonist for the satirical news tabloid *El Malcriado* (The Brat), a nickname which was often used for Venegas himself. Many of his plays and vaudeville reviews are now lost, but his only known novel, *The Adventures of Don Chipote or When Parrots Breast-Feed,* was recently rediscovered by Nicolás Kanellos, publisher of Arte Publico Press, and brought back into print, this time in English. The story was originally published in 1928 by Los Angeles's Spanish-language daily newspaper, *El heraldo de México,* and is regarded today as the first novel directed to a Chicano readership to address labor conditions and issues of Mexican American identity and culture, particularly the dialect and folklore of the braceros. The book's burlesque tone was common to corridos and popular writings of the time, and its plot and title suggest a connection to Cervantes's classic, *The Adventures of Don Quixote.* As this selection begins, Don Chipote has just been released from the hospital, where he was recovering from an injury incurred as a railroad worker.

IT DIDN'T TAKE DON CHIPOTE LONG TO GET HIS BEARINGS. He went to the Placita, because he didn't know where else to go. Also, there he was sure to come across fellow countrymen who could speak to him in his own tongue. He had already spent the greater part of the morning there, sleeping and smoking, until it appeared as though he was getting drunk again. In the end, he was getting bored and extremely sunburned.

Not knowing how to kill time, he thought about taking a stroll along Main Street. So he hit the pavement, just to rid himself of the doldrums.

That's how, step by step, he happened across a movie house and went inside, drawn by the comic always posted at the front door to lure people inside. The announcer was shouting himself hoarse, yelling about the attractions, which according to him were the season's best, and that they had the best movies ever. He was practically shoving passersby into the theater by force.

Don Chipote, who couldn't find anything to do and was excited by the announcer's spiel, asked how much a ticket cost. After finding out that it only cost ten cents, he bought his ticket and went inside to be entertained.

Skinenbones [his dog], upon seeing his master go inside and realizing he didn't even buy him a ticket, chased after him so that he too could watch the "sho."

Never in his life had Don Chipote seen a cinematographic projection—that is to say, he didn't even know that the "sho" would be in the dark. So when the house lights grew dim and he couldn't see anything, he wanted to run out of the theater, for he thought that he had descended into hell. And with the lights completely dark, he couldn't see where he was going and smacked into one of the pillars in the auditorium.

Skinenbones caught up to his owner. But Don Chipote didn't want to let go of the pillar that he had run into. Skinenbones whimpered as Don Chipote's knees knocked.

Little by little, his eyes finally adjusted to the darkness and he began to make out the seats and everything around him. Once he could get a good look at things and see well, he took to the aisle. And without looking at where he was sitting down, he plopped himself down before the silver screen. It wasn't until Don Chipote realized that the fellows who appeared on the big screen were moving on their own that he began to get nervous; or more clearly stated, he started to get scared. So he made the sign of the cross, entrusted his soul to Divine Providence, and prepared to make a dash for the exit. But he stopped, thinking that he might fall while running, and that after he fell, they would do him in.

In the end, he decided to just bow his head and not look around, praying that Our Lady of Perpetual Help would get him out of this fix.

He had already spent some time with his head down beseeching God's grace when a cry of laughter grabbed his attention away from his predicament. Unable to withstand his curiosity, he lifted his head and watched the screen as a funny-looking actor threw a cake at an old man but hit his girlfriend instead. The rest of the audience continued to laugh at the lunacies which comprised the comic scenes. Don Chipote felt the blood rush back into his veins and also felt like laughing at those wise guys' shenanigans. It didn't take long for him to let fly with his guffaws and for him to shake the room with his chortles, which called the attention of the others, who, now being entertained by watching him, stopped watching the screen to laugh at Don Chipote instead. He thought that those pictures were so hilarious that they made him want to laugh even harder than he had on his honeymoon, when his Doña Chipota had tickled him in the morning so that he would wake up laughing with her, which made him fall more deeply in love.

Don Chipote then confessed to himself that he had no reason to be scared and that his fears were the seeds of his ignorance, because he now realized that if he were being dragged down into hell, they wouldn't have made him pay first. Once pacified by this thought, he occupied himself with watching the entertainment on the screen. And so that Skinenbones could see too, he picked him up and placed him on his lap and showed him what he was looking at. Of course, the pooch didn't give a straw about what was making his master laugh so hard, but he felt swell sitting on his lap, because it had been a long time since Don Chipote had so much as petted him.

Don Chipote, all the while, kept rocking back and forth with laughter, giving the others in the crowd reason to laugh at him.

While he was still laughing at the screen, and the others at him, the movies ended and it was announced that the variety show was to follow shortly. Even though Don Chipote had no idea what this was, he remained seated, only because the rest had stayed put as well. He began to get annoyed by so much waiting around, when to his delight he saw a musician with a drum make himself comfortable next to the piano. And he thought, without a doubt, that they were going to dance the *matachines* like back home.

The piano maestro arrived at last. After giving the keyboard a few general passes, he attacked the piano furiously, in harmony with his sonorous companion, playing the *pasodoble,* which even the local barn owls recognize as *"Sangre Mexicana."* After they thought they had played the tune, for in reality nothing could be heard except for the drumming and crashing, the curtain rose and a dame appeared wearing almost nothing at all, making Don Chipote cover his face, which turned red from the embarrassment of seeing a woman in such regalia. And don't go thinking that this was false modesty on the part of our compatriot, for as you well know, in his homeland he had never seen the body of any woman—dare we say, not even his wife—higher up than the ankle. So you can just imagine what happened to him when seeing that dollface showing off her legs to the crowd, looking more like streams of *atole* than legs.

Because temptation is the worst thing that mankind can face, enabling the devil to take us away, Don Chipote could not resist. And, little by little, he went opening his fingers to see what would startle him once more. And that's how, little by little, he continued until he peeled his hand from his face straight away and began to study the beautiful performer and even drool with delight.

When the dull monotonous singing had ended, Don Chipote's sweet temptress gave her thanks and took off. People in the audience stomped their feet, yelled out loud, and applauded. And our pal, corrupted by the others, cheered until suddenly he stood up and let Skinenbones fall from his lap with a crash, for he could not resist joining the tremendous ovation, and howled his approval, which redoubled the cheers because the crowd thought that it was the performer who had started singing again from the middle of the song.

The poor song-and-dance gal was not the greatest, but for the Mexican masses before her, she was out of this world, especially for Don Chipote.

The singer let the crowd go wild for a few moments, then decided to repeat the number, only, this time—and you should understand that what really made the audience go bonkers was the exhibition of her scrawny chicken legs—she sang and danced while trying to reveal herself all the way up to where her bloomers were fastened. With such an artistic display, the reader can imagine how the crowd must have reacted, particularly Don Chipote, who was going blind with ecstasy. Fortunately, now that he had nearly lost his sight, the artist wrapped up her routine and exited the stage to the cheers and stomping feet of the audience which wanted her, at all cost, to do more of the same.

The pack of Mexicans went rabid. They shouted and did all they pleased and could do to compel an encore, but that piece of eye-candy didn't come back out. Instead, a guy dressed like his compatriots in the audience—who had taken their turns with distilled cactus juice—attempted to win their praise as well by telling them jokes and babbling baloney as dirty or more bawdy than his predecessor's songs and legs. In short, that buffoon gave them a kick, not so much from his jokes, but rather because the pantomime he did made them recall getting hooched up back home. And that's why they awarded his evil deeds with a salvo of applause, which he received while doing cartwheels off the stage, his heart full of gratitude for those who knew how to recognize his talents so warmly. Surely, he thought, they would make him do an encore, but as soon as he was out of sight backstage, the clapping came to an end.

Another number followed; rather, it was basically the same, only this time, both performers came out on stage. The woman was now dressed like a country girl and the comedian just as before, only this time he didn't have on his *huaraches* and instead carried a *charro's sombrero,* which in its day had been braided with gold, but now shone with a mountain of sequins embroidered onto it. In these getups, our artists engaged in a street dialogue which they presented as a novelty, but even children know it by heart.

Following this lovely exchange, in which they exhausted their vast repertoire, the maestro started in on his piano with thumps on the keyboard, sending out the discordant chords of the *"Jarabe Tapatío,"* while the artists par excellence started more or less into stomping their heels and kicking their legs to the music.

The row created defies description. The dust cloud cannot be described either, for with each one of the dancers' steps, enough dirt came out of the slits between the stage's floorboards to build an adobe house.

The horde of Mexican performers who entertain in the United States know that the Chicano community goes crazy when something reminds them of their blessed cactus land. And, naturally, they exploit it all the time. Thus wherever there are theaters or even the humblest stages, whether the performers are good or bad, there will always be a drunken tramp with or without a *charro*; and if a comic goes to one of these places and doesn't know how to do the penniless tramp and dance the *"Jarabe Tapatío,"* he will be deprived of a contract and presumed to be a Bohemian.

My readers will forgive me for introducing them to both the good and bad of the Los Angeles theatrical ambiance. But my little aside was only to give the performers, who continued to dance the *jarabe,* the opportunity to finish, while at the same time allowing the dust cloud to clear.

After Venus and the funny guy completed the required steps, the audience was in the aisle with applause and whistles and catcalls, as was the custom. The show was over and the curtain came down. The theater went dark. And then, the movies continued.

Some of those attending the performance got up and left. Others stayed in their seats. As for Don Chipote, he didn't know what to do, whether to stay or to go. But noticing that no one said anything to those who remained, he made himself as comfortable as he could and started to watch the movie, which he didn't understand, but which entertained him very much, just because the pictures moved as if they were real people. And all the while, Skinenbones snored away at his master's feet.

Not to make this story longer than it already is, I'll just tell you that Don Chipote got completely involved in the movie and then watched the variety show a second time. He would have certainly stayed there until they kicked him out were it not for Skinenbones, who showed signs of boredom and hunger, making Don Chipote notice that his stomach too was now empty and starting to growl.

Thanks to this, Don Chipote abandoned the theater at last and went out into the street, somewhat surprised, thinking—the result of course of having been in the dark for too long—that the world had been painted yellow.

from

✻ Radios and Chicanos

anonymous

c. 1930

The corrido form, of which this is an example, is a long–
standing musical tradition in Mexico. These ballads portraying
tragedies and misadventures that epitomize Mexican and
Mexican American culture and experience were especially
popular in and around the Revolution of 1910, and the form
is very much alive today, with special attention paid to drug
traffickers and disgraced celebrities. The Carranza referred to
in the fourth line is probably Venustiano Carranza, the first
president (1917–1920) of the Mexican republic after the
thirty-five-year dictatorship of Porfirio Díaz.

At last he came to this country and rented an apartment
Without knowing that in this town one dies working in the cement.
When he felt that he had money he began to buy on time;
And when he bought ill–fitting suits he felt himself equal with Carranza.
It is true, it is true, it seems a lie that being a Chicano
So spirited and so healthy that he would come from over there.

He rented a radio and aerial with light bulbs and buttons
Because his house was very quiet without music or songs.
At the hour that they transmit the concerts to Chicanos
It happens that they advertise pork and the best country gravy.
It is true, it is true, it seems a lie that in place of songs
Those city people would advertise cantaloupes.

After three-quarters of an hour they sing us some fox-trot,
Then they announce the lady who makes good tepache.
Other subjects follow, illustrating the bargains
That they will make to the dead if they buy good coffins.
It is true, it is true, it seems a lie that they would vex us
In these places, those of the city; it seems a lie, that they would vex us,
those of the city.

from

✹ Hoyt Street

Mary Helen Ponce

1993

Mary Helen Ponce was born in 1938 in the San Fernando
Valley. Educated in Chicano studies, anthropology, women's
studies, history, and literature, she has taught at universities
in California and New Mexico and has been prominently
involved with several Mexican American and women's
rights organizations. She is the author of three collections
of fiction and an autobiography, *Hoyt Street: Memories of a
Chicana Childhood* (1993).

MEXICAN AMERICANS WERE NOT WELCOME in all the theatres. Although
no one tried to keep us out, we knew where we were welcome and
where we were not. We exchanged stories of the many times we were
made to feel unwelcome at a movie house. Concha told of the time her
sister and her date were told to move to the Mexican section. Others
told of how when they laughed aloud, the Anglo ushers stuck a flashlight in their faces:

"Hey you, not so loud!"

"We wasn't doing nuthin'."

"Shut up or we'll kick you out."[…]

Of the three movie places in town, we were made to feel welcome
only at the San Fernando Theater, next door to Thrifty Drugs. It was like
most others, except that it was shabbier, with worn carpeting in the
lobby and seats held together with electrical tape. At the entrance was a
small booth that dispensed snacks; behind it was a wide mirror where we
could see who was walking in. Two narrow doors with red velvet drapes
swung open each time someone went through; they led to the seats
below. The girls' bathroom had two toilets, both of which leaked. One

of the seats was cracked in the middle. If I wasn't careful, I tended to get my behind caught in the crack.

A wide mirror lined an entire wall of the girls' bathroom; an aluminum shelf below could hold makeup and assorted hairpins. The line to the girls bathroom was always long; I often missed the best part of a movie. Right before el chow began, the girls' bathroom was a beehive of activity.

"Gimme the comb."

"Hurry up, the chow is startin'."

"I gotta pee…"

Across town was the Rennie Theater. Larger, with a wide lobby carpeted in rich maroon and two snack bars, this place was off limits to the chicanada, the Mexican Americans, of Pacoima and "Sanfer." It catered mostly to Anglos. Not until after World War II did Mexican Americans become socially acceptable at local movie houses and restaurants. Men from the barrio, it became known, were also wounded and killed while fighting for their country, the good old USA. It was unpatriotic to turn away nonwhites in uniform, especially those with medals and Purple Hearts pinned to their chests.

And so we were made welcome and allowed to sit in any section of the theaters: in the loges, as the upstairs was called, or smack in the front, where the picture appeared to come out at us. By this time however, we had already chosen to attend the San Fernando Theater, where the owner was friendly and made us feel most welcome.

Mort was Jewish and tolerant of other minorities. His was the only theater that allowed Negroes in, too, although there were less of them than of us. Mort was also a good businessman and made sure the snack bar was fully stocked. He was among the first to hire Mexican kids as ushers, and he rarely called the cops on the pachucos. For the Mexican Americans of "Pacas" and "Sanfer," the fun place on Sunday afternoons was the San Fernando Theater, on Brand Street. […]

One year George S., or "Chochis," as his mother called him, asked me to go with him to a matinee. I wasn't too thrilled; Chochis was un gordito. The fact that I too was chubby was of no consequence to me. I mean, we didn't both have to be gordinflones! At first I told him I had promised Virgie and Concha I'd sit with them, but when I saw his downcast eyes and pouting mouth, I changed my mind; I told him to meet me in the theater lobby. I dreaded having my friends see me with fat George! But when he whispered "I wanna pay your way," I forgot my embarrassment and quickly joined him in line.

It was fun to sit with George; he ate all during the movie. He loaded up beforehand, his chunky arms laden with sodas, popcorn, and candy.

During intermission he waddled down the aisle to buy more dulces. Just before the movie ended, he shoved his way to the lobby once more to stuff his pants pockets with chocolates. To be with him was to partake in a continuous feed. Food was happiness for Chochis and for me.

There was a certain security in being with him. He was content to stuff himself during the movie and to leave me alone. He would plunge his hands into a popcorn bag, tearing it in the process, then bring his buttery paws to his wide mouth, stuff it with popcorn, and chomp away. When finished with the popcorn, he wiped his hands on his pants, then from a shirt pocket he slipped Milk Duds and Milky Ways into my eager hands.

Chochis was so busy eating he never had time to get fresh with me; all he ever did was put his arm around me. One arm on my shoulder, the other buried in a big bag of buttered popcorn. While the other girls were kept busy fighting off los frescos, I munched my way contentedly through the movie, mesmerized by the antics of Pauline and Nyoka, secure with an array of my favorite candies.

Sometimes the movies included leftover news of World War II. Black-and-white scenes of battles, soldiers, and tanks flashed on the screen: the fighting men of the USA! These newsreels were boring. My friends and I thought the war was over or at least about to end, what with Hitler dead and the Japanese daily committing hari-kari. The war news was like another movie, part of the entertainment offered to youngsters on a Sunday afternoon.

One time during intermission, they showed a short propaganda movie. It included a funny jingle that the audience was urged to sing:

Stinky Jap, off the map,
Benito's jaw, oh, ho, ho.

We sang several verses, all funny and clever. I stopped eating just enough to sing along. We sang and sang; the theater rocked with shouts of laughter and jeers.

But it felt wrong to be making fun of olive-skinned Japanese and swarthy Italians. *We* were neither blond nor blue-eyed, but brown. Morenos, trigueños, prietos, not white enough to be accepted in the Rennie Theater, yet encouraged to laugh at others who, like our Mexican ancestors, had fought and lost a war against this country. People who to this day were mocked and called "dirty Mexicans."

I was grateful that this "short" was not screened again. My parents were not racist; neither was I. Mort, I think, disliked the film, too. Or perhaps he thought it old, dated, and in poor taste. In any event, he never showed it again.

from

✸ La Mollie and the King of Tears

Arturo Islas

1996

Arturo Islas was born in 1938 in El Paso, Texas, and grew up along the U.S./Mexico border before leaving to study neuroscience on scholarship at Stanford University. Once in college, he switched his focus to literature and received a Ph.D. in English. An award-winning professor of English for twenty years, he introduced Chicano literature into the Stanford curriculum as one of the first Chicano professors of English in the country. He was working on his third novel, *La Mollie and the King of Tears* (1996), when he died of AIDS-related complications in 1991.

San Francisco, 1973

I shoulda told la Mollie I'd be back to her place right after the gig. But I knew she wouldn't believe me, specially cause we were playing at Big Eddie's, this sleazebag jazz joint in the Mission close to where my old girlfriend Sonia lives. But after them shots, man, all I wanted to do was drag this plaster leg of mine back to la Mollie so she could touch it with those magic hands of hers and make the hurt go away. Instead, here I am back in this emergency room waiting to hear if I'm ever gonna feel her fingers on me again.

All morning, la Mollie kept talking about some comet and the end of the world. Right in the middle of my giving it to her the way Rhett gives it to Scarlett the night he lugs her up them red velvet stairs after almost crushing her skull between his hands, la Mollie says, "It's the end of the world!" And I'm saying, "Oh yeah, baby," and she says, "Not this, stupid," ruining my concentration and turning me into that pansy Ashley Wilkes. I hate it when she does that, man.

"Kahoutek," she says, letting it slide out like a wet noodle.

"Ka-who what?" I ask her.

"Kahoutek! Kahoutek!" she screams like I'm deaf. "It's a comet the Russians discovered and it's coming tomorrow. Don't you know nothing, Louie?"

Of course, she says "anything" cause la Mollie's been to college and talks English real good—not like me—and she gets a big kick outta correcting me in front of her big-shot Anglo friends.[…]

Yesterday when she was going on and on about that Russian comet I started getting real mad but I didn't let on. I just told her I needed some time to myself before going to the gig in the Mission. What I was really hoping for is that she'd give the commies and their comet a rest and beg me to stick around so's we can play Deborah Kerr and Burt Lancaster all afternoon. I could feel the waves crashing over our hot, wet bodies. You know what I mean?

Instead, la Mollie started right in on Sonia with no reason at all, cause I haven't seen her for about two months and ain't said nothing about her for even longer than that. But that's when I shoulda realized that comet meant me no good. "I bet Sonia knows about the comet and I bet she believes in mysticism," was what la Mollie said in a real soft and wicked voice.

"No," I tell her. "Sonia believes in God."

"Just like a nice Mexican girl should," la Mollie says, and I feel like Cary Grant before he knocks Tracy Lord on her fancy Philadelphia cream cheese ass.

La Mollie knows that Sonia lives in the Mission by Big Eddie's. After a while, in my best in-control Cagney-at-the-breakfast-table voice, not mad or nothing, just real even with my eyebrows level, I ask her, "Well, when did it come the last time?"

"What?" she says, buttering more toast for me real hard and punching holes in it. I hate toast with holes, man.

"That comet with the weird name." Now Cagney is starting to get mad and there's no grapefruit around.

"I don't know. About fifty years ago. Maybe a hundred," she says, kinda annoyed like it don't matter. I can tell she don't know when.

"Well, did the world end then?" I give her my Clark Gable smile.

"God, Louie, what are you talking about?" That's when she transfers the butter from the tip of her finger to the tip of her tongue, so pink and fresh I feel like I'm melting with it inside her mouth.

"You said the last time this Ka-who-tack…"

"Kahoutek! -tek! -tek! -tek!"

"Okay, okay. Tek, tek, tek. You said the last time it showed up, the world was supposed to end. We're still here. Look around you." And I get up and do a Montgomery Clift walk to the window, hoping she'll notice. Outside in the garden, all the hydrangeas are blooming and the tulips I planted are having an acid party thinking they're real.

La Mollie is too quiet though, so I turn around and look at her like Basil Rathbone studying a bug. She is looking at the eggs on my plate and rocking again. That rocking makes me feel like Charles Boyer and I wanna pick her up and put her on my lap and hold her in my arms. "Well," she says real soft so I can hardly hear, "maybe not *end* exactly. But I know, Louie. I feel something real bad is going to happen and that Kahoutek has something to do with it. Just you wait and see, Louie Mendoza." She pronounces it "Men-doze-uh" and now I know I want her there in my lap.

"Oh, baby," I say to her, praying she'll fling out her arms to me like Ginger Rogers to Fred Astaire in that dance where he's kept her from killing herself. "That's all superstition. Something bad happens every day." But Astaire and Rogers vanish[...]

Face it, we guys can be fuckers. And we wanna conquer everything. I got this theory that war starts between a man's legs. Could you ever tell your dick what to do, man? It did it, whether you wanted it to or not, including just hanging there like a rag when what you wanted it to do more than anything in the world was stand at attention. And so guys start playing with substitutes. Women don't have no penis envy. Men do, and where we are is between two bunches of old farts—one bunch high on vodka and the other on old-time religion—playing mine's bigger than yours. It's real scary, man, so scary that if it weren't for women, we woulda blown ourselves to bits by now. A good woman and her power all around you like electricity, man—that's what you need to survive. And for me, music, too, cause if I didn't have that, I woulda killed myself or someone else a long, long time ago.

So there I was, staring right at la Mollie and not seeing her, even with her looking like Rita Hayworth in that movie where she comes down to earth and nothing dances the way she wants it to. But I don't tell la Mollie none of that. Instead, I say real casual like James Dean pretending he don't care one way or another, "Baby, you wanna mess around? I'm not too tired."

I knew she was gonna say "No!" cause she don't never like to make it in the daytime with the sun shining bright into the bedroom. La Mollie's real conventional about that and only really feels like it in the dark so she can pretend I'm Marlon Brando or whoever is turning her on that month. I don't mind, man, cause when I need to, I always bring her back around to me. So it knocks me out when she says "Okay," and I tango over sideways to pick her up off the chair.

But after a coupla long kisses, she slips away and says, very Barbara Stanwyck, "Stop right there. We'll finish it up tonight. After the gig." I'm hooked in *Double Indemnity* then, man, feeling like Fred MacMurray getting took and knowing it, all helpless and telling the story into the office dictaphone thing before he drops dead. I had to sit down.

"Who's going to drive you home?" she asks, cold as Cruella De Ville.

"Tito," I tell her. "He's borrowed the van for his drums just for tonight." I'm lying cause I know that Tito can only get that little VW bug that looks like a cockaroach and ain't got no brakes. It's a certified death-mobile.

"Come on, Mollie, let's fool around," I say, feeling like Jimmy Stewart standing all hangdog in the snow.

"Tonight," she answers. "After the gig." Then she kisses me on the nose like I'm some poodle. "And I better not smell another woman on you, Louie," and she turns away from me in that put-down way she has.

Well, that got the blood outta my crotch and into my head and I grabbed her from behind, whirled her around to face me and said, better than George Raft, "Maybe Sonia will show up." I force my eyes not to blink when I see la Mollie starting to smile back at me. "Sonia ain't no Shirley Temple from the Good Ship Lollipop," I tell her, real vindictive. "She comes to where I play. She ain't scared of nothing, not even some stupid comet with a Russian name nobody can pronounce."

So it's my fault what happened cause I didn't believe la Mollie. I let her go, man, like I was dropping a tissue, grabbed my jacket and sax, and as cool as cool can be, like I'd rehearsed that exit all my life, I walked out the back door without saying good-bye or nothing. I just left her to the Indians, man, like John Wayne on his way to the Red River with all them cows.

✹ The Coupe de Ville

Elías Miguel Muñoz (translated by Elías Miguel Muñoz and Karen Christian)

1989

Cuban American poet Elías Miguel Muñoz explores America's consumer culture and its effect on relationships in the following piece. His poems "Returning" and "Little Sister Born in this Land" are also included in this anthology.

to Jorge

You shut the trunk
with the slightest touch
to show me the bewildering power
of your new palace.
I returned your smile
of an accomplished young man.
The warmth of your chest,
richly adorned by Calvin Klein,
made me weaken,
or perhaps it made me wake up from my failed
attempt to understand you.

Then followed your list.
And you looked at me with pride,
at your dashboard,
each button a surprise.
And you became a tiny god,
owner and master of the Coupe de Ville.
While the cold air of your machine
freezes my bones.

While in the back,
from the speakers, rain out
the drums and guitars
of British rock and roll.

You don't see me when I shrug,
you don't see my hands resting
on the warm silk of the seat.
"Isn't this like flying, Brother?"
My wish to fly (and not in your car),
my wish to be far,
or to be close the way we never were.

The way we never will be.

♛ The Low Riders

Victor Hernández Cruz

1989

Victor Hernández Cruz was born in 1949 in Puerto Rico
and immigrated to New York when he was five years old.
He published his first collection of poetry when he was
seventeen and followed with a second collection two years
later, shortly after he moved to the San Francisco Bay Area.
He has taught at universities in California and Michigan
and was a co-founder of both the East Harlem Gut Theatre
in New York and the Before Columbus Foundation, which
bestows the annual American Book Awards. He has written
several volumes of poetry and co-edited the anthology
Paper Dance: 55 Latino Poets (1994).

Who first in the human planet invented the wheel, its use as
transport, now see it someone caressing a mountain
watching rocks and pebbles rolling, coming to a stop in
front of their toes, just picture, gee, if we were ants
clinging, or something more minute unnamed creatures of
the tropical berserk, an orange pinhead moving with eight
legs, the ancients must have said how quickly this carries it
through the terrain. Now the first hatchback would have
been inside rocks, or in the dream to be a pelota
flying through a Taíno park, send a message which travels
distance and I can catch it with my fingers.
　　Out here puffing, jamming, moving down boulevard,
deep into the industry of tires, red wheels, blue tires,
metal sunk low around it, like a closed eye or a blink,
constructions floating, homemade interiors, Roman
Chariots dodging, trunks full of batteries. In Peru the

llama was freight carrier over through mountain paths
whose history they were starting, for gasoline they gave
them Chicha and coca leaves, zoom through streams, atop
where it's cold down to the hot flatlands, edges of towns
where they traded woven blankets and disappeared into the
clouds. And that petro took them through sky tree branches,
the llama white and bushy, serene, a caravan of miniature camels.

When I am in this room that flies it is as if I invented
rubber. Like San Jose low riders' interiors, fluffy sit
back, unwind, tattoo on left hand, near the big thumb a
cross with four sticks flying, emphasizing its radiance,
further up the arm skeletons, fat blue lines, Huichol
designs on the copper flesh, the arm of the daddy-o
on the automatic stick. A beautiful metal box which many
call home. It doesn't matter if the manufacturer was Ford
or General Motors, their executives in the suburbs of
Detroit watching home movies, vacationing in weird
Londons, when the metal is yours you put your mark on it,
buying something is only the first step, what you do to it is
your name, your history of angles, your exaggeration,
your mad paint for the grand scope of humanity,
the urbanites will see them like butterflies with
transmissions. Take it to Mexico and get a round figure to
the maniacs of Tijuana, who break it down to slices, throw
it back together, slice it up again.

Once a circus caravan of riders from Watsonville took
twenty cars down, puffing and flying and bouncing all the
way; only stopped twice by Highway Patrol, but they looked
so loony that the officers, perhaps behind a beer or two,
let them go, saying this can't be real, plus they were clean
as a Mormon in Salt Lake City, license and registrations,
and hydraulics well hidden.

Zoom, all enroute toward TJ to get their interiors
laid out, they know who to see, one tall Tony, another guy
called Gordo, talk right adjust your price, Tiger, Zebra,
velvet, polka dots, colors your dream, shit never heard of,
tugged in tight, last you a century, you go before your car
will, blazing stuff shag rug pink running across dashboard.

Twenty cars rolling, eating the road from here to Tijuana,
from here to Tía Juana, music from the Pioneers. All the

mozos some with mozas sporting lumberjack shirts, leaning, brown hands, the tattoo cross where Christ was tortured, on the steering wheel cutting edges, a mosaic of tongues rattling, can we say unidentified flying objects, private discos, patterns, a piece here and a piece there, if that don't work enter the garage of spare parts.

Mission Street is El Camino Real, is the old road of Christianity, if you start riding from 24th you could go in a straight line all the way to the gates of gold. From path to road from road to street to avenue from avenue to boulevard from boulevard to airport from airport continue to space station, looking for those white crystals, don't kid yourself the Northern proposition has always been vertical, an uptown kind of motion, towards the mechanics who lay out your interior, how real is the Camino, El Camino Irreal where car junkies glide into the southern and northern lights.

The scene on the road must be here comes Ali Baba and his twenty machines, going South to get to their North. But wait, how long will this oil supply last. 2050, you cannot replace it like coffee or tobacco, Colombian oil gives its own seeds, but the blood of the earth once it's taken out leaves space. Do you figure they will be able to equip motors with new gadgets that will allow them to digest an alternate source of energy, *si no, se acabó la Honda*. The whole landscape will be full of rust, only the low riders' pleasure boats will be assigned to museums. Tony blows: And my hand against that dashboard, in my studio roving, dazzling right below the mini charro hat swinging from the rearview mirror, with its embroidery in gold and silver, gold rings you bunch of susus, exhibit relaxation, the State of California made the roads for us, the princesses in shiny cabins.

Who invented wheels invented roads, but movement which is before avenues, before circles invented itself, it made enough of itself to be available to all, to be interpreted according to each, it's like you enter and perform, like the full fleet of twenty cars riding towards TJ will each have its own coat, their common language is their closeness to the ground, they want to kiss the earth, they want to penetrate the many disguises of their mama land, have we been in touch with you are we rubbing you right, to be on this

road is this the way we say love dangling from a window
driving Smokey Robinson and the Miracles, OoooooBaby,
Baby OoooooooBabyBaby, green light go, stoplight red stop,
yellow light put your feet down tight, in the hot rod land
what can we do with our hands but attack the street, mold it,
make it unique, each will be different for the same purpose.

Hector blows: When my cacharro goes down there's not
even room to stick a nickel in at the bottom. The steering
wheel is the handle of measurement, skinny ones, made of
silver chains, prisoner chains, industrial chains, smoking
chains, the smaller steering wheels allow for quick jerky
precise turns, tricks that only roadrunner could perform,
beep beep, make room for the modern car yachts of the
Watsonville Road Kings, monarchs of the boulevards, never
bored always going somewhere, now enroute south, towards
the land of the articulate mechanics, who work with their
eyes closed and create short of putting a toilet in the back. A
style of craftsmanship, concentration, it features remnants
of a classical point of view, the car is the living room, like
Gothic mixed with Toltecas, my space to freak you out, come
delight in my red peach fuzz sofas, enjoy the stereo sound
from my Pioneer speakers, picture the chromo hanging like
a painting in a gallery, car club emblems showing through
the back windows: Watsonville Road Kings, jumping and
moving, cleaning the surface, when the gasoline stops
pumping the vehicles will run on perfume and music.

from

☗ Lucky Alley

Alejandro Murguía

1994

Alejandro Murguía was born in 1949 in California and grew up in Mexico City. Murguía has been involved in the Central American solidarity movement since the early 1970s, and his experience as a member of the Sandinista brigade during the Nicaraguan insurrection of 1979 fueled the short-story collection *Southern Front* (1990), which won an American Book Award. He was the founding editor of *Tin-Tin,* a journal of Latino literature and art, and is currently a professor of Raza Studies at San Francisco State University. He published his latest book, *This War Called Love: Nine Stories,* in 2002.

I NEVER UNDERSTOOD WHY THEY CALLED THIS GRAFFITI-SCARRED alley lucky. Still the same as when I lived here—littered with abandoned shopping carts, broken-spring couches, pools of dirty oil, and a million shards of glass. Vatos living in parked cars swigging beer and dealing dope, clouds of black flies buzzing over mounds of garbage, and stray cats under stoops with yellow fear in their eyes. Piss smell so thick in the air, even weeds, sprouting through cracks in the asphalt, look like they want out of this place. At sundown the hazy light filtering between Victorian-vintage tenements makes even the dust motes seem dangerous, and you know nothing but bad luck is going to happen here.

Going by Lucky Alley always reminds me of Catarino Maraña— drove a pearl-white sports car, a '60 Triumph with canvas top. I sold him the top after wrecking my own Triumph. Funny that when I think of other people's bad luck I think of my own. During my bad days I wrecked plenty of cars; the last one, a signal-red TR3, happened one

Saturday night when I turned, piss-drunk, into Lucky Alley and never saw the street light step in front of me—I woke up in General Hospital, an intern stitching my forehead like he was mending a sock, leaving this crescent scar to remind me.

I wrecked the Triumph after an all-night celebration drinking shots of tequila with beer chasers. My girlfriend, Alba, had agreed to move into my studio apartment, 25 Lucky Alley. I'd just left her old flat, and her face was the last thing I flashed on before the pinwheel of nausea exploded in my head; then, like in a movie, everything faded to darkness.

Alba is the most beautiful woman in the Mission. She has brows that are charcoal smudges and eyes like a pampas night. She's Argentine, elegant as a pedestal, and can't stand stereotypes—hates tangos, Juan Perón, and the films of Armando Bo and Isabel Sarli. Perón kicked her family out of Argentina, and she's lived her whole life here in La Mission, like everyone else I know. Her main love is films. Always with a Super-8 camera, she'd film a sparrow's burial if she could. But I'd been into movies way before I met her.

She appeared one day at the Ribeltad Vorden—that place across Precita Park where I tended bar—a red beret cocked over one ear, a light meter around her neck, asking if she could film the poets, locos, revolutionaries, and anarchists who hang out there. Why not? I said, and offered her an Anchor Steam.

She filmed the junkies nodding in the park, the drunken poets reading from up on the little stage, even me, pouring a draft. I got her number before she left and a week later took her to dinner, then a double feature at the New Mission, *El Santo contra el Médico Asesino* and another one I forget. El Santo, the Mexican wrestler with white mask and tights, *el enmascarado de plata*, in one scene he drives a white Corvette into an alley and about seven thugs jump him. The bad guys attack with two-by-fours, chains, and clubs while El Santo fights back with all his champion-wrestler moves, flying kicks and all. Cut to the next scene: El Santo is having dinner at someone's house and you never know how he escaped. We laughed, it was so bad.

Later that night we wound up at my studio in Lucky Alley, a couple of blue candles lit for atmosphere. We were fooling around on the mattress when she picked my hand off her breast.

"Would you ever lie to me?"

Her mouth was so beautiful I felt I was in a foreign movie, something by Lina Wertmüller.

"Never," I said, and meant it.

"Not telling is also lying," she said.

My tongue was already dipping into her navel, and her words were lost on me. I grunted what sounded like agreement.

"Good," she said, "because I never forgive a liar."

That's how our affair began.

When I met Alba she was a film student at the Art Institute and worked nights at El Gaucho on Mission Street, serving drinks in a fluffy skirt and low-cut blouse. I could never reconcile to that part of her. In those days Alba wore spike-heeled shoes, red ones, looked like one of those Helmut Newton models, all legs. Would wear them when we made love. Even after everything that's happened between us—the deal with Catarino, and her chasing other men—I can't stop loving her, not even now when things aren't so good for us and there's no art or glory in our lives. She burns steady, just enough and every day; I like to fire up both ends and the middle. I guess our contradictions unite us.

I didn't know Catarino in those days I was wrecking cars, but he lived on Folsom Street, around the corner from Lucky Alley. I met Catarino a few months after my last wreck. I'd gone to the North Beach office of Revolutionary Films, a foreign film distributor, to rent *Mexico, the Frozen Revolution,* about government corruption after the 1910 Revolution. I wanted to impress Alba by starting a Latino film society in the Mission, a cine club to bring underground classics like *Memorias de Subdesarollo* and *Reed-México Insurgente,* something really political, to the barrio, an alternative to the telenovela mentality.

Catarino was sitting in their snazzy offices, at the edge of the front desk, rapping a mile a minute on the phone, a huge orange-and-brown poster of Zapata on a wall behind him. He sported wire-rimmed glasses, a big mustache, the tips waxed and curled to a fine point, and a tie loosely knotted and looped around his neck like a strip of film, or a noose. He cupped the receiver on his thigh to greet me, pushed the glasses back with one finger, then asked the receptionist to send a memo. He set the receiver down while he stuffed an envelope with publicity flyers and explained the hardships of the movie business to me. The problem was cash flow, he said. In three seconds he returned to his phone conversation, like I wasn't there. He smoked as he talked, mouthing his words around a cigarette stub like Bogart in *Treasure of the Sierra Madre.* I barely got a word in before he rushed out for a business lunch, telling the receptionist he'd taken a twenty from petty cash.

My father started me on movies. His addiction goes back to the first reels carried on mule back over narrow trails to his small town in Jalisco. At dusk, silent movies on a stretched cotton sheet hung in the open-air plaza, the flickering projector light blinding the fruit bats swooping through the royal palms. Later, in Mexico City, the classic leading men of the golden age of Mexican cinema were his idols, but in particular that scowling film-noir legend, Pedro Armendáriz. My father fashioned his life after those Mexican matinee idols, except he didn't sing or ride a horse. Rigid in his honor, brave around men, courteous to women. That's where I got my code of honor that a man's word is worth his life. And about women—if she leaves you for another man, burn every scrap of her memory like Cortés torching Tenochtitlán. I didn't know any other way. That's how I'd been since that movie with Pedro Armendáriz where María Félix tells him she's been raped by a troop of soldiers, and he responds with utter contempt, "You should have let yourself be killed instead." That was me.

The third *cine* club night at the Precita Community Center, some sprockets tore while I was on the phone with Alba; by the time I heard the audience howling, several hundred feet of good film lay piled on the floor like black spaghetti. I refunded the gate to placate the mob. What money was left I used to pay for the damaged film. Somehow it didn't seem right to continue with the *cine* club, so I filed away the idea and chalked it up to experience.

A couple of weeks after the last *cine* club showing, a pearl-white Triumph pulled up outside the Ribeltad Vorden. But a Triumph without the top isn't so hot.

Right away I recognized Catarino when he slid up to the long mahogany bar and ordered an Anchor Steam. I said hello, reminded him about our meeting at Revolutionary Films, and slipped him a draft on the house—but hell, I did that for everyone. No one I knew ever went thirsty when I worked the plank.

Catarino's voice was like a rasp file, the words scraped from deep in his chest where the cigarette smoke collected. At thirty-seven, he was fifteen years older than me, he knew plenty about the movie business, and spoke with authority about films, directors, and life. You'd maybe not guess he'd spent ten years in the joint, but he had, for possession of heroin—a kilo and a half. When he told me I wasn't shook by it. Cat, as he liked to be called, never sat still, always moving around the bar, beer in hand, sleek and intense, always ready. I liked that about him. You might call him a hustler—*vivo,* my father would say. Neither would be wrong.

Catarino came from El Paso, where he learned early about girls, *mota,* and Johnny Law. In and out of Texas reform schools, he survived by hustling and dealing. After the ten-year stint in Huntsville picking cotton for the Texas Rangers, he came out to the coast and settled in the Mission.

I offered him the white canvas top, the only thing I salvaged from the Triumph I wrecked in Lucky Alley. I asked a hundred but took eighty and got fifty, the rest an IOU I still have. That's when I learned Cat was often a little short, light in the wallet, he'd say with a sly smile. Glen, who managed the Ribeltad and was an old friend of Cat's, often let him run up a tab. Glen used to say, "Forgive your friends their sins or you'll live a lonely life."

When Revolutionary Films folded, literally went under, Cat started hanging out more often at the Ribeltad. The times when he appeared flush with cash—I never asked where it came from since it wasn't my business—he always paid off his tab and left a nice tip.

One slow night Cat cruised into the Ribeltad and invited me to the storage room. There, among stacked beer cases, he fired up a wheat-paper rolled joint. After a couple of tokes, he laid a pair of tickets on me to a special screening of Les Blank's *Chulas Fronteras.* "For the free beers, Felix," he said. High on that purple smoke, I figured Cat a *vato* who'd give you the last sip of beer in his mug.

A few nights later Cat dropped in near closing time and helped me shoo out the last customers. I dimmed the bar lights so cruising cop cars wouldn't see us, and, with the bar closed up, we drank free till four in the morning and talked films—Fellini, Herzog, Buñuel. The burning ember of Cat's cigarette reflected in his deep-set, beer-bottle-colored eyes.

This became our ritual. Two, three times a week, Cat would appear around closing time, and after I'd shut down the plank, we'd sit in the dark sharing a pitcher or two of steam beer. One of those nights, well into our third pitcher, I'm not sure which of us had the idea to lease the York Theater on 24th Street in the heart of the Mission. The York had been closed for years, but as a kid I'd spent many Saturdays mesmerized in the plush-velvet seats, and during intermission I'd sit back and, looking up at the ceiling, trace every curlicue on the gold-leaf design. To this day, the smell of roasting popcorn conjures up the York Theater and those Saturday afternoons.

At first I wasn't sure, but little by little, night after night, in the empty bar draining pitchers of Anchor Steam with Cat, I started going for the idea. I knew the theater was an architectural gem, and a gala pre-mier featuring the golden age of Mexican cinema, movies like *Los Olvidados, Nosotros los Pobres, La Mujer del Puerto,* would blow everyone away.

Cat located the owner of the York, a guy in Hollywood named Brody. We needed a five-grand deposit for a one-year lease. Cat said he had a thousand, could I raise the rest? I had to think about this. Alba and I had two grand saved for her to finish school; we'd even mentioned get-ting married. Alba really wanted her degree more than she wanted mar-riage. But it was something to think about, since my studio in Lucky Alley was tightly crammed. Every Saturday we'd go looking for a bigger flat; we looked at some real dogs and some nice ones we couldn't afford.

Those nights after drinking and talking with Cat, I'd come home to Lucky Alley, my head full of ideas about the York, and I'd lie awake think-ing how to tell Alba. I knew already what she'd say. Alba is a practical, food-on-the-table, all-the-bills-paid kind of woman. Like her mother. Don't come to her with get-rich schemes 'cause she'll tell you every reason why they'll fail.

So I called this one alone—and took the two grand from the sav-ings. It was my money, too, and I figured it'd be better not to give Alba a choice, just present her with the done deal. Glen co-signed for the other two grand from a loan company at 22 percent so we could make the deposit. That was the biggest debt I'd ever had in my life, and when I signed on the dotted line the pen was trembling.

The next day Cat came into the Ribeltad Vorden with ten crisp hundred-dollar bills, and I turned over my share in a white envelope. We called Brody from the bar phone and he agreed to fly in on Saturday to show us the theater and sign the papers. Cat said he'd get a cashier's check for Brody. We toasted to success with a pitcher of Anchor Steam, on the house.

The rest of the week I'm so high I can barely eat. I'm bursting inside to tell Alba, 'cause I want this for her just as much as I want it myself. I know she's tired of waitressing at El Gaucho, tired of the cheap tips and lewd comments. And her negatives piled in boxes. So each night while she's sleeping I'm thinking of running the York, of that moment we throw open the doors for the grand premiere and the house lights dim, the cred-its come on, and the faces light up. Alba can even show her own films. One of her *cinema vérité* black-and-whites that haunt you days later with their powerful images. That's what film is all about—subliminal messages. Film is also about forgetting, just sitting in a darkened theater losing yourself in those evanescent images, forgetting everything. You should see Alba's Super-8s, very much influenced by Shirley Clarke. They showed one last year at the Roxie, an interview with a woman who'd been waitressing twenty-four years, and they gave her a standing ovation. Alba still talks of making feature films, and she will, but for now she's editing commercials for Channel 5. She hates it, says she wants to do subversive work, not this garbage.[...]

After laying the money on Cat, I waited all week, tense as a death row inmate, jumping each time the phone rang. Every glance I stole at Alba tied loops in my stomach.

Alba keeps house so clean you can eat off the floor, but that Thursday night for some reason there's a *cucaracha* poking two thin feelers around the edge of the kitchen table, unsure whether to come out into the light. I had one eye on Alba, one eye on the *cuca,* but I was thinking of Cat.

Finally, like I'd just learned to talk, the words came and I told Alba where I'd put all our money. She thought I was kidding. No, I said, I'm serious as the Ten Commandments. She stared at me like I had burned her negatives and smashed her cameras, her eyes pinpoints of black light. "How could you without telling me?" is what she said. "And if it doesn't work out, can you trust Catarino?"

Trying to hide my doubts, I kept talking about things taking off for us. Then I stopped. She had me pinned with those Argentine eyes of hers, but she wasn't seeing me, she was seeing her dreams slipping away like a boat from the dock.

Then she locked herself in the bedroom and wouldn't open the door, but I could hear her smashing things. The lamp. A framed picture of us when we first met. I slumped in the kitchen, my scar throbbing like an open vein, feeling like I had slept with another woman, or worse, and nothing since has made me feel as bad.

For a long time I stared at the bubbled-up linoleum floor, followed the cracks across the kitchen wall. The sour odors in the woodwork we tried so hard to scrub away seemed to rise up and mock me. When the lousy cockroach finally made a dash across the kitchen table, I put my thumb on it and squashed it into the next world.

Friday morning, the brown egg yolk of the sun tried to break through the dirty industrial haze of the city. Glen, the manager of the Ribeltad, woke me with an urgent call. He wanted to meet at the Hall of Justice on 7th

Street. Something urgent. Wouldn't say what it's about till we're going down the hot, piss-smelling elevator to the morgue. At the mention of Catarino's name, my heart wrinkled up like a balloon without air.

A sheriff, pale as a maggot, led us to a walk-in freezer that smelled of chrome and formaldehyde. He pulled back the white sheet on a corpse laid out on a gurney and there's Cat—dead and naked, one eye closed and one partly open, face and chest a gray, pasty color. Death had stripped away his cool-as-ice look. There's a smudge of gunpowder and a little burn hole on Cat's forehead like the dot on a question mark. Anger, rage, I don't know, made the scar on my forehead want to burst.

Can we identify the body? It's Catarino all right, that's his mustache still waxed and curled, though the tips looked a bit singed. In a monotone voice, the sheriff told us the district attorney would be holding an inquiry, but it was pretty much a routine case. Catarino and a partner were scoring some Mexican heroin, but the deal was a setup, the dealer an undercover narcotics agent.

There wasn't much I could do for Catarino, he seemed at peace, much more at peace than I was. I wondered what movie his eyes were looking at now. *Pobrecito.* Then I thought, why should I feel sorry for him when I have Alba and myself to feel sorry for? Then I got angry, thinking—damn it, Cat, what were you doing? And what about your friends, did you ever think of them? Anger pulled me one way, betrayal another.

✴ Little Sister Born in This Land

Elías Miguel Muñoz (translated by Elías Miguel Muñoz,
Karen Christian, and Miguel Gallegos)

1989

See "Returning" and "The Coupe de Ville" in this volume
for more poetry by Elías Miguel Muñoz.

to Vicky

When you slip
slowly and lovingly
through my fingers
I cannot hold you
and explain a thousand things
Each time you smile
and show me your shoes with buckles
or tell me a story
of space flights
(How you would love to be a princess
in those absurd and bloody wars)
Each time you intrigue me
with your riddles
with your words
that will always be foreign
to our experience

It isn't a reproach
sister
Little sister born in this land
It's just that you will never know
of hens nesting

(Is there anywhere in your childhood
a similar feeling?)
Once upon a time
there was a boy
on paving stones so white
and excursions on foot
toys made of tin
There was also mystery
in the ravines
There were evil pirates
and brave corsairs
There were lessons
for carving men
out of stone
There was caramel candy
and sweet potato pudding

It isn't a reproach
sister
Little sister born in this land
It's just that you have only
the joy of Disney heroes
Because you will smile
when the ingenious man
behind the cartoons
makes of you
of every child
a little clown
plastic and ridiculous

When you slip away
slowly and lovingly
I cannot invent
another childhood for you
cannot offer you mine
also nourished by heroes
but tasting of palm leaf
and *mamoncillo*
It did not suffer the mockery
of expensive toys

that the deceptive
ghost of December
brings to you

When you slip away
slowly and lovingly
we cannot bury together
in the backyard
(That warm and always
open earth)
the models
that will take hold of you
that already stalk you
from their cardboard boxes
and their printed letters
on a glass of milk
or Coca-Cola

It isn't a reproach
sister
Little sister born in this land

from

✹ Mocha in Disneyland

Gary D. Keller (El Huitlacoche)

1980

Gary D. Keller was born in 1943 in San Diego and grew up on the U.S./Mexico border, working at a young age to support his family. Keller is the founder of the *Bilingual Review* and Bilingual Press, and Project 1000 and Project Prime, programs working to create educational opportunities for minority students. He has edited more than fifteen books of poetry, fiction, and scholarly text, and he is the author of several collections of short stories, including *Zapata Rose in 1992 and Other Tales* (1997). He currently teaches at Arizona State University, where he has been a Regents Professor of Spanish since 1988.

ABOUT 7:00 A.M. PANCHOLÍN WAS IN MY ROOM, making weird noises. He wouldn't wake you up exactly, he knew he wasn't supposed to disturb his daddy. But he'd play in the room. First, he'd start with a whisper. He'd re-create intergalactic battles and summon the Incredible Hulk and Wonder Woman to his side. By 7:30 the whispers had given way to loud zaps and rat-a-tat-tats as ray guns and stun pistols reverberated from the legions of molded plastic figurines that were propped strategically around the bedroom.

"You want breakfast?"

"What you got?"

"I've got Rice Krispies. I've got Cheerios. Take your pick."

"You mean you don't have Count Chocula?"

"You know I don't keep that sugary garbage around. Your mother lets you eat that stuff?"

"No."

"Well, then?"

"I was just asking."

"Boy, when I was your age all I got was a cup of black coffee and a stale bolillo. Then I had to work all day hunting for tin cans and scrap metal."

"That must have been funnnnnnnnnn. You know what? I want both. Rice Krispies and Cheerios all mixed up. Say, Daddy, do you think we could send away for this magic ring? Only two box tops and twenty-five cents."

"I've got something better than that for you." I opened the top drawer of the chest and took out my Phi Beta Kappa key. "See this!"

"Wow! It's gold, isn't it?"

"Sure!"

"Is it pure gold? Or is it just gold on top like what rubs off?"

"Pure gold!"

"Wow! What is it?"

"It's the sacred key to the Order of the Golden Carp."

"Is that what I get if I make Carp First Class?"

"None other."

"And what am I now? A tadpole, right?"

"Right. But if things go well, by tomorrow you'll be a Carp First Class."

"What are you, Daddy? What class carp are you? Second? Third? Ninth?"

"No, you're going the wrong direction. First is the highest of the classes. Me, I'm a...a Goldfish Supreme."

"Is that the highest?"

"Oh, that's definitely the highest. As a matter of fact, I'm one of the senior carps in the system."

"Oh boy, the highest number of counting of carps. What comes after Carp First Class?"

"Well, uh, there's Star, and then, Life, and then, Goldfish Supreme."

"But why a goldfish? I thought you was a carp!"

"Yeah, well, I am. Goldfish is another word for carp. Only it's the secret word. You're not gonna tell anybody, are you?"

"Naw. I won't tell anybody, except for other carps. Who else is a carp, Daddy?"

"Who else? Well...uh...all the Chicanos. All the Chicanos who make the grade that is. If you ask one and he doesn't know what you're talking about, then you can be sure they've passed him by and he's nothing more than a Chicken Chartreuse Esquinkel."

Pancholín fell down laughing. "Right! Right!" Then he turned serious. "What about Mommy? Is she one?"

"Well, not exactly. She approves of them though. She's a corresponding member of the academy."

"Why don't we start up a Silver Carps? For mommies and girls."

"Not a bad idea. Maybe we should bring it up in August. You know, on the convention floor."

"Tell me again, Daddy. What do I have to do to be a Carp First Class?"

"Well, lots of things."

"Like what?"

"Lots of things. You'll find out as we do them. But every First Class Carp has got to do these two things. One, he's got to find a treasure. And two, he's got to spend the night out-of-doors, in a scary place."

"Yikes! And we're gonna spend it on Tom Sawyer Island, in the old cave!"

"Right you are, none other."

"Yikes!"

"You're not scared, are you?"

"Naw. You'll be there, right?"

"Definitely."

"Think there's any bats in that cave?"

"I'll have the dromedary scare them away."

Pancholín looked at me dubiously.

"Think there are any snakes in that cave?"

"Naw. Snakes like to snuggle into little holes and crevices, kind of like kitty-gato does. Caves are more for big game like wolves and bears."

"Yikes! Maybe the six wolves all live in the cave."

"What six wolves?"

"You know. The wherewolf, the whatwolf, the which, the when, the why, and the whowolf."

"Oh, those guys. Those are just made-up wolves. Those are wh-wolves. They wouldn't be in Tom Sawyer's Cave."

"I thought they were real wolves! You see, you make up everything! I know the wherewolf is real. I've seen him on TV."

"So it's real if you've seen it on TV? Never mind that anyway. We've got to get ready." I brought the gear that I'd stowed away for the outing. "Think we've got everything?"

"Oh boy! A flashlight! Can we make animals with our fingers against the wall of the cave?"

"Hey, that's a great idea! We'll do all kinds of fun things."

"Wanna see my rabbit? I make a beautiful rabbit. ¡Mira qué precioso!"

"Not now. In the cave."

"You know what? You're missing one thing."

"What would that be?"

"A weapon."

"Naw, we don't need a weapon. We'll vanquish any enemies we may encounter with our bare hands."

"Suppose they've got dogs?"

"Dogs at Disneyland? Naw, they wouldn't do that."

"Why don't you pack some hamburger with sleeping drugs in it? If some dogs come around we'll give them a little snooze." Pancholín chortled.

"Pretty good idea. Only I don't have any sleeping drugs and who wants to carry around some smelly old raw meat in a knapsack all day?"

By 8:00 p.m. we were on our last legs. We had done it all, especially anything that whirred, whipped, whirled, whined, whistled or whizzed (six wh's over Disney) including the Jungle Cruise, Star Jets, Grand Prix Raceway, 20,000 Leagues Under the Sea, Snow White's Scary Adventures, Dumbo the Flying Elephant, the Mad Tea Party and Mr. Toad's Wild Ride.

As darkness came upon us, Pancholín grew more and more apprehensive. It was a typical syndrome of his so I didn't pay it that much mind. We went back to the locker where we stowed away the knapsack and we got it out.

"Daddy, you remember those hippos and alligators on the Jungle Cruise? That's not the water around our island, is it?"

"Not at all. They keep those big lugs out of the way of the paddle wheeler. Besides, you're not scared of those silly guys? They're no more real than your Creature Cantina or Luke Skywalker. Giant hunks of molded plastic, that's what they are."

Pancholín was dubious, very dubious.

"Well my man, the last vessel moves out in five minutes. Which will it be, Tom Sawyer's Rafts or Captain Fink's Keel Boats?"

Pancholín sighed. "We might as well take the Keel Boats. They look safer."

On the boat he began whimpering and rubbing his eyes, all the while making a herculean effort to hold in the tears. "Do we have to spend the whole night on this silly island? I'm cold!"

"Pancho! Be quiet! You want everybody to know our business? My God, it's the hottest night in the valley. Besides, I packed a blanket."

"Are you sure there's no bats in that cave? Maybe dogs go in there and pee on the floor."

"They don't let dogs in Disney's land. No way."

"Well, we're not supposed to stay in here after dark. What'll they do with us if they catch us?"

"Maybe they'll throw us in that pirate's dungeon over in Adventureland."

He started whimpering some more. "You're always teasing me. Why don't you stop teasing me?"

"I'm sorry. I tell you what. We'll go to the island and visit Fort Mark Twain and fire the rifles and explore the caves for bats. If you want to stay, fine, and if you don't, pues, ¡qué carajo! ¡Fuímonos!"

"And if we go, do I still get to have the Order of the Golden Carp?"

"You know I can't do that. But you can always try again next year when you're a bigger boy."

Pancholín sighed again like the weight of the world and his culture was on him, but by the time we had explored each and every path on the island, each crevice and cave or mine shaft, each sharpshooter's niche and the secret tunnel out of the fort, he was singing a different tune, like I figured he would.

"This place is neat! Can we sneak up to the lookout after everybody leaves?"

"Maybe, if it seems safe."

Soon enough the bell came for the last raft to leave the island. We slipped away and hid way in the bowels of Old Jim's Cave, "quiet like mouses."

"Ya se van, ¿verdad?"

"Pues sí, gringos mensos. ¡Que aquí hay dos chicanitos escondidos de deveras!"

"Papi, ¿ya nos podemos salir?"

"Todavía no. Mira, aquí voy a tender la manta. Acuéstate un ratito. Vamos a hacer animalitos con la luz del flashlight. Ya te diré cuando podemos salir a regir la islita."

"Yo quiero ser el rey. No, mejor el principe. Que tú seas el rey."

"¡Andale pues! Pero por ahora quietito como si fueras la momia de la cueva de Drácula."

We must have been playing in the cave for at least an hour or two. It was so quiet and peaceful. We had ventured out and filled up two pillow cases I had packed with leaves and grass. We were all set. I even considered making a fire, but then thought twice about it.

"Do you want to know why I tease you a little?"

"Yeah. Why?"

"Because sometimes we play in a way that we're like brothers. You know, I had lots of brothers. And we teased each other a lot. I teased them and they teased me. There was Pancracio and Curro and Tecolote and Joselito-Joey and…"

"How come you don't still tease your brothers?"

"Never see them anymore. Curro's been dead fifteen years now. Tecolote's designing hydraulic screws for the space project, Pancracio and Joselito still hauling scrap metal…"

"How come I don't have any brothers?"

"You were going to have some. Your mommy and I were planning to, but we didn't get the time."

"Why would you tease your brothers?"

"Because they teased me."

"Well, I don't tease you, but you still tease me."

"I guess so. The trouble is, once you're a teaser then you're always stuck a teaser. Es un vicio como cualquier otro. I'll try not to tease you so much."

"You'd better. 'Cause if not, maybe I'll pull some more hair out of your head. Why'd the cops shoot your brother?"

"¡Qué sé yo! I wish I knew. Some cops don't like people who look too dark. When you're an older boy we'll have to talk about that more. Ley fuga. Or maybe 'cause they figured they couldn't pin a rap on him in court."

"What's a rap?"

"When they say you've done something wrong."

Then we heard a sound from outside. We heard it again, a dog barking, a little closer.

"What are we going to do?" Pancholín asked.

"Jesus, I wish I had that poison meat." I packed up our gear. "We've got to make tracks."

"Daddy! Let's go to the Tree House. We'll be way up in the tree. Nobody'll get us there."

"That's a damn good idea. Only one problem, we've got to get across this channel. Look, you wait here! I'm going to swim across and untie the raft and bring it back here."

"No way! If you're swimming out of here, I'm swimming with you."

I could see he was determined. "Look, I'll just be back in a minute. You don't want to get soaked. I'll be right back with the nice dry raft."

"No way!"

"You're going to come with me in the water?"

"Uh huh!"

"You swear to God you'll never tell Mommy!"

"I swear. I swear to God and hope to die."

The dog barked. It was too close for comfort.

"Yikes! We've got to get out of here. You grab my waist real tight. We're going to walk in the water. No heroic stuff now. Nice and easy, walking in the water. That's right, nice and easy."

Halfway across the channel, I asked him, "Feel any fish nibbling at your leg?"

"No. Do you?"

"No, but if you do, don't worry. They're friendly carp."

"Okay."

We were on the other side in a jiffy. We hid in the wooden boat-house where the customers queue up for the rafts. We peered over the rim. Two patrolmen were coming, one from each direction. We ducked down into the shadows of the hut.

"Hey, Bud," one said to the other, "you on again tonight?"

"Yeah, third night in a row Disney sticks me with the graveyard shift. See anything exciting?"

"What's to see? Minnie Mouse's underpants? Say, Bud. What's the matter, somebody over in the central office don't like you?"

"I don't know. Maybe so."

"You better watch over your old lady, Bud. Somebody in central's got you on graveyard duty." The guard walked away, chortling all the while.

Bud stopped and lit a cigarette. He flicked the match our way and cursed Donald Duck's mother. Then he moved on.

Once they were gone we could hardly suppress our mirth, even soaked as we were.

"Can you believe that? Can you believe it!"

"What a guard, Papi! ¡Qué loco! He looks up Minnie Mouse's dress! ¡Es el más grande de todos los guajolotes!"

While Pancholín wasn't looking I planted on the ground a silver five-peso piece, un Hidalgo that I had gotten as a present when I was a kid and which had been rattling around the bottom drawer for three decades. "You know what? I think you must be the bravest kid in the valley. I've got a mind to buck you straight up to Star."

"Star! Wow! But I haven't even found a treasure."

"Gee, that's right. That's too bad. Say, what's that silvery flashing thing?"

"Look, Daddy. It's a silver coin." Pancholín grabbed for it. "It's the biggest silver coin in the world!"

"It sure looks like it. What does it say?"

"It says cinco pesos."

"Do you know what that means?"

"Yeah, five bucks."

"Yeah, but it means it's Chicano money. It's a Chicano treasure!"

"How did it get here?"

"Maybe somebody originally buried it here for good luck. Or maybe...." I look over to the water.

"The carp, right Daddy?"

"I don't know."

"Maybe it's the carp that shot it up here out of the water."

"I don't know. Let's go look."

We looked into the water, long and hard. There was nothing. We looked and looked. Then there was a ripple out in the channel.

"He's out there all right," Pancholín said. "The carp that looks out for Chicanos." We both shivered with that incisive sense of revelation that only young children can experience.

"Okay," I said. "We're moving out to the Swiss Family Tree House."

We crossed the lighted walkway into the unlit bosom of shrubbery, first one, then the other, like guerrillas on assignment. Carefully we made the journey to Adventureland. Then over the puny fence and up the staircased Swiss Family Tree, platform by platform and tree-room by tree-room to the topmost platform. We took off our clothes and hung them to dry. Pancholín wrapped himself in the blanket. We looked down from the tree crown on the Magic Kingdom. Main Street was all lit up and so was Cinderella's Castle. Above, starry heavens capped the sultry night and in the channel prescient carp bided the golden dawn. All was well in the valley.

"Ready to sleep?"

"Yes. I love you Daddy, all the way to the last number of counting."

We hugged and kissed and Pancho went to sleep and I sat up looking out from the tree, thinking warm thoughts about the great chain of being, especially of my father who during one period of his life raised geese to be industrial watchdogs and the way he carried on the day I got that fellowship, my mother in the background, biting her fingers, scared to death and with reason, because I'd be breaking the cycle of tirilones, pachucos and pochos, with their papiamento of street caliche and devious calques, and emerging into the alienating, mainstream Other. God knows, even she had no inkling then I would fall in love with and marry una del otro estirpe. And the walks we took in the barrio past the chicharronería ("sin pelos, ¿eh?"), past the molino de nixtamal, past El Mandamás del Barrio, a beer for my father and a nieve to sweeten my mouth. My father with his moral paradigms, the Chicano Aesop discussing the virtue of geese. "Never take for granted other persons or animals, you must always work toward them, make great effort, is like fine art, a ritual of love." He rolled up his sleeve. "You see this scar on my arm? You see that, the patrón made me go and get it stitched today because it didn't want to heal. You know Doña Jacinta, the big she-goose? She's the one I trained first, she's been with me as a watchdog now for over four years. And what a fine guardian she is. She will hiss like a siren and peck out the eyes of any stranger unless she's well leashed. But last week I got careless. Who knows what I did, walked in this manner instead of that, failed to greet her in my usual soothing way, had on a funny hat, most of all I forgot that she had just hatched goslings who were under the wooden stairs. Before I know it, peck, peck, and my arm was damn near sliced off before she recovered form and hid herself in shame. But it's my fault, I say. I tell the patrón I well deserved this moral lesson, because love is not a cheap commodity. It must be won time and over again."

As often occurs with me, moral quandaries rise up from their repressed bottleneck and beset me just as I fall asleep. I remember thinking that on the one hand it was deceitful to have fixed a false mythos on Pancholín with a silver Hidalgo, on the other the fix or rather feelings were real, and as Thomas Merton had once said (I paraphrase), mysticism was nothing more than the concerted return to the childhood condition of feckless faith. Ultimately it was good, I thought or dreamt, to care or feel deeply.

"Hey, motherfucker! What do you think you are? Some kind of tree-house owl?"

I woke up groggy. The sun was just over the barranca and in my eyes.

"Say, these brown boys are in their birthday suits."

"Look, gentlemen, we got lost in the cave over on the island. We heard some dog barking and we swam over here."

"Yeah, I bet. Just who the hell are you? The Frito Bandito? And while you're answering, stick out your hands for these cuffs."

"I won't do that."

"What do you mean, Pancho? You won't do *what*?"

"Take it easy, fella. I'm going to put on my clothes now, nice and easy. Then I'm gonna go with you just where you say. Don't get my son riled up."

"¡No te dejes, Papi! ¡No te dejes!"

"You're gonna do what I tell you, boy, and that means these sturdy cuffs!" The guard raised his stick menacingly.

"¡No te dejes, Papi! ¡No te dejes!"

The other guard looked through my pants and my watery wallet. "Say, Bubba, take it easy on this sumbitch. He's some kind of perfesser. We'd better get the PR man."

from

✳ Rancho Hollywood: "A California Dream"

Carlos Morton

1983

Carlos Morton, one of the most widely produced Chicano playwrights, has worked with numerous theaters, including the San Francisco Mime Troupe, the New York Shakespeare Festival, and the Puerto Rican Traveling Theatre. Several volumes of his work have been published, including his first collection, *The Many Deaths of Danny Rosales and Other Plays* (1983), from which the following excerpt was taken. He currently teaches Chicano and Latin American theater and playwriting at the University of California, Riverside.

PLACE: LOS ANGELES, CALIFORNIA
TIME: 1840S TO THE PRESENT

ACT I

At rise the Director is assisted by his cameraman as they shoot a movie entitled "Ye Olde California Days." The principals are offstage preparing themselves for their entrances: Ramona, an ingenue, fiery Latina type; Joaquín, a young man dressed as a peon; Sinmuhow, a Native American woman; Victoria, an older matronly type, Spanish-looking; and Rico, a dark debonair older Mexican male.

DIRECTOR: *(To his cameraman.)* If everybody's here, let's shoot the balcony scene. *(Noises backstage, people talking.)*

CAMERAMAN: Attention everybody! Quiet on the set.

DIRECTOR: The fiery impetuous Ramona *(Enter Ramona.)* is pacing nervously on her balcony waiting for her demon lover, Cisco. Stamp your feet, clap your hands, say your line! A medium shot here, camera.

RAMONA: Oh no, this cannot go on. Where is my sultry Cisco? I want him to take me away to the Rancho Grande of ecstasy!

DIRECTOR: That's good, Ronnie, but I need more of an accent. Say "dis" instead of "this" and "wan" instead of "want." And throw in a few "olés." Zoom in on a close-up on "olé."

RAMONA: Dis cun nut go on. I wan heem to take me away. Olé!

DIRECTOR: Wonderful! I love it! Remember, this is nineteenth-century California, just before the Gold Rush, when all those gay caballeros and sexy señoritas were dancing fandangos until dawn. Now then, what's missing?

CAMERAMAN: You forgot the peon.

DIRECTOR: Of course, where is my sleepy peon? *(Enter Joaquín.)* There you are. Oh, I love your outfit, it's so…I don't know…native. What's your name?

JOAQUÍN: Joaquín.

DIRECTOR: Walking?

JOAQUÍN: No, Joaquín. Like in Joaquín Valley.

DIRECTOR: Mind if I call you Jack? Up against that wall. Now squat. *(Placing a sombrero that covers up his face.)* There!

JOAQUÍN: Do I have any lines?

DIRECTOR: Lines!

CAMERAMAN: No lines.

DIRECTOR: Sorry, Jack. Move your sombrero a bit from time to time so we know you're not a statue. Who's next?

CAMERAMAN: The passerby. A lady of the night.

TONTA: I am Sinmuhow. *(Entering.)*

DIRECTOR: Oh, you're Native American. Look everybody, a real honest-to-goodness Indian! We're going to have such good karma! *(He hugs her.)* Now then, this part calls for a Mexican, but I'm sure you can pass. At the very start of the scene you walk on undulating your hips like so. *(He walks across the set undulating his hips.)*

JOAQUÍN: Yes, and that's my cue. I lift the brim of my sombrero, stick out my tongue, and pant.

DIRECTOR: Good. *(To Cameraman.)* Couldn't we put some fruit on her head! You know, then she could do the cha-cha-cha.

CAMERAMAN: That's old hat.

DIRECTOR: All right, forget it. Who's next?

CAMERAMAN: Victoria the maid. *(Enter Victoria.)*

VICTORIA: I was under the impression I was supposed to be her mother.

DIRECTOR: You are, dear, but you're also the maid. Aren't all mothers? Johnny, what is she supposed to be doing?

CAMERAMAN: *(Reading script.)* It says here, "enter making a tamale."

DIRECTOR: Oh, how ethnic. Well, where's your tamale? You little hot tamale you! *(Laughing at his own joke.)* Cut to a long shot.

VICTORIA: *(Pulling out a fake tamale.)* Ay, que ridículo.

DIRECTOR: Great! You speak Spanish! Throw in a few words every once in a while. Doesn't matter what you say, just as long as it sounds good. Give me your line.

VICTORIA: Ay Ramona, forget that no count Cisco, he is no good for you!

DIRECTOR: More accent!

RAMONA: Ay Mamá, I lub heem, he sets my heart on fi-errrr.

DIRECTOR: What happens then?

CAMERAMAN: Her debonair, slightly graying Spanish grandee father enters cracking his whip and drinking tequila.

DIRECTOR: Father! Father! Where's the Father?

RICO: Ay voy, I'm coming!

DIRECTOR: These people! *(To Cameraman who nods in agreement.)* You'd think this was the land of mañana! *(Joaquín gets up to stretch.)*

VICTORIA: He's here!

RICO: Excuse me, I was getting made up. *(He enters with an excess of white powder on his face. The Director does not really see him.)*

DIRECTOR: Let's go! We have a tight schedule! I'm going to have to be a bitch about this!

CAMERAMAN: Places! Places! *(Joaquín squats back into place.)* Quiet! Quiet on the set! Ye Olde California Days, take one.

DIRECTOR: Lights! Camera! Wait. *(He runs up and places a plastic rose between Ramona's teeth.)* Action! *(The lady of the night strolls by dancing salsa. The Peon lifts up the brim of his sombrero and starts panting, grabbing his groin.)*

RAMONA: *(Stamping her feet and clapping her hands.)* Olé! O, dis can nut go on. Wear es my sultry Cisco? I wan heem to take me to El Rancho Grande of Ecstasy!

VICTORIA: *(She drops her tamale as she enters.)* Ramona, forget dat no count Cisco, he es no goot for you.

RAMONA: Ay Mamá! You dropped your tamale. But I love heem, he puts my hard on fi-eerrrrr.

VICTORIA: Well, put de fi-errrrr out! He es un bandido, un desesperado! If your Papá finds out he weeel keeel you!

RICO: *(Enter cracking his whip and drinking tequila from a bottle.)* Andale! Andale! Arriba! Arriba! *(Like Speedy González, like Trini López trilling and shouting.)* Ajúa! Trlllllingg!

DIRECTOR: Cut! Cut! *(To Cameraman.)* Has Central Casting gone color-blind! I asked for a white Spanish grandee and they give me a dark farmworker!

VICTORIA: ¡Qué insulto!

RICO: Por eso me tardé tanto. Me pusieron todo este polvo.

DIRECTOR: Hey, no offense fellah, but you don't look very Spanish. You're supposed to be Ramona's father, the Spanish grandee.

RICO: Sir, I don't understand, even if I am as dark as a Moor, I could still be Ramona's father.

VICTORIA: That's right, Ramona is a mestiza.

DIRECTOR: A what?

VICTORIA: A mestiza. Half and half. If I, as her mother, am fair, and the father is dark, then the child is like café con leche.

RAMONA: I've never been described that way before.

VICTORIA: Yes, but that is what the Mexican people are, a mixture of Spanish and Indian.

RICO: And Arab and Jewish and African…

DIRECTOR: That is very quaint, that is very informative. But this film is supposed to be about the Spanish Californios!

RICO: Mr. Director, with all due respect, I am afraid you have little conception of the Californio reality. The people of that time were Mexican, not Spanish.

RAMONA: Jed, honey, listen to these people, they're trying to tell you something.

CAMERAMAN: It says here in the script that Ramona's father is "a Spanish grandee type, representative of the early aristocratic Californios."

RICO: But did you know that many of the founding families of the City of Los Angeles were black? The last Mexican governor of California was a mulatto. His name was Pio Pico.

RAMONA: Who told you that?

RICO: I read it in a history book. They showed photos of him.

VICTORIA: That's right. All that stuff about the Spanish is pure bunk!

RICO: Look, I'm sure if you approached this film a bit more realistically, by doing some research, you'd find I could do this part.

DIRECTOR: All right! Have you all had your little says now? If you people ever want to work in this town again, you'll play your parts exactly the way I tell you to. Or you will never work anywhere in Hollywood again! Let's go! *(He exits followed by the cameraman.)*

RICO: Oh, damn it! Now I did it!

JOAQUÍN: Listen, I agree with you one hundred percent. I'm sick and tired of playing these demeaning roles.

TONTA: Me too, but I'm also sick and tired of carhopping at the Red-E-Go Drive-In.

RAMONA: I'll try and talk to him. Maybe I can cool him down a bit. *(Exits.)*

VICTORIA: (To Rico.) You did right in speaking out. Are you well versed in the California days? Oh, those must have been wonderful times, halcyon days. *(The lights fade, except for a spot on Rico and Victoria. An old waltz from the period starts to play.)*

RICO: I saw an old photo of the governor's wife. She looked like you, very fair, very Spanish.

VICTORIA: They must have been very happy, before the gringos came.

RICO: *(At this point Rico and Victoria are dancing a waltz downstage. Another spotlight shines upstage to reveal Joaquín and Ramona in an embrace bidding adieu.)* Yes, but they were living on borrowed time. They had barely gained independence from Spain and secularized the missions when other problems arose.

VICTORIA: What could have possibly shattered such an idyllic dream?

RICO: The Indians, for one thing. *(As Rico says this Tonta enters and puts her head to the keyhole to eavesdrop.)* They were becoming increasingly bolder, attacking settlements, running away with livestock, killing our people.

VICTORIA: That would be solved in time. We would all become one race!

RICO: Perhaps, but then there was the constant bickering between those of us in the North and those from the South. *(Rico sees Joaquín and goes for him. Exit Joaquín and Tonta. A door slams.)* That young man is not to darken this door again!

VICTORIA: Don't get upset, dear, I was chaperoning them.

RICO: I don't care, he is not to set foot in this house again!

RAMONA: Why do you dislike Joaquín so much? Aside from the fact he is from the North?

RICO: I'll tell you why. He drinks, swears, reads suggestive books, shoots his pistols in the air, duels, and plots insurrections. Is that enough?!

VICTORIA: *(Aside to Ramona.)* Just like your father did when he was young.

RAMONA: Good God in heaven!

RICO: And there she goes, using the name of God in vain again!

RAMONA: Why don't you admit the real reason you dislike him is because he is in the forefront of steering a new and independent course for us Californios.

RICO: There she goes, using that word again—Californio!

VICTORIA: But Rico, it's just a word the young people use to describe themselves nowadays.

RICO: Not good enough to call themselves Mexicanos como sus padres.

VICTORIA: Don't you remember we used to call ourselves "Criollos" to distinguish us from the Españoles?

RICO: That was yesterday. Today we are Mexican. And we shall always remain Mexican. To call ourselves anything else is treason. I am the governor of this territory and I refuse to hear that word in my house!

VICTORIA: You are as unbending as a mountain; no wonder all the youth are rebelling.

RAMONA: There's some other reason why Papá hates Joaquín so much. Why don't you come out with it!

RICO: Mira, mira! Don't speak to me in that tone of voice. For one thing, his people are barely gente de razón. They are but one generation removed from the savages.

RAMONA: Papá, with all due respect, you claim to dislike Joaquín because of his lower-class origins, yet mother tells me your grandparents were poor shepherds of the humblest class. *(Victoria is making frantic gestures and shaking her head "no.")*

RICO: So, your aristocratic mother, descendant of the conquistadores, told you that, eh?

VICTORIA: Your father comes from good stock, dear, good sound stock.

RICO: Yes, there's no comparison between myself and that young rogue. Why, he's practically a coyote, a half-breed.

RAMONA: You're calling him a coyote! What are you? What am I?

VICTORIA: Ramona, show your father more respect!

RAMONA: I see now, you dislike him because he is not "Spanish."

RICO: He's also the black sheep of the family, he is, esa bola de indios...

RAMONA: Well, let me tell you something, that "indio" asked me to marry him and I said "yes!"

VICTORIA: Why Ramona, how improper! You know that the parents have to be consulted before a girl receives a proposal of marriage!

RICO: You will do no such thing!

RAMONA: Yes I will!

RICO: Get me a switch! I will beat her within a very inch of her life! Listen to me, young lady, you will marry only within your own class! You will marry someone of pure Spanish blood.

RAMONA: What difference does it make! You're not Spanish, I'm not Spanish!

RICO: Yes you are. Call yourself anything else and no gentleman will ever ask for your hand in marriage. Ramona, you don't know prejudice like we do.

VICTORIA: Listen to your father, he means well.

RICO: When I married your mother in Mexico City, her relatives looked down on her because I looked like a Moor!

VICTORIA: It's true, hija, that's why we came back to California.

RICO: I don't want the same thing happening to you!

RAMONA: My God, this is so confusing! Papá, don't you see, you're being a hypocrite!

RICO: *(Raising his hand to slap her. Victoria restrains him.)* Why can't you be like the little girl I once knew, who used to sit on my knee and listen to stories of why the sea is so salty, or why the full moon has the face of a rabbit.

RAMONA: I don't want to hear any more stories!

RICO: I used to tell her the reason people got dark is because they drank too much chocolate. But you're right, those days are past. Still, I have the final word in this house. You shall not see Joaquín again. I shall banish him to the farthest corners of this territory.

RAMONA: Noooooooooo! *(Ramona exits defiantly.)* We shall elope!

RICO: *(Trying to go after her.)* Ramona! Come back here!

VICTORIA: Let her go, give her time to cool her heels. You know, even if she marries the whitest man in California, if you can find one, their children could still be as dark as you. You never told her your grandmother was a mulatto, did you? *(Tonta reenters the scene and listens.)*

RICO: Why trouble our daughter with inconsequential matters concerning my lineage?

VICTORIA: Not so inconsequential when she has to explain to her husband why the child looks like the Queen of Sheba.

RICO: Listen here, woman, don't make fun of me!

VICTORIA: Rico...

RICO: I never denied my origins. My grandmother may have been a mulatto but my parents were mestizos. I, in turn, have become a gente de razón, a citizen with all the rights and benefits thereof.

VICTORIA: Where else but California could you begin life as a Negro and end up as an Español?

RICO: Listen to me! I have heard of places where one drop, just one little drop of black blood automatically makes you a slave, what they call a "nigger." I may have some black blood in me, but I am no slave.

VICTORIA: No Señor, you are not a slave. *(She embraces him.)*

TONTA: *(Rushing in.)* Señores! Señores! The Yankee clipper ship has been sighted in the harbor!

VICTORIA: Oh, Rico, let's go down to the wharf and get our pick of things before the others!

RICO: Now you know why we're getting into debt! But it's too late, we'll go in the morning.

VICTORIA: I have a better idea. Why don't we invite the captain for dinner? We'll have a light supper and then maybe a small baile afterwards.

RICO: *(As they walk away.)* My dear, it is precisely this ostentatious style of living which will be the ruin of us.

TONTA: *(Aside.)* A mulatto, his grandmother. I knew it! That wooly headed old vieja was as black as Cleopatra!

DIRECTOR: *(Breaking up the scene.)* I've been watching it all. I love it!

RAMONA: *(By his side.)* So you see, Jed, they were real people with real problems.

CAMERAMAN: I'm concerned about the father; he's somewhat of a racist.

DIRECTOR: Exactly! Exactly!

RICO: *(Re-entering.)* It's something that the Mexican people would work out in time. Don't you see, they *talked* about it.

DIRECTOR: You know, we could do a California "West Side Story." What happens next?

RICO: The Anglos came. Some hiked in over the mountains, others sailed in on the clipper ships.

TONTA: They brought their slaves.

DIRECTOR: We could get O. J. Simpson to play the slave. Now we need a big-name star for the, uh, captain of the clipper ship. Someone with charisma, poise, good looks…I got it! I got it!

CAMERAMAN: Got what?

DIRECTOR: I'll play the part. *(The cameraman groans.)* You play my slave. Where are we? Where are we? *(The other actors disperse, leaving the Director and Cameraman to set up the next scene.)*

CAMERAMAN: On a boat. Out in the harbor.

DIRECTOR: Oh, I love this. It's so Brechtian. What am I doing?

CAMERAMAN: You could be singing...a popular song of the day.

DIRECTOR: *(Becoming Jedediah Smith.)* "Oh Susana, oh don't you cry for me...for I'm bound to Californee with my banjo on my knee."

✳ The Spirit of Sitting Bull No Longer Protects Us

Juan Velasco

2002

Juan Velasco is the author of many scholarly articles on ethnicity, race, and nationalism, several chapbooks of poetry, and one novel, *Enamorado,* published in Spain in 2000. He teaches Latino literature, composition, and film courses at the University of Santa Clara and is currently working on the book *Labyrinths of Self,* a study of Mexican American identity texts.

Westerns lie. Their heroes
Are made of colorless plastic fleeing
A hound of heaven that has hunted them down
Since the invention of the wheel.

Hollywood movies swing alone
In parks full of children, stealing
What belongs to us, their heroes
Wallowing in mourning.

Deserts lie. Their lonely tracts fetch no playthings.
Even Santa Claus has hands of lye, his white beard
swelling with mint and chocolate.

Westerns hide in hotels.
When night arrives they hop on the bed, pretend they are
women, and vomit cold ice cream.

from

✴ The Crystal Frontier

Carlos Fuentes (translated by Alfred Mac Adam)

1995

The author of more than twenty books, Carlos Fuentes
(b. 1928) has also contributed to major newspapers and
magazines, including the *Los Angeles Times,* the *New York
Times,* and *Newsweek.* He has won many awards as an
essayist, commentator, and novelist, including the 1987
Cervantes Prize, Spain's equivalent of the Nobel Prize. He
has been a professor of Latin American studies at Harvard
University since 1987. In the following selection from
"Spoils," one of the nine stories that make up the novel
The Crystal Frontier (1995), chef, critic, visiting lecturer,
and TV game-show wizard Dionisio Rangel muses on
California's consumer culture.

HOW COULD THE SUCCESSORS OF FORREST GUMP understand that, when a
single Mexican city, Puebla, can boast of more than eight hundred dessert
recipes, it is because of generations and generations of nuns, grandmothers, nannies, and old maids, the work of patience, tradition, love, and wisdom? How, when their supreme refinement consisted in thinking that
life is like a box of chocolates, a varied prefabrication, a fatal Protestant
destiny disguised as free will? Beavis and Butt-head, that pair of half-wits,
would have finished off the nuns of Puebla by pelting them with stale
cake, the grandmothers they would have locked in closets to die of
hunger and thirst, and of course they would have raped the nannies. And
finally, a favor of the highest order for the leftover young ladies.

Baco's students stared at him as if he were insane and sometimes,
to show him the error of his ways and with the air of people protecting

a lunatic or bringing relief to the needy, would invite him to a McDonald's after class. How were they going to understand that a Mexican peasant eats well even if he eats little? Abundance, that's what his gringo students were celebrating, showing off in front of this weird Mexican lecturer, their cheeks swollen with mushy hamburgers, their stomachs stuffed with wagon-wheel pizzas, their hands clutching sandwiches piled as high as the ones Dagwood made in his comic strip, leaning as dangerously as the Tower of Pisa. (There's even an imperialism in comic strips. Latin America gets U.S. comics but they never publish ours. Mafalda, Patoruzú, the Superwise Ones, and the Burrón family never travel north. Our minimal revenge is to give Spanish names to the gringo funnies. Jiggs and Maggie become Pancho and Ramona, Mutt and Jeff metamorphose into Benitín and Eneas, Goofy is Tribilín, Minnie Mouse becomes Ratoncita Mimí, Donald Duck is Pato Pascual, and Dagwood and Blondie are Lorenzo and Pepita. Soon, however, we won't even have that freedom, and Joe Palooka will always be Joe Palooka, not our twisted-around Pancho Tronera.)

Abundance. The society of abundance. Dionisio Rangel wants to be very frank and to admit to you that he's neither an ascetic nor a moralist. How could a sybarite be an ascetic when he so sensually enjoys a *clemole* in radish sauce? But his culinary peak, exquisite as it is, has a coarse, possessive side about which the poor food critic doesn't feel guilty, since he is only—he begs you to understand—a passive victim of U.S. consumer society.

He insists it isn't his fault. How can you escape, even if you spend only two months of the year in the United States, when wherever you happen to be—a hotel, motel, apartment, faculty club, studio, or, in extreme cases, trailer—fills up in the twinkling of an eye with electronic mail, coupons, every conceivable kind of offer, insignificant prizes intended to assure you that you've won a Caribbean cruise, unwanted subscriptions, mountains of paper, newspapers, specialized magazines, catalogs from L. L. Bean, Sears, Neiman Marcus?

As a response to that avalanche of papers, multiplied a thousand-fold by e-mail—requests for donations, false temptations—Dionisio decided to abandon his role as passive recipient and assume that of active transmitter. Instead of being the victim of an avalanche, he proposed to buy the mountain. Why not acquire everything the television advertisements offered—diet milkshakes, file systems, limited-edition CDs with the greatest songs of Pat Boone and Rosemary Clooney, illustrated histories of World War II, complicated devices for toning and developing the muscles, plates commemorating the death of Elvis Presley or the wedding of Charles and Diana, a cup commemorating the bicentennial of American independence, fake Wedgwood tea sets, frequent-flyer offerings from every airline, trinkets left over from Lincoln's and Washington's birthdays, the tawdry costume jewelry purveyed by the Home Shopping Channel, exercise videos with Cathy Lee Crosby, all the credit cards that ever were...all of it, he decided, was irresistible, was for him, was available, even the magic detergents that cleaned anything, even an emblematic stain of mole poblano.

Secretly, he knew the reasons for this new acquisitive voraciousness. One was a firm belief that if, expansively, generously, he accepted what the United States offered him—weight-loss programs, detergents, songs of the fifties—it would ultimately accept what he was offering: the patience and taste to concoct a good *escabeche victorioso*. The other was a plan to get even for all the garbagey prizes he'd been accumulating—again, passively—by going on television and competing on quiz shows. His culinary knowledge was infinite, so he could easily win and not only in the gastronomic category.

Cuisine and sex are two indispensable pleasures, the former more than the latter. After all, you can eat without love, but you can't love without eating. And if you understand the culinary palate you know everything: what went into a kiss or a crab *chilpachole* involved historical, scientific, and even political wisdom. Where were cocktails born? In Campeche, among English sailors who mixed their drinks with a local condiment called "cock's tail." Who consecrated chocolate as an acceptable beverage in society? Louis XIV at Versailles, after the Aztec drink had been considered a bitter poison for two centuries. Why in old Russia was the potato prohibited by the Orthodox Church? Because it wasn't mentioned in the Bible and therefore had to be a creation of the devil. In one sense the Orthodox clergy were right: the potato is the source of that diabolical liquor vodka.

The truth is, Rangel entered these shows more to become known among larger audiences than to win the washing machines, vacuum cleaners, and—*mirabile visu!*—trips to Acapulco with which his successes were rewarded.

Besides, he had to pass the time.

A silver-haired old fox, an interesting man, with the looks of a mature movie star, Dionisio "Baco" Rangel was, at the age of fifty-one, something of a copy of that cinematic model personified by the late Arturo de Córdova, in whose films marble stairways and plastic flamingoes filled the background of neurotic love scenes featuring innocent fifteen-year-old girls and vengeful forty-year-old mothers, all of them reduced to their proper size by the autumnal star's memorable and lapidary phrase: "It doesn't have the slightest importance." It should be pointed out that Dionisio, with greater self-generosity, would say to himself as he shaved every morning (Barbasol) that he had no reason to envy Vittorio De Sica, who moved beyond the movies of Fascist Italy, with their white telephones and satin sheets, to become the supreme neorealist director of shoeshine boys, stolen bicycles, and old men with only dogs for company. But still, how handsome, how elegant he was, how surrounded by Ginas, Sophias, and Claudias! It was to that sum of experience and that smoothness of appearance that our compatriot Dionisio "Baco" Rangel aspired as he stored all his American products in a suburban warehouse outside the border city of San Diego, California.

The problem was that girls no longer flocked to our autumnal star. The problem was that his style clashed badly with theirs. The problem was that as he stared at himself in the mirror (Barbasol, no brilliantine, no brilliant ideas) he had to accept that after a Certain Age a star must be circumspect, elegant, calm—all so as not to succumb to the maximum absurdity of the aged Don Juan, Fernando Rey, in Buñuel's *Viridiana,* who possesses virgins only if he dopes them up first and then plays them Handel's *Messiah.*

"Unhandel me, sire."

Dionisio had therefore to spend many solitary hours, on his lecture tours and in television studios, wasting his melancholy on futile reflections. California was his inevitable zone of operations, and there he spent a season passing time in Los Angeles observing the flow of cars through that headless city's freeway system, imagining it as the modern equivalent of a medieval joust, each driver a flawless knight and each car an armor-covered charger. But his concentrated observation aroused suspicion, and the police arrested him for loitering near the highways: Was he a terrorist?

American oddities began to command his attention. He was pleased to discover that beneath the commonplaces about a uniform, robotic society devoid of culinary personality (article of faith), there roiled a multiform, eccentric world, quasi-medieval in its corrosive ferment against an order once imposed by Rome and its Church and now by Washington and its Capitol. How would the country put itself in order when it was full of religious lunatics who believed beyond doubt that faith, not surgery, would take care of a tumor in the lungs? How, when the country was full of people who dared not exchange glances in the street lest the stranger turn out to be an escaped paranoid authorized to kill anyone who didn't totally agree with his ideas, or a murderer released from an overcrowded mental hospital or jail, or a vengeful homosexual armed with HIV-laden syringes, a neo-Nazi skinhead ready to slit the throat of a dark-skinned person, a libertarian militiaman prepared to finish off the government by blowing up federal buildings, a country where teenage gangs were better armed than the police, exercising their constitutional right to carry rocket launchers and blow off the head of a neighbor's child?

Sliding along the streets of America, Dionisio happily gave to that single country the name of an entire continent, gladly sacrificing in favor of a name with lineage, position, history (like Mexico, Argentina, Brazil, Peru, Nicaragua...) that name without a name, the ghostlike "United States of America," which, his friend the historian Daniel Cosío Villegas said, was a moniker like "The Neighborhood Drunkard." Or, as Dionisio himself thought, like a mere descriptor, like "Third Floor on the Right."

A good Mexican, Dionisio conceded all the power in the world to the gringos except that of an aristocratic culture: Mexico had one, paying the price, it was true, with abysmal, perhaps insurmountable inequality and injustice. Mexico also had conventions, manners, tastes, subtleties that confirmed her aristocratic culture: an island of tradition increasingly whipped and sometimes flooded, though, by storms of vulgarity and styles of commercialization that were worse, because grosser, cheaper, more disgusting, than those of North Americans. In Mexico even a thief was courteous, even an illiterate was cultured, even a child knew how to say hello, even a maid knew how to walk gracefully, even a politician knew how to behave like a lady, even a lady knew how to behave like a politician, even the cripples were acrobats, and even the revolutionaries had the good taste to believe in the Virgin of Guadalupe. None of that consoled him in his ever longer moments of middle-aged tedium, when classes were over, when the lectures had come to an end, the girls had left, and he had to return to the hotel, the motel...

IDENTITY

from

♛ The Circuit

Francisco Jiménez

1997

Francisco Jiménez was born in 1943 in Mexico, immigrated
to the United States when he was four years old, and started
working in the fields with his family two years later. He has
edited numerous anthologies and written several children's
books about the lives of migrant farmworkers. *Breaking
Through* (2001), his most recent publication, is the sequel to
his autobiographical young-adult novel *The Circuit* (1997),
excerpted here. He has won numerous teaching awards,
many in his current position as a professor of modern languages at Santa Clara University.

IT WAS THAT TIME OF YEAR AGAIN. Ito, the strawberry sharecropper, did
not smile. It was natural. The peak of the strawberry season was over,
and in the last few days the workers, most of them *braceros,* were not
picking as many boxes as they had during June and July.

As the last days of August disappeared, so did the number of
braceros. Sunday, only one—the best picker—came to work. I liked him.
Sometimes we talked during our half-hour lunch break. That is how I
found out he was from Jalisco, the same state in Mexico my family was
from. That Sunday was the last time I saw him.

When the sun had tired and sunk behind the mountains, Ito signaled us that it was time to go home. *"Ya esora,"* he yelled in his broken
Spanish. Those were the words I waited for twelve hours a day, every
day, seven days a week, week after week. And the thought of not hearing them again saddened me.

As we drove home Papá did not say a word. With both hands on
the wheel, he stared at the dirt road. My older brother, Roberto, was also

silent. He leaned his head back and closed his eyes. Once in a while he cleared from his throat the dust that blew in from outside.

Yes, it was that time of year. When I opened the front door to the shack, I stopped. Everything we owned was neatly packed in cardboard boxes. Suddenly I felt even more the weight of hours, days, weeks, and months of work. I sat down on a box. The thought of having to move to Fresno and knowing what was in store for me there brought tears to my eyes.

That night I could not sleep. I lay in bed thinking about how much I hated this move.

A little before five o'clock in the morning, Papá woke everyone up. A few minutes later, the yelling and screaming of my little brothers and sister, for whom the move was a great adventure, broke the silence of dawn. Soon after, the barking of the dogs accompanied them.

While we packed the breakfast dishes, Papá went outside to start the *Carcachita*. That was the name Papá gave his old black Plymouth. He had bought it in a used-car lot in Santa Rosa. Papá was very proud of his little jalopy. He had a right to be proud of it. He had spent a lot of time looking at other cars before buying this one. When he finally chose the *Carcachita,* he checked it thoroughly before driving it out of the car lot. He examined every inch of the car. He listened to the motor, tilting his head from side to side like a parrot, trying to detect any noises that spelled car trouble. After being satisfied with the looks and sounds of the car, Papá then insisted on knowing who the original owner was. He never did find out from the car salesman, but he bought the car anyway. Papá figured the original owner must have been an important man because behind the rear seat of the car he found a blue necktie.

Papá parked the car out in front and left the motor running. *"Listo,"* he yelled. Without saying a word Roberto and I began to carry the boxes out to the car. Roberto carried the two big boxes, and I carried the two smaller ones. Papá then threw the mattress on top of the car roof and tied it with ropes to the front and rear bumpers.

Everything was packed except Mamá's pot. It was an old, large galvanized pot she had picked up at an army surplus store in Santa Maria. The pot had many dents and nicks, and the more dents and nicks it acquired the more Mamá liked it. *"Mi olla,"* she used to say proudly.

I held the front door open as Mamá carefully carried out her pot by both handles, making sure not to spill the cooked beans. When she got to the car, Papá reached out to help her with it. Roberto opened the rear car door, and Papá gently placed it on the floor behind the front seat. All of us then climbed in. Papá sighed, wiped the sweat from his forehead with his sleeve, and said wearily, *"Es todo."*

As we drove away, I felt a lump in my throat. I turned around and looked at our little shack for the last time.

At sunset we drove into a labor camp near Fresno. Since Papá did not speak English, Mamá asked the camp foreman if he needed any more workers. "We don't need no more," said the foreman, scratching his head. "Check with Sullivan down the road. Can't miss him. He lives in a big white house with a fence around it."

When we got there, Mamá walked up to the house. She went through a white gate, past a row of rosebushes, up the stairs to the house. She rang the doorbell. The porch light went on and a tall, husky man came out. They exchanged a few words. After the man went in, Mamá clasped her hands and hurried back to the car. "We have work! Mr. Sullivan said we can stay there the whole season," she said, gasping and pointing to an old garage near the stables.

The garage was worn out by the years. It had no windows. The walls, eaten by termites, strained to support the roof full of holes. The dirt floor, populated by earthworms, looked like a gray road map.

That night, by the light of a kerosene lamp, we unpacked and cleaned our new home. Roberto swept away the loose dirt, leaving the hard ground. Papá plugged the holes in the walls with old newspapers and tin can tops. Mamá fed my little brothers and sister. Papá and Roberto then brought in the mattress and placed it on the far corner of the garage. "Mamá, you and the little ones sleep on the mattress. Roberto, Panchito, and I will sleep outside under the trees," Papá said.

Early the next morning Mr. Sullivan showed us where his crop was, and after breakfast, Papá, Roberto, and I headed for the vineyard to pick.

Around nine o'clock the temperature had risen to almost one hundred degrees. I was completely soaked in sweat, and my mouth felt as if I had been chewing on a handkerchief. I walked over to the end of the row, picked up the jug of water we had brought, and began drinking. "Don't drink too much; you'll get sick," Roberto shouted. No sooner had he said that than I felt sick to my stomach. I dropped to my knees and let the jug roll off my hands. I remained motionless with my eyes glued on the hot sandy ground. All I could hear was the drone of insects. Slowly I began to recover. I poured water over my face and neck and watched the dirty water run down my arms to the ground.

I still felt dizzy when we took a break to eat lunch. It was past two o'clock; we sat underneath a large walnut tree that was on the side of the road. While we ate, Papá jotted down the number of boxes we had picked. Roberto drew designs on the ground with a stick. Suddenly I noticed Papá's face turn pale as he looked down the road. "Here comes the school bus," he whispered loudly in alarm. Instinctively, Roberto and I ran and hid in the vineyards. We did not want to get in trouble for not going to school. The neatly dressed boys about my age got off. They carried books under their arms. After they crossed the street, the bus drove away. Roberto and I came out from hiding and joined Papá. *"Tienen que tener cuidado,"* he warned us.

After lunch we went back to work. The sun kept beating down. The buzzing insects, the wet sweat, and the hot dry dust made the afternoon seem to last forever. Finally the mountains around the valley reached out and swallowed the sun. Within an hour it was too dark to continue picking. The vines blanketed the grapes, making it difficult to see the bunches. *"Vámonos,"* said Papá, signaling to us that it was time to quit work. Papá then took out a pencil and began to figure out how much we had earned our first day. He wrote down numbers, crossed some out, wrote down some more. *"Quince,"* he murmured.

When we arrived home, we took a cold shower underneath a water hose. We then sat down to eat dinner around some wooden crates that served as a table. Mamá had cooked a special meal for us. We had rice and tortillas with *carne con chile,* my favorite dish.

The next morning I could hardly move. My body ached all over. I felt little control over my arms and legs. This feeling went on every morning for days until my muscles finally got used to the work.

It was Monday, the first week of November. The grape season was over and I could now go to school. I woke up early that morning and lay in bed, looking at the stars and savoring the thought of not going to work and of starting sixth grade for the first time that year. Since I could not sleep, I decided to get up and join Papá and Roberto at breakfast. I sat at the table across from Roberto, but I kept my head down. I did not want to look up and face him. I knew he was sad. He was not going to school today. He was not going tomorrow, or next week, or next month. He would not go until the cotton season was over, and that was sometime in February. I rubbed my hands together and watched the dry, acid-stained skin fall to the floor in little rolls.

When Papá and Roberto left for work, I felt relief. I walked to the top of a small grade next to the shack and watched the *Carcachita* disappear in the distance in a cloud of dust.

Two hours later, around eight o'clock, I stood by the side of the road waiting for school bus number twenty. When it arrived I climbed in. Everyone was busy either talking or yelling. I sat in an empty seat in the back.

When the bus stopped in front of the school, I felt very nervous. I looked out the bus window and saw boys and girls carrying books under their arms. I put my hands in my pant pockets and walked to the principal's office. When I entered I heard a woman's voice say, "May I help you?" I was startled. I had not heard English for months. For a few seconds I remained speechless. I looked at the lady, who waited for an answer. My first instinct was to answer her in Spanish, but I held back. Finally, after struggling for English words, I managed to tell her that I wanted to enroll in the sixth grade. After answering many questions, I was led to the classroom.

Mr. Lema, the sixth-grade teacher, greeted me and assigned me a desk. He then introduced me to the class. I was so nervous and scared at that moment when everyone's eyes were on me that I wished I were with Papá and Roberto picking cotton. After taking roll, Mr. Lema gave the class the assignment for the first hour. "The first thing we have to do this morning is finish reading the story we began yesterday," he said enthusiastically. He walked up to me, handed me an English book, and asked me to read. "We are on page 125," he said politely. When I heard this, I felt my blood rush to my head; I felt dizzy. "Would you like to read?" he asked hesitantly. I opened the book to page 125. My mouth was dry. My eyes began to water. I could not begin. "You can read later," Mr. Lema said understandingly.

During recess I went into the restroom and opened my English book to page 125. I began to read in a low voice, pretending I was in class. There were many words I did not know. I closed the book and headed back to the classroom.

Mr. Lema was sitting at his desk correcting papers. When I entered he looked up at me and smiled. I felt better. I walked up to him and asked if he could help me with the new words. "Gladly," he said.

The rest of the month I spent my lunch hours working on English with Mr. Lema, my best friend at school.

One Friday, during lunch hour, Mr. Lema asked me to take a walk with him to the music room. "Do you like music?" he asked me as we entered the building. "Yes, I like *corridos*," I answered. He then picked up a trumpet, blew on it, and handed it to me. The sound gave me goose bumps. I knew that sound. I had heard it in many *corridos*. "How would you like to learn how to play it?" he asked. He must have read my face because before I could answer he added, "I'll teach you how to play it during our lunch hours."

That day I could hardly wait to tell Papá and Mamá the great news. As I got off the bus, my little brothers and sister ran up to meet me. They were yelling and screaming. I thought they were happy to see me, but when I opened the door to our shack, I saw that everything we owned was neatly packed in cardboard boxes.

from

♛ Pocho

José Antonio Villarreal

1959

José Antonio Villarreal was born in 1924 in Los Angeles to Mexican immigrants and grew up in Santa Clara. After three years in the navy during World War II, he returned to California for college and published his first short stories. His debut novel and most famous work, *Pocho* (1959), one of the definitive works about pachuquismo, was the first Chicano novel to be published by a major press, earning its author the informal title "founder of Chicano literature." In addition to being the author of three novels and many short stories and articles, Villarreal has worked as an editor, translator, journalist, newscaster, advertiser, public speaker, professor, and speech writer, and as a counselor in juvenile correction facilities.

IT WAS 1940 IN SANTA CLARA, AND, AMONG OTHER THINGS, the Conscription Act had done its part in bringing about a change. It was not unusual now to see soldiers walking downtown or to see someone of the town in uniform. He was aware that people liked soldiers now and could still remember the old days when a detachment of cavalry camped outside the town for a few days, or a unit of field artillery stayed at the university, and the worst thing one's sister could do was associate with a soldier. Soldiers were common, were drunkards, thieves, and rapers of girls, or something, to the people of Santa Clara, and the only uniforms with prestige in the town had been those of the CCC boys or of the American Legion during the Fourth of July celebration and the Easter egg hunt. But now everybody loved a soldier, and he wondered how this had come about.

There were the soldiers, and there were also the Mexicans in ever-increasing numbers. The Mexican people Richard had known until now were those he saw only during the summer, and they were migrant families who seldom remained in Santa Clara longer than a month or two. The orbit of his existence was limited to the town, and actually to his immediate neighborhood, thereby preventing his association with the Mexican family which lived on the other side of town, across the tracks. In his wanderings into San Jose, he began to see more of what he called "the race." Many of the migrant workers who came up from southern California in the late spring and early summer now settled down in the valley. They bought two hundred pounds of flour and a hundred pounds of beans, and if they weathered the first winter, which was the most difficult because the rains stopped agricultural workers from earning a living, they were settled for good.

As the Mexican population increased, Richard began to attend their dances and fiestas, and, in general, sought their company as much as possible, for these people were a strange lot to him. He was obsessed with a hunger to learn about them and from them. They had a burning contempt for people of different ancestry, whom they called Americans, and a marked hauteur toward México and toward their parents for their old-country ways. The former feeling came from a sense of inferiority that is a prominent characteristic in any Mexican reared in southern California; and the latter was an inexplicable compensation for that feeling. They needed to feel superior to something, which is a natural thing. The result was that they attempted to segregate themselves from both their cultures and became truly a lost race. In their frantic desire to become different, they adopted a new mode of dress, a new manner, and even a new language. They used a polyglot speech made up of English and Spanish syllables, words, and sounds. This they incorporated into phrases and words that were unintelligible to anyone but themselves. Their Spanish became limited and their English more so. Their dress was unique to the point of being ludicrous. The black motif was predominant. The tight-fitting cuffs on trouser legs that billowed at the knees made Richard think of some long-forgotten pasha in the faraway past, and the fingertip coat and highly lustrous shoes gave the wearer, when walking, the appearance of a strutting cock. Their hair was long and swept up to meet in the back, forming a ducktail. They spent hours training it to remain that way.

The girls were characterized by the extreme shortness of their skirts, which stopped well above the knees. Their jackets, too, were fingertip in length, coming to within an inch of the skirt hem. Their hair reached below the shoulder in the back, and it was usually worn piled in front to form a huge pompadour.

The pachuco was born in El Paso, had gone west to Los Angeles, and was now moving north. To society, these zoot-suiters were a menace, and the name alone classified them as undesirables, but Richard learned that there was much more to it than a mere group with a name. That in spite of their behavior, which was sensational at times and violent at others, they were simply a portion of a confused humanity, employing their self-segregation as a means of expression. And because theirs was a spontaneous, not a planned retaliation, he saw it as a vicissitude of society, obvious only because of its nature and comparative suddenness.

From the leggy, short-skirted girls, he learned that their mores were no different from those of what he considered good girls. What was under the scant covering was as inaccessible as it would be under the more conventional dress. He felt, in fact, that these girls were more difficult to reach. And from the boys he learned that their bitterness and hostile attitude toward whites was not merely a lark. They had learned hate through actual experience, with everything the word implied. They had not been as lucky as he and showed the scars to prove it. And, later on, Richard saw in retrospect that what happened to him in the city jail in San Jose was due more to the character of a handful of men than to the wide, almost organized attitude of a society, for just as the zoot-suiters were blamed en masse for the actions of a few, they, in turn, blamed the other side for the very same reason.

As happens in most such groups, there were misunderstandings and disagreements over trivia. Pachucos fought among themselves, for the most part, and they fought hard. It was not unusual that a quarrel born on the streets or back alleys of a Los Angeles slum was settled in the Santa Clara Valley. Richard understood them and partly sympathized, but their way of life was not entirely justified in his mind, for he felt that they were somehow reneging on life; this was the easiest thing for them to do. They, like his father, were defeated—only more so, because they never really started to live. They, too, were but making a show of resistance.

Of the new friends Richard made, those who were native to San Jose were relegated to become casual acquaintances, for they were as Americanized as he and did not interest him. The newcomers became the object of his explorations. He was avidly hungry to learn the ways of these people. It was not easy for him to approach them at first, because his clothes labeled him as an outsider, and too, he had trouble understanding their speech. He must not ask questions, for fear of offending them; his deductions as to their character and makeup must come from close association. He was careful not to be patronizing or in any way act superior. And, most important, they must never suspect what he was doing. The most difficult moments for him were when he was doing the talking, for he was conscious that his Spanish was better than theirs. He learned enough of their vernacular to get along; he did not learn more, because he was always in a hurry about knowledge. Soon he counted a few boys as friends, but had a much harder time of it with the girls, because they considered him a traitor to his "race." Before he knew it, he found that he almost never spoke to them in English, and no longer defended the whites, but, rather, spoke disparagingly of them whenever possible. He also bought a suit to wear when in their company, not with such an extreme cut as those they wore, but removed enough from the conservative so he would not be considered a square. And he found himself a girl, who refused to dance the faster pieces with him because he still jittered in the American manner. So they danced only to soft music while they kissed in the dimmed light, and that was the extent of their lovemaking. Or he stood behind her at the bar, with his arms around her as she sipped a Nehi, and felt strange because she was a Mexican and everyone around them was also Mexican, and felt stranger still from the knowledge that he felt strange. When the dance was over, he took her to where her parents were sitting and said good night to the entire family.

Whenever his new friends saw him in the company of his school acquaintances, they were courteously polite, but they later chastised him for fraternizing with what they called the enemy. Then Richard had misgivings, because he knew that his desire to become one of them was not a sincere one in that respect, yet upon reflection he realized that in truth he enjoyed their company and valued their friendship, and his sense of guilt was gone. He went along with everything they did, being careful only to keep away from serious trouble with no loss of prestige. Twice he entered the dreamworld induced by marijuana, and after the effect of the drug was expended, he was surprised to discover that he did not crave it and was glad, for he could not afford a kick like that. As it was, life was too short for him to be able to do the many things he knew he still must do. The youths understood that he did not want it and never pressed him.

Now the time came to withdraw a little. He thought it would be a painful thing, but they liked him, and their friendliness made everything natural. He, in his gratefulness, loved them for it.

I can be a part of everything because I am the only one capable of controlling my destiny....Never—no, never, will I allow myself to become a part of a group—to become classified, to lose my individuality....I will not become a follower, nor will I allow myself to become a leader, because I must be myself and accept for myself only that which I value, and not what is being valued by everyone else these days…like a goddamn suit of clothes they're wearing this season or Cuban heels…a style in ethics. What shall we do to liven up the season this year of Our Lord 1940, you from the North, and you from the South, and you from the East, and you from the West? Be original, and for Chrissake speak up! Shall we make it a vogue to sacrifice virgins—but, no, that's been done.…What do you think of matricide or mother rape? No? Well—wish we could deal with more personal things, such as prolonging the gestation period in the *Homo sapiens*; that would keep the married men hopping, no?

He thought this and other things, because the young are like that, and for them nothing is impossible; no, nothing is impossible, and this truism gives impetus to the impulse to laugh at abstract bonds. This night he thought this, and could laugh at the simplicity with which he could render powerless obstacles in his search for life. He had returned to the Mexican dance hall for the first time in weeks, and the dance was fast coming to a close. The orchestra had blared out a jazzed-up version of "Home, Sweet Home" and was going through it again at a much slower tempo, giving the couples on the dance floor one last chance for the sensual embraces that would have to last them a week. Richard was dancing with his girl, leading with his leg and holding her slight body close against his, when one of his friends tapped him on the shoulder.

"We need some help," he said. "Will you meet us by the door after the dance?" The question was more of a command, and the speaker did not wait for an answer. The dance was over, and Richard kissed the girl good-bye and joined the group that was gathering conspicuously as the people poured out through the only exit.

"What goes?" he asked.

"We're going to get some guys tonight," answered the youth who had spoken to him earlier. He was twenty years old and was called the Rooster.

The Mexican people have an affinity for incongruous nicknames. In this group, there was Tuerto, who was not blind; Cacarizo, who was not pockmarked; Zurdo, who was not left-handed; and a drab little fellow who was called Slick. Only Chango was appropriately named. There was indeed something anthropoidal about him.

The Rooster said, "They beat hell out of my brother last night, because he was jiving with one of their girls. I just got the word that they'll be around tonight if we want trouble."

"Man," said Chango, "we want a mess of trouble."

"Know who they are?" asked the Tuerto.

"Yeah. It was those bastards from Ontario," said the Rooster. "We had trouble with them before."

"Where they going to be?" asked Richard.

"That's what makes it good. Man, it's going to be real good," said the Rooster. "In the Orchard. No cops, no nothing. Only us."

"And the mud," said the Tuerto. The Orchard was a twelve-acre cherry grove in the new industrial district on the north side of the city.

"It'll be just as muddy for them," said the Rooster. "Let's go!"

They walked out and hurriedly got into the car. There were eight of them in Zurdo's sedan, and another three were to follow in a coupe. Richard sat in the back on Slick's lap. He was silent, afraid that they might discover the growing terror inside him. The Rooster took objects out of a gunnysack.

"Here, man, this is for you. Don't lose it," he said. It was a doubled-up bicycle chain, one end bound tightly with leather thongs to form a grip.

Richard held it in his hands and, for an unaccountable reason, said, "Thank you." Goddamn! he thought. What the hell did I get into? He wished they would get to their destination quickly, before his fear turned to panic. He had no idea who it was they were going to meet. Would there be three or thirty against them? He looked at the bludgeon in his hand and thought, Christ! Somebody could get killed!

The Tuerto passed a pint of whiskey back to them. Richard drank thirstily, then passed the bottle on.

"You want some, Chango?" asked the Rooster.

"That stuff's not for me, man. I stick to yesca," he answered. Four jerky rasps came from him as he inhaled, reluctant to allow the least bit of smoke to escape him, receiving the full force of the drug in a hurry. He offered the cigarette, but they all refused it. Then he carefully put it out, and placed the butt in a small matchbox.

It seemed to Richard that they had been riding for hours when finally they arrived at the Orchard. They backed the car under the trees, leaving the motor idling because they might have to leave in a hurry. The rest of the gang did not arrive; the Rooster said, "Those sons of bitches aren't coming!"

"Let's wait a few minutes," said the Tuerto. "Maybe they'll show up."

"No, they won't come," said the Rooster, in a calm voice now. He unzipped his pants legs and rolled them up to the knees. "Goddamn mud," he said, almost good-naturedly. "Come on!" They followed him into the Orchard. When they were approximately in the center of the tract, they stopped. "Here they come," whispered the Rooster.

Richard could not hear a thing. He was more afraid, but had stopped shaking. In spite of his fear, his mind was alert. He strained every sense, in order not to miss any part of this experience. He wanted to retain everything that was about to happen. He was surprised at the way the Rooster had taken command from the moment they left the dance hall. Richard had never thought of any one of the boys being considered a leader, and now they were all following the Rooster, and Richard fell naturally in line. The guy's like ice, he thought. Like a goddamn piece of ice!

Suddenly forms took shape in the darkness before him.

And just as suddenly he was in the kaleidoscopic swirl of the fight. He felt blows on his face and body, as if from a distance, and he flayed viciously with the chain. There was a deadly quietness to the struggle. He was conscious that some of the fallen were moaning, and a voice screamed, "The son of a bitch broke my arm!" And that was all he heard for a while, because he was lying on the ground with his face in the mud.

They half dragged, half carried him to the car. It had bogged down in the mud, and they put him in the back while they tried to make it move. They could see headlights behind them, beyond the trees.

"We have to get the hell out of here," said the Rooster. "They got help. Push! Push!" Richard opened the door and fell out of the car. He got up and stumbled crazily in the darkness. He was grabbed and violently thrown in again. They could hear the sound of a large group coming toward them from the Orchard.

"Let's cut out!" shouted the Tuerto. "Leave it here!"

"No!" said the Rooster. "They'll tear it apart!" The car slithered onto the sidewalk and the wheels finally got traction. In a moment, they were moving down the street.

Richard held his hands to his head. "Jesus!" he exclaimed. "The cabrón threw me with the shithouse."

"It was a bat," said the Rooster.

"What?"

"He hit you with a goddamn baseball bat!"

They took Richard home, and the Rooster helped him to his door. "Better rub some lard on your head," he told him.

"All right. Say, you were right, Rooster. Those other cats didn't show at all."

"You have to expect at least a couple of guys to chicken out on a deal like this," said the Rooster. "You did real good, man. I knew you'd do good."

Richard looked at his friend thoughtfully for a moment. In the dim light, his dark hair, Medusa-like, curled from his collar in back almost to his eyebrows. He wondered what errant knight from Castile had traveled four thousand miles to mate with a daughter of Cuahtémoc to produce this strain. "How did you know?" he asked.

"Because I could tell it meant so much to you," said the Rooster.

"When I saw them coming, it looked like there were a hundred of them."

"There were only about fifteen. You're okay, Richard. Any time you want something, just let me know."

Richard felt humble in his gratification. He understood the friendship that was being offered. "I'll tell you, Rooster," he said. "I've never been afraid as much as I was tonight." He thought, If he knows this, perhaps he won't feel the sense of obligation.

"Hell, that's no news. We all were."

"Did we beat them?" asked Richard.

"Yeah, we beat them," answered the Rooster. "We beat them real good!"

And that, for Richard Rubio, was the finest moment of a most happy night.

♛ At the Rainbow

Robert Vasquez

1995

Robert Vasquez was born in 1955 in Madera, California, and grew up in Fresno. He is the author of *At the Rainbow* (1995), which won the San Francisco Foundation's James D. Phelan Award, and he has won three Academy of American Poets prizes, three National Society of Arts and Letters Awards, and many other honors. He currently teaches at the College of the Sequoias in Visalia, California.

for Linda, Theresa, and Phyllis

At fifteen, shaving by then, I passed
for eighteen and got in, in where alcoves
breathed with ill-matched lovers—
my sisters among them—who massed
and spun out their jagged, other selves.
I saw the rhythmic dark, year over

year, discharge their flare: they scored
my memory, adrift now in the drifting place.
Often I watched a slow song empty
the tabled sidelines; even the old poured
out, some dragged by wives, and traced
odd box shapes their feet repeated. *Plenty*

and *poor*: thoughts that rose as the crowd
rose—my sisters too—in the smoked air.
They rise on....They say saxophones
still start up Friday nights, the loud,

troubled notes wafting out from where
I learned to lean close and groaned

into girls I chose—no, took—and meant it.
In the Rainbow Ballroom in Fresno
I sulked, held hands, and wheeled among
the deep-bodied ones who reinvented
steps and turns turned fast or slow,
and this body sang, man to woman, song to song.

from

✸ And a Voice to Sing With

Joan Baez

1987

Joan Baez was born in 1941 in New York to an English
Scottish mother and a Mexican American father. Baez is
best known as a folksinger/songwriter affiliated with the
protest movements of the sixties and seventies, and she
remains heavily involved with public service and peace
organizations. In addition to her autobiography, *Daybreak*
(1968), and her memoir, *And a Voice to Sing With* (1987), she
has more than fifty musical albums to her name. The following excerpt recalls her teenage years, with her sisters Pauline
and Mimi, in Redlands, California.

ONE OF THE FIRST PROBLEMS I HAD TO CONFRONT in junior high school
was my ethnic background. Redlands is in southern California and had
a large Mexican population, consisting mainly of immigrants and illegal
aliens who came up from Mexico to pick fruit. At school they banded
together, speaking Spanish—the girls with mountains of black hair,
frizzed from sleeping all night long on masses of pin curls, wearing gobs
of violet lipstick, tight skirts and nylons, and blouses with the collars
turned up in back. The boys were *pachucos,* tough guys, who slicked back
their gorgeous hair with Three Roses Vaseline tonic and wore their
pegged pants so low on the hip that walking without losing them had
become an art. Few Mexicans were interested in school and they were
ostracized by the whites. So there I was, with a Mexican name, skin, and
hair: the Anglos couldn't accept me because of all three, and the Mexicans
couldn't accept me because I didn't speak Spanish.

My "race" wasn't the only factor that kept me isolated. The 1950s were the heart of the Cold War, and if anyone at Redlands High School talked about anything other than football and the choice of pom-pom girls, it was about the Russians. I had heard that the Communists had rioted at the University of Baghdad when my father taught there, and that some of them always warned him to keep away when there was going to be trouble. But in America during the overheated McCarthy years, *communism* was a dirty word and the arms race a jingoistic crusade. In my ninth-grade class I was almost alone in my fear of and opposition to armaments (to me they made the world seem even more fragile) and was already considered an expert on anything political.

It wasn't that I knew so much but rather that I was involved, largely because of the discussions taking place in my own home. And the family attended Quaker work camps, where I heard about alternatives to violence on personal, political, national, and international levels. Many of my fellow classmates held me in great disdain, and some had been warned by their frightened parents not to talk to me.

I don't know how Pauline felt about politics in those days. She was an excellent student but suffered terribly from shyness. I idolized her because she got good grades, never carried a wrinkled lunch bag, wore a ponytail which didn't make her ears stick out, and smelled of violets. Also because she was white. She never said a word about social issues. And Mimi—well, my own pacifism did not yet extend to Mimi, who was avoiding me in public because I was brown.

It was the sense of isolation, of being "different," that initially led me to develop my voice. I was in the school choir and sang alto, second soprano, soprano, and even tenor, depending on what was most needed. Mine was a plain, little girl's voice, sweet and true, but stringy as cheap cotton thread, and as thin and straight as the blue line on a piece of binder paper. There was a pair of twins in my class who had vibratos in their voices and sang in every talent show, standing side by side, each with an arm around the other, angora sweaters outlining their develop-ing bosoms, crinoline slips flaring. They swayed to and fro and snapped their fingers, "Oh, we ain't got a barrel of money..." I heard a teacher comment that their voices were very "mature." I tried out for the girls' glee club, and when I wasn't accepted, figured it was because (1) I was not a member of the in crowd and (2) I had no vibrato so my voice wasn't mature. Powerless to change my social standing, I decided to change my voice. I dropped tightrope walking to work full time on a vibrato.

First I tried, while standing in the shower, to stay on one note and force my voice up and down slowly. It was tedious and unrewarding work. My natural voice came out straight as an arrow. Then, I tried bobbing my finger up and down on my Adam's apple and, to my delight, found I could create the sound I wanted. For a few brief seconds, I would imitate the sound without using my hand, achieving a few "mature"-sounding notes. This was terrific! This is how I would train!

The time it took to form a shaky but honest vibrato was surprisingly short. By the end of the summer I was a singer.

At the same time I was giving myself a new voice, I was also under the tutelage of my father's much loved physics professor, Paul Kirkpatric, P.K. for short, conquering the ukulele. I knew the four basic chords used in ninety percent of the country-and-western and rhythm-and-blues songs then dominating the record market, and I was learning a few extra chords to use if I needed to sing in a key other than G. Some of my favorites were "You're in the Jailhouse Now," "Your Cheatin' Heart," "Earth Angel," "Pledging My Love," "Never Let Me Go," and the Annie series—"Annie Had a Baby," "Work with Me, Annie," "Annie's Aunt Fanny" (I was disgusted with the watered-down "white version," "Roll with Me, Henry")—as well as "Over the Mountain," and "Young Blood." These songs all could be played with five chords, most only with four. All were either melodic and sweet, upbeat and slightly dirty, or comic. I even did a vile racist version of "Yes Sir, That's My Baby" called "Yes Sir, Zat-a My Baby," and Liberace's inane "Cement Mixer, Putty Putty." And this list is only a bare beginning of what I listened to on my little gray plastic bedside radio. I cannot describe the satisfaction I got from memorizing tunes by ear and scribbling down words anytime, day or night; finding the right key (the choices were C or G); and making the songs my own.[…]

Before long an exhibitionist impulse overcame me. I took my ukulele to school. At noontime I hung around the area where the popular kids ate lunch and waited for them to ask me to play, which they did soon enough. I sang "Suddenly There's a Valley" and when they applauded and asked for more, I sang the current hits of the day: "Earth Angel," "Pledging My Love," and "Honey Love." I was a big hit and came back the next day for a command performance. This time I did imitations of Elvis Presley, Della Reese, Eartha Kitt, and Johnny Ace. Before the week was out I had gone from being a gawky, self-conscious outsider to being something of a jesterlike star.

Someone suggested that I try out for the school talent show. At the tryouts, while standing at the microphone, I rested my foot on the rung of a stool to feign calm, and discovered that my knee was shaking. Afraid I would rattle the stool, with seeming nonchalance I raised my foot off the rung and held my knee suspended in the air, foot dangling, my entire leg trembling. The rest of my body was impressively composed, and I sang "Earth Angel" all the way from start to finish with a "mature" vibrato. Nobody noticed my shaky knee, and I discovered that I had an innate poise and a talent for bluffing. Clearly I would "make" the talent show. I hoped to win the prize.

For my first stage performance I wore my favorite black jumper, polished my white flats, and even dabbed on some lipstick. I was terrified, but was told later that I had been "cool as a cucumber." As the crowd clapped and cheered I grew so nervous and thrilled I thought I would faint. They wanted me back for an encore, so, knees watery, I went back out and sang "Honey Love."

There had been nothing showy about my performance. I had walked out and sung exactly the way I would in my room or on the back porch. The actual time in front of an audience was both frightening and exhilarating, and afterwards I was euphoric.

I did not win the prize. It went to David Bullard, the only black in the show. The judges had picked the only horse darker than me. David had befriended and defended me in the fifth grade and I loved him. He was tall and smoky black, had perfect teeth, and may have been the only person in that school who smiled as readily as I did. He also had a good voice. The fact that I didn't win the prize I'd been expecting dampened that day only a little. For all the anxiety, I knew I'd been really good and that, in some strange way, my peers loved me and were proudly claiming me as one of their own, as someone who truly *belonged* to Redlands High School. My sense of having arrived was almost as heady as my satisfaction with the performance.

from

♖ A Long Line of Vendidas

Cherríe L. Moraga

1983

Cherríe L. Moraga was born in 1952 in Whittier,
California, the daughter of an Anglo and a Chicana. Her
Loving in the War Years: Lo que nunca pasó por sus labios (1983)
was one of the first books published by an openly gay
Chicana. An activist for gay, ethnic, and women's rights, she
founded the equal-opportunity Kitchen Table: Women of
Color Press and has written several award-winning plays.
The anthology she co-edited with Gloria Anzaldúa, *This
Bridge Called My Back: Writings by Radical Women of Color*
(1981), won a 1986 American Book Award. Moraga has
taught drama and writing courses at colleges across the
United States and is currently an artist in residence in the
drama department at Stanford University.

para Gloria Anzaldúa, in gratitude

MY BROTHER'S SEX WAS WHITE. MINE, BROWN.
If somebody would have asked me when I was a teenager what it means
to be Chicana, I would probably have listed the grievances done me.
When my sister and I were fifteen and fourteen, respectively, and my
brother a few years older, we were still waiting on him. I write "were" as
if now, nearly two decades later, it were over. But that would be a lie. To
this day in my mother's home, my brother and father are waited on,
including by me. I do this now out of respect for my mother and her
wishes. In those early years, however, it was mainly in relation to my
brother that I resented providing such service. For unlike my father, who

sometimes worked as much as seventy hours a week to feed my face every day, the only thing that earned my brother servitude was his maleness.

It was Saturday afternoon. My brother, then seventeen years old, came into the house with a pile of friends. I remember Fernie, the two Steves, and Roberto. They were hot, sweaty, and exhausted from an afternoon's basketball and plopped themselves down in the front room, my brother demanding, "Girls, bring us something to drink."

"Get it yourself, pig," I thought, but held those words from ever forming inside my mouth. My brother had the disgusting habit on these occasions of collapsing my sister JoAnn's and my name when referring to us as a unit: his sisters. "Cher'ann," he would say. "We're really thirsty." I'm sure it took everything in his power not to snap his fingers. But my mother was out in the yard working and to refuse him would have brought her into the house with a scene before these boys' eyes which would have made it impossible for us to show our faces at school that following Monday. We had been through that before.

When my mother had been our age, over forty years earlier, she had waited on her brothers and their friends. And it was not mere lemonade. They'd come in from work or a day's drinking. And las mujeres, often just in from the fields themselves, would already be in the kitchen making tortillas, warming frijoles or pigs' feet, albondigas soup, what have you. And the men would get a clean white tablecloth and a spread of food laid out before their eyes and not a word of resentment from the women.

The men watched the women—my aunts and mother moving with the grace and speed of girls who were cooking before they could barely see over the top of the stove. Elvira, my mother, knew she was being watched by the men and loved it. Her slim hips moved patiently beneath the apron. Her deep, thick-lidded eyes never caught theirs as she was swept back into the kitchen by my abuelita's call of "Elvirita," her brown hands deepening in color as they dropped back into the pan of flour.

I suppose my mother imagined that Joe's friends watched us like that, too. But we knew different. We were not blond or particularly long-legged or "available" because we were "Joe's sisters." This meant no boy could "make" us, which meant no boy would bother asking us out.

Roberto, the Guatemalan, was the only one among my brother's friends who seemed at all sensitive to how awkward JoAnn and I felt in our role. He would smile at us nervously, taking the lemonade, feeling embarrassed being waited on by people he considered peers. He knew the anglo girls they visited would never have succumbed to such a task. Roberto was the only recompense.

As I stopped to wait on their yearning throats, "jock itch" was all that came to my mind. Their cocks became animated in my head, for that was all that seemed to arbitrarily set us apart from each other and put me in the position of the servant and they, the served.

I wanted to machine-gun them all down, but swallowed that fantasy as I swallowed making the boy's bed every day, cleaning his room each week, shining his shoes and ironing his shirts before dates with girls, some of whom I had crushes on. I would lend him the money I had earned housecleaning for twelve hours, so he could blow it on one night with a girl because he seldom had enough money because he seldom had a job because there was always some kind of ball practice to go to. As I pressed the bills into his hand, the car honking outside in the driveway, his double date waiting, I knew I would never see that money again.

Years later, after I began to make political the fact of my being a Chicana, I remember my brother saying to me, "*I've* never felt 'culturally deprived,'" which I guess is the term "white" people use to describe third world people being denied access to *their* culture. At the time, I wasn't exactly sure what he meant, but I remember in retelling the story to my sister, she responded, "Of course he didn't. He grew up male in our house. He got the best of both worlds." And yes, I can see now that that's true. *Male in a man's world. Light-skinned in a white world. Why change?*

The pull to identify with the oppressor was never as great in me as it was in my brother. For unlike him, I could never have become the white man, only the white man's *woman*.

The first time I began to recognize clearly my alliances on the basis of race and sex was when my mother was in the hospital, extremely ill. I was eight years old. During my mother's stay in the hospital, my tía Eva took my sister and me into her care; my brother stayed with my abuela; and my father stayed by himself in our home. During this time, my father came to visit me and my sister only once. (I don't know if he ever visited my brother.) The strange thing was I didn't really miss his visits, although I sometimes fantasized some imaginary father, dark and benevolent, who might come and remind us that we still were a family.

I have always had a talent for seeing things I don't particularly want to see, and the one day my father did come to visit us with his wife/our mother physically dying in a hospital some ten miles away, I saw that he couldn't love us—not in the way we so desperately needed. I saw that he didn't know how, and he came into my tía's house like a large lumbering child—awkward and embarrassed, out of his league—trying to play a parent when he needed our mother back as much as we did just to keep him eating and protected. I hated and pitied him that day. I knew how he was letting us all down, visiting my mother daily, like a dead man, unable to say, "The children, honey, I held them. They love you. They think of you." Giving my mother *something*.

Years later, my mother spoke of his visits to the hospital. How from behind the bars of her bed and through the tubes in her nose, she watched this timid man come and go daily—going through the "motions" of being a husband. "I knew I had to live," she told us. "I knew he could never take care of you."

In contrast to the seeming lack of feeling I held for my father, my longings for my mother and fear of her dying were the most passionate feelings that had ever lived inside my young heart.

We are riding the elevator. My sister and I pressed up against one wall, holding hands. After months of separation, we are going to visit my mamá in the hospital. Mi tía me dice, "Whatever you do, no llores Cherríe. It's too hard on your mother when you cry." I nod, taking long deep breaths, trying to control my quivering lip.

As we travel up floor by floor, all I can think about is not crying, breathing, holding my breath. "¿Me prometes?" she asks. I nod again, afraid to speak, fearing my voice will crack into tears. My sister's nervous hand around mine, sweating too. We are going to see my mamá, mamá, after so long. She didn't die after all. She didn't die.

The elevator doors open. We walk down the corridor, my heart pounding. My eyes are darting in and out of each room as we pass them, fearing/anticipating my mamá's face. Then as we turn around the corner into a kind of lobby, I hear my tía say to an older woman—skin and bones. An Indian I think, straight black and gray hair pulled back. I hear my tía say, "Elvira."

I don't recognize her. This is not the woman I knew, so round and made-up with her hair always a wavy jet black! I stay back until she opens her arms to me—

this strange and familiar woman—her voice hoarse, "¡Ay mi'jita!" Instinctively, I run into her arms, still holding back my insides—"Don't cry. Don't cry." I remember. "Whatever you do, no llores." But my tía had not warned me about the smell, the unmistakable smell of the woman, mi mamá—el olor de aceite y jabón and comfort and home. "Mi mamá." And when I catch the smell I am lost in tears, deep long tears that come when you have held your breath for centuries.

There was something I knew at that eight-year-old moment that I vowed never to forget—the smell of a woman who is life and home to me at once. The woman in whose arms I am uplifted, sustained. Since then, it is as if I have spent the rest of my years driven by this scent toward la mujer.

> when her india makes love
> it is with the greatest reverence
> to color, texture, smell
>
> by now she knew the scent of earth
> could call it up
> even between the cracks
> in sidewalks
> steaming dry
> from midday summer
> rain

With this knowledge so deeply emblazed upon my heart, how then was I supposed to turn away from La Madre, La Chicana? If I were to build my womanhood on this self-evident truth, it is the love of the Chicana, the love of myself as a Chicana I had to embrace, no white man. Maybe this ultimately was the cutting difference between my brother and me. To be a woman fully necessitated my claiming the race of my mother. My brother's sex was white. Mine, brown.

Tattoos

Roberto Tinoco Durán

1987

Roberto Tinoco Durán was born in Bakersfield and grew up working in the fields, eventually becoming involved with the United Farm Workers Organizing Committee. In 1977, three years after publishing his first collection of poetry, which addressed police harassment of Chicanos, he was arrested for assaulting two officers while trying to protect a friend and was sent to prison for four years. Upon his release, he published the chapbook *A Friend of Sorrow* (1980) and returned to college, graduating with a degree from San Jose State University's school of social work.

Tattoo madness
terrible pain
permanent ink stain
anywhere will do
of gun towers
and sad flowers
convicts' arms
tales of power
portrayed in
India black ink
teardrop eyes
La Vírgen de Guadalupe
proudly displayed
on a young warrior's skin
a barrio's tattoos
are always in

La Letty

Michele Serros

1993

Michele Serros was born in 1966 in Oxnard, California, and published her first book, *Chicana Falsa* (1993), a collection of poems and short stories, while still an undergraduate student. Her second book, *How to Be a Chicana Role Model* (2000), debuted at number five on the *Los Angeles Times'* best-seller list, and she has won numerous awards for her poetry. She is currently working on a young-adult novel from her home in New York City.

Her steady hand
outlines inside bottom eyelid,
thick
darkening to deep velvet black.
A finishing touch
ends sixty-minute routine
for this raccoon-eyed beauty.
Turning from the mirror
she says:
"You know what you are?
                    A Chicana Falsa."

"MEChA don't mean shit,
and that sloppy Spanish of yours
will never get you any discount at Bob's market."

"HOMOGENIZED HISPANIC,"
that's what you are."

She
had once been "Leticia,"
"Tish" for short,
but now
only two weeks into junior high,
She is "La Letty"
y que
no mas.

Taught me
years ago,
how to ride a bike.
Doesn't matter now
Chevy Impalas snatch
her from school,
Mexican Cadillacs
low and slow,
done up in candy paint, metal flake
chrome-plated spoke rims
glistening.
Young boys
in hair nets and Dickies
fingers dipped in Old English ink
controlled
chained steering wheels
and La Letty.
Steered her
away from me,
my sister, best friend.
And she fell for them
for it,
the whole creased-khaki
pressed-flannel
medallion-wearing scene.

Every night
after dinner was done
TV clicked off
in Holly Hobbie haven
my naked lids closed

as I listened for
soft car hum
copycat teenage laughter
faint oldies station...
waiting
and waiting
for Tish
       to come home.

✸ I Used to Be Much Much Darker

Francisco X. Alarcón

1985

Francisco X. Alarcón was born in 1954 in California, grew up in Guadalajara, Mexico, and later returned to California. He is the author of more than ten volumes of poetry, several award-winning bilingual poetry books for children, and two textbooks for high school and college Spanish-language courses. The following poem is from his first poetry collection, *Tattoos* (1985).

I used to be
much much darker
dark as la tierra
recién llovida
and dark was all
I ever wanted—
dark tropical
mountains
dark daring
eyes
dark tender lips
and I would sing
dark
dream dark
talk only dark

happiness
was to spend
whole
afternoons

tirado como foca
bajo el sol
"you're already
so dark
muy prieto
too indio!"
some would lash
at my happy
darkness but
I could only
smile back

now I'm not as
dark as I once was
quizás sean
los años
maybe I'm too
far up north
not enough sun
not enough time
but anyway
up here "dark"
is only for
the ashes—
the stuff
lonely nights
are made of

Puertoricanness

Aurora Levins Morales

1986

Aurora Levins Morales was born in 1954 in the United States, moved to Puerto Rico when she was still a child, and returned to the states when she was thirteen. An award-winning writer, historian, news reporter, and documentary producer of Puerto Rican and Jewish descent, she has been lecturing and reading on women's and Jewish studies around the nation for twenty years. Her work includes a book of essays and two experimental cross-genre books, including *Remedios: Stories of Earth and Iron from the History of Puertoriqueñas* (1998), a prose-poetry version of Latina history.

IT WAS PUERTO RICO WAKING UP INSIDE HER. Puerto Rico waking her up at 6:00 a.m., remembering the rooster that used to crow over on 59th Street and the neighbors all cursed "that damn rooster," but she loved him, waited to hear his harsh voice carving up the Oakland sky and eating it like chopped corn, so obliviously sure of himself, crowing all alone with miles of houses around him. She was like that rooster.

Often she could hear them in her dreams. Not the lone rooster of 59th Street (or some street nearby...she had never found the exact yard though she had tried), but the wild, careening, hysterical roosters of 3:00 a.m. in Bartolo, screaming at the night and screaming again at the day.

It was Puerto Rico waking up inside her, uncurling and shoving open the door she had kept neatly shut for years and years. Maybe since the first time she was an immigrant, when she refused to speak Spanish in nursery school. Certainly since the last time, when at thirteen she found herself between languages, between countries, with no land feeling at all solid under her feet. The mulberry trees of Chicago, that first summer, had looked so utterly pitiful beside her memory of flamboyan and banana and…no, not even the individual trees and bushes but the mass of them, the overwhelming profusion of green life that was the home of her comfort and nest of her dreams.

The door was opening. She could no longer keep her accent under lock and key. It seeped out, masquerading as dyslexia, stuttering, halting, unable to speak the word which will surely come out in the wrong language, wearing the wrong clothes. Doesn't that girl know how to dress? Doesn't she know how to date, what to say to a professor, how to behave at a dinner table laid with silver and crystal and too many forks?

Yesterday she answered her husband's request that she listen to the whole of his thoughts before commenting by screaming, "This is how we talk. I will not wait sedately for you to finish. Interrupt me back!"

She drank pineapple juice three or four times a day. Not Lotus, just Co-op brand, but it was *piña,* and it was sweet and yellow. And she was letting the clock slip away from her into a world of morning and afternoon and night, instead of "five-forty-one and twenty seconds—beep."

There were things she noticed about herself, the Puertoricanness which she had kept hidden all these years, but which had persisted as habits, as idiosyncracies of her nature. The way she left a pot of food on the stove all day, eating out of it whenever hunger struck her, liking to have something ready. The way she had lacked food to offer Elena in the old days and had stamped on the desire to do so because it was Puerto Rican: *Come, mija…¿quieres café?* The way she was embarrassed and irritated by Ana's unannounced visits, just dropping by, keeping the country habits after a generation of city life. So unlike the cluttered datebook of all her friends, making appointments to speak to each other on the phone days in advance. Now she yearned for that clocklessness, for the perpetual food pots of her childhood. Even in the poorest houses a plate of white rice and brown beans with calabaza or green bananas and oil.

She had told Sally that Puerto Ricans lived as if they were all in a small town still, a small town of six million spread out over tens of thousands of square miles, and that the small town that was her country needed to include Manila Avenue in Oakland now, because she was moving back into it. She would not fight the waking early anymore, or the eating all day, or the desire to let time slip between her fingers and allow her work to shape it. Work, eating, sleep, lovemaking, play—to let them shape the day instead of letting the day shape them. Since she could not right now, in the endless bartering of a woman with two countries, bring herself to trade in one-half of her heart for the other, exchange this loneliness for another perhaps harsher one, she would live as a Puerto Rican lives *en la isla* right here in north Oakland, plant the *bananales* and *cafetales* of her heart around her bedroom door, sleep under the shadow of their bloom and the carving hoarseness of the roosters, wake to blue-rimmed white enamel cups of *jugo de piña* and plates of *guineo verde,* and heat pots of rice with bits of meat in them on the stove all day.

There was a woman in her who had never had the chance to move through this house the way she wanted to, a woman raised to be like those women of her childhood, hardworking and humorous and clear. That woman was yawning up out of sleep and into this cluttered daily routine of a northern California writer living at the edges of Berkeley. She was taking over, putting doilies on the word processor, not bothering to make appointments, talking to the neighbors, riding miles on the bus to buy *bacalao,* making her presence felt...and she was all Puerto Rican, every bit of her.

 # Aztec Angel

Luis Omar Salinas

1970

Luis Omar Salinas was born in 1937 in southern Texas and moved to California at age nine. He attended California State University, Fresno, studying under Philip Levine and Robert Mezey as a member of the informal Fresno School of poets. He has published several collections of poetry, beginning with *Crazy Gypsy* (1970) and most recently *Sometimes Mysteriously* (1997), and he co-edited *From the Barrio: A Chicano Anthology* (1973).

I

I am an Aztec angel
    criminal
        of a scholarly society
I do favors
        for whimsical magicians
where I pawn
        my heart for truth
and find my way
        through obscure streets
of soft-spoken
                hara-kiris

II

I am an Aztec angel
    forlorn passenger
        on a train
    of chicken farmers
        and happy children

III

I am the Aztec angel
    fraternal partner
        of an orthodox society
    where pachuco children
        hurl stones
    through poetry rooms
    and end up in cop cars
    their bones itching
        and their hearts
    busted from malnutrition

IV

I am the Aztec angel
    who frequents bars
    spends evenings
    with literary circles
    and socializes with spiks
    niggers and wops
        and collapses on his way
            to funerals

V

Drunk
    lonely
        bespectacled
    the sky
        opens my veins
            like rain
        clouds go berserk
            around me
    my Mexican Ancestors
        chew my fingernails

I am an Aztec angel
    offspring of a woman
        who was beautiful

 # Classifieds

Rubén Medina

1986

Rubén Medina has published articles in scholarly magazines in both English and Spanish, and has written one
book-length critical work, *Autor, autoridad y autorización*
(1999), about the works of Octavio Paz. His poem
"Busing" also appears in this anthology.

for David Sternbach

While I look for a job in the newspaper
and my eyes rise and fall along the columns
—bilious yellow—I imagine:

> Honorable Lady from La Jolla
> solicits Third World poet
> to teach her to write
> poems like Rod McKuen.

But I say no.
Because as a boy I was very Catholic
and I'd really suffer, writing lies.

Later on I read:

> Excellent tourist guide solicited; must
> speak 18th century Spanish and
> love to meet people. Should be very
> sociable and neat in appearance, to show
> our *Nice People* from Latin America

our most important places like
the San Diego Zoo, one of the
most beautiful in the world; the Coronado Hotel;
the Cabrillo monument; the Museum of
Natural History, etcetera.

But I say to myself, no.
I get nervous because I always
have been very orderly but
I've always had problems with arithmetic.

Then, desperate, I read:

Mexican emigrant solicited; with
great desire to learn to cut
hair in the most varied styles.
English not necessary,
only to smile and say yes
in English, German, French, and Japanese.
3 dollars an hour, plus tips.

And then I say, yes. I accept.
I stand up, enthusiastic, to tell my wife.

WORKING

from

✸ The Vaquero

Arnold R. Rojas

1964

Arnold R. Rojas was born in 1899 in California to
Mexican immigrants and grew up riding horses and herd-
ing cattle with vaqueros. He had no formal education but
studied the history and techniques of the vaqueros, becoming a respected authority on horse training and eventually
incorporating this knowledge, as well as his firsthand experiences on the ranchos of Kern County, into several historical fiction and nonfiction books, including *The Vaquero*
(1964), excerpted below. "Chief" Rojas died in 1988.

THE BLOOD OF CABALLEROS, BULLFIGHTERS, Jews, Moors, Basques, and
Indian heroes ran in the vaquero's veins. He was a strange mixture of
races. He admired his Iberian father, but sided and sympathized with his
raped Indian mother. If food was short, he fed his horse before he fed
his wife. Though often a strange contradiction, he was, without a doubt,
the most interesting man in the New World.

He was a descendant of the old conquerors and retained the language of Spain. In living the free life of the nomad he imitated the
Spaniard in the trappings of his horse, and the Indian in his abode. He
spent his wealth on silver-mounted bits and spurs and often left his
home destitute of necessities. He slept on the ground, but rode a silver-
mounted saddle. He may not have combed his hair, but his horse's mane
was trimmed, with one tuft for a colt and two for a bridle horse. He was
named after the saint's day on which he was born; it was often Jesús who
was the most proficient in stealing cattle.

The vaquero would lie on the ground with his saddle for a pillow
even though the rain was falling, and sleep without a word of complaint,

yet he would grumble when his saddle blankets got wet. Wet saddle blankets make a horse's back sore.

The vaquero's way of life gave him virtues which do not exist in this modern day, and at this distant time no man can judge a man of that era. His life was hard. He would stand shivering in the early morning cold, holding a cup of coffee in his shaking hand, then sit a horse all day in the driving sleet, chilled to the bone. He would ride from dawn to dusk in a cloud of alkali dust, his tongue parched and swollen, with rippling water in a mirage shimmering in the distance, with visions of all the water he had ever drunk or seen wasted haunting his memory, for memory plays queer, cruel tricks. The want of water was the vaquero's greatest hardship in the burning heat of a San Joaquin Valley summer. He often rode in a daze with visions of springs of cool water bubbling out of the pine-scented Sierra, of canals of water from which he had never bothered to drink. And when he came to drink, it would more than likely be out of a reeking water hole that contained the putrid remains of some animal.

But there was another side. A matchless sky overhead. An expanse of wildflowers that spread over the great valley like a purple carpet, so vast that a day's ride would take one only to the middle of it. The bold, brooding Sierra standing in grim outline that stretched away to the northern horizon. A wild chase down a mountainside in the fall when the air is like wine and life is good. The feel of a good horse between one's knees as he sweeps and wheels around a herd of restless cattle. The evening campfire when men broil *costillas,* ribs, on chamiso-root coals and gather around to tell tales of long ago, of Murieta, Vásquez, and García.[…]

When a vaquero was especially skilled, and he was asked how he had reached such a degree of proficiency, his answer would invariably be: *"Me crié entre los Indios,"* I was raised among the Indians. Or when some vaquero had performed his work with great skill, the other men would look at each other, smile approvingly, and say, *"Se crió entre los Indios pues."* Well, he was brought up among the Indians.

Contrary to a lot of false statements, a man took pride in calling himself "Indio." The Indian vaquero was highly respected for his skill and good qualities—that is, by those who knew him. And the proof is that very few of the men who have ridden on the Tejón stayed there any length of time without becoming *"Indios del Tejón,"* Tejón Indians, whatever their true race may have been.

At night around the fire a note of awe would creep into the old man's voice as he told of hard-riding Indian vaqueros who had roped grizzly bears and led wild cattle out of the Sierra, men who had become legends on the Tejón Ranch.

The vaquero, or buckaroo, who herded the cattle on the ranches of California was sometimes a Cahuilla, a Paiute, a mission Indian, or a member of one of the numerous tribes which populated California. Sometimes he was a Sonoreño, that is to say, a native of the state of Sonora in Old Mexico, or a descendant of Sonoreños born in California. Sometimes he was a Californian of pioneer colonial stock, like Don Jesús López. At other times he was from Baja California like Federico Lamas, and sometimes he was a gringo. Once in a while a Chilean was met among the vaquero crews.

The Indian vaquero was sparing in speech and serene under all circumstances. He was pithy in all his expressions and often spoke in metaphor or ironically. One would have to be well acquainted with him to know his meanings. He had a knack for giving names which never failed to correspond to something visible in their owners. To a man on Tejón who rode humped up over his horse, the other men applied the name *El Tacuachi,* the Possum. They would say of a man who showed much Indian blood in his makeup, *"Ese no le debe ni los Buenos Días a los Españoles,"* that one doesn't owe even a "good day" to the Spaniards.

from

✴ The Brick People

Alejandro Morales

1988

Alejandro Morales (b. 1944) published fiction exclusively in
Spanish before writing *The Brick People* (1988), his first
novel in English. His articles have appeared regularly in the
Los Angeles Times Book Review, and his writing can be found
in scholarly journals in the United States, Mexico, and
Europe. He currently teaches film studies and Latin
American and Chicano literature at UC Irvine. A historical
novel, *The Brick People* traces the growth of California from
the nineteenth to the twentieth century, following the
Simons Brick Factory. A Chinese massacre like the one
described below did take place in 1871 in Los Angeles;
some ten percent of the population participated in what has
been called the city's first race riot.

FROM THE EAST WHERE TIME BEGAN, the wind blew hard through the
canyons and cold off the snowy mountains as Rosendo Guerrero waited
in the early gray morning for Joseph Simons to emerge from his office.
The morning brought back memories to Rosendo of his mother and
father, who were murdered by a deranged Frenchman who believed that
the Emperor Maximilian was imprisoned near the Guerreros' home. He
was thirteen when the demented man broke into his home, demanding
to know the whereabouts of Emperor Maximilian, a man whom neither
Rosendo nor his parents had ever heard about. The crazed man shot
wildly at the Guerrero family: Father, Mother, and five children of whom
Rosendo was the eldest. His brothers and sisters did not scream but
watched and turned into small brown rocks. The room filled with the

screams and hand defenses of his father and mother attempting to stop the bullets with torn voice and bloody hands, and the insistent questioning and firing of the Frenchman. Rosendo overcame fear and leaped out through the doorway to survive in the blackness of the North.

For many days, perhaps weeks, there was only blackness before his eyes. He kept advancing on the Flint Knife of the Northern axis of the ancient Aztec coordinates his parents had taught him. He could not go toward the Red Reed axis of the East, nor to the White House of the West, nor dare to look back at the Blue Rabbit of the South. At this time, these colors and images were hidden deep in his mind. Traveling through the pure blackness for seven years, Rosendo followed the brilliantly sharp Flint Knife that opened a path to the North.

Rosendo arrived in Los Angeles to realize that most of his young adult life had been spent journeying to a place that he knew nothing about. He had followed a directional mandala that his parents had inculcated in his psyche.

At the Simons Brickyard in Pasadena in 1892, he now traced the directional mandala in the soft red earth. The morning was one of complete loneliness as he finished the last oval figure of the mandala, which consisted of a center and four ovals interrelated in a continuous unwinding infinite spiral of energy, time, and space. The figure symbolized Rosendo's perception of the cosmos. It represented the pattern Rosendo would follow to construct the buildings on the six acres where the brickyard evolved.

The men had worked for two hours. They had started early and would soon finish a complete order of bricks for a small house to be built on Fair Oaks near the intersection of Glenarm. The Simons Brickyard had achieved the capacity to produce fifty thousand bricks per day. The constant demand for brick projected a lucrative future for the brick business. Joseph Simons, the owner, had given Rosendo the authority to hire and fire the workers. At this time the yard had forty men, interviewed and selected by Rosendo. Most of the men hired were from Guanajuato, Rosendo's home state.

Rosendo tossed away the stick with which he had traced the figure on the clay. He looked at the door of the office from which the patron would emerge. He waited and observed the men at work. He, Rosendo Guerrero, did not labor; he directed and ordered. He, the privileged foreman, felt powerful. Physically, he feared no one. He respected Joseph's business capabilities and the abilities of the labor organizers who mounted strikes against men like Joseph. Rosendo's job was to keep the Mexicans producing constantly and remaining content with what they had, as well as function as sheriff of the town of Simons. Thus far no trouble had arisen and Rosendo did not expect any.

Bricks were in demand and production continued to expand daily. Although Joseph knew a great deal about the production of brick, it was Rosendo who had taught him about clay and formulas for the preparation of mud, information which Rosendo had acquired from John V. Simons, Joseph's cousin. Joseph listened carefully and experimented to improve his company's products. For the first year and a half, he labored side by side with Rosendo and the workers. He built molds, trays, and long-drying racks; mixed, poured, and formed red mud into bricks; dried and stacked the bricks into monolithic kilns for firing. Joseph acquired knowledge and business sense from Rosendo, whom he recognized as a business mentor.[…]

Joseph let go of the reins and approached Rosendo. "I want ten more men hired. Remember, no Chinamen."

"Yes, we have a lot of work." Rosendo crossed his arms.

"Within a year I'll double the crew," Joseph smiled.

"The ten men you want to hire, where will they sleep?" Rosendo asked cautiously.

Joseph laughed. "They can sleep in the barn or share the bachelors' quarters. You don't expect them to complain, do you?"

Rosendo shook his head, but with eyes, mouth, and hands communicated that to prevent their leaving, the men should have something better.

"I'll order wood to build cottages. Meanwhile, they can live in tents. You suggested a place for the cottages. Where?" Joseph waited.

Rosendo stepped out in front of Joseph for a better view of the place in question. "The west side of the yard. In the White House of the West."

Rosendo made statements that Joseph could not comprehend; however, he respected the meaning and importance Rosendo gave to them. There was always an abstruse logic which Rosendo brought to the surface. Joseph had a high regard for Rosendo's linguistic ability. Since the time that they had met, Rosendo had spoken English well.

"Why the west side? Aren't we going to dig there?" Joseph asked.

"No. The pit in the south is rich. For many years we will get clay out of it. We will dig towards the north from the furthest point in the south. Towards the center of the yard. From the center we will gradually go down, deeper. The deepest point will be the furthest away from the center.

We have houses on the east now and we should build more on the west separating the workmen. We will have two sources of energy, two sources of labor. The brick works and the new machines will be on the north side of the center, on the north side of the east-west axis. The office is located at the center. From there you can observe the world you create." Rosendo seemed satisfied.

"I'm convinced, Rosendo. But you know I want you to move into the office. It will be the foreman's quarters."

Rosendo welcomed the change and opportunity to be at the center of the evolving directional mandala.

On that gray morning of changes, Joseph had an appointment at a Pasadena bank to finalize the purchase of two stiff-mud brick-making machines. The parts had been delivered and in the afternoon the mechanics would assemble the apparatus. Joseph planned to observe the arming of the technological beasts. Rosendo would also be present to learn their operation. On schedule was a trip to the property on California Street which Joseph had bought to build several homes for his family. The houses would be constructed with Simons brick, of course.

"Rosendo, I want you to handpick the best brick, the best material for my house. Start on that today. I'll see you in the afternoon with the mechanics."

Joseph grabbed the reins, mounted the horse and galloped out from the center of his company, following the north-south axis to the outside world. Rosendo marched through the yard, watching the men to make sure that the production was maintained at approximately fifty thousand bricks per day.

With the installation of the new machines, the digging in the clay pit became more intensified and in six months the Mexicans had gouged out of the earth twice as much clay as Joseph and Rosendo had estimated for that period of time. An immense red hole began to form, a wound located in an unnoticeable place on the earth's precious skin. Rosendo hired more Mexicans, who fell into the pit as laborers who dug, molded, and created the material that built small to large pyramids.

Joseph, satisfied with the progress of his company, valued the Mexican worker and, in his opinion, endeavored in every way possible to keep his peons happy. Above all, he did not want outside labor voices heard inside the brickyard. There were labor movements in the country that inspired unmeetable demands and lethal strikes. If his workers demanded fewer hours and more money, the company's economic progress would be greatly retarded. In different parts of the world social movements threatened to destroy established world powers. Brown men nibbled away at portions of the British and Spanish colonies. In the United States, unionism became stronger and urged labor to fight for fair pay and improved working conditions. Unions and radical socialists compared the situation of exploited workers in Latin America, Africa and Asia to laborers in the United States and urged the people to guard against unjust treatment. Joseph, aware of what could happen if extreme idealists infiltrated his workers, did whatever was necessary to keep their spirits high, without damaging the company's profits.

In the afternoon, Joseph chose to ride alongside Rosendo as he made his rounds through the directional mandala of the brickyard. As they neared the ridge of the pit, several workers ran excitedly toward them.

"¡Don Rosendo! ¡Difuntos! We have discovered thousands of cadavers!"

Rosendo heard the cries with a puzzled expression which soon turned to a serious look.

"I won't enter the hole anymore! It's sacred ground!"

"I'm afraid the dead saw me!"

"We might awaken them!"

Joseph steadied the horse and waited for an explanation from Rosendo, who searched beyond the men toward the pit.

"The men have found a burial ground. Probably Indian," Rosendo said as he moved away from the screaming men. Abruptly he turned the horse.

"¡Cálmense! If you're afraid, go to work in the drying racks! Cowards! The dead won't harm you; they only scare you!" he shouted.

Rosendo daggered the workers' pride. He had questioned their machismo. They were not cowards, but they had been frightened, shocked into running like children away from what under normal circumstances would be considered simply a corpse in the natural process of decomposition. They had been taught to respect the dead and not violate their right to peaceful rest. Four men followed Rosendo as he advanced to the pit. One remained behind and walked slowly away to the center of the yard. Joseph recognized the contorted expression of terror on the man's face as he left.

By the time the group arrived, the work had stopped at the pit. The men, in a red field of clay, circled and stared down into several deep cavities in the earth. Silence dominated the area. A slight breeze passed from the north to the south as Rosendo and Joseph dismounted and moved into the nearest circle. Both men studied the grave and noticed a strange logic to its whole. In the center was a clothed and preserved body. Contrary to what the observers expected, the body had not decayed. Around the mummified remains, almost in a perfect arrangement, parts of other bodies reached out from the clay wall to touch the body at the center. Joseph saw a hand, an arm, a foot, a leg, and buttocks extending to the center. None of the cadavers was dismembered, but they were contorted in an exaggerated way to emphasize a specific part of the human body.

Joseph turned away, yet curiosity made him join another circle of men staring at the human remains. He moved to another and then another. To his surprise, most of the mummified bodies, clothed in Chinese garments with hair and beards arranged in the Chinese tradition, looked up through Asiatic eyes. Ten holes had been filled with corpses. Joseph understood about the land being a sacred burial ground for the Indians, but why hundreds, perhaps thousands of Chinese were buried there was beyond his comprehension.

"Massacre, massacre," Rosendo repeated, with a disgusted, angry tone.

The many accounts of the massacre had rendered the infamous occurrence a blurry memory in the community's conscience. Most people believed that the Chinese were apt to spin tales against the Anglo Americans and that the story of the massacre was a legend brought from China. Few people were convinced that the massacre had taken place. But Joseph and Rosendo peered down at hundreds of Chinese bodies with bullet holes, stab wounds, and crushed craniums. Bodies, piled four and five deep, comprised the proof that a horrendous massacre had occurred in the recent past.

Joseph and Rosendo ordered the men to continue digging and to place the remains in a pyramid at the center of the main pit. Some of the workers simply refused and left. The majority, motivated by pity, morbid curiosity, or the desire to give some kind of acceptable ritual burial, stayed to exhume the victims so that their souls would sleep in harmony with God. While the pyramid of flesh grew, the bodies began to dance in Joseph's mind.[…]

Joseph notified the authorities of the discovery.

The reply was a simple "Burn the remains," a statement made by an unidentified messenger who rode off as suddenly as he had arrived.

There were now five large heaps of bodies in the central pit. A strong stench of death reeked in the air. The workers kept digging and extricating more cadavers. As the mounds grew, so did the flowers that the women were bringing to surround the heaps of bone and leathered flesh.

From a distance, sobbing women with playful children gathered to pray the rosary. They mourned for the unknown dead, for the loss that had never been recognized. Joseph and Rosendo watched and periodically expressed disbelief as to what was happening, what they were directing.

Earlier they had discussed the possibility of abandoning the site and beginning another pit on the west side of the yard, but the best clay was located under their feet and Joseph refused to alter the master plan that Rosendo had envisioned and explained. Joseph was prepared to eliminate anything from the past that might halt the successful progress of the plant.

The bodies would be exhumed and cremated. Joseph would follow the orders given to him by the messenger. He ordered Rosendo to bring in straw, logs, and fuel. Rosendo organized some of the men to prepare the bodies for the burning. As men placed logs and fuel on the heaps of cadavers, the women brought more flowers and covered the faces of the dead with beautiful, colored embroidered doilies, quilts, mantillas, aprons, and tablecloths. When finished, the crematoriums appeared to be multichromatic mountains of flowers.

As night enveloped the scene, Joseph asked for volunteers to keep the fires burning throughout the night and if necessary through the next day. The cadavers had to be eradicated, reduced to gray ashes. Rosendo selected ten young men to accompany him during the vigil. Joseph went to his horse and gave orders to torch the bodies. The flames rose rapidly. An explosive hissing sound competed with the chorus of women praying the rosary. Gradually, the stench gave way to the burning smell of wood, bones, and leathered flesh. All night and part of the next day, Rosendo put wood on the fire. By the late afternoon Joseph Simons got his wish. The only physical evidence left of the dead were five mounds of ash, blown away that evening by a strong warm wind that came from the east and flew to the sea.

from

✹ The Original Sin

Nellie Quinn, as told to Anthony Quinn

1972

Manuela (Nellie) Quinn was the mother of two-time
Academy Award–winning actor Anthony Quinn
(1915–2001). She moved with her Irish Mexican husband
and their children from Mexico to California when Anthony
was a child, eventually settling in East Los Angeles. She
worked on job sites alongside men to support her family and
retold the following story of her early days in California in
her son's autobiography, *Original Sin* (1972), which has been
translated into more than eighteen languages.

FRANCISCO WAS IN ALL HIS GLORY IN GLAMIS. I'd never realized how well
he spoke English. There in Glamis I heard him for the first time. We had
gone to the little grocery store by the side of the tracks and he began to
talk to the man behind the counter. The man was obviously surprised
too, because he said, "Oh, you speak English?"

Francisco said, "Yes, what's so funny?"

"Nothing, except that most of these people who work on the rail-
roads are Mexicans."

"I'm Mexican too," said Francisco.

"Oh, well…" The man got nervous and didn't know what to say. I
didn't understand too well why Francisco had gotten angry. He handed
the man a piece of the paper that entitled him to groceries from the railroad company. The man took the paper and filled up a bag with groceries.
As we were going out, he called Francisco back. He put out his hand.

"No offense was meant. If you care to, you are welcome to come and
work for me anytime you want. I could use somebody that understands
these people's lingo." Francisco shook his hand and said he'd think about it.

They became very good friends after that. I told Francisco to accept the man's offer. Somehow I couldn't imagine that beautiful man, your father, working like an ox on the railroad.

He said no, that he had talked Glafiro into coming to work on the railroad and that he would work beside him.

It used to break my heart to see those men go out into that broiling sun each morning. Their job was to fix the railroad bed and lay new tracks.

At the end of a few weeks, most of the men gave up. They said that there was too much work and too little pay. Many went back to El Paso and some of them just headed across the desert for Los Angeles. Finally, Glafiro and your father were the only ones left. I suppose the reason they were still there was because neither one would admit to the other he couldn't take it.

Even the inspector who came by one day wondered how they had gone on doing the work by themselves. They needed one man to hold the spikes on the railroad ties while the other two men hammered them in. Otherwise, it slowed them down terribly. It wasn't a very difficult job, but very important.

The inspector said he'd bring a man to hold the spikes. Francisco asked him how much the job would pay.

"Same as you get."

"Just for holding a spike?" asked Francisco, surprised.

"It's still work."

"Never mind getting another man," said Francisco. "I have a friend who will do the job."

"That's okay with me," said the inspector. "Just so the job is done."

"That night Francisco said to me, "Nellie, how would you like to ride with me to work tomorrow morning?"

The men used to go to work on this handcart that they put on the rails. They made it go by pumping handles up and down. Often you and young Glafiro would get on it and Francisco would let you ride for a mile or so, then you'd walk back. I liked the idea of riding the handcart.

Next morning I left with Glafiro and Francisco. They both pumped the handle and we rolled down the rails very fast. It took us about an hour to get to where they were working. I had thought I was just going along for the ride, but when we got there Francisco handed me some long pincers and told me to hold the spike in place while he and Glafiro hammered it into the railroad tie.

I helped the men all that morning until we stopped for lunch. I had prepared Francisco's basket early that morning. Glafiro had his own.

We all went and sat under the shade of a scraggly tree and had our lunch. It was almost like a picnic.

Then Francisco asked me if I thought I'd like to come to work with him every day. "All you have to do is hold the spikes while Glafiro and I hammer them in. You will get the same money we're getting."

I hadn't thought of it as a job. I thought we were just out on a picnic, but the work wasn't hard and I knew we could use the money, so I agreed.

I had been working with the men for a week or so when the inspector came around unexpectedly. He was surprised so much work had been done. Even though we were alone—the three of us—we worked a full day.

"You boys are doing a very nice job. Where's the other man you hired?"

"He couldn't take it out here so I got her to help us." He pointed.

"The inspector looked at me. He thought it was some trick, I guess, to collect the extra wages.

"You mean this girl is doing a man's work?"

"She's as good as any man around," said Francisco. "Come on," he said to me, "let's show him."

The two men and I nailed down about ten ties. The inspector shook his head.

"I wouldn't have believed it. Who is she?"

Francisco hesitated for a little bit, then he said, "She's my wife."

"Well, it's your business. I don't care who does the job as long as it gets done."

He gave the two men their salaries, then he handed me fourteen dollars! That was the most money I'd ever had at one time in my life. I offered it to Francisco; after all, he was the head of the family. But he pushed it back to me.

"You've worked hard for it. It's yours, keep it."

"All I need money for is the family. I have no use for money for myself."

With that he handed me ten dollars from his salary and told me I was to keep the money from then on to run the house.

We were really getting to be husband and wife by then. That night when we got back to our boxcar, Francisco told his mother that now that I was working on the railroad with him, it would be her job to do the cooking and that she would have to watch the children. The way he said it, he wasn't asking her as a favor, he was telling her. She agreed.

A few weeks later we had laid so much rail that it was now taking us longer to reach the end of the line. The inspector said we'd have to move our wagons closer to the work. Shortly after that an engine arrived. They hooked the wagons to the engine and we moved further down the line.

I suppose nowadays all this sounds unbelievable. It might even sound strange, a young girl working on the railroad, but we Mexican women were used to it. We fought beside our men and found it only normal to work beside them. I loved working hard beside Francisco. When we came home at night we were both tired and hot. We understood each other's pains. That is almost more important than sharing each other's happiness.

Sometimes it was so hot out there in the sun that the barrel of water we brought out in the mornings would be boiling hot. We tried everything; we even buried it in the sand. Nothing helped.

You know, they make fun of Mexicans sleeping, I mean taking the siesta, but let anyone who laughs go out and work from six o'clock in the morning until twelve in that hot sun and see how long they last on their feet. No human could stand working in that fire between twelve and two-thirty. There was nothing else to do but find some shade and wait for the heat to pass.

Nobody was there checking on us. We were on our honor. We never cheated the railroad company of one second of their time. We gave them a full eight hours' labor for their dollar a day.

I learned a lot about your father at that time. Don't forget he was still a young boy. He was only twenty-one or twenty-two. He was not afraid of hard work. As a matter of fact, he enjoyed it. But, more than that, he took pride in his work. He wanted to do his best.

Once he found two ties that were just a little bit crooked. Nobody would have noticed and it certainly didn't affect the safety of the trains, but he said it looked bad. Glafiro and I argued with him for an hour. He wanted to take up fifty feet of rails and straighten out the railroad ties. It meant losing a whole day's work, but we helped him. If we hadn't, he would have done it himself.

Next day, when we were finished, he looked over the work and said, "There, doesn't that look better?"

Yes, it did, I had to admit—but was it worth all that work and sweat? To him it was. Imagine working overtime with nobody paying you just to make it a little bit better!

One day, a very hot day, I almost fainted in the sun. During the lunch break I wasn't able to eat a bite. Up till then I'd always been able to keep up with the men, but that day my womanhood showed up. I fell fast asleep during lunch. Francisco tried to wake me up around three but I couldn't make it. He and Glafiro went back to work by themselves. With one hand Francisco tried to hold the pincers that held the spike and with the other hand he swung the hammer. It was almost impossible to do it. The hammer was very heavy. You needed two hands to lift it. Even then, after a few minutes it weighed a ton.

He worked like that for an hour or so, then I guess his arm got tired. He reached down to straighten out the spike with his hand. Glafiro couldn't stop the swing of the hammer and drove the spike into Francisco's hand.

The quiet had awakened me. I saw Glafiro bending over Francisco. His hand was a mass of blood. I let out a scream and ran to him. We put him on the handcart and started pumping our way home.

His hand was still bleeding quite badly. I tore off part of the hem of my dress and bandaged it the best I could. The blood still gushed out. He told me to tie his arm tight above the elbow.

When we got to our boxcar, everybody rushed to see what had happened. Francisco was very pale by then. Doña Sabina started screaming and crying. Francisco was furious.

"It's nothing. Shut up! You'll only scare the children."

All night we bathed Francisco's hand in hot water and salt. About midnight I heard his moaning. I woke up and took his hand out of the basin of water. It was turning dark blue.

Sabina became terrified: "Gangrene is setting in."

In the distance I heard a train whistle. I ran out into the night. There was no stop there. The trains just went by us. The nearest was about twenty or twenty-five miles west.

I stood in the middle of the tracks and tried to flag the train. It was coming very fast. I hoped that the engineer was looking out and would see me, otherwise he was going to kill me, but I wouldn't leave the tracks.

God was with me. The engineer put on the brakes and the train pulled to a stop. I ran up and told him my husband was dying, that he had to go to a doctor. Two men ran over to our boxcar. Francisco already had a very high fever and was delirious. One of the men looked at his hand and told the other to help him pick up Francisco. He was such a big man we all had to help carry him to the train.

I wanted to go along with Francisco; I didn't want to leave him alone, but the engineer said I'd only be in the way. He said they would see he got to a good doctor.

The train pulled away. We all stood there by the rails long after it had disappeared around the bend.

Later I learned that the engineer had stayed with Francisco until he got him to a hospital in Los Angeles. They had stopped in some small town to see a doctor, who said he could only give momentary relief. Francisco would lose his hand unless he had the best medical attention. Since Los Angeles was the nearest place where a top doctor could be found, the engineer had taken Francisco to Los Angeles the same night.

He left him at the hospital and disappeared. We never knew his name.

We suffered, Doña Sabina and I, not having any news of Francisco. Three whole days passed before a note tied around a piece of coal was thrown from a speeding train.

"Your husband is doing fine. He is in a hospital in Los Angeles. It is on Washington Street and Central Avenue."

That's all it said. No name or anything. But Sabina and I were relieved and happy. We didn't know how to write Francisco. We would just have to wait for him to come back. We had spent so much of our life waiting for him, we were used to it.

We were afraid that the inspector would take our jobs away so Sabina, Inez, and I went to work every morning with Glafiro. Sabina and Inez took turns swinging the other hammer. Poor fine ladies. The revolution had certainly not made their life better; I suppose that is what is meant by equality.

One day the inspector came and caught us working. He had already heard from someone about Francisco. He told us that he would be back in a few weeks. He made no comment about the fact that we women were doing the work of men. He paid us each a man's salary. He was a good man.

A week or so later the man who ran the little grocery store back in Glamis came with a letter for me. It was from Francisco:

Nellie,
    I am not coming back to Glamis. Tell my mother she can do what she wants. She can go back to El Paso or come to Los Angeles with you and the children.
    Tell the inspector I have already talked to the railroad people and they are willing to give my family passage to Los Angeles. I signed some paper saying my accident was not their fault, and they are giving me the tickets for signing.
    The inspector will put you on the train and tell you where I am in Los Angeles.
Francisco Quinn

Doña Sabina, of course, decided to go to Los Angeles with us.

Inez broke down in tears the day we left. She thought it was some kind of trick to get away from her. She was furious at Doña Sabina for abandoning her. She felt that since she was the younger sister of Doña Sabina, she should stay with her.

"My place is with my son and his family," said Sabina, as we boarded the train. Inez walked off and never bothered to wave to us as we pulled away. Glafiro and his children did.

If El Paso had seemed to me the biggest city in the world, you can imagine what Los Angeles looked like. When we got out of the station and saw the miles and miles of buildings, I thought to myself, "Well, here we are, on another new adventure."

The minute I saw Los Angeles I fell in love with it. I knew I wanted my family to grow up in that city.

We went out into the street. We had never seen such traffic. All the noise, automobiles backfiring, streetcars clanging, fire engines screaming down the street. It was like a huge sideshow! We stopped and asked some people where Washington Street was. It was about twelve long blocks from the train station.

What with you two children in tow and all our belongings on our back, it took us forever to walk those twelve blocks.

Almost everybody we met in Los Angeles spoke Spanish, especially on Grand Avenue. That was the street where most of the Negroes and the Mexican people lived.

At the hospital, I found a nurse who spoke Spanish. I told her I was looking for my husband, Francisco Quinn. She smiled when she heard his name. She told me to go up by myself, that children were not allowed to go into the patients' rooms.

Francisco was in a room with another man who had his legs all bandaged up. Later, I found he had third-degree burns. He was from Canada.

When I walked in, Francisco and the man had been laughing. Francisco had a tube stuck in his bandaged hand. The tube emptied into a bottle by the side of the bed. I had been so anxious to see him that I had forgotten about my appearance. I had been up all night. My dress was the same one I had left Glamis in. I guess I didn't look my best.

We just stood there looking at one another.

"How do you feel?" I asked.

"Better. Where are the children?"

I explained to him that they were downstairs, that they weren't allowed in.

He made me tell him everything that had happened since he had left. Then he introduced me to the man in the other bed, "This is Nellie."

He didn't say, "This is my wife" or "This is Mrs. Quinn."

The man in the other bed said, "How do you do, Mrs. Quinn? Have you found a place to live?"

He spoke Spanish with a very big accent, but I understood what he was saying.

"No, we just arrived and we don't know anyone in Los Angeles."

He took a pencil and paper and wrote down an address. He said the woman there would help me find a place, and to mention his name.

After a while, I said good-bye to Francisco and left to look up the woman. Sabina and I walked down Main Street, each one carrying a child and a roll. We found the lady. I didn't know what her relationship was to the Canadian, but she moved very fast and found us a house on Clover Street, right off Main.

When I saw the house I was sure it must be some kind of mistake. It was a palace. It had one big room and two small ones. The rooms were painted in a very pretty blue color. It even had a basement downstairs and, Tony, electric lights!

Oh, Tony, I wanted that house so much but I knew there was some kind of mistake.

"How much does this cost?" I asked her.

"Do you like it?"

"I love it. But we have very little money. There must be something cheaper."

"Don't you worry about it. You move in, we'll straighten it out later."

I never knew what arrangements had been made. Maybe it was one of Francisco's secrets. He always had secrets from me. Nevertheless, we moved in.

That first night, Sabina and I didn't know where to sleep. We were so used to living in one room. We became hysterical with laughter because we couldn't decide where to sleep. Imagine having such a problem!

from

✳ My Horse Gonzalez

Fernando Alegría (translated by Carlos Lozano)

1964

Fernando Alegría was born in 1918 in Santiago, Chile. He taught at UC Berkeley for twenty years and Stanford University for more than thirty, and served as a cultural attaché from Salvador Allende's Chilean government to the United States for the three years before Allende was assassinated. A noted novelist, poet, biographer, and literary critic, he was awarded Chile's prestigious Premio Municipal for literature for *Caballo de copa* (1958), translated and excerpted below. The novel takes place in San Francisco, where a young Chilean has gone to study but instead finds himself washing dishes and dreaming of a better life.

SOME TIME AGO, I WAS WASHING DISHES in a San Francisco restaurant. Don't ask how I had sunk so low. I earned my keep and a few dollars extra by washing dishes. It was a worthy job. Worthy of a dog. In those days I was preparing for higher things which, at the time, were far from clear. Dishwashing gave me time to think and let my imagination soar. It taught me the stoic virtues of patience and understanding and, in a subtle way, served to beat down the false sense of gentlemanly dignity I had brought with me from Chile. After hours on end of scraping off the gravy they pour over mashed potatoes around here, if your stomach doesn't turn at the sight of that brownish green goo, you are either a hero or a martyr. Mashed potatoes make my hair stand on end; as for the gravy, it clouds my mind, and I'd howl if they put a spoonful of the stuff to my lips.

I was rescued from that martyrdom by a fellow countryman who dropped into the restaurant by chance one day. Without hearing me say a word, how did Hidalgo guess that I was Chilean? It must have been the sixth sense we develop abroad that makes us smell a *paisano* a mile away. Or maybe it was my looks, for I have the map of Chile on my face.

I am an auburn-haired, brown-eyed, wine-drinking Chilean, of ruddy complexion with a fine network of blood vessels on my cheeks and nose. In addition, I sport a mustache that is a riot of color, with blonde and red predominating. I come from the Central Valley of Chile. I have a big mouth, thick lips, and I laugh easily. Dress me like an Eskimo and I'd still look like a Chilean *huaso*. Maybe that's the reason Hidalgo picked me out so quickly. I was busy at the counter sink when he approached me for a match. He asked for it in Spanish. I was not surprised because I was used to the Mexicans and Basques on Broadway. As he returned the matches, he asked:

"You Chilean, ain't you?"

"Yes, friend," I replied.

"Jesus, we're countrymen," he said. "Who woulda thought it?"

"I came to San Francisco not long ago. No kidding, so you're Chilean, too?"

"Yes. I'm from the North. I was born in Antofagasta, but don't ask me anything about it because I've spent the better part of my life in Santiago."

Hidalgo's dark skin was beginning to bleach out slightly in the U.S.A. His straight black hair was stiff over the brows and the nape of his neck. When his thin lips attempted a smile, the result resembled a snarl more than anything, and his dark eyes held a scornful look. An ugly scar bisected his left cheek. A knifing? A whiplash? There was something humble about him and he seemed cowed; but his expression had a trace of mockery also and an instinctive disdain for everyone and everything. He was very small. In Chile he would have been considered a runt and dubbed *"chico"*; here in the U.S.A. he was a pygmy. He listened politely but without showing much interest, saying little. At first I thought he was shy, that perhaps he was ashamed of his poor education and believed he saw in me a more cultured and superior being. I soon realized my mistake: there was nothing shy about Hidalgo. If in the past he had lived in poverty and had been denied an education, such things were unimportant to him now. He simply didn't talk unless he had something to say. And when he did talk, he found the right words and put them in the right place, like chairs in a sparsely furnished room: you could sit on them. It was clear that he had taken a liking to me. I was obviously so green and young, my experience in this gringo country was so limited that, given his character, it was only natural that he should want to protect me.

Hidalgo settled down at a window for a couple of hours, drinking black coffee and chain-smoking, while waiting for me to get off my job. At times he read a newspaper filled with photos of horses and jockeys. Absorbed for minutes on end, he would look up occasionally, stare blankly at the people going by outside, then return to his perusal of the racing news, ticking off with a red pencil the names of the winners.

When we left the restaurant at nightfall, he asked briefly, "Where to?" and I said, "First of all, I've got to go to my hotel to change into some clean clothes, then we'll go out on the town."

We started a routine that night that we kept up for a week or two. First there would be a trip on one of the cable cars that climb up and down the San Francisco hills, past leafy parks full of statues of Italian firemen, where couples walked about arm in arm or lay on the grass making love openly and unashamed. Usually we got off at Powell and Market, where people were lined up to go to the movies, and where neon signs blinked on and off in green, red, purple, yellow, where hundreds of lightbulbs and reflectors bathed the walls of buildings, lighting up earth and sky, where monstrous posters lewdly advertised everything from deodorants to motor cars. And in the midst of this make-believe world were dark alleys where trash cans were stacked before mysterious doors and where furtive shadows prowled—hungry bums looking for scraps, queers looking for other queers, thieves looking for victims. Market Street had the atmosphere of a fair, with dark cafés where women danced almost naked, where God's age was discussed, palms were read, and jukeboxes lit up in a thousand colors could be made, for a nickel, to produce any song you wanted to hear. In these cafés, perched on stools, we drank more cheap alcohol than we were able to hold, and picked up or were picked up by dubious women who laughed too loud and had 100-proof breaths.

One night I suddenly noticed how my pygmy companion rode his bar stool: shoulders hunched, his short bowed legs dangling, his eyes watching a distant goal as if he wanted to gallop into the mirror, and occasionally his legs wrapped round the foot of the stool exactly as if wrapped about the belly of an invisible horse. We were both in a talkative mood, waging a bitter duel with a trumpet rendering an obscene version of something that sounded like a hymn from a synagogue.

"Why should I lie to you?" Hidalgo suddenly said. "Just now when you were telling me about your travels, I was thinking about my own plans. Oh yes, I have my plans. The main thing is to have dough, plenty of dough, and the only place to make dough is at the races."

"The races?"

"Sure, at the races."

"Are you...by any chance, a pickpocket?"

"Pickpocket your grandmother."

"Are you a jockey?"

"Well, I used to be a jockey. If you'd known me in Chile you wouldn't recognize me today. I was the famous 'Seven Millions.' Imagine me, now a stable boy hustling shit out of the stalls. Who'd have thought it! A stable boy, goddamn. But even so, I earn some dough, and as soon as I get a few bucks together, I intend to take off for Chile and marry a well-stacked dark broad who's waiting for me down there."

At that hour, full of cheap alcohol, the marriage idea seemed great.

"Great!" I said.

"But do you want to know why I want the dough?" he asked.

"To support your woman?"

"No. For some time I've been thinking about a project, one of those things you get to thinking about living among gringos; for the truth is that for practical and mechanical talent there ain't no one who can touch them. Of Chile's resources, do you know what should really be exploited most?"

"Women? Horses?"

"No, stupid. Fishing, that's what. The industriation...bah! The industrialization of fishing and the moderni...the moderzani...the monerdiza...hell."

"The modernization."

"That's it, of fishing. You may not believe it to look at me, but my ambition is to get ten thousand bucks, that's all, to set up a fishing fleet with all the latest improvements. Brand-new boats, good motors, and everything else. Oh, man, to be able to set up shop near Coquimbo, to sail the seas, comb them, tame them; to run my hand along their backs like horses and take out their multicolored gold: conger eel, corbina, hake, bass, and albacore. How the dough would flow in!"

Without stopping to get his breath, Hidalgo gulped down his drink.

"There is a beach near Mejillones where the sand is like a silk skirt. I'd like to spend my life there, stretched out with my face against the warm sand, breathing in the sea air. It's like having your face between the legs of a real soft woman, with that smell that comes from the sea and sets all the juices flowing. Goddamn! Squeeze me a lemon over a raw mussel, and I'm in heaven!"

Hidalgo spoke like one transfigured and from his subconscious, as from a murky pool whose clear waters appear when its surface is disturbed, the spirit of the good Creole began to rise—all the longings of a man of the sea chained to strange catacombs. He began to insist aggressively on the superiority of Chilean women and Chilean cooking. At times I couldn't tell whether he was savoring a drumstick or a woman's leg. He made everything sound sweet, whether corn pie or the kisses of a former mistress. He had got it into his head to play the jukebox and asked for "Ay, Ay, Ay" again and again, insisting that it was Chilean, not Mexican. He kept saying, "Chile, Chile, Chile." Some thought he was talking about Mexican *chili* and each time Hidalgo said "*Chile*," a drunk added by way of explanation: "*Chili* con carne, he means *chili* con carne."

That night as usual lasted until dawn and at dawn, as usual, I found myself walking along the almost empty streets with Hidalgo, zigzagging from sidewalk to the middle of the street and back again, while he kept on talking long after I had stopped listening. The air was fresh; I shivered. We finally reached the bus terminal and sagged against a wall below a sign that read "Don't Spit. $500 Fine."

The gray sky had turned pink when we reached Hidalgo's rooming house on Taylor Street, both of us as blinking and helpless as nighthawks in the first level rays of sunshine. Together with the rumble of the cable cars that were beginning to climb the hills, day was rising slowly from the sea, soon to touch the hilltops, on its way dragging the fog off the Golden Gate Bridge, stripping it from its towers in tatters, drenching itself in the green dampness of the mown lawns of the Presidio. I have seen so many dawns in 'Frisco that I can recall each phase and almost with my eyes closed can see the gray and milky hues tear away reluctantly from the black mass of the buildings and warehouses on the docks. After that, pink clouds climb to Nob Hill, then jump to the rooftops of mansions and hang there like chasubles. Then a thousand chips of light flash from the windows along Sutro and Balboa, while in the depths of the city, on the wet asphalt of Chinatown, lampposts trace in white the night's route, punctuated here and there by the slippery shadow of a hobo.

from

✳ A Pitcher's Story

Juan Marichal, with Charles Einstein

1967

Juan Marichal was born in 1937 in the Dominican
Republic. He started playing baseball as a child and was the
star pitcher in local amateur leagues as well as on the
Dominican Air Force team. Known as the "Dominican
Dandy" during his sixteen years as a pitcher for the San
Francisco Giants, he was named to nine all-star teams and
was elected to the Baseball Hall of Fame in 1983.

FOR BASEBALL EQUIPMENT when you were a farm boy in the Dominican
Republic there seldom was money, but you seldom needed it. All you
needed was fifty cents, to pay the shoemaker, and you were in business.

You made your bats, cutting them from the branches of the *vasima*
tree, which is like an apple tree, only bigger. Then you would let them
dry in the sun, and the wood would become lighter when the sun got
to it. You would then trim the bat and rub it so the handle part was
smooth. Now you had a bat.

Gloves were no problem. You took a piece of burlap, framed it
around a sheet of cardboard, sewed up the sides with fishing line, and
bent the whole thing in the middle. Now everybody's glove looked like
a first baseman's mitt. But you had a glove, and the glove even had
padding—the cardboard.

Then you would go to the golf links at Monte Cristi and find an old
golf ball and take the inside—the center—from this golf ball, then take a
woman's stocking, unravel it, and wind it patiently around the center until
it was the right size. Then you took your fifty cents and went to a shoemaker and gave it to him to sew a leather cover onto the ball.

So that was what the shoemaker and the fifty cents were for, but if you did not have fifty cents you could get almost the same effect by wrapping the ball with friction tape instead.

Carl Hubbell, who now is director of the Giants' farm system, was asked about me when I first came up to the big leagues. I had not had too long a time in the minor leagues—a season at Michigan City, a season at Springfield, Mass., half a season at Tacoma—and Hubbell was asked, "How long has he been pitching?"

"I don't rightly know," Hubbell said.

"How long would you guess?"

"All his life."

He was very close to being right when he said that.

I did not finish high school. I quit instead to play baseball. I am not proud of that, for I would have had a better future if I had finished my schooling. Even when you say you did not finish high school, it sounds as though you had gone to school up to that point where you stopped going to school—but not even that was truly so in my case, for many days I started off to school and never arrived. Or, if I did arrive, it would be late, after classes had started, and afterward the teacher would come to my mother.

"Juan is stopping on the way to school," they would tell her. "To play ball."

It was a sorrow in the life of my mother, I know. But my brother, and later my sister's husband too, were baseball enthusiasts as well. From my brother Gonzalo came my first lessons in the game, my first tips about pitching. Some of the lessons actually were conducted on horseback, for whenever I could I would ride a horse to Monte Cristi to watch Gonzalo play for the town team, and afterward he and I would both ride the same horse back to our home in Laguna Verde, and we would talk baseball on the way.

I was throwing a curve ball—a *good* curve ball—when I was perhaps ten years of age. At that time, I threw sidearm—almost underhand. Before I was fifteen, I was even experimenting with a screwball. I would work, and work, and work—at baseball, doing the things that Gonzalo showed me. In pickup games here and there I might play one position or another, but for the most part, and from the very beginning, I was always a pitcher.[...]

Today, I have purchased a new home for my mother, and she has appliances which are served by electricity furnished by a gas generator. Two miles from the river, it is already in desert country, but a new power line, running the 291 kilometers from Santo Domingo to Monte Cristi, runs directly overhead.

It may sound strange if I say that no family in Laguna Verde has use of the power line, even though it runs directly over our heads. This is because we would all have to chip in to provide the money to erect a transformer—a substation—to tap into the main line, and also because of the fire hazard, for the leaf thatching of most of the homes makes electric wiring a hazardous thing.

The farm now is larger, totaling 1,665 acres, and my brother Gonzalo works there full time. From my early baseball earnings I was able to buy a twelve-thousand-dollar tractor—a tremendous and marvelous machine—for the farm, and in addition to crops and dairying, we now have beef cattle as well.[…]

My 1960 totals with Tacoma were 11 wins, 5 losses, 12 complete games in 18 appearances, 139 innings pitched, 121 strikeouts against 34 walks. If that does not sound like a full season's work, it is because it was barely half a season's work, for almost as soon as Tom Sheehan succeeded Bill Rigney as manager of the San Francisco Giants, he called me up from Tacoma.

I was twenty-one years old at the time, and the only big-league baseball I had ever seen was on television, mainly the Cub games when I was playing with Michigan City.

With the San Francisco club there already were Felipe Alou, from the Dominican Republic, and Orlando Cepeda, from Puerto Rico. Within a year we would be joined by Felipe's brother Matty, José Pagan, and Manny Mota, and ever since that time we have had at least a couple of Spanish-speaking players, including, for a short period of time, a rookie shortstop who could not find the ball park.

The presence of Felipe was especially fortunate for me when I first joined the Giants, because he lived next door to a wonderful grandmotherly woman named Mrs. Blanche Johnson, and she and her husband took me in as a boarder, and when Matty Alou came up from Tacoma they took him in too.

Mrs. Johnson was "Mama," and I was "Baby," and it even said so on the towels in the bathroom. She taught us English, and how to live in the United States, and in turn we taught her how to cook chicken and rice and other Dominican dishes, except that I think she was being polite. Maria, Felipe's wife, knew how to cook, but Matty and I were not very good at it. Even worse, we actually preferred American food a lot of the time, but "Mama" thought we would get homesick if we did not have a lot of Dominican dishes, and we found a place on Fillmore Street where you could get the same kind of fish as in the Dominican Republic.

So my American education began in earnest—largely on a Dominican diet.

"Mama," I said to her one time, "the best way to learn how to eat a steak like an American is for us to have a steak for dinner."

"You already know how to eat a steak," she said.

"I would like to practice some more."

"Practice on the rice and the chicken. Then you will feel right at home."

Gradually, we became Americanized, and the food became a magnificent blending of our dishes and hers. To this day, she comes often to our house, and we go to hers, and there is always activity in the kitchen, and music, and singing.

Also, "Mama" has given up on insisting that we speak only English in her presence—not because she quits easily, but because she feels, and correctly, that her main job—teaching us the new language—had been completed.

A Red Palm

Gary Soto

1995

Gary Soto was born in 1952 in Fresno to Mexican
American parents who worked as farm laborers. A poet,
short-story writer, essayist, novelist, playwright, and editor,
Soto has written more than forty books of fiction, poetry,
drama, and autobiographical essays for adults and children.
He has taught English and ethnic studies at the University
of California and traveled the country as the Young People's
Ambassador for California Rural Legal Assistance and the
United Farm Workers of America.

You're in this dream of cotton plants.
You raise a hoe, swing, and the first weeds
Fall with a sigh. You take another step,
Chop, and the sigh comes again,
Until you yourself are breathing that way
With each step, a sigh that will follow you into town.

That's hours later. The sun is a red blister
Coming up in your palm. Your back is strong,
Young, not yet the broken chair
In an abandoned school of dry spiders.
Dust settles on your forehead, dirt
Smiles under each fingernail.
You chop, step, and by the end of the first row,
You can buy one splendid fish for wife
And three sons. Another row, another fish,
Until you have enough and move on to milk,
Bread, meat. Ten hours and the cupboards creak.

You can rest in the backyard under a tree.
Your hands twitch on your lap,
Not unlike the fish on a pier or the bottom
Of a boat. You drink iced tea. The minutes jerk
Like flies.

　　　　It's dusk, now night,
And the lights in your home are on.
That costs money, yellow light
In the kitchen. That's thirty steps,
You say to your hands,
Now shaped into binoculars.
You could raise them to your eyes:
You were a fool in school, now look at you.
You're a giant among cotton plants.
The lung-shaped leaves that run breathing for miles.

Now you see your oldest boy, also running.
Papa, he says, it's time to come in.
You pull him into your lap
And ask, What's forty times nine?
He knows as well as you, and you smile.
The wind makes peace with the trees,
The stars strike themselves in the dark.
You get up and walk with the sigh of cotton plants.
You go to sleep with a red sun on your palm,
The sore light you see when you first stir in bed.

from

❅ The Plum Plum Pickers

Raymond Barrio

1969

Raymond Barrio (1921–1996) was born in New Jersey and lived most of his life in California. As much a visual artist as a writer, he taught art and literature at several San Francisco Bay Area colleges and wrote articles for art, travel, and literary magazines. His seventh and most famous book, *The Plum Plum Pickers* (1969), is considered by many to be the first major novel about Chicano migrant workers to be published in the United States. It was originally turned down by every publisher Barrio offered it to, so he published it himself, and within two years it had become an underground classic, selling more than ten thousand copies. It was then published by Harper & Row and is now widely respected both as an effective indictment of an unjust economic system and as a masterful piece of writing.

LIFE IS LIKE A RIVER, FLOWING RELENTLESSLY.

The nascent Guadalupe River of San José, starting its life as a vast hopeful network of tiny brooks and freshets high up among the rocky crevices of the Santa Cruz range, finding out what life was about, rushes down the hilly sides, gathers, then slowly peters out. It meanders north alongside Almaden Road all through the city of San José, a crooked charming chasm hidden behind rows of residential MJB boxes, beneath overhanging weeping willows, its IBM slopes at times cemented in, and limps past San José's SOC Airport. It then skirts Laurelwood Road, passes near the Southern Pacific's magnificently unguarded r.r. crossing at Lafayette Street, ambles past acres of broad, open tomato fields, flows past Agnews State Mental Hospital, trickles past sinking Alviso, past stinking garbage pits, past sunken Drawbridge, and finally disgorges itself into the enormously profitable salt flats abounding in and around the southern tip of San Francisco's bay.

If the vast Santa Clara tomato fields, bursting green with red life, heavy with a quarter of a million round, hard fruit per acre, reaching easily to the moon and back, were aching to be picked; if they had not been well cared for, well cultivated, well planted, well manured, well weeded, and well irrigated, they were also somehow to some extent dependent upon thousands of miserable tomato pickers trying their best to keep up with nature's glut and at the same time trying to work their own way out of their misery. Every fruit identical, sweet, delicious, bugless, bulging with nutriments, hundreds of thousands of tomato-bearing plants had done their work well, impeccably, impersonally, perfectly, in this most ideal of all benign climes.

Next project on the board's agenda: why not turn the ant people into automatic pickers and save the cost of an internal

HOW TO PICK CANNING TOMATOES
—by the Agricultural Extension Service of the
University of California—

★

THE tomato harvest is very important in
California. Many people share the income from
it—pickers, farmers, truckers, cannery
workers, can manufacturers, chemical
manufacturers, and many others.

machine? Every plant would by then be absolutely perfect. Every picker perfect too. No complainers. In marked contrast, in their own board meetings in the fields, all that the

A LITTLE "know-how" will make your work
easier and will help you to earn more money.

miserable migrants had to worry about was their everlasting hunger, their basic insecurity, and their miserable worthless existence, where they plotted whether they really existed or not.

And in all that heady gardening, all the growers growing everything they could, mightily, greenbacks back to back, and all the glands of agri-combines owned by holding companies holding their regular hoard meetings, engendering still more agriblobconglomerates up and down the agricoast, the ups and downs of the greedy agridollar coasters had also to be computed. Plant more. Make more. Raise more. Sell more. Eat less. Many happy combines, thank you. Sappy happy company heads. Paying off their collegiate kids. Threading pears to the moon. And all those lands were all owned by, controlled by, inflated by still vaster holders buried in the ticker-tape emporiums, far from the madding migrants. What golden crops could be sown. When they were to be planted. When to be rotated. Rotation is great. What projects. Plans encompassed even an unborn city upon these very sinking salt marshes as part of the biggest master plan of all—to fill in the whole San Francisco Bay entirely. Just leave a little trickle of a stream locked in a cement-lined tube under Main Street, where the Golden Gate used to be. No more bay. No more cool waters. No more lapping waves. An enormous greed was growing, a greed that knew no bounds. Why should it? Wasn't greed the greatest, the most powerful human emotion, after killing? And who or what was powerful enough around to stop it? Nothing. And so the growers and the corporations and the holding companies and the combines grew bigger and happier and tighter and fatter and wealthier and smarter and kindlier

IN THIS leaflet, we offer suggestions that may
be helpful to both new and experienced tomato pickers.

★

WEAR COMFORTABLE clothes. Old ones
are fine. A straw hat to shade your head. Some
workers wear cloth or rubber gloves to protect
their hands from tomato leaf stains. Tomato
juice will remove these stains from hands.

disposed to hypocritical charity drives. And why not? Everything paid, paid well, nay, paid handsomely.

It was therefore only natural that the most bootlicking, short-sighted, inhumane, egotistical, inchoate, despicable, contemptuous, tawdry, and most deceptive trick on earth was to exhume some lordly profit out of human misery. And among the most knowledgeable in-group, it was almost universally conceded that Fredrick C. (Combine) Turner managed neatly to turn this trick, antwise and otherwise, and also to appear virtuous at it as well, with no excrementa showing, without experiencing even the slightest tinge or nidge of inner pain or shame. And Turner, in turn, all full of good intentions on his way to hell, was all pure, pure-all.

He was a great sparkling symbol of California's grand wine and dine club, eat and be merry, give 'em cake, me fustest with the mustest, combining everything: land, water, taxes, corruption, population, levies, pickers. Turner, consistently one of America's ten best-dressed men, his flaming ascot fluffed boldly out of his scrawny neck, to show how nonconformist he was when he felt like it, to hell with the kids, rated highly in Fortune—also in southern Texas—as well as in Dun & Brad—even in the USSR—and, of all places, last but not least, in the BBR, the Bastards' & Brothers' Roasting. There sure was nothing like saintliness for getting next to holiness and godliness, the good lord knew, though few mortals knew, but Turner also knew.

Meanwhile, however, back at the raunchy ranch, the tempestuous tomatoes kept right on ripening and growing wildly, as though there were nothing more important in the world as their

> TAKE a (10) ten (10) minute cotton-picking
> rest period midmorning & afternoon.
> YOU'LL pick just as many tomatoes
> AND you won't be so tired.
>
> ★
>
> BRING two sandwiches with you.
> EAT one in the morning.
> AND one in the afternoon.
> A little food will give you more energy.
> THE grower will furnish drinking water.
> AND toilets near where you are picking.

ripening inexorably toward their only possible solution—getting picked—so someone could eat them.[...]

Manuel's eyes clicked open inside the blackness of the tent. He saw nothing. Three days' steady [strawberry] picking. And another night's nervous sleep. His mind suddenly awakened fully, as though snapped on by a switch. His body ached from the previous day's picking, aches that were drugged partially but not entirely wiped out by the relieving drafts of wine he took before falling asleep. All his muscles were stiff. The tiredness would wear off. He would just walk around a little and stretch his legs. He knew he would get his strength back, to go at it again for another straight eight, ten, twelve hours' picking.

Lupe, still sleeping, was breathing deeply. Baby Cati, her plump round little body wedged between them on the ground, was also asleep. So were Manuelito and Mariquita, on their lumpy pads. Manuel was proud of his neat little family. He worried over Lupe's constant worrying about their constant scurrying about, their never seeming to get ahead. He could not answer. He did not know the answers. He was strong and healthy, wasn't he. She worried too much. That was woman for you. Wasn't he healthy and strong? "But what will I do if something happens to you, Manuel?" Do? How did he know? Why must she worry so? She had nothing to worry about. They slept. They traveled. Oh yes, sure, they sure traveled all right. But wasn't he healthy and strong? That was the only answer he had. The only answer he could have—for he had no future.

The cotton pad they slept on was shaped by sharp clots of painful earth and rocks beneath them which they were too tired to do anything about. Stupid dogs knew how to get off sharp rocks, as California's great golden Governor (Howlin Mad) Nolan astutely pointed out, from his own movie-making days, because they are lively and full of energy. But dog-tired human beings somehow had a much harder time coping with such a simple problem as how to sleep on lumpy clods of earth at night when you put your bedding out in the dark. Oh yes, the güeros do like to go camp-ing, but somehow that didn't seem like the same thing. And Lupe was beyond comprehension as to how anyone could like going camping. The tarp shielded the moisture but not the cold from below. Manuel wished he could sleep more. It was no use. He lifted himself carefully on one elbow so as not to waken the others. The children's innocence let them sleep deeply. The sleep he was losing would haunt him late in the day, like an uppercut. He knew that. Wine would relax him. He was already looking forward to it. Wine would also bring along with it an overpowering urge to simply pass out on the works, in the rows, on the ground, or in the Sun and bake, if he made it that far.

They were getting along nicely—The Sun and He.

In summer everything ripened at once. It was imperative to get in all the outside work possible. It was good to have so much work avail-able. He wished it would never run out. He would like to pick fruit all year round, if only they'd invent year-round trees so as to make the work steady. For when he worked he could feed his whole family handily. [...]

Lupe's recurrent daytime nightmares kept tormenting her. Ants and roaches and earwigs and hundreds of mice scurrying around her, from under the house, cockroaches getting inside the coffeepot, fighting small wars over luscious scraps of fresh ripe garbage. Burrowing into the soft cool mother earth. Poison sprays would stop them—they sprayed. The despicable bugs with their baleful looks disappeared. But they came back again a little later, starting all over, in bigger droves, as big as horses, bigger and more ferocious and more daring. They needed newer and more powerful insecticides because the coked roaches kept on getting bigger, fattening on the poison, and her children kept getting smaller as though they weren't getting enough food. It drove her mad. Many times at night, Manuel had to wake her out of her turbulent sleep when she started in moaning or screaming. Had she known that Fred Turner had to do the same for his wife, Jean, Lupe might have felt better.

What a mess her hair was in. How could she ever comb it? It wasn't often she felt so depressed. Washing the baby's pañales, steamy water, sloshing, squidging, squeezing, one window pane cracked, another broken, cardboard, row of bric-a-brac, two avocado trees, one empty pit, one dried chile plant, shriveled black little chiles once so fair and plump and green now so bare and gaunt, and little paper cutouts from Manuelito's drawings. A Christmas scene. And some rocks she'd picked up at the beach, an old ashtray…

She knew she was simply being nervous. Or bitter. In her bitter moments she sometimes lost her self-control. She gave thanks, gracias a Dios, that this time it was only her period that was making her so tense and nervous.

"Frijoles, mujer!" He knew how to make her smile. "Where are my blessed frijoles, woman?" Manuel could not keep his stomach full without beans. She knew so many intricate ways to cook the delectable bean. Boiling and softening them, she could fry, mash, smash, and then refry them. She mixed them with rice to make delicious morisqueta. Tacos were marvelous with their fine heart of chopped meat, topped with a fiery smiling chile sauce. Cheese-melting enchiladas, and frijoles refritos. Chiles rellenos, long hot green chile peppers filled with sardine, dipped in egg batter and fried along with frijoles refritos. Everything went better with beans. And there was always maíz. Beans from the moon and corn from the golden sun. Corn for thick plump tamales, corn for tortillas—

"What are we having tonight, corazón?" She would try to shut off her anxieties by thinking of things that could go wrong. What would she do if something happened to her Manuel? Suppose he got sick? Well that, even that wouldn't be the worst. They'd always managed sickness. But—hurt? Or—worse? Well, she was strong. She could work herself. She could always find something. But—the children? Here was Manuelito already six and she still couldn't get him into kindergarten, they moved around so much.

She sat, licking the end of the thread, trying to sew the long tear in Cati's playsuit, given to her by Olive Pope. And what was all this struggling for? Suppose Mr. Turner sold his land? Or his business? Or simply went to Mexico to retire? Or stopped giving Manuel work for any number of unforeseeable reasons? What would they do? Travel north to Oregon and Washington again? Was it only that she wanted to have more? Was it a sin to want more? Wasn't it a sin not to have enough to live decently? When you saw everyone around you, and you wanted what they had, was that sinful? What sin, dear God? Padre, is it immortal sin that I shall have to carry to my grave on my dying day to wish to see that evil old Mr. Turner hanging from the Hangman's Tree in place of the straw dummy? The very evilness of the thought made her shudder.

"Manuelito, ven acá!" She could work. She had already worked. The strawberries, true, were too hard for her. She did better in the prunes. She saw other families, living in their own homes nearby, go out to the prunes for a few days or weeks, pick all they could or wanted to, get paid, and go home each night. She could see that. That wasn't too bad. And as part-time extra work, for extra income, it was fine. But she also had to take care of her own children. When the children were bigger, like Serafina's, then they surely would be able to earn more. Lupe vowed to herself that she would spark ambition in her own children, somehow. She would have to. The next, the most immediate problem was how to get Manuelito into school this next fall. If they had to move again, there would be no chance to get him started. May dear God—

She saw that Margarita also suffered. Such a young girl, and already so much a woman. Lupe's motherly heart went out to her. A woman didn't need a profession; only had to get herself a good man. Margarita was getting an education; she studied hard. Still, she was unhappy. Why was Pepe so strict with her? Was her heart struck? Margarita would know how to raise her own children. She was serious. Had she known what love was? Had she fallen in love with Ramiro? Would Ramiro come back? For two weeks now he'd been gone; it was sad, a sadness no tears could wash away. But she was young. She still had plenty more years to grow sadder by.

Picking fruit was only a part-time evil. The insecurity was the worst of it. It was evil to get trapped, to be on tap, to be used like a faucet, on and off when beckoned, instead of being fed T-bones every blessed day. The picking part of it was healthy enough; the meager pay and the insecurity were the evil.

"Mamacita!" Then, after she had convinced herself and had convicted the system, Manuel came home with absolutely wonderful news: "Mamacita! You must guess, guess—!" Mr. Schroeder had actually offered him a job, him of all workers, to work part-time in his nursery. Part-time through the winter, and maybe full-time by spring. Mr. Schroeder couldn't afford another full-time worker just yet, but it was steady work. "Permanent and steady work mamacita, and for a year!" Manuel could easily pick up extra odd jobs in his leftover time. But now, now they had a base that would let them stay put in one place. They might even rent a house, a poor one of course, but their own house. Maybe they could even get a credit card. Lupe burst into tears.

"Caramba, mujer, why are you crying? You are not happy with such wonderful news?"

"Sí, sí, sí, of course, corazón—" She sobbed uncontrollably, out of sheer joy. "You ah you are not fooling me, you, Manuel?" They were happy tears. The first happy tears she'd shed in she didn't know how long. They felt so good. So clean. Did that also mean…that they might start Manuelito in school next…next month? Soon?

"Sí, sí, mi corazón. Of course."

She had so much to be grateful to America for, so grateful now, so many happy tears. And maybe now, dear God, ay Dios—perhaps, maybe now she would also be able to plant her very own little Mexican avocado tree in a permanent spot too, her very own tree!

from

 # Macho!

Victor Villaseñor

1991

Victor Villaseñor was born in 1940 in Carlsbad, California,
to Mexican immigrants. Struggling with dyslexia severe
enough to interfere with his speech and comprehension, let
alone reading and writing, Villaseñor dropped out of high
school and went to work in the fields. In his determination
to master language, however, he discovered his passion for
literature and has since produced more than sixty short stories and eight novels, including the highly acclaimed *Macho!*
(1973), the national best-seller *Rain of Gold* (1991), and its
sequel, *Thirteen Senses: A Memoir* (2001). He is also the
author of a book of nonfiction, a screenplay which was produced by PBS, and a book of short stories for young adults.
Villaseñor currently travels the country speaking about
dyslexia, his writing, and his nonprofit peace organization,
Snow Goose Global Thanksgiving.

AT FIVE-THIRTY A LITTLE LIGHT began breaking in the east. They drove
around. They saw a light in the kitchen of a work camp. They went in. It
was a huge kitchen with enormous pots. There was only one cook. He
was making coffee. They asked for coffee. He said, sure. They asked about
the melons. He told them the melons had not started. There was no work
in town. The cantaloupes began here in six weeks. Now the melon work
was farther south. In Huron. Or anywhere around Bakersfield. They
thanked him for the coffee, got back in their car, cursed the family who
had given them the wrong information, and drove off.

Now as they drove through town they could see that this town was
indeed deserted. Windblown. Resembling a ghost town. And yet, in six

weeks, with the melons, this same town would be bursting with men. Booming! Like a gold-rush town. All the bars full. All the sidewalks covered with men. All the markets open most of the night. They now drove out of the ghost town and headed east to catch big Freeway 99 and shoot south. They would try Huron first; then, if they didn't have any luck, they'd go on to Bakersfield and out toward Pumpkin Center, Greenfield, and Weed Patch.

After many more bad leads and a lot of arguments about the gas, they found work in the melons south of Bakersfield, at the foot of the great mountains between Bakersfield and Los Angeles. There, in Kern County, one of the richest farmlands in the world, they found plenty of work, and they worked at the melons, one of the physically hardest of all farm labor. Starting with the first light of day, they would straddle a row, bend down, and pick with heavy sacks on their backs. There were six men on each side of each truck, and every man would have his own row and he would walk along bent over, move the leaves, select only the large, three-quarter-size, ripe melons, pick them, toss them over his shoulder into his sack, fill the sack, and trot quickly to the truck, race up the two-by-twelve ramp which dragged along behind the truck, dump his sixty or eighty pounds of melons, race down the other board, jump over the rows of melons, get to his own row, straddle it, bend over, and start selecting, picking, and tossing them over his shoulder, filling his sack. Quickly. The faster the better, for soon the sun would be too hot, and they were getting paid so much per truck.

Each *cuadrilla,* group, had twelve men, and each *cuadrilla* was paid so much per truck, and so they hurried. They ran bent over in the fields, they trotted quickly to the ever-creeping-along-beside-them truck and trailer, and then raced up the two-by-twelve board. Short quick steps, trying to keep balance, holding the sack of melons from swaying, yelling at the driver, who's always trying to creep ahead faster than the men can pick, slow down, dammit! Or we'll quit loading you! The driver would act like he didn't hear, but still he'd slow down for a little while.

Then it was ten in the morning and the sun was hot and the men didn't run anymore. They began to walk, to lug up the ramp, flip-flop down the ramp, wipe the dripping sweat out of their eyes, line up at the five-gallon water tank tied to the side of the truck, take the empty can of Coors with a wire tied to it like a handle, fill it half up with ice-cold water, rinse, spit, drink, pass it to the next man, and return to the field. Refreshed. And so they would briskly walk out two or three or six rows, straddle, bend over, and begin selecting. Now it was truly hot. It was eleven, and all the melons were beginning to look bad. Too green. Too small. Too burned by the sun. And, for these bad ones, one didn't get paid. They'd get thrown out at the packing shed. Only the good ones were taken from the truck, boxed, and shipped, and one got paid by the number of boxes shipped per truck.

Then it was noon, and Roberto was still racing. He straddled, he bent over, he walked along selecting fast. Picking with his left hand, passing to his right hand, and tossing over his right shoulder into the sack. He picked and tossed and tossed and tossed. He yelled at Luis and Aguilar and Ramón.

"The melons! They're heavy over here!"

"Good," said Luis, and moved over to him. "They're thin here."

"I got plenty," said Ramon.

"Don't pick the green ones!" said Aguilar.

Ramón and Luis were all right, but Aguilar was tired and he was working near the ever-creeping truck. He was drained. The sun was blazing. It was at least a hundred and eight degrees in the shade, but they were not in the shade. They were out in midfield, ten to thirty degrees hotter than the shade. The melons themselves that were not shaded by leaves were burning into wrinkled-up little balls. Roberto came at a trot over the rows with a full sack of melons. Aguilar saw him. He smiled. That boy could truly work. They'd already filled six trucks and trailers. As much as the best *cuadrillas,* and this boy was still running. There he went, back bent under his load of melons. So many melons that they were up over the top of his sack. Three, four, resting on his back. Two others in his left arm in front. A good eighty or ninety pounds, and he hit the two-by-twelve at a run. Short quick steps, working to keep balance. He dumped, he turned, and came running down the other ramp as the truck moved forward. Aguilar called him.

"Boy, not so fast. Don't do work for the others. Save your strength for the whole harvest season. You know we all twelve split the number of boxes at the end of the day." Roberto smiled. Dripping with sweat. Soaking through all his clothes with dark wetness. Eight salt tablets a day he took. "Yes. But there is so much melon." He raised up his new American straw hat. A big golfer's type hat. "We're going to get rich! Six trucks and trailers today so far. Twelve loads. Maybe we can make fifteen or sixteen by two o'clock. Yesterday we made twelve." He wiped his face with his long-sleeved shirt. He blew his nose by putting a finger on one side and then on the other side. Dirt and sweat and snot blew out. He smiled hugely. Wiping his hands on his pants. "God, we'll maybe make thirty-five dollars apiece today." And he rushed over the rows, yelling at the six men on this side of the truck. Six men took six rows on each side of the always creeping truck. "Hurry! Pick only good ones! Fill up these trucks! And by God! I'll do more than my share!" Some men laughed and yelled back at him. They liked him. He was truly a good, strong, enduring workman. Others said nothing. They just grumbled. They didn't like him. He was too good. He made them look bad, and yesterday, because of him, two men had been fired by the *cuadrilla* boss. Each *cuadrilla* had a headman who was elected by the men to keep count of the trucks, keep check on the men, and make sure of the division of their pay. This *cuadrilla* boss liked Roberto, liked the way he worked and talked and pushed the men in a good-happy manner, and yesterday he had reported to the foreman that he had two slow men in his *cuadrilla* and he wanted them replaced. The foreman, proud of this fast-working *cuadrilla* which made him look good to the field boss, took the two men and put them on a slow *cuadrilla* of old men and winos. These bad *cuadrillas* filled only two or three trucks and trailers in a whole day. And they made only twelve or fifteen dollars per man a day.

At twelve-thirty the lunch truck came. The men stopped work, the headman went and got their boxes of lunch. They all gathered around the truck they were loading and lay down in its shade, panting and sweating like dogs on a chase, and began to eat. Each man was given a brown paper bag with six tacos. Three of bean and three of dried-out beef stew. They bitched about Gordo's cooking. They laughed. They ate. Mouths open. The tacos were warm because of the sun. They drank water to wash them down. Coke and beer were available but cost extra. Twenty-five cents a can. Either one. Same price. And, in the wino *cuadrillas,* some wino would have a cold gallon jug of cheap mountain red and sell a canful for seventy-five cents. A fantastic profit.

With lunch over, the good *cuadrillas* would go back to work. Quickly. Renewed. Refreshed. And strong. While the bad *cuadrillas* would buy more beer, more wine, more Coke, and collapse.

Like that they worked hard all week, and many men were fired off the good *cuadrillas* and put on the bad ones, and in the bad ones two men collapsed that week. Fell down with their sacks on their backs, and that was that. They were winos, they were old men, they were no good for the melon work, and they were taken off the job. But in Roberto's *cuadrilla* no one fell. They were the best, and they worked on and never looked back. The pay was good and the season was short and they had to get all they could. Now! Quickly! Pick the melon, fill the trucks. The trucks were filled and the boxes were shipped east by rail, and the cantaloupe business was in full swing. Their grower–shipper–owner was moving fifteen thousand boxes per day and making good money. Depending on the day's market. Some days he'd make as much as $2 per box. His cost was at a steady $4.50 per box, and the daily market was keeping at $6 and $6.50 per box. That made him $22,500 to $30,000 per day. Everyone was making money. It was one of the best years in the last five years for cantaloupes.

Roberto earned $235.50 that first week for a seven–day week and was given $216.50, and out of this he spent only $35 for his living: $24.50 for his board and room and $10 more for 7-Up, beer, and a few personal things. Aguilar took another $50 from him. That was their deal. One–fourth of his earnings. He had $121.50 left. He kept the $21.50 and had the rest sent home to his sister through the office. He figured he had now sent home a total of $160 American, so he now wrote the letter to his sister and told her to give some money to their father so he could buy a milk cow. But for her not to give him the money until he promised not to drink the money. For her to read this letter aloud to him in front of the whole family.

"Father," he added to the letter, "this is my money. I've worked hard to earn it. If you do not do as I ask, I will not send you any more money. On the other hand, if you do as I ask, I will keep sending money and I will bring you home any gift you, personally, wish. A rifle? Or a many-shot shotgun if you wish? Or a radio that plays with batteries? Anything. There is much money to be made here. But understand, it is not easy like we think back home. Here, in one day, I work harder and sweat more than in a week at home. We are not in the mountains. We are in a valley. Flat and deep and hot, and richer than your highest dreams. The soil, you can smell its richness. And the rivers, they lose not one drop of water. They are enclosed in concrete.

"This land has water and soil and machinery and crops, such huge crops of the deepest richest green, that ten days on a horse would not cross half of them. And each hectare is like gold. The soil's that rich.

"Father, take care of my money. It is ours. Our family's. And if I can keep finding work, we will soon be able to buy a ranch, and cattle, and be a people to whom the word 'Don' will be addressed."

Then he wrote some words of warmth to his mother…to his mother and to the children and to his sister Esperanza, who would be in charge of the money, the correspondence, and all legal papers of their different purchases.

He breathed.

He lay down and dreamed of the future. He fell asleep. The alarm went off. He got up. Heavy. He was getting tired. This was not so good. But after eating he was strong once more and he worked all day, and the days passed, the weeks passed, and all was good for him, a strong young man. He worked seven days a week. He worked and ate and slept and had no time to notice how the faces were changing in his *cuadrilla*. The weaker were being put aside.

Then the melons were done. No more work. But they, the strong, were told to go north, and they were given a paper with an address. And these strong ones got rides on buses and cars, and they went a few miles north, and the work continued.

✺ Cotton Rows, Cotton Blankets

Diana García

2000

Diana García was born in 1950 in a labor camp in California's
San Joaquin Valley. A single mother, she worked odd jobs
along the way to becoming a professor of creative writing and
world literatures. She has taught college courses on the East
Coast and in Germany and is now teaching at California
State University, Monterey Bay. Her work appears in several
anthologies, and her first volume of poetry, *When Living Was a
Labor Camp* (2001), won an American Book Award.

Sprawled on the back of a flatbed truck
we cradled hoes, our minds parceling rows
of cotton to be chopped by noon. Dawn stuck
in the air. Blackbirds rang the willows.

Ahead, a horse trailer stretched across the road.
Braced by youth and lengths of summer breeze
we didn't give a damn. We'd be late, we joked,
stalled by a pregnant mare draped in sheets.

Later, backs to the sun, bandannas tied
to shade our brows, hands laced with tiny cuts;
later, when the labor contractor
worked us through lunch without water; our dried
tongues cursed that mare in cotton blankets
brought to foal in the outlines of summer.

✳ Aching Knees in Palm Springs

John Olivares Espinoza

2002

John Olivares Espinoza was born in 1978 in Indio,
California, and spent his youth landscaping with his brothers
and father, a Mexican immigrant. He is the author of two
poetry chapbooks, *Gardeners of Eden* (2000) and *Aluminum
Times* (2002), and was the recipient of a Paul and Daisy
Soros Fellowship for New Americans. A graduate of the
University of California, Riverside, he is currently earning
his M.F.A. in creative writing at Arizona State University.

One gray Thursday in winter break, Albert
And I plucked patches of grass from petunia
Beds wide as swimming pools, within a condo
Complex—these are one-story stucco blocks
For old men wiping sweat with dollar bills.
We spent our school vacations in shivers:
Raking, trimming, and mowing frosted yards
With Dad. During the eighth hour of kneeling,
The weight on my knees was too much for me
To go on—I was no big-league catcher.
For each fistful of grass, I stood up to stretch
And let the cold air sneak under my shirt.
When Dad noticed the weeds slowly filling
The can, he turned to me red-faced and said,
"You're packing down the dirt, kneel on the lawn
And weed the beds from there." I said, "Being bent
Down since nine this morning, I'm at least entitled
To some circulation." I kept the truth

From slipping past my chapped lips,
How I didn't care about dirt
And weeds from a bourgeois
Garden, these few men I learned
About in sociology class—
Who raked in more hundred-dollar
Bills than I did citrus leaves
In a long day. I wanted to tell
Dad that these men didn't care
If Mexicans spent ten hours—
Or even a full lifetime—
Bent as old limbs of lemon wood,
Weeding again the same bed
The following week. To only tell
Him about the hours I felt wasted
When we could've rested our sore backs
On a bed, and drowned in a lake
Of a much-deserved sleep, or sailed
Through Tierra del Fuego, us standing
On the deck and never bowing,
Not even to the sun.
Or how he could have learned to read
And I would finally show him
A poem I wrote. But I didn't.
Because I knew what he would say:
"It's the only way to put you
Through school, this oily sweat."
I kept my tongue hidden

Behind my teeth, and watched
My young brother hunched over,
Tossing fresh weeds and years
Inside a green plastic can
Without a single word.

from

✸ Where the Sun Don't Shine

Dagoberto Gilb

1993

Dagoberto Gilb was born in 1950 in Los Angeles to a
Mexican American mother and German father. Gilb earned
an M.A. in philosophy and religion but worked in construction for more than a decade before publishing his first
short-story collection, *The Magic of Blood* (1993), which
won the 1994 PEN Hemingway Award and was a PEN
Faulkner Award finalist. He is the author of another short-
story collection and one novel, and his stories have
appeared in several magazines, including the *New Yorker,
Ploughshares,* and *Harper's Magazine.* He has taught writing
at colleges in California, Arizona, and Wyoming and is currently a professor at Southwest Texas State University.

USUALLY SAL ENJOYED HIS BREAKS BETWEEN JOBS and he acted like some
kid who had legal ID and enough money to buy his partners a few
rounds, a short to take a pretty barmaid for a ride, and a few quarters to
lag at a circle. But not this time. This time took too long, and his unem-
ployment money would run out soon and his daughters wanted some
new clothes for starting school and his wife was getting worried because
she was pregnant. Sal had even stopped going down to the Bar de Los
Angeles. Instead he sat around his house and watched TV.

So it felt good when he got on at a luxury condominium, its
structural steel just coming out of the hole, on the edge of Beverly Hills.
It was a big job, twenty above and four down, and he could get at least
nine months out of it, more if they liked him, and, if they liked him
enough, more still at some other rich high-rise they could transfer him

to. That had happened to him before, because the big shots usually liked his work. All the men said that he should be a foreman, that he'd make a great foreman. It wasn't just wishful thinking on his part to think good things about this job.

And it was even better than that since down at the bottom of the dark hole, D-level of parking it would be, Sal's first five minutes were filled with shaking the hands of old carpenter and laborer buddies from other jobs. It was a lot easier, among good friends, to lift his boots out of moist, ungraded dirt, to drive double-headed nails in the heat of 250-amp lamps, and Sal settled into the job quickly. And it wasn't long before lunch break was just another time to sit around with the guys and talk about the mysteries of sex, the high cost of everything, or the incompetence of men in every trade but their own. Or the poor way the men with the shiny white hardhats made the men with the scruffy orange and blue and green hardhats work.

"I remember that job downtown," Augustín said, "and they wouldn't give us a morning coffee break. Sal says, 'I was looking for a job before I found this one!' and sits down with the ironworkers on this pile of rebar. So this foreman goes, 'That sounds good to me!' and heads to the office and everybody knows Sal's gonna get his check. But this guy sits there like nothing in the world bothers him and gets back to work only after the ironworkers do. And nothing, not a thing happens to him! A week later we're all taking a coffee break."

"Why don't we get a morning break no more?" Sal asked the union steward, cutting through the chuckles that surrounded him.

"It's not in the contract. The company doesn't have to give us a break if it doesn't wanna."

"That's bullshit."

"That's the times. Too many hungry men on the books. The company figures that they don't hafta go outa their way being nice."

Sal shook his head with disgust, knowing that the man spoke the truth, and soon he was back in the hole forming columns and walls, helping his foreman lay some grade marks for the first slab. No matter what, he needed to get healthy first, and he got along good enough with the foremen, all except the general foreman who nobody got along with, who for some reason hated just about everyone's guts, especially, rumor had it, those that didn't begin at lily pink lips. He was a hard man to disregard since he made a special point of watching and checking over everything the men did. But Sal promised his wife he'd ignore it, though he didn't like it, though the other men already talked, because they knew Sal and anticipated another one of his memorable confrontations.

"Down at that Figueroa Street job," Rudy was telling the apprentice Jamaal, "Salvador was decking out this ramp that curved, and this redneck foreman come up to him and told him he was doing it all wrong. Salvador didn't pay any attention to the shit and that got him really pissed. So they started saying 'Fuck you!' to each other and calling each other names and came to blows. The whole job site stopped working to watch that. Salvador kicked the shit out of him and they both ended up in the office. We got to fuck around until quitting time, and the next day that foreman didn't come back. They told us he got transferred."

"It musta been a hundred degrees that day," Sal explained.

"And when Salvador got rehired a few days later it was in the eighties, the cabrón," said Rudy.

Two weeks went by as well as possible. Sal was getting a lot of the job's overtime, even the double time, and he and the general foreman rarely spoke to one another, even so much as to say good morning or good night. Then, in the eleventh hour twilight of a very long, humid day, Sal, this man, two laborers, and two other foremen were fighting to push a cement hose into a long, narrow dirt opening so they could pour an odd footing. They'd been battling with it for a good forty minutes and sweat made the dank hole dirt smear them in more places than their clothes and body, and now Sal was translating the general foreman's instructions into Spanish for the two laborers.

"It's not that they don't understand what you want," Sal said as patiently as he could, "and not that we're not trying hard enough. It's that it can't be done this way."

"We've got eight yards of cement waiting on us and a driver who wants to go home and this has to be done tonight. Now are we gonna stand here and talk or do you wanna get the job done? "

"Tell him how you want to do it," Benito told Sal in Spanish. Elario nodded in agreement.

"I have this idea," Sal said with contempt disguised as modesty. "You wanna hear it?"

"Jesuschrist!" the general foreman fumed, stomping away from them.

"What is it?" the labor foreman asked Sal.

"We take some wire and we feed it through the hole, then we tie the wire around some rope, pull the rope through, then tie the rope to the hose and pull it through."

"Do it," the carpenter foreman said.

While they stood around, ten minutes later, listening to the cement slop in, filling up the footing hole, the men relaxed and talked and Sal thought he'd try to break the ice with the general foreman. And so he asked, good-naturedly, "Are you buying the beer tonight?"

The man looked at him, scowled, walked over to the scaffold stairs and stepped up three metal flights to the office trailer.

There was a time when Sal wouldn't have let something like that pass by, but the union books were full, the wait was long, and he needed hours to keep up his medical benefits. And he'd promised his wife. For once he would say nothing, he would leave it to someone else. All the men had the same problems with this man, he reasoned, so why not let someone else play hero for a change? He wouldn't let it bother him.

And so he practiced. When an ironworker working above him with a torch and goggles showered him with glittering hot slag, Sal held in his rage and walked away from his own work area and waited until the man finished, and then he asked him to be more careful. He didn't say anything when the ironworker did the same thing an hour later to another carpenter, though he felt better that the carpenter, who screeched, also told the steward. It was, after all, the steward's job to watch out for safety. And then finally the ironworker was done working this level, and it'd be a week or so before they'd have to worry about him above them again.

And he didn't say anything when a foreman had the carpenters help the laborers move about fifty very heavy form panels, misloaded on C-level, down to D-level and all the way over to its opposite side, though it was another hot, muggy day, though a small caterpillar laced the dusty air with fat black exhaust as it graded the dirt, though the company didn't supply fans to ventilate the stagnant pit.

He even controlled himself a week later when they were working on their second hour of double time, and he'd been watching the pour, patching and fixing the columns that leaked and blew out. The general foreman was stewing because of all the blowouts and he was right to be, and soon they started pouring the last column of the day, which was now evening. It looked like the column would be okay, and Sal told Elario and Benito to keep their eye on it and holler to stop if they saw anything, because they pumped from the deck above and couldn't see and he needed to take a walk. He went to the toolshed to put the ram set away, even though that was really a laborer's job and his to watch the pour, and when he got back, all smiles because it was the end of another long day, he took out his hammer to tap the plywood and see how much was in it, and, stepping forward, sank his boot in an ankle-deep mush of fresh gray concrete.

The general foreman was screaming so much at him that Sal stopped listening, and he helped Elario and Benito shovel the yard or so of cement away, telling them in Spanish not to worry about it, it was nothing, it was too dark, maybe it just popped out right then like the labor foreman said, that he should have been there, that the mother should have been built right in the first place.

They all talked about what it was that made the general foreman hate Sal so particularly after that, because it wasn't just that incident, which might make the man think Sal was a fuckup, and it wasn't the one prior to that, which might have made the man look bad and Sal disrespectful. It was something else, and everyone had an opinion.

"It's your drinking," said Augustín. "He's a Mormon and Mormons don't like people that drink. You gotta stop drinking with us Sal. You gotta stop getting drunk!"

"Augie's sorta right, Sal," said Rudy, "but it's not beer or whiskey, it's women. It's that secretary who's been hanging all over you after work. The pendejo's jealous cuz he thinks you're getting some of his own private stuff. It's ever since you took her home that night and brought her back the next morning. Come on, Sal, tell the truth, you are getting some, aren't you?"

"She had car trouble. I took her home and brought her to work the next day because her car was being fixed."

Nobody completely believed that one.

"It's that the old dude is white and Sal's brown," said Jamaal.

They all laughed about that one, mostly because Jamaal said it and they'd never heard him say much before.

"I think because Salvador speak Spanish and he don't," Benito said in English, trying to agree somewhat with Jamaal.

"The guy's under a lot of pressure," said the carpenter foreman. "They wanna rush rush and he's worried. And he thinks you don't care enough. He's like a football coach, you know?"

"I'll tell you what I think, Sal," offered the labor foreman. "I think you're better than him and he knows it. I think he's afraid to have you around here. He's got a hard-on to get you."

Sal did have his own thoughts. He believed it had something to do with the men sitting with him before work and at lunch and after work, and laughing, and talking, and his getting along with them as white or black or mejicano. He thought the man sensed that Sal didn't care to be a boss, that he liked laborers as much as, or even more than, the super-intendents. But what he said to the other men, what he gave as his exclusive opinion on the subject, was, "He's such a miserable sonofabitch that the more I ignore him the more I like this job and the longer I stay. Other than that he can stick it where the sun don't shine." And that made the men laugh.

So Sal went on with his work, ignoring the fact that the general foreman wasn't letting him have the overtime, not saying anything about the small irritations thrown his way, like never having a laborer to find material or to bring him a tool, or getting all the dirtiest jobs in the dirt-iest places, or about his getting a new partner every day and a half or less, his having to start at the beginning with each of them, telling them now this is a column clamp, and it goes around like this, and we have to work together, and when I set my pin in you have to make sure you can get yours in, and we'll put nails in at these measurements, and the rest. Instead he thought of the pretty dresses he was buying for his pretty daughters, the happy face of his wife when he got home to a sirloin steak in a cast-iron pan with onion and chili and tomato staining the apron that hugged her round stomach.

It was all to make a decent living, even Efren had to make a decent living, and that's why Sal didn't say anything bad to him about the col-umn he fucked up and Sal was sent over to fix. The tall, spindly column, which was beside the driveway ramps and exposed to the Mercedes coupes and sedans that would eventually drive up and down them, seemed twisted at the top, and when Sal looked it over he discovered that the clamps were biting wrong, so he and Efren took them off, about mid-form, and put them on again. But that wasn't the problem. He looked it over once more and checked the square. That was okay. He looked over everything he could think of, climbed up and down the scaffolding, back and forth across the planks, and from the top he pondered, staring down forty feet at the unfriendly dowels staring back out of the hard cement below him. It was a bitch of a problem, and he was almost stumped, but just to make sure, he asked Efren to tell him, one more time, exactly what he did when he built it. And there it was. He heard what the measure-ments were supposed to be, and figured out that Efren had managed to cut the panels fourteen inches at the bottom to almost sixteen at the top.

Efren was so relieved to know what was wrong that he ran off to the shitter, and Sal began unbuttoning the column by himself. He'd noticed the general foreman watching him for a while, but Sal didn't think much of it because the man so often watched him work. Sal's mouth dropped open when the man walked across a steel beam and hopped onto the scaffolding.

"So now what the fuck you doing with this damn thing?"

Sal began to explain.

"You mean you been working on this damn thing all day and yesterday and you don't got it cut right?!"

Sal was speechless. He'd been there two hours and figured the man knew that. He knew the man knew that.

"What the fuck kind of carpenter are you?! You think I pay you to be an apprentice?! You're no goddamn carpenter!"

The man often got hoarse and his voice was just starting to break up now. Sal blushed with anger. He swallowed. He said nothing. He heard his wife's voice. He listened to that. He listened.

The general foreman screamed and Sal didn't say anything. The men watched from below, waiting for Sal to push him off the scaffold, incredulous that the man knew nothing of Sal's pride and temper. But Sal didn't say anything, and the general foreman stomped back across the beam to the deck and screamed even louder that he was getting Sal's check, to pick up his gear.

Sal climbed down. He didn't talk and the men didn't talk to him. He picked up his toolbox and loaded it on his shoulder and walked. He heard Rudy say to someone, "Fucking Salvador's gonna kill that man, he's really mad now, he's gonna kill him."

Sal went to the Bar de Los Angeles and drank and stayed late and picked a fight with two cholos and took home a bruised face and the next morning his wife shook him to wake up.

"You're gonna be late! Your lunch is made. Go take a shower."

"I'm not working there no more."

She sat on the bed. "What happened?"

"We had an argument."

"You can go apologize. Go tell him you need the job."

"I already hit him," he told her.

"Why, Sal? You promised. You promised me!"

Cannery Town in August

Lorna Dee Cervantes

1981

Lorna Dee Cervantes was born in 1954 in San Francisco and grew up in San Jose. Her two volumes of poetry, *Emplumada* (1981) and *From the Cables of Genocide: Poems on Love and Hunger* (1991), have won numerous awards, including a 1995 Lila Wallace–Reader's Digest Fund Writers' Award, a Pushcart Prize, a 1981 American Book Award, and a nomination for the 1992 National Book Award.

All night it humps the air.
Speechless, the steam rises
from the cannery columns. I hear
the night bird rave about work
or lunch, or sing the swing shift
home. I listen, while bodyless
uniforms and spinach-specked shoes
drift in monochrome down the dark
moon-possessed streets. Women
who smell of whiskey and tomatoes,
peach fuzz reddening their lips and eyes—
I imagine them not speaking, dumbed
by the can's clamor and drop
to the trucks that wait, grunting
in their headlights below.
They spotlight those who walk
like a dream, with no one
waiting in the shadows
to palm them back to living.

✴ Rosario's Graveyard Shift at JFK Memorial Hospital

Rigoberto González

1999

Rigoberto González was born in Bakersfield, California, and raised in Michoacán, Mexico, the son of migrant farm-workers. His first book, *So Often the Pitcher Goes to Water Until it Breaks* (1998), was selected to be published as part of the National Poetry Series, and he has won a University Award from the Academy of American Poets. He is currently working on *Soledad Sigh-Sighs,* a children's book; *Butterfly Boy,* a memoir of his childhood; and *Crossing Vines,* a novel, all forthcoming in 2003 and 2004.

At 2:00 a.m. the light in the hallways sticks
to the walls. The fluorescence swallows
her uniform and she marches undetected,
her face peering out of a clipboard, white as her nurse's cap.

She is safe in her camouflage, having to walk
from wing to wing unarmed, without a needle
or a bottle of tablets rattling in her hand. She's
bold when she glances to the sides at this hour,

and for one quick look she is unashamed
to think: whose abuelos are these, these gauze-
haired mannequins who stoop each morning over
a clutter of plastic utensils, a bedpan, and a cup

or a bowl of green Jell-O? Metal bars surround
their oversized cribs. Do they mind their wrists

handcuffed to a small machine that counts
up or counts down to some booked destination? They cough

and wheeze, using up their words like pills. Yet even
when they speak they are too tired to call, these old
dolls that prop themselves up to unstick their lids,
each time leaning back to blink. Only Rosario's ear,

whisper-sensitive and paper cup clean, can admit to hearing
them manage a whimper or a groan. Even then she's quite
invisible rubbing their pale skins with oil
while they turn to the door and visitors gawk like birds

in their flowered shirts and dresses. What
do the passersby see that they won't find
in any other room with Rosario in it? Blank-eyed people
see only a sickness with weak limbs, see only

whiteness. Rosario, brown-faced, dissolves away
unnoticed, frequently ignored. Here, Rosario
is only part of the curtain. During linen changes,
she is only an extension of the sheets. Will Rosario

reach some compromise with the patients, at that point
when they open their eyes, glassy as if to offer her
a drop of water, and when her arm unfolds to find
the pitcher? Or when they attempt a smile

in the morning, a row of imperfect teeth
that pretend to possess a rind of light,
and when she smiles back, accepting their humble
gift, letting them think they own something?

There must be a middle ground where they can meet,
naked of these four-cornered cloths and pillows
designed to muffle cries at night. A place
where stitches can pass for wrinkles, scars

for stretchmarks, and where body parts are nailed
back on without the concern of matching color

or proportion, without that ceremony that ends
with short-lived roses and balloons that deflate

overnight. At 2:25 the nurse's light goes on
in room 308. Rosario pulls out a surgical mask
from her pocket and fades out of one dimension,
only to reappear discreetly in the next.

Manos Morenas

Michele Serros

1993

Michele Serros has published two books, been a commentator on NPR's *Morning Edition* and *All Things Considered,* released a spoken-word CD, toured with Lollapalooza as a "road poet," and contributed to the *Los Angeles Times'* children's fiction section. She regularly speaks at inner-city schools, universities, and correctional facilities across the country. Her poem "La Letty" is also included in this collection.

Maria is a poet
but it is her hands
that speak the memories

The Chilean activist/artist
held mine
as he tongue fed me
homemade wafer cookies
 in between overdone kisses.
"You have working hands,"
he whispered.
I pulled away
embarrassed
of my calloused income.
He took them back
assuring me,
"You don't want
to look like those
gabachas on Wilshire

manicured and ready
...to do nothing."

My co-worker, Yolie,
shook her head in shame
at the sight of these fingers:
"No color
no tips
no wedding band.
A woman
is as good as her
porcelain set
and the rock
a man gives her
to wear."

Between a flagging career
and city college night courses,
my mother's
own tired hands
patted homemade masa
coaxed roses out of dead soil
nurtured two babies
typed term papers till
three in the morning
never clenched a bottle neck
or leather belt
free of nicotine stains
seldom lifted a paintbrush
but died an artist.

I remember
all of this
when I see Maria's hands.

Tierra y libertad

Carol Zapata-Whelan

2002

Carol Zapata-Whelan was raised in both California and Argentina. Her fiction and creative nonfiction have appeared in publications including *Newsweek,* Argentina's *Diario Uno,* and *El Andar* magazine. She currently teaches Spanish and Spanish American literature at California State University, Fresno, and is working on a screenplay set in Latin America and the San Joaquin Valley.

Another time it will be like this, another time: things will be the same, sometime, someplace. What happened long ago, and which no longer happens, will be again—it will be done again—as it was in far-off times: Those who now live, will live again. They will live again…

—Nahuatl proverb

THE DAY THAT GENERAL EMILIANO ZAPATA cursed the fang marks that a rattler had just left him, a young campesino, Tranquilino Tiburcio Rodríguez García, galloped faster than the poison and pulled death out of his hero with a bite more potent than the snake's. Tranquilino himself had been stung by countless snakes—and lived. So it was said that he carried the blood of Quetzalcoatl, whose icon is the plumed serpent. And when Tranquilino himself died of a snake bite, his legend, ironically, was confirmed.

A warped sepia portrait—the only one ever taken—of Tranquilino, stiff as his winged mustache, belies a life of ambition, altruism, and a rash courage that sifted, in varying measures, to a few of his descendants, those who faithfully lit candles and left white roses for his spirit by an image of Our Lady, *la virgencita.*

One of the descendants who left roses for Tranquilino was his granddaughter, María Guadalupe, a sturdy young woman with a kind expression and waist-long hair the color of cinnamon. Though she should have been called María Guadalupe, or even Lupita, in honor of Nuestra Señora de Guadalupe, María lost half of her identity when she was naturalized by an INS official with a crew cut and no-nonsense stamping pad. That was the day María Guadalupe Rodríguez Castañón painstakingly unfolded her documents and shyly signed on to a new life as Maria Rodriguez. (Months, years later, María would hide her cinnamon hair in a disposable hair net and bend over moving bridges of golden raisins. She would have learned a few more English words than the ones she memorized the night she arrived in the U.S., or the day her name was abbreviated to change her life.)

María never had time to stop and think if her future had improved. She was too busy working assembly lines when packing houses called, cleaning homes when customers didn't cancel, caring for other women's children, attending daily Mass and driving a wood-paneled station wagon with a magnetic Our Lady of Guadalupe on the dashboard, a rosary swinging from the rearview mirror, and bags full of clothes for the poor. When she married Carlos Zúñiga, an immaculate young mechanic who sang with the choir and whose mustache smelled of lemon, she took a day off.

Another of Tranquilino's descendants who never forgot to leave white roses for him by Our Lady's statue was María's younger sister, Dulce Esperanza. Dulce Esperanza had onyx eyes, perfect features, and an Arabian air. She got to keep her full name because she entered the United States in the trunk of a Mustang driven by a *coyote,* a sullen man with bad breath and a dirty beard who couldn't care less how many names Dulce Esperanza gave herself as long as she paid in American dollars. During her trek, Dulce Esperanza, perpetually unwashed and thirsty, hallucinating with fear and exhaustion, prayed to Our Lady and asked Tranquilino for protection. She was not let down. The rodents that made their daily rounds left her unmolested, and one morning she was awoken by a little rattling noise that turned out to be a divine sign. The rattling belonged not to a snake but to the maraca of a small boy chanting to himself at the window of a dismal way station. The small boy smiled as Dulce Esperanza asked, *"¿Cómo te llamas?"* Tranquilino Rodríguez, he answered, with a shake of the snake rattle.

Dulce Esperanza never forgot the divine sign her great-grandfather and Our Lady sent her during the harrowing cross. And like the snakes her grandfather could charm, she shed useless old shapes and started to gain ground imperiously in her new territory. Unlike Maria, Dulce Esperanza learned English quickly and soon was the unofficial interpreter of their barrio, a liaison between the Irish priest and his Hispanic faithful, the organizer of food drives and charity raffles. Dulce Esperanza was the one who led the St. Sebastian's *Posadas* to celebrate Christmas and who made sure that the day of Our Lady of Guadalupe was properly honored in flashy procession, with a wide embroidered banner of Juan Diego's vision, mariachis with glossy guitars, youths in metallic Aztec dress, painted candles, and blooming flowers.

Because Dulce Esperanza, like her great-grandfather Tranquilino, was as strong and resourceful as the plumed serpent of myth, she tolerated well her outdoor labor in the harshest climate California had to offer. She was always the only woman reaching up from a ladder in the shag of the orange groves, stooping at the neat green rows of strawberry fields, or laying grapes on the drying trays of a dusty vineyard.

One infernal Valley afternoon, when burning asphalt rippled the horizon and the air in the grove turned thick as marmalade, the familiar sound rose, dry and deadly. Young José Hernández, dropping his shears in the crusty furrows, never heard or saw it. As the other men hesitated, faces stunned by the heat, it was Dulce Esperanza who tore off her plaid flannel overshirt, tied it around the boy's leg, and did what had made her grandfather a legend.

When María heard about the snake, she told her sister to clean air-conditioned houses with her. *"No hay víboras allí,"* she admonished. Not the kind on the ground, retorted Dulce Esperanza, rattling off in the old station wagon, leaving a trail of dark oil in the driveway of their tiny stucco house.

Everything would have been fine for Dulce Esperanza if she had taken her grandfather Tranquilino's advice in a dream and stayed with María to clean a mansion flanking the vast eucalyptus trees of a country club. No, *ni modo*, said Dulce Esperanza while María had begged, *"¡Un favorcito, Dulce! It takes me ten hours to clean that castle and la señora* always puts on that face."

Of course there was another reason that María wanted company, but she couldn't tell her sister or any future cleaning partnership would be jinxed for sure. Twice, when María was dragging a mop across the marble floors in the upstairs bathrooms, the doorbell rang. Twice, María descended wearily down the spiral staircase to open the door—to no one. *"¿Abuelito?"* she called out. It wouldn't have been the first time Tranquilino had paid an unannounced visit at someone else's home. But the silence that answered was not Tranquilino's. (And he usually arrived with a light menthol fragrance.)

María felt her arms turn to chicken skin. She carefully shut the door and resigned herself to dusting the living room with its dark antiques. Because the theory that neighborhood children might have been playing a game never occurred to María, she did what anyone else would have done when the third bell rang: she dropped the Old English and ran.

"Is there someone there who can *habla inglés?*" asked a woman on the phone who identified herself as Sylvia Wilhelm, pronouncing each word carefully.

"I espeak," said Carlos Zúñiga with unconvincing confidence.

"Well, please tell María she spilled lemon oil all over the Persian rug and left the French doors wide open, so Ashley ruined the side of the couch!"

"María ruin your couch with ashes?"

"No, no," said Mrs. Wilhelm patiently. "Ashley is my cat, and she's having like a—Oh, never mind! Just tell your wife if she wrecks anything else, I'll dock her pay."

"Okay!" said Carlos brightly.

María convinced her sister to help clean the Wilhelm house and told the truth. "It's probably just *el Abuelo,*" shrugged Dulce Esperanza. Tranquilino had come to her recently in the dream, trying to scold—or warn—her about something, but Dulce Esperanza never paid much attention to her grandfather in dreams, especially if he appeared to be giving advice. "No matter how brave, old people are always afraid of everything," she would complain to María.

"They're here to guard the house," said Mrs. Wilhelm, gesturing to two men in sweats on the porch and a white van at the curb. (Behind her, across

the garage doors, sloppily scrawled in red enamel was, "HEiL WiLHELm.")
Inside the van was a dead-serious bald man handling a walkie-talkie.

"My husband's had death threats from the labor union," Mrs.
Wilhelm added, offhandedly. "You don't know labor unions! Someone left
dead flowers on our porch this morning. The phone's been ringing off the
hook and the *doorbell's* been going nuts...." Mrs. Wilhelm was a tiny red-
haired woman who might have been pretty had it not been for a peculiar
combination of suspicion and confusion that marked her features.

"Now that the bell has guards, you don't need me," said Dulce
Esperanza, craning her neck at the stone turrets of the house's faux-castle
facade. "I'm going to the fields. I'd rather kill snakes."

The overcrowded van full of farmworkers that transported Dulce
Esperanza ran a stop sign and took a mortal sideswipe, plowing helplessly
into a vineyard. Eight people were loaded onto ambulances in zipped body
bags and four were lifted by helicopter to the Valley's main trauma center.
Though Dulce Esperanza Rodríguez had never ridden through the air, she
was unable to marvel at the` systolic sound of helicopter blades beating
across the sky.

While Dulce Esperanza, tethered to this earth only by tubes,
lines, and beeping blue screens, wavered between worlds, Tranquilino
waited, the only soul allowed across the threshold of the ICU.

"Am I dead, *Abuelito?*" she asked as he stood near, his hand on
her dry, hot forehead.

"*¡Cabeza dura!*" he said angrily.

"It's a good thing I have a hard head! Or I wouldn't be here.
Abuelito, am I...'here'?"

"Didn't I warn you? I even tried to tell María and she took off as
if she'd seen a—"

"You rang all the doorbells, *Abuelo?*"

"I even left flowers!"

"You've never done that before," said Dulce Esperanza in disbelief.

"I arranged them myself!" said Tranquilino proudly. "I should have
put them in water..."

"*¡Ay!* Would you please answer me, Tranquilino! Am I alive?"

"You have work to do, *mi hija.* You know, you are very lucky I did
not save as many people from the snakes as they say I did, because by
now, I would be taking it easy in heaven."

Dulce Esperanza awoke exactly three days after her conversation with Tranquilino. She had no memory of the visitation and had no way of knowing that the future obligations that had spared her life would be harder than crashing through a vineyard.

It was as if the accident had left Dulce Esperanza out of focus. "I don't know what's happened to you," said María in exasperation one day. Dulce Esperanza regarded her sister with that new faraway look that had taken over her eyes. She never seemed to be able to answer simple questions like, "Do you want *pan dulce* or *churros* with your chocolate?" or "What's your favorite color?" It was as if she were deliberately stalling for time, holding off commitment with a vague "Ah…" Sometimes María wanted to shake her sister, but then felt guilty, sorry, and explained redundantly to no one in particular: *"El accidente, pobrecita."*

But the accident left other things intact, things which caused the maternal cousin of José Hernández (whom she had saved from the snake), Eliseo Benavides, to fall in love with Dulce Esperanza. She seemed fond enough of the ambitious young gardener, whose menacing good looks belied a pure soul, but nobody could tell if his devotion was reciprocated. Whenever the question came up—which was daily—Dulce Esperanza retreated to her lost look and all-purpose "Ah…"

It was not long before Dulce Esperanza, weary of trick questions, planned the perfect white wedding and married Eliseo Benavides. With his abundant slicked hair and borrowed black tux, Eliseo cut the figure of a matinee idol, while she creaked regally down the aisle, looking like a nervous meringue. Father O'Leary, who said the wedding Mass, had practiced his Spanish relentlessly for the occasion, cornering parishioners at every opportunity to help him roll his *r*'s. And when the priest had successfully married Dulce Esperanza and Eliseo Benavides in a flawless Castilian marred only by his tripping over his own Irish name (which Father O'Leary inadvertently said in Spanish), the congregation gave its pastor a standing ovation before the groom kissed the bride.

Pregnancy made Dulce Esperanza more absentminded than ever. There were times when she became incensed at the friendly pats to her belly—until she remembered, *"¡El bebé!"* And there were days when she spoke of the baby in plural, as if she were having more than one or already had a few children. This type of talk brought María to her wit's end, as she was already forced to suppress a guilty rivalry with her sister—she had been unable to conceive despite every rosary and novena, every strategy of modern science and ancient magic. What if Dulce Esperanza were, after all, having multiple births! It was too unfair for María to even consider.

The subterranean currents between the two sisters became so strong that Eliseo Benavides realized it was time to separate the families, which until then had been comfortably sharing the same tiny stucco house. "I have saved enough," he assured Dulce Esperanza, and found a bigger stucco house in a neighborhood with sidewalks.

The trouble started as most troubles start, on an invisible scale. The new neighbors, unlike the families in the old barrio, never came by to say *"bienvenidos,"* to offer a hand, a phone, or a plate of warm tamales. There were a few friendly faces, a few people who waved "hi" while sponging off a car or walking a dog, but it gradually became apparent to Dulce Esperanza that she and Eliseo had not only moved "up" in the world, they had landed in a different universe.

One afternoon, as Dulce Esperanza, big with child, was dragging bags of groceries across the yard, she came face-to-face for the first time with her next-door neighbor, a square, florid-faced man whose silver hair was still sharp from a buzz cut. She smiled at the man and extended her hand, which he ignored.

"I'm tired of you people parking on my property," the neighbor said by way of greeting. Momentarily taken aback, Dulce Esperanza set down her bags and assured the man politely that her car would never again cross his property line.

"And if you play that music of yours too loud, I'm calling the cops!" he bellowed before ducking into his stucco house.

A fist came down on the kitchen table. Eliseo was not as accommodating as his absentminded wife. "No man treats my family with disrespect!" he said, loud enough for the neighbors to hear. Dulce Esperanza was also caught off guard by her husband's response. Eliseo was normally a good-natured, fair-minded man who did not anger easily or respond irrationally to small annoyances.

But the trouble escalated, with the next-door neighbor and his young grandsons making surly trips across the Benavides's front yard— for no good reason. And once a lawnmower "accidentally" made a dent the size of a toaster on the side of the Benavides's old Chevy Impala. Dulce Esperanza did her best to ignore the comments and heated monologues pointed over the fence while she strung borrowed baby linens on the clothesline.

María got home as the answering machine clicked. She had just missed catching Dulce Esperanza, and excitedly hit a button to hear if the baby was on its way. What the machine played back, instead, jolted her blood: "Oh, María!" said her sister, a suppressed sob jarring her voice. "I need a lawyer. I'm in jail!"

Madre santísima, how could this possibly have happened? Who can I call? Where do I go? What time is it? Where is Eliseo? María's thoughts were like birds trapped in a room, fluttering wildly about with no exit in sight. She lit a candle before Our Lady and was distractedly making the sign of the cross when the phone rang again.

"María? This is Sylvia Wilhelm. Where did you put my—"

"*Ay! Gracias a Dios.* Mrs! My sister is in the jail!"

"Good Lord, María! Let me get Leonard."

Mrs. Wilhelm took an eternity to locate her husband in their castle, but María could finally hear the echo of Mr. Wilhelm's voice growing less faint: "Isn't she the one who's out of it? Didn't she stick my dress shoes in the toy box?"

"Just get me a notepad!" reproached Mrs. Wilhelm.

"What could that girl possibly be arrested for?" asked Mr. Wilhelm. "Felony confusion?"

Dulce Esperanza had been arrested for Assault with a Deadly Weapon, Section PC245A1 of the Penal Code, her bail set at twenty thousand dollars, her arraignment scheduled after a long holiday weekend. Mr. Wilhelm was able to find a golfing buddy to get Dulce Esperanza out of the County Detention Facility on her own recognizance.

Mrs. Wilhelm even visited Dulce Esperanza before she was released, taking along a cosmetics sample bag and a Bible, not knowing that the Bible and the makeup would go in a lobby locker while she chatted with Dulce Esperanza through bullet-proof glass.

Mrs. Wilhelm had never seen anyone—much less an expectant mother—in jail. "That forest-green looks cute on you," she said uncomfortably, taking in Dulce Esperanza and her vast belly in the jail jumpsuit. "Is that maternity size?"

Dulce Esperanza ignored Mrs. Wilhelm's good intentions and started to give her a clear and precise account of how she landed in jail instead of making it to a comadre's house to pick up another bag of baby clothes.

The day before, when Dulce Esperanza had settled heavily into a borrowed truck (the Chevy Impala was having its toaster-sized dent fixed) which she had absentmindedly parked a few feet over her neighbor's property line, the block was deserted. Then, just as the truck's engine sounded, Mr. Hacker, the neighbor, came out for his newspaper.

"Suddenly, I hear a loud thump. He had thrown the newspaper at the back of the truck," said Dulce Esperanza. "So, I pretended like nothing happened because I didn't want no trouble."

As Dulce Esperanza backed out the truck, Mr. Hacker stooped to pick up his paper. Flustered, and most scattered of all in the mornings, she never noticed her neighbor bending down behind the bumper until she heard the bloodcurdling howl—and braked violently. Then Mr. Hacker limped over to the driver's window, cursing and hollering: "You hurt me! You hurt me!"

"Was he really injured?" asked Mrs. Wilhelm.

Dulce Esperanza widened her eyes. "No! Because he got up in his truck and drove his little grandson to school! And the grandson was laughing!" She held onto her belly as if for support.

"An hour later two policemen knocked to arrest me for hurting Mr. Hacker. They put handcuffs on me in my kitchen. I said, 'I can't believe this is happening!' They said, 'Believe it!'"

As she was being led to the plain white squad car, Dulce Esperanza wondered if she might need a lawyer and brought this idea up, uncertainly, to the police. But both men assured her that her case would look better to any judge if she would "cooperate fully."

As Dulce Esperanza retraced the last twenty-four hours and drew conclusions from her story, Mrs. Wilhem realized that María's younger sister had never spoken more eloquently or looked more alert. Even her complexion seemed brighter.

What the van accident had done to Dulce Esperanza, the day in jail seemed to reverse. She had gotten back her old verve; she was Tranquilino Rodríguez's granddaughter again. And what was more, Dulce Esperanza Rodríguez Castañón de Benavides had acquired a new vision.

Despite the frenetic demands of motherhood—of a perfect, hardheaded cinnamon-haired baby called Ezequiel, who grew into a perfect, harder-headed boy called Zeke—or maybe because of them, Dulce Esperanza worked for her high school diploma, went to college, and made a career in…law enforcement. And because police department employees are not immune to false charges, once again, Dulce Esperanza needed legal defense. This time she was not handcuffed or arrested. She was sued.

"Race discrimination?" Dulce Esperanza asked in shock, looking up from an official-looking document.

"And sexual harassment," said her brother-in-law, Carlos, now a new associate at Sanson and Carrasco Law Offices.

Dulce Esperanza was being sued because she and her immediate superior, an African American police chief, were accused of thwarting the careers of three men—who were Caucasian. The truth was, the police chief was "set up" by an elaborate legal intrigue built on an old vendetta. The sexual harassment charge—part of the conspiracy—was thrown in against Dulce Esperanza by a wilting middle-aged man who sent her saucy e-mails and even tried to warn her about the lawsuit in one of them.

"This lawsuit starts with a fairy tale: that people of color have the same rights as everyone else—that justice is blind," ranted Dulce Esperanza one afternoon in Carlos's tiny congested office.

"Do you know when justice is blind?" said Carlos. "When the police find a Hispanic boy running to his *abuelita's* house and *zas!*—he's on the ground, handcuffed for stealing a van. But it's a case of mistaken identity. They let him go after he celebrates Easter in juvenile hall."

The night before the trial began, Tranquilino came to caution Dulce Esperanza in a dream: "The other attorney has the eyes of a snake. Never look in his face."

The trial was like an endless sentence for everyone trapped in the ring of that wood-paneled courtroom. And then, finally, just when Dulce Esperanza felt she couldn't state her own name in a believable tone of voice, Tranquilino sent a sign.

The attorney with the soft voice and the eyes of a snake (magnified by glasses) was about to try to confuse her again, make her say that black was white, down was up. He was handing out a document, passing the same papers to the judge, the other lawyers, the jury. Dulce

Esperanza glanced down at her copy, looked up and looked down again—and started to laugh—she had to laugh—and laugh—and laugh. And she was echoed by Carlos—and the jury! Even the bailiff's shoulders began to shake. But the one who laughed hardest of all was the judge, who was forced to slam his gavel for the first time.

"What's so funny?" the soft-voiced lawyer finally asked, only his voice wasn't so soft in the marble corridors.

"Counselor, you have made a 'global change' to this document in your computer?" asked Carlos.

"Yes, I had our staff in Los Angeles standardize all reference to race. My paralegal appropriately converted the word 'black,' wherever it was stated, to 'African American.'" He added matter-of-factly, "My document doesn't reflect the conversion yet."

"Well, you have converted more than you think," said Carlos, flashing his paper. "You have submitted this to Judge 'Seamus S. African American.'"

Not long after Tranquilino's sign, the lawsuit against Dulce Esperanza and her chief was dismissed. There were not enough facts to support the case. The night of the decision, Tranquilino appeared to his granddaughter in a dream.

"Our victory today was small, Dulce."

"There's nothing small about justice."

"Better if the facts had piled high as a mountain against you and your chief."

"Go home, *Abuelito.* You never make sense when I'm asleep."

"You are still far away—from *tierra y libertad,* the land, the freedom I fought for with *mi general.*"

"Go home, Tranquilino. We got the snake."

"No, *mi hija*: when people of color finally rise or fall through the free will God gave them, swift and strong as the plumed serpent, then you will be closer to *tierra y libertad. Andale,* Dulce Esperanza."

"*Vaya con Dios, Abuelo.*"

And I, Tranquilino Tiburcio Rodríguez García, did just that.

POLITICS

from

✸ The Organizer's Tale

César Chávez

1966

César Chávez was born in 1927 near Yuma, Arizona, the
son of a Mexican immigrant and a first-generation
Mexican American. As part of the mass relocation of
migrant workers following the Great Depression, Chávez
moved with his family to California, where as a child he
experienced firsthand the injustices done to farmworkers
by labor contractors and landowners. He worked nights for
the Community Service Organization, educating workers
and registering them to vote, and in 1962 he organized,
with Dolores Huerta, the National Farm Workers Union
(now known as the United Farm Workers of America) in
Fresno. Chávez's demands for better wages and improved
conditions for workers directly influenced California's labor
laws, and he is honored each March 31st (his birthday) in
California as one of America's greatest civil rights activists.
He died in 1993. The following piece was originally published in *Ramparts* magazine in 1966.

FOR SIX MONTHS I TRAVELED AROUND, planting an idea. We had a simple
questionnaire, a little card with space for name, address, and how much
the worker thought he ought to be paid. My wife, Helen, mimeographed
them, and we took our kids for two- or three-day jaunts to these towns,
distributing the cards door-to-door and to camps and groceries.

Some eighty thousand cards were sent back from eight Valley
counties. I got a lot of contacts that way, but I was shocked at the wages
the people were asking. The growers were paying $1 and $1.15, and

maybe 95 percent of the people thought they should be getting only $1.25. Sometimes people scribbled messages on the cards: "I hope to God we win" or "Do you think we can win?" or "I'd like to know more." So I separated the cards with the pencilled notes, got in my car, and went to those people.

We didn't have any money at all in those days, none for gas and hardly any for food. So I went to people and started asking for food. It turned out to be about the best thing I could have done, although at first it's hard on your pride. Some of our best members came in that way. If people give you their food, they'll give you their hearts. Several months and many meetings later we had a working organization, and this time the leaders were the people.

None of the farmworkers had collective bargaining contracts, and I thought it would take ten years before we got that first contract. I wanted desperately to get some color into the movement, to give people something they could identify with, like a flag. I was reading some books about how various leaders discovered what colors contrasted and stood out the best. The Egyptians had found that a red field with a white circle and a black emblem in the center crashed into your eyes like nothing else. I wanted to use the Aztec eagle in the center, as on the Mexican flag. So I told my cousin Manuel, "Draw an Aztec eagle." Manuel had a little trouble with it, so we modified the eagle to make it easier for people to draw.

The first big meeting of what we decided to call the National Farm Workers Association was held in September 1962, at Fresno, with 287 people. We had our huge red flag on the wall, with paper tacked over it. When the time came, Manuel pulled a cord ripping the paper off the flag, and all of a sudden it hit the people. Some of them wondered if it was a Communist flag, and I said it probably looked more like a neo-Nazi emblem than anything else. But they wanted an explanation, so Manuel got up and said, "When that damn eagle flies—that's when the farmworkers' problems are going to be solved."

One of the first things I decided was that outside money wasn't going to organize people, at least not in the beginning. I even turned down a grant from a private group—$50,000 to go directly to organize farmworkers—for just this reason. Even when there are no strings attached, you are still compromised because you feel you have to produce immediate results. This is bad, because it takes a long time to build a movement, and your organization suffers if you get too far ahead of the people it belongs to. We set the dues at $42 a year per family, really a meaningful dues, but of the 212 we got to pay, only 12 remained by June 1963. We were discouraged at that, but not enough to make us quit.

Money was always a problem. Once we were facing a $180 gas bill on a credit card I'd gotten a long time ago and was about to lose. And we *had* to keep that credit card. One day my wife and I were picking cotton, pulling bolls, to make a little money to live on. Helen said to me, "Do you put all this in the bag, or just the cotton?" I thought she was kidding and told her to throw the whole boll in, so that she had nothing but a sack of bolls at the weighing. The man said, "Whose sack is this?" I said, "Well, my wife's," and he told us we were fired. "Look at all that crap you brought in," he said. Helen and I started laughing. We were going anyway. We took the $4 we had earned and spent it at a grocery store where they were giving away a hundred-dollar prize. Each time you shopped they'd give you one of the letters of M-O-N-E-Y or a flag; you had to have M-O-N-E-Y plus the flag to win. Helen had already collected the letters and just needed the flag. Anyway, they gave her the ticket. She screamed, "A flag? I don't believe it," ran in and got the $100. She said, "Now we're going to eat steak." But I said no, we're going to pay the gas bill. I don't know if she cried, but I think she did.

It was rough in those early years. Helen was having babies and I was not there when she was at the hospital. But if you haven't got your wife behind you, you can't do many things. There's got to be peace at home. So I did, I think, a fairly good job of organizing her. When we were kids, she lived in Delano and I came to town as a migrant. Once on a date we had a bad experience about segregation at a movie theater, and I put up a fight. We were together then, and still are. I think I'm more of a pacifist than she is. Her father, Fabela, was a colonel with Pancho Villa in the Mexican Revolution. Sometimes she gets angry and tells me, "These scabs—you should deal with them sternly," and I kid her, "It must be too much of that Fabela blood in you."

The movement really caught on in 1964. By August we had a thousand members. We'd had a beautiful ninety-day drive in Corcoran, where they had the Battle of the Corcoran Farm Camp thirty years ago, and by November we had assets of $25,000 in our credit union, which helped to stabilize the membership. I had gone without pay the whole of 1963. The next year the members voted me a $40-a-week salary, after Helen had to quit working in the fields to manage the credit union.

Our first strike was in May 1965, a small one but it prepared us for the big one. A farmworker from McFarland named Epifanio Camacho came to see me. He said he was sick and tired of how people working the roses were being treated, and he was willing to "go the limit." I assigned Manuel and Gilbert Padilla to hold meetings at Camacho's house. The people wanted union recognition, but the real issue, as in most cases when you begin, was wages. They were promised $9 a thousand, but they were actually getting $6.50 and $7 for grafting roses. Most of them signed cards giving us the right to bargain for them. We chose the biggest company, with about eighty-five employees, not counting the irrigators and supervisors, and we held a series of meetings to prepare the strike and call the vote. There would be no picket line: everyone pledged on their honor not to break the strike.

Early on the first morning of the strike, we sent out ten cars to check the people's homes. We found lights in five or six homes and knocked on the doors. The men were getting up and we'd say, "Where are you going?" They would dodge, "Oh, uh…I was just getting up, you know." We'd say, "Well, you're not going to work, are you?" And they'd say no. Dolores Huerta, who was driving the green panel truck, saw a light in one house where four rose workers lived. They told her they were going to work, even after she reminded them of their pledge. So she moved the truck so it blocked their driveway, turned off the key, put it in her purse, and sat there alone.

That morning the company foreman was madder than hell and refused to talk to us. None of the grafters had shown up for work. At 10:30 we started to go to the company office, but it occurred to us that maybe a woman would have a better chance. So Dolores knocked on the office door, saying, "I'm Dolores Huerta from the National Farm Workers Association." "Get out!" the man said, "you Communist. Get out!" I guess they were expecting us, because as Dolores stood arguing with him, the cops came and told her to leave. She left.

For two days the fields were idle. On Wednesday they recruited a group of Filipinos from out of town who knew nothing of the strike, maybe thirty-five of them. They drove through, escorted by three sheriff's patrol cars, one in front, one in the middle, and one at the rear with a dog. We didn't have a picket line, but we parked across the street and just watched them go through, not saying a word. All but seven stopped working after half an hour, and the rest had quit by mid-afternoon.

The company made an offer the evening of the fourth day, a package deal that amounted to a 120 percent wage increase, but no contract.

We wanted to hold out for a contract and more benefits, but a majority of the rose workers wanted to accept the offer and go back. We are a democratic union so we had to support what they wanted to do. They had a meeting and voted to settle. Then we had a problem with a few militants who wanted to hold out. We had to convince them to go back to work, as a united front, because otherwise they would be canned. So we worked—Tony Orendain and I, Dolores and Gilbert, Jim Drake and all the organizers—knocking on doors till two in the morning, telling people, "You have to go back or you'll lose your job." And they did. They worked.

Our second strike, and our last before the big one at Delano, was in the grapes at Martin's Ranch last summer. The people were getting a raw deal there, being pushed around pretty badly. Gilbert went out to the field, climbed on top of a car, and took a strike vote. They voted unanimously to go out. Right away they started bringing in strikebreakers, so we launched a tough attack on the labor contractors, distributed leaflets portraying them as really low characters. We attacked one—Luis Campos—so badly that he just gave up the job, and he took twenty-seven of his men out with him. All he asked was that we distribute another leaflet reinstating him in the community. And we did. What was unusual was that the grower would talk to us. The grower kept saying, "I can't pay. I just haven't got the money." I guess he must have found the money somewhere, because we were asking $1.40 and we got it.

We had just finished the Martin strike when the Agricultural Workers Organizing Committee (AFL-CIO) started a strike against the grape growers, DiGiorgio, Schenley Liquors, and small growers, asking $1.40 an hour and 25¢ a box. There was a lot of pressure from our members for us to join the strike, but we had some misgivings. We didn't feel ready for a big strike like this one, one that was sure to last a long time. Having no money—just $87 in the strike fund—meant we'd have to depend on God knows who.

Eight days after the strike started—it takes time to get twelve hundred people together from all over the Valley—we held a meeting in Delano and voted to go out. I asked the membership to release us from the pledge not to accept outside money, because we'd need it now, a lot of it. The help came. It started because of the close, and I would say even beautiful, relationship that we've had with the Migrant Ministry for some years. They were the first to come to our rescue, financially and in every other way, and they spread the word to other benefactors.

We had planned, before, to start a labor school in November. It never happened, but we have the best labor school we could ever have in the strike. The strike is only a temporary condition, however. We have over three thousand members spread out over a wide area, and we have to service them when they have problems. We get letters from New Mexico, Colorado, Texas, California, from farmworkers saying, "We're getting together and we need an organizer." It kills you when you haven't got the personnel and resources. You feel badly about not sending an organizer because you look back and remember all the difficulty you had in getting two or three people together, and here *they're* together. Of course, we're training organizers, many of them younger than I was when I started in CSO. They can work twenty hours a day, sleep four, and be ready to hit it again; when you get to be thirty-nine it's a different story.

The people who took part in the strike and the march have something more than their material interest going for them. If it were only material, they wouldn't have stayed on the strike long enough to win. It is difficult to explain. But it flows out in the ordinary things they say. For instance, some of the younger guys are saying, "Where do you think's going to be the next strike?" I say, "Well, we have to win in Delano." They say, "We'll win, but where do we go next?" I say, "Maybe most of us will be working in the fields." They say, "No, I don't want to go and work in the fields. I want to organize. There are a lot of people that need our help." So I say, "You're going to be pretty poor then, because when you strike you don't have much money." They say they don't care about that.

And others are saying, "I have friends who are working in Texas. If we could only help them." It is bigger, certainly than just a strike. And if this spirit grows within the farm labor movement, one day we can use the force that we have to help correct a lot of things that are wrong in this society. But that is for the future. Before you can run, you have to learn to walk.

There are vivid memories from my childhood—what we had to go through because of low wages and the conditions, basically because there was no union. I suppose if I wanted to be fair I could say that I'm trying to settle a personal score. I could dramatize it by saying that I want to bring social justice to farmworkers. But the truth is that I went through a lot of hell, and a lot of people did. If we can even the score a little for the workers, then we are doing something. Besides, I don't know any other work I like to do better than this. I really don't, you know.

✶ Homenaje a la tercera marcha de Delano; manifestación contra la uva gorda y blanca, Domingo 8 de Septiembre, 1968, San Francisco, Califas

Roberto Vargas

1968

Roberto Vargas was born in 1941 to Nicaraguan parents and was raised in the Mission district of San Francisco. An activist on behalf of Latinos in the United States and elsewhere, he founded the Brown Berets activist group, organized the Third World Liberation Front at San Francisco State College, worked as a Nicaraguan ambassador to the United States, and helped found numerous programs which supported the Latino arts community in California. The following poem commemorates a Brown Berets march on San Francisco's city hall in support of striking farmworkers in Delano, California.

primer canto

Domingo.......
En el sol del medio día
Old prayers chant to notes
of New Guitar Strings
Air....Heavy incense
Proud Sonrisas of Young Brown Berets
Adding to the richness and splendor
De este Domingo
En el sol del medio día/

The "Huelga" Banners (Black and Red)
Point silent proud fingers
To the witness clouds…
That softly glance by

Picket signs que reclaman
En espectáculo silencioso las injusticias
A nuestra RAZA…on this Domingo
Y miles y miles pasados

5000 Bodies melting in human ether
singing/breathing/dancing of oneness
5000 Minds crying…of truth and lies
            crying…of death and rebirth
            crying…of newfound awareness
5000 heartbeats marching death
                        to the American Dream
5000 Guides marching in
                the new order of consciousness
FEET STEP FEET STEP
EYES MEET EYES THEY KNOW
                    THEY KNOW
        Vanguard of Proud Blacks/on chrome and
        iron camels roaring in the lead
        they know…Goddamn they know

Gentle fluttering Indio Feathers
Dancing Red in Sunday unison
Dancing away forked tongues
and BROKEN TREATY/PROMISES
Heralding the Coming of the Buffalo
They know…verdad…they know

        Asian Brothers and Sisters
        in half somber songstep
        keeping cadence
        With Hiroshima thoughts
        in their hearts and wise eyes
        and they know…por Dios…they know

segundo canto

Ay Raza Vieja
Raza nueva y orgullosa
Sun bronzed and arrogant
Con el Espíritu de Che y Sandino
Con el ardor de Malcolm X y Zapata
Now Marching Against Exploitation
Now Marching Against Shit and Frustration
Now Marching Against the Bastard Grape
Grapes of Wrath/Grapes of Paradox
and bittersweet madness
grapes of big white houses
That mold or destroy
                the innocent lives of our children
Children that starve
                while pigs feed off their backs
children of brown eyes in Delano
Delano the epitome of America
Delano of César el santo
                who fasts in their consciences
Delano of the 10 o'clock Mexican Curfew
Delano the mississippi of California
Delano of the 3 thousand year Huelga
                Huelga that Rings in Hunger's own belly
                huelga Que Inspira Revolución
                y descubre al vendido
Hoy Sí mis hermanos

This is the year of the last stolen banana
And the Rape of Coffee Beans must cease
This is the year of the bullet (and frenzied Pigs)
that Run with Grape-Stuffed mouths
And they know....Shit yes *They* know

        EN ESTE DÍA DOMINGO
        BAJO TODOS LOS SOLES
           QUE SIGUEN/

from

☷ The Revolt of the Cockroach People

Oscar Zeta Acosta

1973

Oscar Zeta Acosta was born in 1935 in El Paso, Texas, and grew up in California near Modesto. After four years in the air force and time spent in Panama as a Baptist missionary in a leper colony, he returned to California to attend college and earn his juris doctorate. He first practiced law for the East Oakland Legal Aid Society and later moved to East Los Angeles, where he became known for his political activism and legal work on behalf of Chicanos. Acosta wrote two novels, *The Autobiography of a Brown Buffalo* (1972) and its sequel, *The Revolt of the Cockroach People* (1973), before his mysterious disappearance in Mexico in 1974.

IT IS CHRISTMAS EVE IN THE YEAR OF HUITZILOPOCHTLI, 1969. Three hundred Chicanos have gathered in front of St. Basil's Roman Catholic Church. Three hundred brown-eyed children of the sun have come to drive the money changers out of the richest temple in Los Angeles. It is a dark moonless night and ice-cold wind meets us at the doorstep. We carry little white candles as weapons. In pairs on the sidewalk, we trickle and bump and sing with the candles in our hands, like a bunch of cockroaches gone crazy. I am walking around giving orders like a drill sergeant.

From the mansions of Beverly Hills, the Faithful have come in black shawls, in dead fur of beasts out of foreign jungles. Calling us savages, they have already gone into the church, pearls in hand, diamonds in their Colgate teeth. Now they and Cardinal James Francis McIntyre sit patiently on wooden benches inside, crossing themselves and waiting for the bell to strike twelve, while out in the night three hundred greasers from across town march and sing tribal songs in an ancient language.

St. Basil's is McIntyre's personal monstrosity. He recently built it for five million bucks: a harsh structure for puritanical worship, a simple solid excess of concrete, white marble, and black steel. It is a tall building with a golden cross and jagged cuts of purple stained glass thirty feet in the air, where bleeding Christ bears down on the people of America below. Inside, the fantastic organ pumps out a spooky religious hymn to this Christ Child of Golden Locks and Blue Eyes overlooking the richest drag in town.

All around us, insurance companies with patriotic names are housed in gigantic towers of white plaster. Here prestigious law firms perform their business for rich people who live next to jaded movie stars. The Bank of America, Coast Federal Savings, and all those other money institutions that sit in judgment over our lives keep the vaults across the street behind solid locks. But the personalized checkbooks now sit on the pews of St. Basil's, under siege by a gang of cockroaches from east of the Los Angeles River, from a "Mexican American" barrio there called Tooner Flats.

It is dark out on the sidewalks. Cars pass along Wilshire Boulevard and slow down when they see us. Most of our crowd are kids. Most of them have never attacked a church before. One way or another, I've been doing it for years. And for this and other reasons, I have been designated *Vato Número Uno,* Number One Man for this gig.

The young wear clothes for battle, the old in thick woolen ponchos, gavans, and sarapes. College-age kids in long hair and combat garb: khaki pants, olive-drab field jackets, and paratrooper boots spit-shined like those of the old *veteranos* who once went to war against America's enemies. Girls with long mascara-eyes, long black hair done up *chola* style, with tight asses and full blouses bursting out with song.

Three priests in black and brown shirts pass out the tortillas. Three hundred Chicanos and other forms of Cockroaches munch on the buttered body of Huitzilopochtli, on the land baked pancake of corn, lime, lard, and salt. Teetering over our heads are five gigantic papier-mâché figures with blank faces, front-lipped beaks, stonehead bishop dunce caps. A guitar gently plucks and sways "Las Posadas" to the memory of the White and Blue Hummingbird, the god of our fathers. We chew the tortillas softly. It is a night of miracles: never before have the sons of the conquered *Aztecas* worshiped their dead gods on the doorstep of the living Christ. While the priests offer red wine and the poor people uptilt earthen pottery to their brown cold lips, there are tears here, quiet tears of history.

When the singing has ended and the prayers for the dead and the living are complete, I step forward and announce that we have been permitted to enter St. Basil's. A Chicano sergeant from Judd Davis's SOC Squad just told me we could enter if we left our "demonstration" outside.

"Do we need special passes?" I had baited him.

"This is a *church,* Brown. Just tell them to hold it down when they go in. It's being *televised.*"

I knew that, of course. We were at the home base of the holy man who encouraged presidents to drop fire on poor Cockroaches in far-off villages in Vietnam. From, behind these stained glass windows, this man in the red frock and beanie, with the big blue ring on his knuckle, begs his god to give victory to the flames.

"Viva La Raza!" the crowd shouts at my announcement.

We turn and start walking up the cement steps. But at the top, the fifteen-foot doors of glass are shut in our faces. And when we try them, they are locked. Left out, once again; tricked into thinking we are welcome. An usher with a dark blue suit and red hair flops his lips against the thick soundproof glass: *No More Room.*

There is a stirring. Pushing towards the front. What do they mean? No more room. Locked out. Period. Just like Jesus.

The wind is still cold. Everyone huddles together on the steps. Our leaders regroup in one corner. It's up to us. This is the nut, our test of strength. Are we men? Do we want freedom? Will we get laid tonight if we cop out now? And what would our children say?

"Fuck it, *ese.* Let's get in there!" Gilbert shouts at the student intellectuals who want to organize outside.

"Yeah, fuck these *putos,*" Pelón puts in. Both are regular *vatos locos,* crazymen.

"But what will happen?"

"Oh, fuck that, *ese.* Let's go on in."

A dozen men and women trudge through the questioning crowd. We are going in to find out what's going on, we say. Wait for us. And with that we run around the side of the monster with steeples pointing to a star that no longer shines.

But whoops! Wait! What is this in the parking lot? Black and white and mostly blue. The SOC Squad desperados standing in formation. Clubs and pistols with dumdum bullets. Solid helmets with plastic visors from the moon of Mars. Ugly ants with transistor radios, walkie-talkies and tear gas canisters dangling from their hips. There are fifty pigs waiting for us to make the wrong move. But do they see us?

"Come on," our lawyer exhorts. I, strange fate, am this lawyer.

In the darkness we find a door leading to the basement. We are smiles again. Hah! We have a crack!

Yet caution: I peek into the basement. No mops. No brooms. It is a chapel, filled with the overflow of the Faithful. They are on their knees, clasping fingers and hands in front of their faces. Beads are being kissed, little black crosses dangled about in a cloud of incense. I see no room for us. Beside me is a stairway. We scramble up fast.

We enter a blue room, the vestibule inside the main entrance. There sits holy water in bowls beside the four huge doors. And through the glass we see the Cockroaches outside: faces in a sea of molasses. Teeth and bright-colored clothes. The Chicanos are a beautiful people. Brown soft skin, purple lips and zaftig chests. Their fists are raised in victory, though all we may hear is the most reactionary voice in America sing "Joy to the World."

"Hey, what are you doing in here?" Again, the carrot-top usher with the dark blue suit. He looms before us out of nowhere.

"We are here to worship, sir," Risco, the *cubano,* says.

"No more room, boys. You'll have to leave."

"How about up in the choir loft?" I say.

"Nope. We don't let nobody up there."

Outside, we see white teeth and feel fists banging on the doors. But we hear nothing. The glass is four inches thick. Mouths are moving and bodies are agitated. Things are tense.

"Hey, man. Why can't we just stand here?" Gilbert asks.

"In here? This isn't, uh…Sorry, boys. All the room is taken up. You'll just have to leave."

We all crowd around the usher. He is big but nervous; he keeps looking to his side. The vestibule is dark. The floors, walls, and ceiling are all deep blue velvet. A soft room for worship. The light is dim and nearly yellow. Some of the women cross themselves. Some also dip their fingers in holy water and bless themselves.

Then Black Eagle says, "Hey, man. Why don't you just open up that door and we'll listen to the service from here?"

The usher looks up and down at Black Eagle's immense black beard and militant gear. I know he wants to say how that isn't dress for civilized worship.

"No, I just can't do that. All of you will have to leave right now. Or I'll be forced to call the police."

"Well, fuck it, *ese!*" Gilbert shouts at the man.

"Hey, come on, Gilbert," one of our law students reprimands.

"You'd better leave, boy!" The usher is now obviously worked up.

Gilbert reaches for the horizontal panic bar to one of the outside doors.

"Stop!" The usher screams but makes no move.

Gilbert stops. "You said to get out." But the door is somehow open a bit.

"Not that way! You'll have to leave the same way you got in." The man is sweating now. He is looking at the crowd of Chicanos banging away on the glass. With the door cracked open we can hear what they have been chanting all along:

LET THE POOR PEOPLE IN! LET THE POOR PEOPLE IN!

Just about then, the choir and the congregation begin to sing. The choir and the organ are in a loft right above the door leading to the main church. This loft overlooks the vestibule and, occasionally, the choir director, waving his baton madly, peers at us over the low wall.

"You leave right now!" he shouts.

So naturally, Gilbert and Black Eagle again reach for the panic bars. Out of desperation the usher grabs Gilbert by the back of his coat and swings him against the bucket of holy water. Black Eagle stops and turns. We all move into a circle with the usher in the middle.

"Touch me again, you *puto,* and I'll let you have it!" Gilbert shouts. Glroosh-flut! The usher has struck Gilbert, the black frog, in the kisser. We stare and wait for the fog to clear. We are in a church, remember.

Gilbert reaches for the door once again. Flluutt!! The usher has struck Gilbert Rodriguez, the poet laureate of East L.A., right in the eye.

For two seconds no one moves. How in the fuck are you going to strike an usher? A *Catholic* usher. What would Gilbert's grandmother say? For two seconds time is suspended. And then it comes upon us in a wave: it isn't an usher. The police have tricked us again!

Boom! A solid uppercut to the pig's jaw. Then a scream. He hollers, "Sergeant Armas! Sergeant Armas!" Black Eagle finally opens the front door. Gilbert takes one in the stomach. *Vato Número Uno,* Warrior Number One, does not move. The lawyer stands and watches.

A wall curtain jumps and Sergeant Armas, the real boss of the SOC Squad, bowls in with twenty men. The vestibule explodes as men in blue run in formation swinging two feet of solid mahogany. Five other "ushers" run out of nowhere pulling out badges from inside their coats and pinning them on their breast pockets. Then they pull out little canisters and systematically squirt stuff into the faces of Chicanos who are entering now, pushing in through the front doors. And there is swinging and screaming and shouting and we are into a full-scale riot in the blue vestibule of the richest church in town. But I am standing stock still. All around me bodies are falling. Terrified women and children are wailing while the choir sings above my head:

> *O come all ye faithful, joyful and triumphant,*
> *O come ye, O come ye, to Bethlehem...*

I see Gilbert, the fat Corsican pirate, grappling with a burly cop. Wearing his Humphrey Bogart raincoat, he's on the pig's back. His small brown hands are stuck in the eyes of the monster with the club. They pass me by.

Black Eagle has squared off with two ushers. One squirts Mace in his face while the other kicks him in the balls. Down and down he goes, crashing to the velvet floor. I watch it all serenely while the choir and congregation entertain. I wear a suit and tie. No one lays a hand on me. I take out my pipe and wade through the debris. Crash-crattle and krootle! A thirty-six-inch cement ashtray flies through the plate-glass door. Sticks to hold up posters fly over the crowd. Candles for the gods become missiles in the air. A religious war, a holy riot in full gear. Then, sirens screaming outside, the rest of the SOC Squad bursts in to join its brothers. The choir never misses a beat:

> *Come and behold Him, born the king of angels...*

I watch a red-haired girl with glasses and a miniskirt rush through the door to the main church, which has opened momentarily. It is Duana Doherty, the street nun who once worshipped wearing black robes while her head was bald. Then she joined up with the Chicanos and became a Cockroach herself. I take a few steps to see what she is up to.

Inside another usher, a real one, sees us. I have on my pin-striped blue Edwardian and I've put my pipe back in my pocket. Duana has creamy peach skin. She has the face of an angel. The usher has no hair. The three of us make one of a kind.

"I think there's a seat up front," he says.

Duana doesn't stop for an answer. She runs down the length of the aisle. The Faithful in furs, in diamonds and hats of lace, are staring straight ahead at the altar where seven priests perform for TV.

"Just keep on, my children. Pay no attention to the rabble rousers out there," Monsignor Hawkes is exhorting them, his red hands cupping the mike.

The usher can't keep up with Duana. She makes it to the front, turns, and addresses the congregation, "People of St. Basil's, please, come and help us. They're killing the poor people out in the lobby! Please. Come and help!"

Two ushers finally grab her around the belly and carry her out. I stand aside and watch them pass. And almost at the same moment I see another woman running at full-bore. It is Gloria Chavez, the fiery, black-haired Chicano Militant. She charges down the aisle in a black satin dancing dress that shows her beautiful knockers and she carries a golf club in her pretty hands. I am aghast! The Faithful are petrified. No one makes a move for her. Her big zaftig ass shakes as she rushes up to the altar, turns to the pie-eyed man in the red cape, and shouts:

¡QUÉ VIVA LA RAZA!

Swoosh, swoosh, swoosh! With three deft strokes Gloria clears off the Holy of Holies from the altar of red and gold. The little white house with its cross falls. The little white wafers which stick to the roof of your mouth just before you swallow, the Body of Christ is on the red carpet.

It is too astounding a thing to believe. No one lifts a finger to stop this mad woman with her golf club as she hotfoots it down the aisle toward the vestibule. The ushers, the worshippers, and myself simply stand and stare. The congregation has long since stopped singing. It is just the choir:

O come let us adore Him, O come let us adore Him…

The golden chalice, the cruets for the wine and water are scattered on the floor before the bleeding Christ and the Madonna with child in arm.

"CHICANO POWER!" Gloria shouts as she vanishes inside the battle zone.

I follow her. I stop in the doorway and see Gloria being taken by three huge pigs. The pigs have already backed the scum out into the streets.

"Just a minute, Officer…You don't have to hit her," I say.

"Get out of the way, Mr. Brown," Sergeant Armas says to me.

Gloria is kicking and cussing and slapping away. Her legs are shooting up at the three men who are hustling her to the floor.

"*¡Pinches, cabrones, hijos de la chingada!*" she screams.

I move. I grab the arm of one of the cops. He turns to slug me with his baton, but Armas stops him.

"Leave Brown alone! He's their lawyer," Armas tells the man.

When they have carried her away, I stand and scan the battlefield. The floor is covered with debris. Sand from the ashtrays, broken glass from the doors, papers listing our demands, a shoe, an umbrella, eyeglasses with gold frames, banners with *La Vírgen de Guadalupe* drawn in color. Garbage galore litters the holy blue vestibule.

I walk carefully outside. It is the same on the steps. The street is lined with police vans, red lights glaring, sirens howling in the night. And on the other side, hundreds of Chicanos standing or walking around aimlessly.

I see Gilbert and Black Eagle being whacked over the head with batons as they are hauled into a car. I run down the steps, toward the street. Cops hold me back. I struggle, I shove, I kick away. For God's sake, I want to be arrested! "Don't touch the lawyer," they say to one another.

I run back toward St. Basil's, which now has helmeted pigs standing in a skirmish line at the bottom of the steps. They are tense, their hands gnarled around the batons held before them at parade rest. Fear is in the eyes of black and Chicano cops. So I say to them, "Why don't you guys relax? You ought to see yourselves, you'd be ashamed." I see murder in their eyes. They have to take this shit. Armas, their tough Chicano sergeant, has told them to keep their bloody hands off me.

The St. Basil's side of Wilshire is filthy with cops and Wilshire itself is still clogged with police wagons. Beyond them the Chicanos are waiting for a call to regroup. I cup my hands to my mouth and shout, "Hey, *Raza*...Go home now. Go home and rest up. Tomorrow, during Christmas Mass, let's meet here again."

I walk up and down the street on the sidewalk. Nobody touches me as I shout at them to go home, shower up, and regroup here tomorrow for another battle. To go home, bandage the wounded, and heal the sick.

When it is done, the big pig, Sergeant Armas, comes up to thank me. "You're OK, Brown. Things got out of control here tonight. Thanks a lot."

"Ah, fuck you, you asshole!"

✳ The Twenty-Ninth

Luis J. Rodríguez

1991

Luis J. Rodríguez was born in 1954 in El Paso, Texas, lived briefly in Mexico, and grew up in Watts and East Los Angeles. His experience as a pre-teen gang member influenced much of his later work, which includes award-winning journalism, photography, criticism, autobiography, poetry, and children's literature. The following excerpt is from *The Concrete River* (1991), which won a PEN West Josephine Miles Award for Literary Excellence. The piece retells the events of August 29, 1970, the day the high-profile Mexican American journalist Ruben Salazar was killed by a police deputy following a Chicano-led march protesting the Vietnam War.

AUGUST 29, 1970—I EMERGED OUT OF AN OLD, BUMPY BUS on the Atlantic Boulevard line and entered a crowd snaking through the steaming streets and by the red-dirt yards of the city's east side. I hadn't been fully aware of my own sense of outrage until, melding with other marchers, I found myself raising a fist in the air. I was a street kid then: sixteen years old, in gang attire and earring. I had no idea how significant the protest would be. Frankly, I had only come to party.

We continued past stretches of furniture stores, used-car lots, and cemeteries. Many storekeepers closed early, pulling down rusty iron enclosures. Others, small vendors of wares and food, came out to provide drink—relief on that broiling day. Around me marched young mothers with babies in strollers, factory hands, *cholos,* uniformed Brown Berets (the Mexican version of the Black Panthers) in cadence, a newlywed couple (still in tuxedo and wedding gown)—young and old alike.

We turned onto Whittier Boulevard, joined by people from the neighborhoods. Instances of battle flared up at alleys and side streets.

Young dudes and cops clashed. But most of us kept up the stride. At Laguna Park, the multitude laid out on the grass. Children played. Beer got passed around. Voices burst out in song. Speeches, music, and street theater filled the air. I made my way to a nearby liquor store. The store had closed early. A number of us wanted to get more to drink. A shotgun, pushed against my head, caused me to jerk backward. "Move, or I'll blow your fuckin' head off," a sheriff's deputy ordered. I left, wandering through feet and bodies, coolers and blankets.

At the park edge, a brown line of deputies—armed with high-powered rifles, billy clubs, and tear gas launchers—began to swagger toward the crowd. Those who hesitated were mowed down by swinging clubs. A group of people held arms to stop the rioting police from getting to the families. I turned toward the throng of officers. One guy told me to go back, "We'll fight tomorrow." Then it hit me: there are no more tomorrows for me. I had enough at the hands of alien authority. So come then, you helmeted, marching wall of state power. Come and try to blacken this grass, this shirt of colors, this festive park filled with infants and mothers and old men, surging forth in pride. Just try and blacken it with your blazing batons, shotguns, and tear gas canisters. I'm ready.

A police officer in a feverish tone told me to move. I said, "*Chale,* this is my park." Before I knew it my face was being smeared into the dirt, a throbbing in my head. Officers pulled my arms back, handcuffing me. On the ground, drops of red slid over blades of green. By then the battle of Laguna Park had burst open. Bodies scurried in all directions. Through the tear gas mist could be seen shadows of children crying, women yelling, and people on the grass kicking and gouging as officers thrust blackjacks into ribs and spines. Several people tried to run into the yards and living rooms of nearby homes. Deputies followed in a murderous frenzy, pulling people out of backyards and porches.

A deputy pushed me into the back of a squad car. Somebody lay next to me, his hair oiled with blood. I didn't want to look for fear his brains were coming out. I managed to give him a piece of my shirt, my favorite, soon to be soaked. From the East L.A. jail, where we were crowded into a holding tank for hours, we went on long rides to the Los Angeles county jail, to juvenile hall, and county jail again. At one point, while we sat chained to one another in a county jail bus, officers sprayed Mace into the windows; it burned our skin, eyes.

There were three other young dudes with me: another sixteen-year-old, a fifteen-year-old, and his thirteen-year-old brother. They put us in with the adults—with murder, drug, and rape suspects. But nobody bothered us. There was an uprising outside and we were part of it. One guy recalled the Watts uprising and shook our hands. At one point, deputies took the four of us to the Hall of Justice, known as the Glasshouse. They threw us into "murderers row," where hard-core youth offenders and murder suspects were awaiting trial or serving time. I had a cell next to Charles Manson.

I was placed with a dude who had killed a teacher and another who had shot somebody in the Aliso Village housing projects. At first the dudes threatened me, pressing a stashed blade to my neck. But I knew, no matter what, never show fear. Soon we played cards, told jokes and stories. That night we heard that the "East L.A. riot" (this is what the media was calling it!) had escalated through much of Whittier Boulevard. Stores were being burned, looted. Police had killed people. Fires flared in other communities like Wilmington and Venice.

Then a radio reporter announced that Chicano journalist Rubén Salazar had been killed in a bar by sheriff's deputies. Salazar had been a lone voice in the existing media (he was a former *Los Angeles Times* reporter and KMEX-TV news director) for the Mexican people's struggle in the United States. Now silenced. At word of his death, the tier exploded into an uproar of outrage. Inmates gave out yells and rattled the cell bars.

For five days, I disappeared. My parents searched for me throughout the criminal justice system. They checked for my name in court records and arrest sheets. Nothing. Finally, in the middle of night, a guard awakened me, pulled me out of the cell and led me down brightly lit corridors. Through a small, thick-glassed window I saw my mother's weary face. When they finally brought me out, with dirt and caked blood on my clothes, she smiled—a lovely smile. I remember telling her, "I ain't no criminal, ma." She looked at me and replied, "I know, *mijo,* I know."

Rachel

Roberto Tinoco Durán

1993

Roberto Tinoco Durán has won several awards for his poetry
and in 2001 co-produced a short experimental film and
accompanying spoken-word CD called "86ed Again."
Another poem by Durán, "Tattoos," is also included in this
volume.

The so-called movement
took the best years
leaving the lines of loyalty
on your dedicated face

I remember you
leader of picket lines
who dared burly six-foot
two-hundred-pounders
to cross her path

I remember you
at the top of your voice
as the safe and lucky supermarket patrons
stepped on your lungs
coming out of stores in San Jose
saluting you with middle fingers
sometimes stopping in front of your face
to eat grapes Julius Caesar–like
and you handed them flyers anyway
La Rachel de San Jose

Notes from a Chicana "COED"

Bernice Zamora

1985

Bernice Zamora was born in 1938 and grew up in
Colorado. She has written two critically acclaimed volumes
of poetry, *Restless Serpents* (1976, with José Antonio Burciaga)
and *Releasing Serpents* (1997). She co-edited *Flor y Canto: An
Anthology of Chicano Literature IV and V* (1980, with José
Armas), and has taught at several universities, including UC
Berkeley and Santa Clara University.

To cry that the *gabacho*
is our oppressor is to shout
in abstraction, *carnal.*
He no more oppresses us
than you do now as you tell me
"It's the gringo who oppresses you, Babe."
You cry "The gringo is our oppressor!"
to the tune of $20,000 to $30,000
a year, brother, and I wake up
alone each morning and ask,
"Can I feed my children today?"

To make the day easier
I write poems about
pájaros, mariposas,
and the fragrance
of perfume I
smell on your collar;
you're quick to point out
that I must write

about social reality,
about "the gringo who
oppresses you, Babe."
And so I write about
how I worked in beet fields
as a child, about how I
worked as a waitress
eight hours at night to
get through high school,
about working as a
seamstress, typist, and field clerk
to get through college, and
about how, in graduate school
I held two jobs, seven days
a week, still alone, still asking,
"Can I feed my children today?"

To give meaning to my life
you make love to me in alleys,
in back seats of borrowed Vegas,
in six-dollar motel rooms
after which you talk about
your five children and your wife
who writes poems at home
about *pájaros, mariposas,*
and the fragrance of perfume
she smells on your collar.
Then you tell me how you
bear the brunt of the
gringo's oppression for me,
and how you would go
to prison for me, because
"The gringo is oppressing you, Babe!"

And when I mention
your GI Bill, your
Ford Fellowship, your
working wife, your
three *gabacha guisas*
then you ask me to

write your thesis,
you're quick to shout,
"Don't give me that
Women's Lib trip, *mujer*,
that only divides us,
and we have to work
together for the *movimiento*
the *gabacho* is oppressing us!"

Oye carnal, you may as well
tell me that moon water
cures constipation, that
penguin soup prevents *crudas,*
or that the Arctic Ocean is *menudo,*
because we both learned in the *barrios,*
man, that pigeon shit slides easier.
Still, because of the *gabacho,*
I must write poems about
pájaros, mariposas, and the fragrance
of oppressing perfume I smell somewhere.

✴ It's About Class, Ese

Margarita Luna Robles

1990

Margarita Luna Robles is a writer, performance artist, and teacher. Her poetry, fiction, essays, and reviews can be found in many anthologies and journals, and she is the author of two books. She helped found several women's writing workshops in Fresno and the San Francisco Bay Area, and she currently teaches at California State University, Fresno, where her husband, Juan Felipe Herrera, is also a professor.

Say, Vato, remember that time you
was in line at the store and some white chick said to you,
You ain't got no class?

I was thinking then it was about style.

But now I think I got it.

It's about how the medical receptionist
looks at you when you walk into the
doctor's office

It's about how the dentist cringes
when he looks at your clothes and
you're thinking you look clean

It's about how your job applications
get put into the reject pile 'cause
no one can pronounce your name

and can you imagine starting the day
with "good morning, how do you
pronounce your name again?" and
maybe having to work with someone
who's brown and god forbid different

It's about maybe not making it at
the top of your class in school
'cause your thinking is different
radical and revolutionary (left over from
the 60's, even)
and maybe you won't even get through
school

It's about your kids being placed in
slower reading groups in school 'cause maybe
even if they don't speak Spanish anymore,
their parents still do so the kids are
still thinking in Spanish as in values (can you take that one?)

It's about everyone in town thinking
you can't cut it 'cause you're less than
how could you be more than if you don't
even make it equal to

That's what class is all about

And no one has to say they don't like
Mexicans anymore 'cause everyone's
too cool

In fact, they like to call us
what we want to call ourselves like
Chicanos
or Latinos
or sometimes people still carefully say
Spanish people
and polite appropriate institutionally correct catch-all can't miss it
Hispanic

And no one has to say anything 'cause
no one wants to be called racist anymore
so instead they don't say anything
and just look at you/stare/
and turn their faces/look away

Ese, I call this American denial
and it's all about class as in value
as in market as in how much you got
I can't give you too much 'cause I don't think you're worth it.

✴ Letter to America

Francisco X. Alarcón (translated by Francisco Aragón)

1987

This poem by Francisco X. Alarcón is from his collection
Body in Flames (1990). Several other poems by Alarcón—"I
Used to Be Much Much Darker," "Guerra Florida," and
two sonnets from *Sonnets to Madness and Other Misfortunes*
(2001)—are also included in this collection.

pardon
the lag
in writing you

we were left
with few
letters

in your home
we were cast
as rugs

sometimes
on walls
though we

were almost
always
on floors

we served
you as
a table

a lamp
a mirror
a toy

if anything
we made
you laugh

in your kitchen
we became
another pan

even now
as a shadow
you use us

you fear us
you yell at us
you hate us

you shoot us
you mourn us
you deny us

and despite
everything
we

continue
being
us

America
understand
once and for all:

we are
the insides
of your body

our faces
reflect
your future

from

The Hidden Law

Michael Nava

1992

Michael Nava was born in 1954 in Stockton, California,
and raised in Sacramento. He started practicing law in 1981
and five years later published his first novel, *The Little Death*
(1986), featuring Henry Rios, the gay lawyer-detective who
stars in seven of Nava's books. He has also written a
nonfiction book, *Created Equal: Why Gay Rights Matter to
America* (1994), and edited an anthology of mystery stories.
Ending his career as a mystery novelist, he published the
final Henry Rios book, *Rags and Bones,* in 2001. He continues to practice law in San Francisco.

I STOOD ON THE SIDEWALK IN FRONT OF CITY HALL in downtown Los
Angeles on a warm April morning thinking of my father, who had been
dead for a long time, and *Dragnet,* his favorite TV series. City Hall was
engraved on the badge that Sergeant Friday flashed weekly in his dour
pursuit of law and order, and my father never missed a single episode. He
was a big believer in law and order. *Dragnet* fueled his black-and-white
vision of the world as consisting of humorless machos like Sergeant
Friday and himself battling the forces of evil. In my father's expansive
view this included most Anglos, all blacks, many Mexicans, priests, Jews,
lawyers, doctors, people on welfare, the rich, and everyone under forty.
He was a great and impartial hater; anyone different from him became an
object of his contempt. Homosexuals, had he allowed that such creatures
existed, would certainly have qualified.

As I started up the steps to City Hall I wondered whether my father
would have hated me more because I was homosexual or a lawyer. Then
I reminded myself that he had never needed a reason to hate me. It was
enough that I was not him. For my own part, I no longer hated my

father, though, admittedly, this had become easier after his death. Forgiveness was still a problem.

I took the steps too fast and stopped to catch my breath when I reached the top. I was forty, and I found myself thinking of my father more often now than in all the years since his death. He was ferociously alive in my memory, where all the old battles still raged on. Sometimes I had to remind myself not only that he was dead, but that I had been there. He had died in a brightly lit hospital room, slapping away my consoling hand and screaming at my mother, *"Más luz, más luz."* It had never been clear to me whether he was asking for more light, or crying out in fear at a light he perceived that the rest of us could not see. He had died with that mystery, as with so many others.

I entered the rotunda of City Hall, a grave, shadowy place, its walls made of great blocks of limestone. Three limp flags hung high above a circular floor of inlaid marble that depicted a Spanish galleon. Around the domed ceiling were eight figures in tile representing the attributes of municipal government: Public Service, Health, Trust, Art, Protection, Education, Law, and Government. I searched in vain for the other four: Expedience, Incompetence, Corruption, and Avarice. Undoubtedly I would encounter them in the hearing I was there to attend.

Six weeks earlier a bill had been introduced in the state senate by Senator Agustin Peña, who represented East Los Angeles. Peña's bill made it a crime to "actively participate in any criminal street gang with knowledge that its members engage or have engaged in a pattern of criminal gang activity." Despite its abridgment of the First Amendment right to free association, the bill had been expected to clear the legislature easily. Even though passage was a foregone conclusion, the senate committee before whom the bill was pending had scheduled a public hearing in Los Angeles.

The committee's motives became clear when a *Los Angeles Times* columnist pointed out that the date of the hearing was also the last day for mayoral candidates to file for the upcoming June primary. The columnist cynically concluded that Senator Peña planned to use the occasion to announce his entry into the race, positioning himself as the law-and-order candidate. When asked about it, Peña, who had been preparing for months to run, coyly declined comment.

A few days later, in mid-March, Peña ran over an old man in Sacramento, killing him. At the time, the senator's blood-alcohol level was twice the legal limit for drunk driving. He was charged with gross vehicular manslaughter. Immediately thereafter, he had entered a drug-and-alcohol rehab called SafeHouse and had not been heard from since.

Two days ago, his office had announced that Peña would be appearing at the hearing to make a statement.

The hearing had become the hottest ticket in town. I entered the city council chamber, where the hearing was being held to a packed house. The minicams were out in force, representing TV stations as far north as San Francisco. Their presence reminded me that Peña was more than simply a local politician. He was perhaps the ranking Latino officeholder in the state, a symbol of the political aspirations of millions and, until his accident, the person most likely to become the first mayor of Los Angeles of Mexican descent in a hundred and fifty years.

Although I had met Peña occasionally over the years, most of what I knew about him came from his campaign brochures and the newspapers. The former still portrayed him as the lean idealist who had marched in the dust of Delano with César Chávez a quarter century earlier. In the latter, he was depicted as a powerful patronage politician. Both accounts agreed that he was effective at his job. Over the years, however, he had become in a vague but unmistakable manner tainted by his success, careless about appearances, arrogant in the pursuit of his objectives. The work shirts and jeans had given way to expensive suits tailored to conceal the growing thickness of his body. From my perspective he was no worse than most politicians, but certainly no better, and I might even have voted for him.

Whether I would've voted for him or not, I thought his bill was a disaster and I had come to testify against it. As far as I was concerned, it was a mandate for police harassment in Latino and black communities, not that the cops needed much encouragement on that front. Only last year, members of the LAPD had been inadvertently videotaped as they pulled a black man out of his car and beat him senseless. His crime was failing to pull over with sufficient dispatch to receive a speeding ticket. The spin doctors in the department asserted "isolated incident," but my clients had been telling me for years about being beaten for what defense lawyers called contempt of cop. I didn't think it was a good idea to turn them loose on every poor black or Latino kid who gave them attitude. I had written a piece for the *Times* to that effect, and I was still getting hate calls three weeks later.

"Rios."

I glanced over my shoulder. Tomas Ochoa lumbered toward me. He was tall, big-gutted, and deliberately graceless as he clomped across the floor, forcing people out of his way. He came up to me like an old friend, crowding the space between us. It was a trick he used on people shorter than himself to force them to look up when they spoke to him. I moved back a step.

Salt-and-pepper hair framed his dark moustached face. His eyes were hidden behind tinted aviator glasses. Ochoa preached the revolution from a classroom podium at the local state college, where he taught in the Chicano Studies Department. On the wall of his office was a yellowing poster that demanded the end to the Anglo occupation of California.

The last time I had seen him was at his school, where we had been on a panel discussing the spread of AIDS among the city's minorities. While the rest of us deplored the indifference with which minority political leaders had responded to the presence of AIDS among their constituents, Ochoa took the position that it only affected elements of the minority communities which they were better off without, homosexuals and drug users. We had not parted on friendly terms.

I was surprised that he had sought me out today.

I said, "Hello, Tomas."

"I read your article in the *Times*," he said. "Where you defended the gangs."

"I didn't defend the gangs," I replied. "All I said was that there are better ways of dealing with them than turning the police loose."

"Listen, Rios, the gangs are the best thing that ever came out of the barrio. With a little political education, they could be urban guerrillas."

"I deal with gang members all the time," I told him. "They're not revolutionaries. They're drugged-out losers who get a little self-esteem by shooting each other."

He frowned at me. "So your solution is to plea-bargain them into prison."

"The solution has to start long before they reach me."

"The solution," he said, raising his voice, "is outside the system that you represent."

A few people had stopped to stare. I answered quietly. "The only thing I represent is my clients, Tomas, and I do it well."

"You represent something a lot worse than that," he said, jabbing a finger at me.

"Well, according to you, AIDS will take care of that," I replied. "Or would you prefer concentration camps like Castro? Or Hitler?"

"Take your choice," he said, moving away.

I watched him disappear into the sea of brown and black faces in the room, with the depressing certainty that he spoke for most of them. Whatever their other disagreements, the races all united in their contempt for people of my kind. The revolution never extended to matters of personal morality.

At the front of the room, the senators had begun to assemble. I found a seat just as the chairwoman of the committee called the hearing to order. Spruce and intricately coiffed, she announced, "These hearings have been called for the purpose of encouraging public debate on SB 22, introduced by Senator Peña of Los Angeles."

She was interrupted by a rising commotion from the audience as a door opened behind her and Agustin Peña walked briskly forward, the minicams sweeping toward him. An aide pulled out his chair and he sat down, saying, "I apologize to the committee for my tardiness. I'd like to make a statement."

The presiding senator replied, "Certainly, Senator Peña. Welcome back."

"Thank you," he said. He raised his hand back over his shoulder. His aide handed him a sheaf of papers. Peña laid them on the desk before him and, for a moment, simply looked out at the crowd thoughtfully. His thick, black hair was brushed back from a long, narrow face that El Greco might have painted, strong and melancholy; it was the face of a man who had passed through something difficult and was not yet certain of his ground. He cleared his voice and began to read from his papers.

"The streets of our poorest communities have become battlefields."

Nearby, someone whispered, audibly, "Yeah, they're full of drunk drivers."

"'It's time for action," Peña continued. "It's time to send a message to the gangsters that the decent people of our cities will not tolerate—"

The same wag quipped, "intoxicated politicians." But this time, someone shushed him.

"Their guns and their drugs," Peña concluded.

The crowd shifted restlessly, waiting for him to address the topic of his political future. At length, he finished with his prepared statement and said, "Now, with the committee's indulgence I would like to address my constituents in the room on another matter."

The room began buzzing again and was gaveled to order, the presiding senator saying, "You have the floor, Gus."

"Thank you, Charlene," he said. "You've been a good friend to me. In the past two months I've had a chance to see, truly, who my real friends are. I'm gonna ask some people to come up here and join me—my wife, Graciela, and my children: my son, Tino, and my beautiful daughter, Angela."

The three got up from the front row and walked awkwardly to the dais where the senators were seated. His wife was a plump, pretty woman who wore a photogenic dress of red and blue silk. She had mastered that vaguely beatific expression that Nancy Reagan had popularized among the wives of public figures. His teenage daughter kissed her father quickly and retreated to the background. His handsome son also kissed his father but remained at his side.

Peña, reaching for his wife's hand as he rose from his seat, said, "This is what life is really about, a loving family, people who stand by you no matter what, and these are the people I know I hurt the most with my alcoholism."

He paused for effect and got it, the cameras clicking, the crowd whispering. I watched his family. His wife's mouth twitched but her expression did not change. The girl retreated farther back. The boy looked straight ahead. Now that he was on his feet, Peña was as relaxed as a talk show host working the crowd.

"I know that some of you in the press expected me to be making a different kind of announcement today, and I would be lying if I didn't tell you I would rather be standing here announcing my candidacy for mayor than admitting that I'm an alcoholic. Still," he smiled, "you roll with the punches." The back-room echoes of that remark were more authentic than what came next. "But maybe by doing this, I can help someone else. All I can say is that I have had to look at my human weakness right in the eye and realize that I have spent so much time caring about and worrying about others that I have not worried or cared enough about myself. I now know that it's time for me to take care of me, to accept my responsibilities and my weaknesses. But I say to others who are as pained and hurt as myself," and here he draped an arm over his son's shoulders while gripping his wife's hand, "I say to you, 'Join me, brothers and sisters. We can make it. We will make it. It's going to be a lonely journey, but I stand and God stands with me.'"

He released his children and his wife. "As you know, I have been at an alcohol rehabilitation center, and I believe that I have been cured of this disease of alcoholism. I have begun to heal my body and my soul."

Looking at the camera rather than her husband, his wife said, "Gus, for you to admit you have this problem and to deal with it has truly lifted a burden from our souls." She gestured vaguely toward the children. "I thank God you have had the strength to realize that you are truly in God's hands. I know for our family this is just a beginning and we, Tino, Angela, and me, we will be with you every step of the way."

"God bless you, Graciela," he said, choking back tears. To my astonishment, people around me were also crying.

The presiding senator hammered the table with her gavel and said, "The committee stands in recess for fifteen minutes."

The media descended on the Peñas, who were soon obscured by flashing cameras and shouted questions. An old gray-haired woman sitting near me cast a skeptical eye on the scene and muttered to no one in particular, in Spanish, "The man has no shame."

The cameras were gone when the hearing was called back to order, as was Peña's family, and the proceeding reverted to its original purpose. Peña had resumed his seat and watched a parade of witnesses through half-glasses, showing increasingly less interest as the morning wore on. He passed a note to his neighbor, smiling like a schoolboy, and lit a cigarette, oblivious of the no-smoking sign posted on the wall just a few feet behind him. This face, that of the bored legislator who knew where the real deals were made, seemed more authentic than the teary penitent.

Still, the speech had served its purpose. The old woman who'd pronounced him shameless was definitely in the minority. His East L.A. constituents had lined up to shake his hand, delaying the resumption of business for nearly an hour.

As I sat and watched him, I wondered whether he would have met with such unquestioning forgiveness had he been a white politician. Minority politicians liked to complain about being held to higher standards than their white counterparts by the press, but within their communities even the most outrageous behavior was often pardoned. I understood the reasons for this: mistrust of the media by people who were usually neglected by it and a hunger for leaders among groups who had for so long been without them. Still, when I analyzed what Peña had actually said in his defense, it amounted to a self-serving statement about the burdens of high office. He hadn't mentioned the fact that he had taken another man's life, much less expressed any remorse for it. His grief seemed directed at the setback to his career. I could have forgiven him for his human frailty but not his arrogance. By the time I heard my name called to testify I was incensed.

"Senators, ladies and gentlemen," I began, "I don't think anyone disagrees that there is a growing problem with gang violence in the poorest neighborhoods of the city. This bill, however, will not solve that problem. It will make it worse. This bill is a blank check for the police to come in and round up young men and women because of how they dress, or who they choose as their friends, or simply because the police don't like their looks."

"Excuse me," Peña cut in. "You are a criminal defense lawyer, aren't you, Mr. Rios?"

"That's right, Senator."

"And isn't it true that you have defended gang members in the past?"

"What is that supposed to mean?"

He lurched forward, startled by my asperity. "Well, Mr. Rios, I don't think anyone's surprised about what side you're taking."

"I defend criminals, Senator, but I'm not one myself. Can you make the same statement?"

Everything got very quiet. Peña nodded slowly, as if he'd taken my measure, but I could see he was struggling for a response that wouldn't make him appear completely hypocritical.

"I guess I'm going to have to get used to that kind of smear," he said.

"You have a homicide charge hanging over your head, Senator. That's not a smear, it's a statement of fact."

"My personal problems don't have anything to do with this hearing," he replied.

"Nor does the fact that I'm a defense lawyer," I snapped back. "So if you'll stop imputing my character, I won't discuss yours."

With a dismissive shrug, he leaned back into his chair and focused his attention on the ceiling. I finished my statement and left the podium, catching sight of Tomas Ochoa, who winked approval. Ignoring him, I headed for the door. I heard someone at my back running toward me. I stopped and turned. It was Peña's aide. Breathlessly he said, "Senator Peña would like to talk to you for a minute."

"About what?"

"I don't know, but he's waiting."

Curious. I followed the aide back up the aisle and through a door that led to a small anteroom behind the chamber. Peña was slouching against the wall, smoking. When he saw me, he dropped the cigarette, crushed it, and extended his hand with a broad grin.

"Henry," he said. "It's nice to see you again." My expression must have been as blank as my mind at that moment because he added helpfully, "Last year at the MALDEF dinner. You were with Inez Montoya.

"Of course," I said, remembering that he had been glad-handing at Councilwoman Montoya's table.

He wagged a genial finger at me. "You were pretty tough on me out there."

"You deserved it," I replied.

He clamped his hand on my shoulder, massaging it with thick fingers. "It's all a show, Rios. Nothing personal."

"Under the circumstances, Senator, that's a remarkably cynical thing for you to say."

He dug his fingers deeper my shoulder. "Henry, truce, OK?"

"Sure," I said.

"Listen, we'll let the courts decide whether my bill is constitutional. That's not what I wanted to talk to you about."

"No?"

He dropped his hand from my shoulder, lit another cigarette, and with a curt nod dismissed his aide. "I fucked up good in Sacramento, Rios. I killed a man, and I hurt a lot of other people." His long face took on a distant, pained expression. "I'm still hurting a lot of people. I read that piece about you in the *Times*," he continued. "You've been where I am."

He referred to a profile that had appeared in the paper a few months earlier under the caption "Gay Crusader Fights for the Underdog." The reporter had been thorough in his research, even prevailing upon my sister to describe our bleak childhood, not to mention my own stays at alcohol rehabs over the years, and the fact that my lover was HIV-positive. He seemed to regard these matters as evidence of my saintliness. Reading his piece had made me want to change my name and move to another state.

I said, "The reporter was looking for a hero."

"I'm looking for a friend," Peña said. "Someone who knows what it feels like to fail a lot of people who look up to him."

"I know what it feels like to fail myself," I replied.

"Yeah, well," he exhaled a plume of smoke, "that's the most humiliating part, isn't it? I made myself into somebody from nothing, Rios, just like you. Sure, I made mistakes along the way, but there wasn't anyone to tell me how to do it right. But I got most of it right, anyway," he said, tapping his chest. "Only this thing that happened up there, I don't understand it."

"What don't you understand, Gus?"

"How I got so out of control. I mean, the one thing I know about is control."

"Control's an illusion, Gus," I said. "Being born is like being tossed from a cliff. Grabbing on to the rocks that are falling around you doesn't keep you from falling. You just fall faster."

He smiled bleakly. "What's the difference if you still hit the ground?"

"You can always learn to fly."

He put his cigarette out on the marble wall behind us. "Is that what you do?"

"I'm still letting go of the rocks myself."

"You're a good man, Rios. Can I give you a call sometime?"

"Of course." I gave him a business card, pausing to write my home number on it.

He examined the card, slipped it into his wallet, and patted me on the back. "Say a prayer for me."

I watched him slip back into the council chamber, ashamed of the way I had taken him on during the hearing, but not entirely convinced that I hadn't just been brilliantly manipulated.

⚜ Days Gone by in Orange County

Gloria Velásquez

1997

Gloria Velásquez was born in Colorado and now lives in
California, where she has been teaching Spanish language
and literature at California Polytechnic State University, San
Luis Obispo, since 1985. She created the *Roosevelt High
School* series of novels for young adults, which includes five
books featuring adolescents from different ethnic back-
grounds, and she has published one collection of bilingual
poetry, *I Used to Be a Superwoman* (1997), which has a companion CD featuring her songs and poetry.

I mourn for those days gone by,
the slim-waisted girl I once was,
dressed in beads,
the bearded Chicano at my side,
screaming obscenities at the crowds,
waving peace signs,
drinking beer in honky-tonk bars
with Cowboy and his dogs,
the Beatles
and the smell of stale muscatel.

I mourn for those days gone by,
Martin Luther King Jr.,
"Nigger lovers," they shouted at us,
welfare lines and food stamps,
Vietnam pouring out of the cracks,
the smell of Fini's burnt skin,

the closed coffin
and my mother's screams.

I curse those days gone by
sitting here in my office
surrounded by mediocrity,
academic pimps,
Martin Luther King Jr. dead on the wall,
letters from Vietnam neatly stacked on the shelf,
no more stale muscatel,
no more bearded Chicano,
no more days gone by.

✳ 187

Leroy V. Quintana

1999

Leroy V. Quintana was born in 1944 in Albuquerque, New Mexico. He is the author of six volumes of poetry and has received numerous awards, including two American Book Awards, for *Sangre* (1981) and *Interrogations* (1992). The title of the following poem refers to Proposition 187, California's 1994 anti-immigration law denying social services, health care, and education to illegal immigrants. The proposition was voted into law but later declared unconstitutional and not enforced.

In California there are one hundred and eighty-seven reasons
for a beating. Everything about you is illegal except your hands.
May they move fast, move fast, then move on.
Pray for rain.

✷ Tomorrow Today

Alfred Arteaga

1995

Alfred Arteaga was born in East Los Angeles and raised in Whittier, California. He has written three volumes of poetry, two scholarly works, and a book of creative nonfiction, *House with the Blue Bed* (1998), which won a PEN Oakland Josephine Miles Award. He has worked as an editor for the literary journals *La Raza* and *Quarry West* and has taught at universities in California and Texas. He is currently a professor in the ethnic studies department at the UC Berkeley.

October 11, 1995

Tomorrow marks
five hundred and three years
since Columbus found his way
to the Americas, half
a millennium and three years
since the story of contact began,
since Europe came west.
Tomorrow marks the anniversary.
Five hundred and three winters
have transpired, as many springs,
summers, and falls. Those seasons
are gone, those times have passed,
there is nothing we can do,
they are gone.
Tomorrow we will remember
October 12th, 1492,
here in the United States,

tomorrow will be Columbus Day;
here in Berkeley,
it will be Indigenous Peoples' Day;
here in Califas, Aztlán,
it will be Día de la Raza.
As many winters have passed,
as many suns have set, as many
minutes and seconds have come
and gone, up to the same tomorrow:
Columbus Day, Indigenous Peoples' Day,
Día de la Raza;
but they are not the same.
For we are different and we mean different
when we celebrate
the discovery of a new world, imagine,
a new world, or different when we solemnize
the most severe genocide in the history
of the world, the most severe, or when
we recognize the birth of a new race,
a new race. For twenty-four hours tomorrow
we can celebrate the greatest act
of the Renaissance and the act of a single man
in Columbus Day,
and we can solemnize
the deaths of tens of millions
of Native Americans and the extermination
of whole peoples, such as those
on the islands of first contact,
remembered in Indigenous Peoples' Day
and we can
recognize miscegenation and the possibility
of contact between races
in the birth of hybrid, mestizo peoples
in the Día de la Raza.
Tomorrow is Columbus Day,
it is Indigenous Peoples' Day,
it is Día de la Raza: all exactly
mark five hundred and three years
and all exactly mark something different.
The events that have happened

in the interim have happened,
nothing can change that.
The first joy at the sight of land
happened. The unspeakable terror
of parents watching their child
fed to conquistadors' dogs happened.
Five hundred and three years of events
took place, we cannot change that.
We cannot stand up like Las Casas
and say this must stop; we cannot
tell the Tainos, on first seeing the Spanish arrive,
to run, to run, and not to stop running.
What was, was.
We cannot change the number of days, nor
can we change the events that happened.
We can, though, choose to remember or forget,
to celebrate, solemnize, recognize.

Last year
my state expressed hatred for my people,
marking in law Mexicans as the common evil,
going as far as denying vaccine
so that those of us not deported, aborted,
or incarcerated could die from childhood disease.
The majority of Anglo Americans, of African Americans,
Asian Americans, the majority of women
supported proposition 187.
Why?
Why is it that Chicanos and some Latinos
are the only people whose majority opposed it?
I am not bitter, but I do not forgive.
Don't all of us know, don't we all realize,
the terrible danger when we allow ourselves
to choose among ourselves and choose one
people for exclusion? Don't we realize
what we do to ourselves when we delude
ourselves and support a solution that marks
one people illegal? Any ultimate solution,
any ethnic cleansing, any racism,
any xenophobia of hate, hurts us all.

Each and every one.
For each small act of exclusion
opens the door for more.

This year,
the regents denied affirmative action.
Those regents who direct the university
that employs me, that educated me,
voted for exclusion.
This year, they met and they voted
to prevent Cal and UCLA,
to prevent Riverside, Irvine, and San Diego,
Santa Cruz, Santa Barbara,
Davis, and San Francisco, to prevent
this university from fair policy,
from policy that opposes the practice of exclusion,
from policy that has made opportunities
for people, including me.
Earlier this year the regents so voted.

Tomorrow, we will not be able to change
five hundred and three years of events:
Columbus did what Columbus did; whole
peoples have been exterminated, nothing can
bring them back. But tomorrow, we can
choose to remember or forget, and if to
remember, we can choose how to recall,
we can decide what all that time, all those events,
what all those acts mean.
And our act is significant.
It is true that the regents have voted,
it is true that they have struck down
affirmative action, but it is not true
that nothing can be done about it:
the matter is not over.
Each regent who voted is still alive
and more importantly, I am alive,
and more importantly still, we
are gathered tonight here and we
say the matter is not over.

Some things cannot be changed
but this can.
Whether any individual regent
voted out of intimidation by the governor,
or to support his presidential bid,
whether out of deep-seated racism, or
naive misconception: it does not matter:
that vote was wrong.
I stand here now and say to you
it is wrong to impede us; any step backward
hurts us all. Those who imagine good
from a politics of exclusion delude
themselves: each selfish gain comes at
a cost to all: we share the university,
we share the state.
Affirmative action is not dead history,
sealed and written, it is a live issue
one that right now we are waging.
I stand opposed to racism,
opposed to sexism,
opposed to ethnocentrism.
I oppose the politics of exclusion.
I affirm our action.

Poem for the Young White Man Who Asked Me How I, an Intelligent, Well-Read Person, Could Believe in the War between Races

Lorna Dee Cervantes

1981

Lorna Dee Cervantes earned a Ph.D. in philosophy and aesthetics, an educational background that is reflected in the philosophical nature of much of her work. She was a founding editor and publisher of *Mango,* a cross-cultural literary and art magazine, and she is currently the director of the creative writing program at the University of Colorado at Boulder. Her poems "Cannery Town in August" and "Beneath the Shadow of the Freeway" are also included in this collection.

In my land there are no distinctions.
The barbed-wire politics of oppression
have been torn down long ago. The only reminder
of past battles, lost or won, is a slight
rutting in the fertile fields.

In my land
people write poems about love,
full of nothing but contented childlike syllables.
Everyone reads Russian short stories and weeps.
There are no boundaries.

There is no hunger, no
complicated famine or greed.

I am not a revolutionary.
I don't even like political poems.
Do you think I can believe in a war between races?
I can deny it. I can forget about it
when I'm safe
living in my own continent of harmony
and home, but I am not
there.

I believe in revolution
because everywhere the crosses are burning,
sharp-shooting goose-steppers round every corner,
there are snipers in the school...
(I know you don't believe this.
You think this is nothing
but faddish exaggeration. But they
are not shooting at you.)

I'm marked by the color of my skin.
The bullets are discrete and designed to kill slowly.
They are aiming at my children.
These are facts.
Let me show you my wounds: my stumbling mind, my
"excuse me" tongue, and this
nagging preoccupation
with the feeling of not being good enough.

These bullets bury deeper than logic.
Racism is not intellectual.
I cannot reason these scars away.

Outside my door
there is a real enemy
who hates me.

I am a poet
who yearns to dance on rooftops,

to whisper delicate lines about joy
and the blessings of human understanding.
I try. I go to my land, my tower of words and
bolt the door, but the typewriter doesn't fade out
the sounds of blasting and muffled outrage.
My own days bring me slaps on the face.
Every day I am deluged with reminders
that this is not
my land
and this is my land.

I do not believe in the war between the races

but in this country
there is war.

VIOLENCE

from

♛ Splendor and Death of Joaquín Murieta

Pablo Neruda (translated by Ben Belitt)

1972

Pablo Neruda was born Neftalí Ricardo Reyes Basoalto in 1904 in Chile and started writing and publishing poetry under the name Pablo Neruda as a teenager. His first major work and biggest best-seller, *Twenty Love Poems and a Song of Despair* (1924), established his international reputation as a writer, but he was also known as a political figure, holding diplomatic positions in several East Asian and European countries and serving as a Chilean ambassador to France under president Salvador Allende. His political career included membership in the Communist Party, election to the Chilean senate, winning the 1953 Stalin Prize, and being exiled from his homeland. He wrote for magazines, edited a literary journal, and produced more than forty volumes of poetry, drama, and translations, including large works like *One Hundred Love Sonnets* (1960) and *Canto General* (1950), a collection of 340 poems. Neruda was awarded the Nobel Prize in Literature in 1971, two years before he died of leukemia in Santiago. The scope of Neruda's work extends to California with the play excerpted here about the life of Joaquín Murieta, an outlaw so legendary that several nationalities have claimed him and many scholars believe he was actually several people.

BLOODHOUND: Jest what do you fellers reckon you're up to? Got yer citizenship papers handy? Or mebbe you're jest natural-born citizens of the *U*-nited States of America. We got laws in this land!

CHILEAN: You mean the law of the land office and the pitchmen: all for me and whatever's left over for you? Sure, mister, we know the law.

BLOODH.: If you take my advice, you'll git off yer asses real quiet and git lost. This ain't the *U*-nited States of Mexico, you know! This here is the *U*-nited States of America. This is Uncle Sam's territory. This is the Union.

CHILEAN: Where we come from, the soil belongs to the people who work it. And just now it's our sweat that's working this sand.

BLOODH.: Listen good, greaser. We don't fancy niggers and Chileans here. We don't take to Mexicans. Mexico's down yonder somewhere, over the border. Now, make tracks! Git back where you come from. It'll be a sight healthier!

MEXICAN: Right here is where I come from, Señor Gringo. I'm proud to tell you I'm Mexican-born and hope to die Mexican. Didn't nobody tell you, Señor Gringo, that the soil we're both standing on was baptized with Mexican sweat? They call it Tejas, San Francisco, Zamora in Mexican.

OTHER: They call it Chapanal, Santa Cruz, San Diego, Calaveras: that's Mexican for "skulls."

OTHER: Los Coyotes, San Luis Obispo, Arroyo Cantova.

OTHER: Camula, Buenaventura—that's Good Luck in Mexican.

OTHER: San Gabriel, Sacramento.

MEXICAN: They call it Sonora in Mexico. They call it Cuernavaca.

CHILEAN: In Chile, it's Chillán Viejo or Valparaíso: like you say, the Valley of Paradise.

MEXICAN: Man to man, tell me, compadre: does that sound like gringo—or Christian?

BLOODH.: *(After a pause.)* Sounds like a mouthful of names and foreigners' talk. Nothin but words on a map…Anyhow, school's out, amigo. It's recess time now…Now you git yer ass out of this schoolhouse! We don't take lessons from foreigners here!…It says further on in my history book that they was a war, and we won it…Wanna real lesson in liberty? Free's free and bullshit is bullshit!

ALL BLOODH.: America fer them that was born here. America for the Americans!

CHILEAN: What's that he's saying?

MEXICAN: He just said: all America for North Americans.

BLOODH.: *(Approaches a small flag stuck in a hummock.)* And what's this rag supposed to mean? Who stuck this white-and-green snot rag up here?

CHILEAN: That rag, 'mano, is the flag of the Republic of Chile.

BLOODH.: We don't take kindly to foreigners' flags in this country. They's only one flag in this country.

CHILEAN: You mean there's a law against Chile?

BLOODH.: Betcher ass! We just passed it. This is white folk's country, compadre. And we happen to be *it*. Ever hear tell of the Benevolent Order of Bloodhounds? We make the laws like we like 'em. Now heist that snot rag offa that stick!

(They move toward the flag.)

CHILEAN: If that's how you want it—

(General free-for-all. The flag is picked off with a volley of bullets and burns like a torch. Then the BLOODHOUNDS turn tail.)

(Exit BLOODHOUNDS, pursued by LATIN AMERICANS.)

VOICE OF THE POET:

So the Posse rides on…Lashing their horses, the Killers went on with
    their murders, till they struck at the life
of my countrywoman, the wife of Joaquín, Teresa Murieta.
It's a very old song. Joaquín, coming out of the shadows, never guessed
his love lay defiled on a foreigner's soil, with a nosegay of blood on
    her breast.

His spurs first caught in the weight of her hair; then he trembled. He
dropped to his knees, kissed her eyes closed, swore by the roses and stars:
"Whatever is fallen or fouled or betrayed, I will redress in her name!"
Then he rose up, a bandit, committed in honor and love to wipe out his
   shame.
Every joy vanished, says the Poem: face to face with his sorrow, wild
with his loss, he paid out his lifetime, avenging, opposing, till the wound
   of her dying was healed
and there in the mud and the gold his blood and his guts were spilled.

(Scene: Facade of Murieta's ranch. Enter two MEN, *one hooded, the other in a
   Texan hat. They bang at the door.)*

VOICE OF TERESA: Who's there? What do you want?

HOODED MAN: Is this the residence of Mr. Murieta, please, ma'm?

VOICE OF TERESA: Joaquín isn't here. He left with the lavaderos this
   morning. He hasn't come back from the hills.

HOODED MAN: In that case, ma'm, we'll presoom on your hospitality.
   We'll come in and wait.

*(They hurl themselves on the door. It opens to their fists. They enter the house.
   Noises. A sound of general wreckage.)*

VOICE OF TERESA: Help! Dios mío! Socorro! Asesinos!

*(They all enter. The noise of ruthless pillage and destruction continues. Then a
   silence. Later a long wail from* TERESA. *Minutes pass. Silence. Then laughter. Two shots are heard from within. The attackers exit on the run. The first
   to leave, unhooded now, is the* GENTLEMAN SWINDLER, *who quickly covers
   up again with his hood. A sound of receding hoofbeats…The windows red-
   den; smoke pours from the house of Murieta. Then* MEN *and* WOMEN *are
   seen rushing to the rescue, including a* BIRD VENDOR *carrying a vertical
   stack of bird cages on his back, with a few pigeons visible. They enter the
   house, pulling out chairs and household chattels at top speed. Suddenly there
   is a piercing cry.)*

VOICE: Ay-y-y! Dios mío! Asesinos! Ratones! Gringos malditos!
   They've murdered Teresa!

OTHERS: Sinvergüenzas! Hijos de perras! It's our little Teresa!

VOICE: She's dead! Joaquín's Teresita is dead!

(The WOMEN *kneel in front of the house. A wailing is heard throughout the remainder of the scene. The* MEN *cluster around the* BIRD VENDOR. *One of them, just out of the house with some plates in his hand, stacks them one by one near the* BIRD VENDOR, *and says more to himself than to the others, in a choked voice:)*

MAN: They raped her and left her for dead!

(A wave of revulsion and hate runs through the group.)

VOICES: Jackals! Hyenas! Culebras! Savages! Savages!

VOICES: Get word to Joaquín!

VOICES: We've got to find Murieta!

BIRD VENDOR: Little playmates, little pigeons—find Murieta. Don't come back without him. Vamos, creaturas!

from

♖ Daughter of Fortune

Isabel Allende (translated by Margaret Sayers Peden)

1999

Isabel Allende is best known as the author of more than
nine fiction and nonfiction books, but she has also worked
around the world as a school administrator, a United
Nations employee, a journalist, an editor, and a television
interviewer. She has written several historical novels, including her latest book, *Portrait in Sepia* (2001), and *Daughter of
Fortune* (1999), which is excerpted below. *Daughter of Fortune*
traces a young Chilean woman's journey to California
during the gold rush and the rise of the legend of Joaquín
Murieta. Though fictional, the novel is based on real inci-
dents, including the hanging of Josefa, who was actually
named Juanita. Allende's memoir *Paula* is also excerpted in
this anthology.

IN THE SUMMER OF 1851 JACOB FREEMONT DECIDED to interview Joaquín
Murieta. Outlaws and fires were the chief subjects of conversation in
California; they kept citizens terrorized and the press occupied. Crime
was rampant and police corruption common knowledge; most of the
force was composed of crooks more interested in protecting their partners in crime than the local populace. After one more raging fire, which
destroyed a large area of San Francisco, a vigilante committee had been
formed by outraged citizens, headed by the ineffable Sam Brannan, the
Mormon who had spread the news of the gold. Companies of firemen
pulling water carts by hand ran uphill and down, but before they reached
a burning building, flames would be leaping from the one beside it. The
fire had begun when Australian "hounds" had splashed kerosene all

through the store of a merchant who had refused to pay them protection money and then torched it. In view of the indifference of the authorities, the committee had decided to act on its own. The newspapers clamored, "How many crimes have been committed in this city this year? And who has been hanged or jailed for them? No one! How many men have been shot or stabbed, hit over the head and beat up? And who has been convicted for that? We do not condone lynching, but who can tell what an indignant public will do to protect itself?" Lynchings were precisely the public's solution. Vigilantes immediately threw themselves into the task and hanged the first suspect. The numbers of these self-appointed enforcers grew day by day, and they acted with such excessive enthusiasm that for the first time outlaws took care to move about only in the full light of day. In that climate of violence and revenge, the figure of Joaquín Murieta was on the way to becoming a symbol. Jacob Freemont took it upon himself to fan the flames of Murieta's celebrity: his sensationalist articles had created a hero for Hispanics and a devil for Americans. Murieta was believed to have a large gang and the talent of a military genius; it was said that he was fighting a war of skirmishes that authorities were powerless to combat. He attacked with cunning and speed, descending upon his victims like a curse and then disappearing without a trace, only to show up a hundred miles away with another attack of unbelievable boldness that could be explained only by magic powers. Freemont suspected that there were several "Murietas," not one, but he was careful not to write that because it would have diminished the legend. On the other hand, he had the inspired idea of labeling Murieta "the Robin Hood of California," which immediately sparked a wildfire of racial controversy. To the Yanquis, Murieta represented what was most despicable about the greasers, and it was believed that the Mexicans hid him and provided him with weapons and supplies because he stole from the whites to help the people of his race. In the war they had lost the territories of Texas, Arizona, New Mexico, Nevada, Utah, and half of Colorado and California, and so for them any attack against the victors was an act of patriotism. The governor warned the newspaper against the rashness of making a hero of a criminal, but the name had already inflamed the public's imagination. Freemont received dozens of letters, including one from a young girl in Washington, D.C., who was ready to sail halfway around the world in order to marry that "Robin Hood," and people stopped Freemont in the street to ask him details about the famous Joaquín Murieta. Without ever having seen him, the newspaperman described Murieta as a young man of virile mien, with the features of a noble Spaniard and the courage of a bullfighter. Quite by accident, Freemont had stumbled across a gold mine more productive than many in the mother lode. He decided he must interview this Joaquín, if the fellow really existed, and write his biography, and if it were all a fable he would turn it into a novel. His work as author would consist simply of writing in a heroic tone to satisfy the common man's tastes. California needed its myths and legends, Freemont maintained. To Americans, it had come into the union with a clean slate; they thought that the stroke of a pen could erase a long history of Indians, Mexicans, and Californians. For this land of empty spaces and solitary men, a land open to conquest and rape, what better hero than a bandit?

Freemont packed his indispensables in a suitcase, stocked himself with a supply of notebooks and pencils, and set off in search of his character. The risks never entered his mind; having the dual arrogance of an Englishman and a journalist, he felt he was protected from any harm. In addition, traveling was by now effected with a certain ease; there were highways, and a regular stagecoach service connected the towns where he planned to make his investigations. It was not the way it had been when he had begun his work as a reporter, riding on mule back, forging a path through the uncertainty of hills and forests with no guide but insane maps that could lead one to wander in circles for all time. Along the way, he could see the changes in the region. Few men had made their fortune with gold but, thanks to adventurers who had come by the thousands, California was becoming civilized. Without gold fever, the conquest of the West would have been delayed by a couple of centuries, the journalist wrote in his notebook.

There was no dearth of subjects, such as the story of the young miner, a boy of eighteen, who after a year's backbreaking effort had gotten together the ten thousand dollars he needed to go home to Oklahoma and buy a farm for his parents. He was walking back to Sacramento through the foothills of the Sierra Nevada one radiant day, with his treasure in a sack over his shoulder, when he was surprised by a band of ruthless Mexicans or Chileans, he wasn't sure which. All he knew for sure was that they spoke Spanish, because they had the impudence to leave a sign in that language, scrawled by knifepoint on a piece of wood: "Death to Yanquis." They were not content with beating and robbing him; they tied him naked to a tree and smeared him with honey. Two days later, when he was found by a patrol, he was raving. Mosquitoes had eaten away his skin.

Freemont put his talent for morbid journalism to the test with the tragic death of Josefa, a beautiful Mexican girl who worked in a dance hall. She arrived in the town of Downieville on the Fourth of July and found herself in the midst of a celebration promoted by a candidate for senator and irrigated with a river of alcohol. A drunken miner had forced his way into Josefa's room and she had fought him off, plunging her dagger deep into his heart. By the time Jacob Freemont arrived, the body was lying on a table, covered with an American flag, and a crowd of two thousand fanatics ignited by racial hatred was demanding the gallows for Josefa. Impassive, her white blouse stained with blood, smoking a cigarette as if the yelling had nothing to do with her, the woman was scanning the faces of the men with abysmal scorn, aware of the incendiary mixture of aggression and sexual desire she aroused in them. A doctor tried to take her part, explaining that she had acted in self-defense and that if they executed her they would also kill the baby in her womb, but the mob silenced him by threatening to hang him, too. Three terrified doctors were marched over to examine Josefa and all three declared that she was not pregnant, in view of which the impromptu tribunal condemned her in a matter of minutes. "Shooting these greasers is not the way to go," said one member of the jury. "We have to give them a fair trial and hang them in the full majesty of the law." Freemont had never had occasion to witness a lynching before, but this one he described in emotional sentences: how, about four in the afternoon, they had started to lead Josefa to the bridge where the ritual of execution had been prepared, but she had haughtily shaken them off and walked to the gallows on her own. The beautiful woman climbed the steps without any help, bound her skirts around her ankles, placed the rope around her neck, arranged her black tresses, and bid them farewell with a courageous *"Adios, señores"* that left the journalist uncertain and the others ashamed. "Josefa did not die because she was guilty, but because she was Mexican. This is the first time a woman has been lynched in California. What a waste, when there are so few!" Freemont wrote in his article.

Following Joaquín Murieta's trail, he passed through established towns, with school, library, church, and cemetery, and others whose only signs of culture were a brothel and a jail. Saloons thrived in all of them; they were the centers of social life. Jacob Freemont would install himself there, asking questions, and so began constructing—with some truths and a mountain of lies, the life—or the legend—of Joaquín Murieta. The saloon keepers painted him as a damned spic dressed in leather and black velvet, wearing outsize silver spurs and a dagger at his waist and riding the most spirited sorrel ever seen. They said he would ride into town, unchallenged, amid a jangle of spurs and his gang of cut-throats, slap his silver dollars on the counter and order a round of drinks for everyone in the house. No one dared refuse; even the bravest of men would down their drinks in silence under the villain's flashing gaze. For the constables, on the other hand, there was nothing splendid about him; he was nothing less than a vulgar murderer capable of the worst atrocities, who had managed to escape justice because all the greasers protected him. The Chileans thought he was one of them, born in a place called Quillota; they said he was loyal to his friends and never forgot to repay a favor, which was why it was good policy to help him, but the Mexicans swore he came from the state of Sonora and was an educated, handsome young man from an old and noble family and had turned to crime out of revenge. Gamblers considered him an expert monte player but avoided him because he had crazy luck in cards and a ready dagger that flashed into his hand at the least provocation. White prostitutes were dying with curiosity because it was rumored that this handsome and generous youth had the tireless cock of a stallion, but the Hispanic girls never expected to find out: Joaquín Murieta never used their services but often gave them tips they hadn't earned; they claimed that he was faith-ful to his sweetheart. They described him as a man of medium height, with black hair and eyes like coals, adored by his men, stalwart in the face of trouble, ferocious with his enemies, and gentle with women. Other people said he had the gross features of a born criminal, with a terrible scar right across his face, and that there was nothing of kindness, breeding, or elegance about him. Jacob Freemont selected the opinions that best suited his image of the bandit, and that was how he portrayed him in his articles, always with enough ambiguity that he could print a retraction in case he should someday meet his protagonist face to face. He looked high and low during the four summer months, without finding Murieta anywhere, but from the many different versions he contrived a fanciful and heroic biography. As he did not want to admit defeat, he invented in his articles brief meetings between cock's crow and midnight in mountain caves and forest clearings. After all, who was going to contradict him? Masked men, he wrote, led him on horseback with his eyes blindfolded; he couldn't identify them, but they spoke Spanish. The same fervent eloquence he had used years before in Chile to describe the Patagonian Indians in Tierra del Fuego, where he had never set foot, now served to pull an imaginary outlaw from his sleeve.

He was becoming enamored of the character, and in the end was convinced that he knew him, that the secret meetings in caves were real,
and that the fugitive himself had commissioned him to write about his
feats because he thought of himself as the avenger of oppressed Spanish
peoples, and someone had to assume the responsibility of according him
and his cause a proper place in the developing history of California.
There was little journalism involved, but more than enough fiction for
the novel Jacob Freemont was planning to write that winter.

from

✺ Zoot Suit

Luis Valdez

1978

Luis Valdez was born in 1940 in Delano, California, and
soon after college joined César Chávez's effort to organize
farmworkers, forming El Teatro Campesino, a now internationally known theater troupe that toured labor camps,
educating workers through one-act plays. Valdez, often
called the father of Chicano theater, made history when his
play *Zoot Suit* (1978) became the first work written and
produced by a Chicano to ever appear on Broadway. A
playwright, director, and producer, his honors include an
Emmy, an Obie, three Los Angeles Drama Critics Awards, a
George Peabody Award, and a Golden Globe nomination
for Best Musical Picture for the film version of *Zoot Suit*
(1981). Valdez also directed *La Bamba* (1987), produced *Like
Water for Chocolate* (1993), and helped found the California
Arts Council and California State University, Monterey
Bay, where he currently teaches for the Center of
Teledramatic Arts and Technology. His newest play, first pro-
duced in 2002, is *Mummified Deer*.

SETTING

The giant facsimile of a newspaper front page serves as a drop curtain.
  The huge masthead reads: LOS ANGELES HERALD EXPRESS, *Thursday,*
June 3, 1943.
  A headline cries out: ZOOT-SUITER HORDES INVADE LOS ANGELES.
U.S. NAVY AND MARINES ARE CALLED IN.

Behind this are black drapes creating a place of haunting shadows larger than life. The somber shapes and outlines of pachuco images hang subtly, black on black, against a background of heavy fabric, evoking memories and feelings like an old suit hanging forgotten in the depths of a closet somewhere, sometime....Below this is a sweeping, curving place of levels and rounded corners with the hard, ingrained brilliance of countless spit shines, like the memory of a dance hall.

ACT ONE

PROLOGUE

A switchblade plunges through the newspaper. It slowly cuts a rip to the bottom of the drop. To the sounds of "Perdido" by Duke Ellington, EL PACHUCO *emerges from the slit.* HE *adjusts his clothing, meticulously fussing with his collar, suspenders, cuffs.* HE *tends to his hair, combing back every strand into a long luxurious ducktail, with infinite loving pains. Then* HE *reaches into the slit and pulls out his coat and hat.* HE *dons them. His fantastic costume is complete. It is a zoot suit.* HE *is transformed into the very image of the pachuco myth, from his porkpie hat to the tip of his four-foot watch chain. Now* HE *turns to the audience. His three-soled shoes with metal taps click-clack as* HE *proudly, slovenly, defiantly makes his way downstage.* HE *stops and assumes a pachuco stance.*

PACHUCO: ¿Que le watcha a mis trapos, ese?
    ¿Sabe qué carnal?
    Estas garras me las planté porque
    Vamos a dejarnos caer un play, ¿sabe?

(HE *crosses to center stage, models his clothes.*)

    Watcha mi tacuche, ese. Aliviánese con mis calcos, tando, lisa,
    tramos, y carlango, ese.

(*Pause.*)

    Nel, sabe qué, usted está muy verdolaga. Como se me hace que es
    puro square.

(EL PACHUCO *breaks character and addresses the audience in perfect English.*)

    Ladies and gentlemen
    the play you are about to see
    is a construct of fact and fantasy.

The Pachuco Style was an act in Life
and his language a new creation.

His will to be was an awesome force
eluding all documentation…
A mythical, quizzical, frightening being
precursor of revolution.
Or a piteous, hideous, heroic joke
deserving of absolution?
I speak as an actor on the stage.
The Pachuco was existential
for he was an Actor in the streets
both profane and reverential.
It was the secret fantasy of every bato
in or out of the Chicanada
to put on a Zoot Suit and play the Myth
más chucote que la chingada.

(Puts hat back on and turns.)

¡Pos órale!

(Music. The newspaper drop flies. El Pachuco begins his chuco stroll upstage, swinging his watch chain.)

1. ZOOT SUIT

The scene is a barrio dance in the 1940s. Pachucos and Pachucas in zoot suits and pompadours.

They are members of the 38th Street Gang, led by Henry Reyna, 21, dark, Indian-looking, older than his years, and Della Barrios, 20, his girl-friend in miniskirt and fingertip coat. A Sailor called Swabbie dances with his girlfriend Manchuka among the Couples. Movement. Animation. El Pachuco sings.

Pachuco: Put on a zoot suit, makes you feel real root
    Look like a diamond, sparkling, shining
    Ready for dancing
    Ready for the boogie tonight!

(The Couples, dancing, join the Pachuco in exclaiming the last term of each line in the next verse.)

The hepcats up in Harlem wear that drape shape
Como los Pachucones down in L.A.
Where huisas in their pompadours look real keen
On the dance floor of the ballrooms
Donde bailan swing.

You better get hep tonight
And put on that zoot suit!

(The DOWNEY GANG, *a rival group of pachucos, enters upstage left. Their quick dance step becomes a challenge to* 38TH STREET.)

DOWNEY GANG: Downey...¡Rifa!

HENRY: *(Gesturing back.)* ¡Toma! *(The music is hot.* EL PACHUCO *slides across the floor and momentarily breaks the tension.* HENRY *warns* RAFAS, *the leader of the* DOWNEY GANG, *when* HE *sees him push his brother* RUDY.) ¡Rafas!

PACHUCO: *(Sings.)* Trucha, ese loco, vamos al borlo
Wear that carlango, tramos y tando
Dance with your huisa
Dance to the boogie tonight!

'Cause the Zoot Suit is the style in California
También en Colorado y Arizona
They're wearing that tachuche en El Paso
Y en todos los salones de Chicago

You better get hep tonight
And put on that zoot suit!

2. THE MASS ARRESTS

We hear a siren, then another, and another. It sounds like gangbusters. The dance is interrupted. COUPLES *pause on the dance floor.*

PACHUCO: Trucha, la jura. ¡Pélenle! *(Pachucos start to run out, but* DETECTIVES *leap onstage with drawn guns. A* CUB REPORTER *takes flash pictures.)*

SGT. SMITH: Hold it right there, kids!

LT. EDWARDS: Everybody get your hands up!

RUDY: Watcha! This way! (RUDY *escapes with some others.*)

LT. EDWARDS: Stop or I'll shoot! (EDWARDS *fires his revolver into the air. A number of pachucos and their girlfriends freeze. The cops round them up.* SWABBIE, *an American sailor, and* MANCHUKA, *a Japanese American dancer, are among them.*)

SGT. SMITH: ¡Andale! (*Sees* SWABBIE.) You! Get out of here.

SWABBIE: What about my girl?

SGT. SMITH: Take her with you. (SWABBIE *and* MANCHUKA *exit.*)

HENRY: What about my girl?

LT. EDWARDS: No dice, Henry. Not this time. Back in line.

SGT. SMITH: Close it up!

LT. EDWARDS: Spread! (*The* PACHUCOS *turn upstage in a line with their hands up. The sirens fade and give way to the sound of a teletype. The* PACHUCOS *turn and form a lineup, and the* PRESS *starts shooting pictures as* HE *speaks.*)

PRESS: The City of the Angels, Monday, August 2, 1942. *The Los Angeles Examiner,* Headline:

THE LINEUP: (*In chorus.*) Death Awakens Sleepy Lagoon. (*Breath.*) L.A. Shaken by Lurid "Kid" Murder.

PRESS: The City of the Angels, Monday, August 2, 1942. *The Los Angeles Times,* Headline:

THE LINEUP: One Killed, Ten Hurt in Boy Wars. (Breath.) Mexican Boy Gangs Operating within City.

PRESS: The City of the Angels, August 2, 1942. *Los Angeles Herald Express,* Headline:

THE LINEUP: Police Arrest Mexican Youths. Black-Widow Girls in Boy Gangs.

PRESS: The City of the Angels...

PACHUCO: *(Sharply.)* El Pueblo de Nuestra Señora la Reina de los Angeles de Porciúncula, pendejo.

PRESS: *(Eyeing the* PACHUCO *cautiously.) The Los Angeles Daily News,* Headline:

BOYS IN THE LINEUP: Police Nab 300 in Roundup.

GIRLS IN THE LINEUP: Mexican Girls Picked Up in Arrests.

LT. EDWARDS: Press Release, Los Angeles Police Department: A huge showup of nearly three hundred boys and girls rounded up by the police and sheriff's deputies will be held tonight at eight o'clock in Central Jail at First and Hill Street. Victims of assault, robbery, purse snatching, and similar crimes are asked to be present for the identification of suspects.

PRESS: Lieutenant…? (EDWARDS *poses as the* PRESS *snaps a picture.)*

LT. EDWARDS: Thank you.

PRESS: Thank you. (SMITH *gives a signal, and the lineup moves back, forming a straight line in the rear, leaving* HENRY *up front by himself.)*

LT. EDWARDS: Move! Turn! Out! *(As the rear line moves off to the left following* EDWARDS, SMITH *takes* HENRY *by the arm and pulls him downstage, shoving him to the floor.)*

3. PACHUCO YO

SGT. SMITH: Okay, kid, you wait here till I get back. Think you can do that? Sure you can. You pachucos are regular tough guys. (SMITH *exits.* HENRY *sits up on the floor.* EL PACHUCO *comes forward.)*

HENRY: Bastards. (HE *gets up and paces nervously. Pause.)* ¿Ese? ¿Ese?

PACHUCO: *(Behind him.)* ¿Qué pues, nuez?

HENRY: *(Turning.)* Where the hell you been, ese?

PACHUCO: Checking out the barrio. Qué desmadre, ¿no?

HENRY: What's going on, ese? This thing is big.

PACHUCO: The city's cracking down on pachucos, carnal. Don't you read the newspapers? They're screaming for blood.

HENRY: All I know is they got nothing on me. I didn't do anything.

PACHUCO: You're Henry Reyna, ese—Hank Reyna! The snarling juvenile delinquent. The zoot-suiter. The bitter young pachuco gang leader of 38th Street. That's what they got on you.

HENRY: I don't like this, ese. *(Suddenly intense.)* I DON'T LIKE BEING LOCKED UP!

PACHUCO: Calmantes montes, chicas patas. Haven't I taught you to survive? Play it cool.

HENRY: They're going to do it again, ese! They're going to charge me with some phony rap and keep me until they make something stick.

PACHUCO: So what's new?

HENRY: *(Pause.)* I'm supposed to report for the Navy tomorrow. (THE PACHUCO *looks at him with silent disdain.)* You don't want me to go, do you?

PACHUCO: Stupid move, carnal.

HENRY: *(Hurt and angered by* PACHUCO's *disapproval.)* I've got to do something.

PACHUCO: Then hang tough. Nobody's forcing you to do shit.

HENRY: I'm forcing me, ese—ME, you understand?

PACHUCO: Muy patriotic, eh?

HENRY: Yeah.

PACHUCO: Off to fight for your country.

HENRY: Why not?

PACHUCO: Because this ain't your country. Look what's happening all around you. The Japs have sewed up the Pacific. Rommel is kicking ass in Egypt but the Mayor of L.A. has declared all-out war on Chicanos. On you! ¿Te curas?

HENRY: Orale.

PACHUCO: Qué mamada, ¿no? Is that what you want to go out and die for? Wise up. These bastard paddy cops have it in for you. You're a marked man. They think you're the enemy.

HENRY: *(Refusing to accept it.)* Screw them bastard cops!

PACHUCO: And as soon as the Navy finds out you're in jail again, ya estuvo, carnal. Unfit for military duty because of your record. Think about it.

HENRY: *(Pause.)* You got a frajo?

PACHUCO: Simón. (HE *pulls out a cigarette, hands it to* HENRY, *lights it for him.* HENRY *is pensive.)*

HENRY: *(Smokes, laughs ironically.)* I was all set to come back a hero, see? Me la rayo. For the first time in my life I really thought Hank Reyna was going someplace.

PACHUCO: Forget the war overseas, carnal. Your war is on the home front.

HENRY: *(With new resolve.)* What do you mean?

PACHUCO: The barrio needs you, carnal. Fight back! Stand up to them with some style. Show the world a Chicano has balls. Hang tough. You can take it. Remember, Pachuco Yo!

HENRY: *(Assuming the style.)* Con safos, carnal.

4. THE INTERROGATION

The PRESS *enters, followed by* EDWARDS *and* SMITH.

PRESS: *(To the audience.)* Final Edition, *The Los Angeles Daily News.* The police have arrested twenty-two members of the 38th Street Gang, pending further investigation of various charges.

LT. EDWARDS: Well, son, I was hoping I wouldn't see you in here again.

HENRY: Then why did you arrest me?

LT. EDWARDS: Come on, Hank, you know why you're here.

HENRY: Yeah. I'm a Mexican.

LT. EDWARDS: Don't give me that. How long have I known you? Since '39?

HENRY: Yeah, when you got me for stealing a car, remember?

LT. EDWARDS: All right. That was a mistake. I didn't know it was your father's car. I tried to make it up to you. Didn't I help you set up the youth club?

SGT. SMITH: They turned it into a gang, Lieutenant. Everything they touch turns to shit.

LT. EDWARDS: I remember a kid just a couple of years back. Head boy at the Catholic Youth Center. His idea of fun was going to the movies. What happened to that nice kid, Henry?

PRESS: He's "Gone with the Wind," trying to look like Clark Gable.

SGT. SMITH: Now he thinks he's Humphrey Bogart.

PACHUCO: So who are you, puto? Pat O'Brien?

LT. EDWARDS: This is the wrong time to be antisocial, son. This country's at war, and we're under strict orders to crack down on all malcontents.

SGT. SMITH: Starting with all pachucos and draft dodgers.

HENRY: I ain't no draft dodger.

LT. EDWARDS: I know you're not. I heard you got accepted by the Navy. Congratulations. When do you report?

HENRY: Tomorrow?

SGT. SMITH: Tough break!

LT. EDWARDS: It's still not too late, you know. I could still release you in time to get sworn in.

HENRY: If I do what?

LT. EDWARDS: Tell me, Henry, what do you know about a big gang fight last Saturday night, out at Sleepy Lagoon?

PACHUCO: Don't tell 'em shit.

HENRY: Which Sleepy Lagoon?

LT. EDWARDS: You mean there's more than one? Come on, Hank, I know you were out there. I've got a statement from your friends that says you were beaten up. Is that true? Were you and your girl attacked?

HENRY: I don't know anything about it. Nobody's ever beat me up.

SGT. SMITH: That's a lie and you know it. Thanks to your squealer friends, we've got enough dope on you to indict for murder right now.

HENRY: Murder?

SGT. SMITH: Yeah, murder. Another greaser named José Williams.

HENRY: I never heard of the bato.

SGT. SMITH: Yeah, sure.

LT. EDWARDS: I've been looking at your record, Hank. Petty theft, assault, burglary, and now murder. Is that what you want? The gas chamber? Play square with me. Give me a statement as to what happened at the Lagoon, and I'll go to bat for you with the Navy. I promise you.

PACHUCO: If that ain't a line of gabacho bullshit, I don't know what is.

LT. EDWARDS: Well?

PACHUCO: Spit in his pinche face.

SGT. SMITH: Forget it, Lieutenant. You can't treat these animals like people.

LT. EDWARDS: Shut up! I'm thinking of your family, Hank. Your old man would be proud to see you in the Navy. One last chance, son. What do you say?

HENRY: I ain't your son, cop.

LT. EDWARDS: All right, Reyna, have it your way. (EDWARDS *and* PRESS *exit.*)

PACHUCO: You don't deserve it, ese, but you're going to get it anyway.

SGT. SMITH: All right, muchacho, it's just me and you now. I hear tell you pachucos wear these monkey suits as a kind of armor. Is that right? How's it work? This is what you zooters need—a little old-fashioned discipline.

HENRY: Screw you, flatfoot.

SGT. SMITH: You greasy son of a bitch. What happened at the Sleepy Lagoon? Talk! Talk! Talk! (SMITH *beats* HENRY *with a rubber sap.* HENRY *passes out and falls to the floor, with his hands still handcuffed behind his back.* DOLORES, *his mother, appears in a spot upstage as he falls.)*

DOLORES: Henry! *(Lights change. Four* PACHUCO COUPLES *enter, dancing a 1940s pasodoble (two-step) around* HENRY *on the floor, as they swing in a clothesline of newspaper sheets. Music.)*

PACHUCO: Get up and escape, Henry…
    leave reality behind
    with your buenas garras
    muy chamberlain
    escape through the barrio streets of your mind
    through a neighborhood of memories
    all chuckhole lined
    and the love
    and the pain
    as fine as wine…

 # El Louie

José Montoya

1992

José Montoya was born in 1932 in New Mexico and grew up moving with his family between New Mexico and California. After serving in the Korean War, Montoya studied art in college, eventually becoming an art professor at California State University, Sacramento, where he taught for twenty-seven years. An accomplished painter, poet, songwriter, and musician, he was one of the founding members of the Barrio Arts Program, the Rebel Chicano Art Front arts collective (later known as the Royal Chicano Air Force), and *El Grito,* one of the first Chicano journals. His diverse body of work includes several collections of poetry, internationally shown paintings, and a CD recording with his band, José Montoya y Casindo. Montoya was named Sacramento's poet laureate in 2002.

Hoy enterraron al Louie.

And San Pedro o san pinche
Are in for it. And those
Times of the forties
And the early fifties
Lost un vato de atole.

Kind of slim and drawn,
There toward the end,
Aging fast from too much
Booze y la vida dura. But
Class to the end.

En Sanjo you'd see him
Sporting a dark topcoat
Playing in his fantasy
The role of Bogart, Cagney
Or Raft.

Era de Fowler el vato,
Carnal del Candi y el
Ponchi–Los Rodriguez–
The Westside knew 'em
And Selma, even Gilroy.
'48 Fleetline, two-tone–
Buenas garras and always
Rucas—como la Mary y
La Helen…siempre con
Liras bien afinadas
Cantando La Palma, la
Que andaba en el florero.

Louie hit on the idea in
Those days for tailor-made
Drapes, unique idea—porque
Fowler no era nada como
Los, 'ol E.P.T. Fresno's
Westside was as close as
We ever got to the big time.

But we had Louie, and the
Palomar, el boogie, los
Mambos y cuatro suspiros
Del alma y nunca faltaba
That familiar, gut-shrinking,
Love-splitting, asshole-up-
Tight, bad news…

　　Trucha, esos! Va 'ver
　　Pedo!
　　Abusau, ese!
　　Get Louie!

No llores, Carmen, we can
Handle 'em.
> Ese, 'on tal Jimmy?
> Orale, Louie!
> Where's Primo?
> Va 'ver catos!
En el parking lot away from the jura
> Orale!
> Trais filero?
> Simon!
> Nel!
> Chale, ese!
> Oooooh, este vato!

An Louie would come through—
Melodramatic music, like in the
Mono—tan tan tran!—Cruz
Diablo, El Charro Negro! Bogart
Smile (his smile as deadly as
His vaisas) He dug roles, man,
And names—like "Blackie," "Little
Louie…"

Ese Louie…
Chale, man, call me "Diamonds!"

Y en Korea fue soldado de
Levita con huevos and all the
Paradoxes del soldado razo—
Heroism and the stockade!
And on leave, jump boots
Shainadas and ribbons, cocky
From the war, strutting to
Early mass on Sunday morning.

Wow, is that 'ol Louie?

Mire, comadre, ahí va el hijo
De Lola!

Afterward he and fat Richard
Would hock their Bronze Stars
For pisto en el Jardin Canales
Y en El Trocadero.

At barber college he came
Out with honors. Despues
Enpeñaba su velardo de la
Peluca pa' jugar pocar serrada
And lo ball en Sanjo y Alviso.

And "Legs Louie Diamond" hit
On some lean times…

Hoy enterraron a Louie.

Y en Fowler at Nesei's
Pool parlor los baby chukes
Se acuerdan de Louie, el carnal
Del Candi y el Ponchi—la vez
Que lo fileriaron en el Casa
Dome y cuando se catio con
La Chiva.

Hoy enterraron al Louie.

His death was an insult
Porque no murio en accion
No lo mataron los vatos,
Ni los gooks en Korea.
He died alone in a
Rented room—perhaps like in a
Bogart movie.

The end was a cruel hoax.
But his life had been
Remarkable!

  Vato de atolle, el Louie Rodriguez.

from

✵ Gods Go Begging

Alfredo Véa

1999

Alfredo Véa was born in 1952 in Arizona, of Mexican and Yaqui Indian ancestry. He worked as a migrant farmworker before being sent to Vietnam, after which he attended law school and became a criminal defense attorney. He is the author of three critically acclaimed novels, and his latest, *Gods Go Begging* (1999), was named one of the best books of the year by the *Los Angeles Times* and won the Bay Area Book Reviewers' Award for Fiction. Jesse, the central figure of *Gods Go Begging,* is, like Véa, an attorney in San Francisco.

TWO GROUPS OF MEN HAD MET ON ONE FACE OF THIS HILL, and their savage intentions had left every tree limb and twig disfigured. Unwatered since the last monsoon rains, the small hill of dry and cracked earth had been sickened to nausea by this forced feeding of burned sulfur and human fluids. Here and there intrepid flowers persisted between fissures and fox-holes, their soft petals and thin stems choked shut by the savage spray, the crimson effluence of exit wounds. Against their will, the living poppies masqueraded as roses.

In one place, a ragged patch of hair follicles and skin soiled the stigma and stamens of a weeping blueblossom, repelling bee after bee. In another, scores of red seeds had erupted from human bodies, bursting violently through the drabness of cloth and skin—seed of stomach, seed of lung, hopeless grains set onto the wind. Everywhere, shell casings littered the garden like brazen chaff.

Among the wide spray of innards was a slice of cerebellum, a single sliver of mind, thrown yards from its previous owner. On a stem of wild lemongrass hung a taste for grape soda and shepherd's pie, the memory of her good-bye, even the newborn baby's impulse to cry when the world was upside down. On a leaf of wild lemongrass specks of sense were stranded and fading—three digits of a phone number, a single syllable from the second verse of a cherished song, and half a glimpse of a woman's entire face.

At the top of the hill, drying in the sunlight, was an array of green pods: plastic bags snapped shut and steaming from within. A chaplain crawled among them, calling out to God and screaming the names of the newly dead at the top of his lungs. His body shook with palsy as he went from bag to bag retrieving a dog tag and their personal effects and marking soiled paperwork with their names and the date of their death.

A sergeant by his side was helping him with the grisly duty. Below them, grunts were laying out more concertina wire, setting new trip flares, and replanting the hill with claymore mines. Behind the landing pad, the bunkers that protected the radio emplacement were being rebuilt by a gaggle of shirtless, wordless men.

"Try to calm down, padre," said the black sergeant. "Tonight's gonna be our last night in this place. I'm sure of that." He had a smooth and soothing Southern accent. His voice was a round baritone with a burnish of gentleness that belied his muscular build and serious eyes. A hint of both French and of Dixieland seasoned every sentence he spoke.

"I just talked to battalion. I gave them a sit-rep from hell and they won't dare leave us hanging like last night. You have my word on that. Now, take some deep breaths, padre. Otherwise you're gonna bust your heart wide open. I've seen it happen. Like the boys always say, keep your shit wired tight."[…]

Down below the sad array of green pods, below the Creole sergeant and the frightened chaplain, a group of young men had gathered to smoke and to calm one another down. Except for a swatch of olive drab here and there, they were all the same color as the clinging red dust around them. They moved and spoke awkwardly, sleepwalking their way through wave after wave of inexpressible grief and fatigue. The hair on the napes of their necks would be standing for hours, their semi-permeable skin would crawl for days.

The ground around them was littered with shell casings, claymore bags, ration cans, discarded harnesses, and torn rucksacks. There were broken sandbags everywhere, smoke grenades, and the ominous wrappings that had once held field bandages. Here and there were the empty pith helmets of the North Vietnamese.

"Jesse," said Cornelius, a young black man from Oakland, "how come a college-boy pogue like you is here with his ass in the grass like all us illiterate grunts? You ain't eleven-bravo, is you?"

Cornelius was referring to the military occupational specialty number for an infantryman.

"You too smart for eleven-bravo. Is you one of those spooky crypto dudes?"

Cornelius was tall and thin, impossibly thin. His skin color had gone past black and looked purple in the sun. All of his classmates at Castlemont High School had been unmerciful with him for four full years. Back home at chicken dinners with his family, his mother had set aside all the gizzards and chicken skins for him to eat, but it had never made any difference in his weight. She'd made rice and gravy just for him using nothing but rice, flour, and pure bacon drippings, but the boy never gained a pound. She made him suck on spoons full of Crisco, but his skin remained stuck to his rib cage. No one knew where he got the strength to lug an M-60 machine gun around. An extra barrel and belt of cartridges were strapped across his narrow back. The letters FTA were written on every square inch of Cornelius's clothing, flak vest, and helmet. Fuck The Army.

"I went to Berkeley for one year, two semesters," sneered Jesse with a distracted, stunned air, "and I'm here because I'm a fucking idiot." His voice was raspy and brittle. He could not keep his teeth from chattering. Death's tongue had reached down into his small intestines. He removed his flak vest as he spoke, then used his T-shirt to wipe the mud and sweat from his face. He didn't mind the questioning. No one did. Conversations after great sorrow were now a necessity of life. They often took strange and unforeseeable twists. The discussions had a life of their own. They had to.

"Jesus," Jesse said softly, "I think I aged ten years last night. I never, ever want to go through that again. My teeth are all loose from the stress. My gums are black. I've had enough of this."

"Now, even I know you ain't no idiot," said Cornelius. "First time I talked with you I could tell right off. Word is you coulda been the driver for a full-bird colonel." He placed both hands on an imaginary steering wheel and managed a smile as he spoke. "Now, that would surely be the gravy train." He smiled. "Colonels don't get shot in this here war. A man who drives for a colonel done fell into a real fat spot."

"Shit," said Jesse, trying hard to shake the fear and shock from his thoughts, "that's ancient history. They offered me that job way down in Bien Hoa when I was still pissin' stateside water. The colonel almost shit when I turned him down. They got so pissed at me that they sent me up to the DMZ, to Dong Ha, the armpit of the fucking world. The day I got there the Têt offensive kicked off. I swear to God, the second I stepped off that chopper some sappers hit the ammo dump. The zips were probing and pounding that place for weeks."

"You avoidin' the question, my man," insisted Cornelius. "I've heard you talkin' that *parlez-vous* French with them Montagnards and talkin' that Mexican lingo with Mendez and Lopez. You must've done something real bad to end up here with all the bloods and spics. How did you get on this hill? And why the fuck are we up here guarding a fucking radio installation in the first place? And why the hell does Charlie give a shit about this place when I sure as shit don't? "

"We're a communications relay," answered Jesse in a hollow and mechanical voice. "Something is happening out there past the free-fire zone and across the border—air strikes, black operations. You saw the crypto guys that they airlifted out of here yesterday?"

"Yeah, just before the feces come into contact with the fan," said Cornelius with a disdainful laugh. He hated army intelligence. They were never right, and they never stuck around to see what happened when they were wrong. Last night they had fallen all over themselves in their mad dash for the safety of the choppers, all the while assuring field command on the hill that there were no NVA units in the area larger than platoon strength. The chickenshits left behind most of their equipment, two half-full cups of warm coffee, and three battalions of seasoned North Vietnamese regulars with mortars and heavy armor just beyond the treeline.

"Those army intelligence officers sure know how to stand by their predictions," sneered Jesse as he recalled the special treatment that had been given those men. They had been hustled off like a gaggle of spoiled, self-indulgent celebrities. By now they would be buying Saigon tea for some half-naked bar girls in Da Nang. Right now they could be eating slices of pepperoni pizza at the Special Forces compound or swimming at the Air Force pool near China Beach. Jesse shook his head in anger. They didn't draft college kids, and the boys with the lowest test scores in boot camp were stuck in the infantry. It was always the sons of the poor who ended up on hills like this.

"I think we're a conduit into Laos from I Corps command in Da Nang; that's why we have both a tropospheric scatter dish and a line-of-sight relay system," explained Jesse.

"Jesús, hijo de Dios!" moaned a voice with a Mexican accent. Someone wanted a translation of that last sentence.

"Someone very far away is talking to somebody just on the other side of the Laotian border," explained Jesse. "It's all scrambled when it comes through here, and they're rotating codes and frequencies every twenty minutes. Everything's in code. Top-secret shit."

"Shit is right," said Cornelius. "It's them CIA fuckups again. I shoulda known it. I shoulda known! I bet the spooks is sticking them poor South Vietnamese rangers in there again, trying to infiltrate the troops that is coming down old Ho's trail. It never fucking works," said Cornelius disgustedly. "Poor bastards always get caught, and the CIA always leaves them twisting in the breeze, pretending it never happened. I tell you, if the CIA ever wants my black ass to do anything, I wants the money up front, in small unmarked bills. Talk about the gravy train, all their fuckups are a secret."

"Yeah," said Jesse, "I've heard it described as an insertion operation. I've been told that the spooks have been pouring money and guns into some turncoat Pathet Lao cadre. They're supposed to help with the infiltration. They've been doing the same thing above the DMZ for years. But hell, for all I know, everything I've heard is bullshit. But getting back to your question about how I got here, the staff sergeant over there convinced me to come. He said that my ass needed to be farther out in the grass, that Dong Ha was easy street compared to the bush. He knew that in my confused heart, I wanted to come and see what the grunts were up to. I know how to fix all the radio equipment up there, and you needed a second RTO, so here I am."

Jesse pointed toward the PRC-25 at his feet, a radio the size of a large rucksack that had a very conspicuous antenna. The first radiotelephone operator was lying in one of the body bags at the top of the hill.

"I speak *pocho* Spanish because I'm Chicano, and passable French because I once had a girlfriend from Quebec. She was one sweet thing. I haven't had much opportunity to speak French until I came to the Nam. A lot of the older folks here still *parlent Français*; some of the Montagnards, some of the bar girls, and all of the Catholic nuns do. Sometimes the Sarge and I practice our French on each other. It comes in handy over here."

As he spoke, the image of Hong Trac's cold body lying by a roadside back in Da Nang pushed its way back into his mind's eye. He could hear the sharp clicking of the photographer's camera. The blond hair of the French woman was the last image to fade from his mind.

"But that's all I'm going to say about my past. It's really not very interesting. Right now all I want is to be any place on earth but here, but I'll settle for a Thai stick, a bath, and two weeks in Singapore. This boonie shit ain't for my ass. I can't believe I volunteered for this." He held his hands out as he spoke. They were still shaking violently. They had been shaking for hours.

"Hit on this," said a voice behind the glowing ash of a joint that had been extended to Jesse. It was Jim-Earl, the Shoshone from the Wind River Reservation. Almost every Indian that had enlisted or who had been drafted by the army had been put directly into the infantry.

Jesse took the cigarette, inhaled deeply, then held his breath for a few seconds before speaking. "Now you guys have to answer a question for me. What was your asshole pucker factor last night? I need some sort of gauge for future reference—just in case there is a future."

"Mine was a definite ten." Cornelius laughed and reached around with his right hand and rubbed his ass. It had leaked. "Good thing this here underwear is green." He reached around and checked the front of his pants, too. "Seems I done leaked from every damn hole. I'll tell you, the army sure has been good for my sex life. Every time I turn around, I'm gettin' fucked."

"It was a definite eleven," said another voice. "Fuck, it still is," added the voice. There was a look of distance and horror in the speaker's eyes. He was a new grunt, a boy from Nevada who had a pronounced overbite and one slow eye.

"That's good to hear. I feel better now." Jesse sighed. "But I really don't think my asshole will ever open again. The damn thing is sealed shut. I didn't know there was that much fear anywhere in the universe. It's been hours and I'm still shaking from it. My heart won't slow down and I'm so numb I can't feel my fingers and my feet. I have deep cuts everywhere and I don't know how or when I got them."

He exhaled deeply as he probed a dozen new lacerations and abrasions. Now he started to feel the pain. Jesse couldn't know it as he spoke, but his voice was no longer the same. Around each forced word that left his lips was a deathly host of sullen harmonics, echoes of savagery, second- and third-order resonances of screams and sighs, sights of explicit mortality, and images of incredible courage that had settled in to infect and to bless each day for the rest of his life.

"Join the club," said a Midwestern voice. "I went my whole first tour of duty without ever getting this close to Charlie. I can't believe it, last night the fuckin' dinks was running right between our bunkers. I could hear 'em talking. I could see their faces. Jesus, I thought I was dead."

"I felt like there were lead weights all over me," continued Jesse, who somehow felt compelled to keep talking, "like I was moving in Jell-O. At first I was too afraid to pull the trigger, then I was too scared to stop. If there had been a Southern Baptist church choir in front of me, I would have shot it to pieces." He turned to gaze at the body bags lined up at the crest of the hill.

"Human life is only worth what we agree it's worth. There's no intrinsic value." Jesse's voice almost broke as he spoke. He had dared to say the ancient secret out loud.

from

✸ Days of Invasion

Juan Felipe Herrera

1992

Juan Felipe Herrera is a writer, professor, graphic designer, performer, theater director, and the founding force behind several multi-media poetry performance groups, including Teatro Tolteca in Los Angeles and TROCA in San Francisco. He has written more than twenty books of poetry, been widely anthologized, and won numerous writing awards, including a Pura Belpré Award, an Americas Award, two Pushcart Prize Poetry nominations, a Smithsonian Award, and an Academy of American Poets nomination for the William Carlos Williams Poetry Award. His poem "Exiles" also appears in this volume.

I DECIDED TO LEAVE FOR CENTRAL AMERICA WITH ZETA. Sure did. I was better off in Panama, maybe. I always ended up doing whatever Zeta got into, anyway. At City College, he used to hang around the teachers after class talking about astrology, Sartre, and French films. French films? Never even had French bread. So I went along. Never said a thing. Nothing. Just kinda smiled. One time even gave everyone a penny. Didn't know what to do or say. Just gave them a penny. Then, at school: *Thus Spoke Zarathustra* on my desk in chemistry lab. My mom was scared; she thought I was getting into devil stuff. It all worked itself out, somehow. Follow Zeta, it's OK, it told me, this thin stuff here inside my gut. Zeta is right, it said.

"I'll tell you about the Marine thing later, man." Zeta was throwing his arms up, pulling at his goatee, swiveling his shoulders, loose, striding, as we stepped out of the wrinkled wagon-bus we had boarded in the open-air depot back in Guatemala City. Later, "They say Edgar has-n't been seen in weeks." Zeta looked concerned as he hung up the phone outside the main plaza in Tegucigalpa. Edgar was a guy on the inside of things—an accountant by day, a sentry for the Left by night.

The white colonial towers bounced light through the trees. I was spinning. Heat thickened the fragrance of the budding flowers. In the plaza, a half-naked boy tumbled over a towel sprinkled with glass sliv-ers. Another blew out fire from his mouth, eyeing the *turistas* rushing by, looking for hotels, cigarettes, taxis.

By nightfall, we had ended up in Panama City, stopped at a cafe. Zeta mumbled something about trekking twenty-five kilometers fur-ther south. We rested and smoked. Then he made a call and got direc-tions to Edgar's place in the hills. Edgar would fill us in—we were close, he said.

In the morning we found Edgar barely alive in a small village.

I thought about all this on the pier.

Crawling through the smoking corn slush, pushing my boots down on the blackened sod, then Zeta found Edgar ahead of me. Bullets burned in his right thigh. A gaping hole by his shoulders. Edgar was dreamy and spurted words as best he could, pointing ahead to a river. The villagers had fled to the border river, he said. Old farmers, women, and children shot down by American soldiers—Edgar kept on repeating this and pointed again; there had been helicopters. Zeta went further. He disappeared and then came up holding the hand of another body along the field.

It was raining—hard rain smashing the wide, red-flared plant leaves along the small roads. I could hear the mad ticking all around and inside of me. The sky lowered and then unraveled its dark knots that had been tightening since dusk and then, thunder. All the tiny things in the earth below were loosening with a music of their own—little bones in water letting go of their cargo suddenly; all around us, the corn fields whitened in a sharp, strange light, a pure light. Zeta! His arms come up, caught in a storm of flickering sheaths, little blazing shards, his face slowly going to the side and the torso—stretching, curling at the edges, the thousand brilliant translucent shells falling to his feet—in a mil-lisecond, not far from me; I lost Zeta to this light. I ran to Edgar and told him I would come back with help.

I can still hear the lightning.

I've been pacing every walkway in San Francisco for the last two weeks thinking about this. Been drinking too much Yukon Jack syrup. Yesterday, it took me two hours to get out of the house—lost the keys in my sweatshirt, left the door open, got back and thought my cassette player had been stolen. Then, remembered I had pawned it for more fast food, cigarettes, and sweet drinks.

Standing.

Thinking in the middle of the street. Shotwell Avenue. Zeta's last mural. I look to the southern sky and try to make the connection between Zeta's crazy acrylics—the swirling elongations of arms, robes, the fleshy ochre whiteness, even the piety of the hands as they reach up towards something dark and unknown—and my last image of him.

There was nothing that could be done in Panama.

I wandered back—caught buses. Bummed money from old pals in Mexico City. Made it to Mexicali to pick up the Chevy we had parked before catching a train. It was slouched over a ravine by the train station. The seats were littered with orange sandwich papers, diapers, and soiled pillows. I dumped the papers and diapers and a knot of newspapers that was stuffed into the door to keep out the cold air. Filled up one of the tires with air and made it to Escondido, California. Bummed more gas money and a dinner from Gabby Vasquez, a good buddy of mine who is the only decent person I know that is happily married—three kids and a wife named Rosemary. In his house there was a filmy kind of steam making everything moist: the wood grain on the door, the television's blackish rubbery plastic molding. Even Rosemary. Her lips, porous, the hair on her arms longer, lighter—having another baby, going to name him Toño, she said. Gabby gets up early. Pulls out his jump rope with a black ball at the end of each cord. Five hundred, he says. Five hundred. I open my hands to my side, tighten my fingers two or three times, then close them into a fist and leave to San Francisco in one straight drive, loop into downtown where the green and silver windows block out everything the sun gives except the abstract noise shooting up from the asphalt. I park the Chevy on Polk, walk away still seeing patches of the corn field in front of me uprooted in yellowish brown heaps and the waxy faces and shoulders falling out of the bloody slush. And the brilliant lights crashing on Zeta.

My mother once told me about what happened before we moved to San Francisco. I was a child and my father, Emilio, was working the tractor as a farmhand out on the edge of a town bordering Arizona. The immigration patrol had snared three Mexicans without papers. They were taunting them and from a large reserve can poured gasoline on one of the men. My father never told anyone else about it. The immigration officers would blame him, he said. He would rub his face hard when he said this, then turn away.

It was getting late. The streets were hurting me—pacing in squares and zigzags, leaning on little restaurant walls I had never visited. My face against the windows. See the thick coats hunched over a bowl of soup, the nervous hands flipping the basket for more French bread. A waitress chewing gum grimaces at a wino that steps in and shoves a menu into him like a knife. Couples with their tiny pink pastry boxes in a bag hang their coats and wait for a glass of water to wash things away. My stomach churns, I tap my cigarette pack against the fleshy part of my palm and light one, slowly eyeing the furniture specials on the street.

The furniture stores still put up the same old Christmas sale signs, I chuckle sourly.

I thought of Zeta and Edgar. There was nothing I could do about Edgar. I told the villagers to go for him. What more could I do?

Central America was always hot. We said it—over a wine cooler or at a poetry reading in the Mission District. None of us would even dare leave San Francisco. And any fire-play out there gave us more reason to stay put.

I couldn't get back into the city—no matter how much I tried to dig into the concrete. Just couldn't get back.

Days are at a standstill. Papers say Noriega lives in the Vatican Embassy now—listens to heavy metal blasting from the Marines' speakers. He doesn't want to show his face.

The old deli had a dim light on. It was a greenish two-story Victorian that stood on the corner facing a Bekins storage facility—maybe the last Bekins building in the Mission District; U-Haul was taking over. Further up, a closed beer brewery was being torn down. People said the City was going to build a school there later in the year. The rest of the block was boarded up except for a few smaller houses scattered here and there. It was very late now. What could I say to Zeta's mom?

I pushed the little button again and again. "It's me, Señora Mendoza." I heard a young man's voice with a funny accent. I tried to think where to start. "Victor?" I said hoping it was Zeta's brother as the door opened.

I wanted to say more but I couldn't. Vic said nothing as he limped ahead, passing the black deli refrigerators towards the back room. I could see the *coquitos* on display by the juices—we used to wrap them in cellophane on weekends so Zeta's dad could sell them to the Mexican candy stores in the District. I smelled candles, medicine, and the coconut oil in the candy. The smell of burnt corn stumps came up. My stomach loosened. "Vic?" I peeped again.

"Victor?" I was louder this time. Nothing came back.

I only had seen him a few times, at dinner or going out with his friends. Now, he wasn't very big; he was frail, the box of his shoulders tight, tiny. Angular face, unshaven; a religious air. Before I could ask him anything, he opened the door to an amber-lit room and just said, "He's waiting for you."

Another silence.

Nothing came back from me this time. I was stopped by the odd breathing coming from the man sitting in a makeshift bed in front of me. "He's been waiting for you." I turned to an old woman at the end of the bed. She moved her lips without looking at me.

Zeta's dead. I left him in Panama. A mortar shell burned him alive. I saw it. All this balled up in my throat and left me speechless. I couldn't say this now. There was nothing I could say. Who was this man? Zeta's mother knelt at the foot of the crooked mattress. I turned to Vic standing by the door. But he motioned with his thin hand, shooing me back.

Zeta's breath was swimming through his lungs. Remember? I thought to myself: the forehead gnarls, things flutter across his face. "Come on, Zeta," I said. Blinking fast, his eyes watered, glaring at mine. His mouth opened and closed, trying to make something inside speak. But he couldn't make it work. The tongue moved and pushed. All I could see were the damn blisters at the back, by the tonsils. And he closed his eyes, dropped his head.

What happened? The strange man spoke with an odd childlike swing to his voice.

"Yes?" I said, awkwardly. He glared. Zeta's mom nodded and stood up, propping one hand on the bedside, walked over to the dresser, and handed me a letter.

I was sweating. Raised a hand and brushed my hair with my fingers. All this had already done something to alter her quiet poise. The envelope did more.

She stood far away and pointed the letter at me. I moved up to her, took the note and heard myself saying: "*Gracias,* Señora Mendoza." A muffled fear trembled in the corners of her eyes. She was turning her eyes to the suited man, then to little Vic. Then to me. I stood there looking at her, there in the dark box burning with an old bulb on the high ceiling. I started to open the envelope.

"Not now, Lopez." I turned to the man. He was sullen. Serious.

"What do you mean, *not now?*"

"Not now," he said.

"Is this about Zeta?" I stammered. "I need to know what's in this letter."

"You never made it to Panama, OK?"

He brushed the stubble on his chin. I wanted to put it in my shirt pocket, but nothing moved.

"You went on a vacation, maybe Acapulco, an old buddy looked you up, maybe."

"What?"

"You saw nothing, punk," he says and he jumps up to me.

"You saw nothing, OK? Or maybe you were running cocaine for the military back there? Maybe you've been doing this for two years now. You and Mr. Zeta. What else could two college dropouts do to keep up with things in the city? And maybe you sold some to your artist friends, you know the ones that wear all those Apartheid and USA out of El Salvador buttons? I got it all here in my notes." He laughs, walking around the bed.

"And then you know what?" Pokes me. "Why don't you ask Mrs. Mendoza and Vicky boy? They're smart."

He reaches inside his coat behind his worn leather belt and pulls out a snub-nosed gun. Waving it in a short, nervous circle, planting it on my right temple.

"Let us say it was going pretty good for a while. You started making fine drug money, eating fine—better than hanging around Berkeley selling rings with the rest of the weirdos. Then you know what?"

He was getting louder. "Your buddy Zeta got an idea: more stuff. Right? But, he didn't have the connections. So you guys went south." He was breathing hard. "You saw nothing, Lopez." He stalled, backed off, stopped: he was sorting things out, shuffling his story into my story—how I smuggled stuff back to the streets and how he could prove it in one easy sweep; how I had seen the American military kill one of our own and how he would pin me so I would stay quiet—he glanced at Zeta's mom, then at me. He brought up the gun again and pointed me towards the little door.

He was pushing me out of the room with the gun at my back. I wanted to turn around and grab at something. Zeta's mom was stiffening, opening her mouth trying to push something out, wheezing, pulling up the bones in her shoulders. She ran up to the headboards and dropped next to the bed.

"Come on, get out, I don't need you," he closed the back door with his free hand. Then he picked up a sandwich by the refrigerator door and took a sumptuous bite. "You say something and I'll get her too, Señor Lopez." A hot bitter liquid came up my throat.

I wanted to turn back to the corn fields—run back through the wetness. The mass graves—up there by the corn fields—the American military had them dug in already, just waiting for the air attack on Panama City. A setup. I was frozen.

He pushed me by the head out the front door onto the street. Something came over me. I jammed my arm through the closing edge of the door lock, grabbed it, and pressed back. I was backing him up now.

"Come on, mister, shoot my brains out." I was talking fast.

"Get the hell outta here, Lopez."

And then what you gonna do, shoot the candies?"

"Shut up!" He was moving further back. A bit more every time.

"You didn't see nothing!" I pushed him.

Zeta's mom was moaning in the closed room. "Blow me away, buddy." My voice was coming from deep down. "You want to know what that letter says?" he barked, shielding the door to the little room. "Go ahead, let's see it, pull it out—let's hear about your vacation." He waved his little gun again.

I held up a picture: a couple of guys with a woman in fancy clothes, snorting powder on the table—drinks, aperitifs, musicians in blue vested suits. "Who's going to believe this crap—this guy don't even look like me. Zeta had straight hair." I wanted to tear the photos, shred them, and fling the pieces at him. Didn't say a word, just stood there, dropped the glossies on the floor. Squinting and wiping the side of my face, turned around, and didn't look back. Walked out. "You saw nothing," he whispered. "Don't come back, Lopez, I swear…" he went on as I shut the front door. It was around four in the morning. The steel street signs above me.

 Her Hair

Francisco Aragón

2000

Francisco Aragón was born in 1965 and raised in San Francisco, the son of immigrants from Nicaragua. He is the author of three volumes of poetry, his poems and translations have appeared in various literary journals, and he was awarded an Academy of American Poets Prize in 1999. He is currently completing his M.F.A. at the University of Notre Dame, where he is the editor of the poetry journal *Dánta*. He began the following poem in the 1980s in response to U.S. involvment in Nicaragua.

Long and black the streaks
of gray, aflutter in the light
wind as she prepares to tell

her story at the Federal Building:
reaching into a tattered sack
she pulls out a doll

missing an eye, balding—
singed face smudged with soot
from the smoke the hut took in

as her village was being shelled.
Next she retrieves what's left
of a book—a few pages

the borders brown, coming
apart in her hands: hesitant,
she raises one, starts to speak:

por la mañana sube el sol y calienta el día
la tierra nos da dónde vivir y qué comer
la vaca nos da leche para beber y hacer mantequilla

It's her daughter's reading lesson
the poem she recited to her
the day they struck—

(in the morning the sun rises and warms the day
the earth provides a place to live and what to eat
the cow gives us milk to drink and make butter with…)

…mid-way through, her voice begins
to shake—her words
like refugees exposed to the night shiver,

freeze: silence
swallows us all…
…her words, drifting

casualities,
gather and huddle
in my throat.

San Francisco

 No Shelter

Naomi Quiñonez

1994

Naomi Quiñonez has written two volumes of poems and co-edited several anthologies, including *Invocation L.A.: Urban Multicultural Poetry* (1989), which won an American Book Award. She is also known for her work in community service and education, and she currently teaches in the Chicano studies department at California State University, Fullerton.

His explosion
was only temporary.
A moment, a blood clot
a red ribbon of anger
tied around her neck
a second of scorn
a fistful of hair.
His bruised ego
imprinted
its black and blue
on her face.
His words shot
like bullets
her spirit
cracked open
the blows
immediate, sharp
as she stumbled over
those few moments
and dragged herself
across the seconds
that split the shattered face
of time.

from

✳ East Side Stories

Rubén Martínez

1998

Rubén Martínez has been a commentator for CNN,
Frontline, Nightline, and *All Things Considered* and has written for many major newspapers and magazines. He is currently an associate editor at Pacific News Service, a correspondent for PBS's *Religion and Ethics News Weekly,* and the
2001–2 Loeb Fellow at Harvard University's Graduate
School of Design. The following selection is excerpted from
the book *East Side Stories: Gang Life in East L.A.* (1998), a
pictorial essay by award-winning photographer Joseph
Rodríguez featuring an interview with Luis J. Rodríguez.
An excerpt from Martínez's most recent book, *Crossing
Over* (2001), also appears in this anthology.

IT IS A BEAUTIFUL HOUSE, AIDA QUILES'S HOUSE. An old two-story wood-
frame with an ample, green front yard. In the living room a twenty-foot-
high ceiling dwarfs the oversize red velvet chairs and couches. A grand
staircase with oak balustrade leads to the upstairs bedrooms.

The house stands at the end of a long row of aging stuccos and
woodframes, just where Arizona Street slams on its brakes and becomes
the Pomona Freeway. The fifteen-foot-high sound barrier does not
silence the consistent roar of cars shuttling white-collar commuters east
and west, between the bedroom communities of the San Gabriel Valley
and the high-rise offices in downtown Los Angeles. It is the constant
hollow soundtrack to the Quiles's lives.

The house also stands in the heart of Marianna Maravilla territory; Marianna is one of the several cliques of Maravilla, one of the largest and oldest of the Eastside gangs.

Aida Quiles, in her late fifties, mother of ten, sits by the tall dining room windows that look out onto Arizona Street. A warm wind has blown the smog away today and the light from a big, cloudless sky casts a blue glow over her face. She keeps glancing nervously into the blue, toward the birdcage in the front yard where her cockatoos chirp and jump. Another cage in the backyard holds eight white doves. In the living room, there's an aquarium with little turtles. Aida is not really looking at the cockatoos, but to the street beyond, as if watching for an expected but unwelcome visitor.

"I didn't sleep at all last night," she confides.

She is worried about her sons, Ramiro, 17, who is locked up in the California Youth Authority, and Daniel, 18, who is in state prison. She is worried about the fallout from the birthday party last weekend for her daughter María, just turned 16. "It was going to be a clean party, no drinking, nothing," she says, but the Los Angeles County Sheriff's Department showed up before the deejay could spin the first record, acting on a tip that weapons were stashed in the house. They found an automatic on the roof by one of the bedroom windows.

She is worried about her eldest son, Joaquín, who was shot at a few days later by some members from Little Valley gang, which claims the territory next to Marianna's. They jumped over the fence behind the garage as he was getting into his dusty Lincoln Mark IV and began firing. Joaquín started the engine and floored it, backing out of the driveway. Aida points to three bullet holes, one on the driver's side of the windshield.

Last night the Little Valley boys jumped over the fence again, fired a couple of rounds at the house, then disappeared into the darkness. Marianna homeboys from all over the 'hood responded, guarding the house all night long, weapons at the ready.

It's life in a war zone. But in the midst of it all, the Quiles family is still that—a family. Yes, the father walked out seven years ago. But Aida remains, at the absolute center of her family, doing everything she can to keep her kids from becoming homicide statistics. In good Mexican Spanish, Aida is *aguantadora*. Enduring, proud of how much abuse she can take and still stand. *Pleitona*. Always ready for a fight, willing to defend the family at all costs—especially when one of her children is involved (even with her own kids, if she feels they've betrayed her trust).

Cariñosa. Tender, on those long nights the kids come home drunk or bloodied or scared out of their wits because they had a close call in some alley where one moment everything is *tranquilo,* the homeboys just kickin' it with their cans of Bud and maybe a little weed, someone's car stereo sending an oldies tune straight into the soft nostalgic part of their souls, and then the car with headlights off careening out of nowhere and the sudden, terrible flash of an automatic and the bodies diving into the dirt...

She loves them unconditionally, no matter what they do when they walk out the door and into their "other family," Marianna. Because they are her children.

Although this neighborhood is part of what is popularly known as "East L.A.," it actually lies a couple of miles east of the Los Angeles city limit, in what is known, for political and demographic purposes, as "unincorporated Los Angeles County." No city council, no mayor. There is a county supervisor, a progressive Latina named Gloria Molina, but she represents more than two million people in a district that extends from the L.A. River halfway to the San Gabriel Mountains—about thirty miles as the crow flies. Of course, there is a congressional representative and a senator. But Aida Quiles doesn't know their names, has never written them a letter, never voted in an election because she never registered. She does not speak English, though she understands it well enough after almost twenty years of her children talking back to her in that foreign tongue.

Aida Quiles and her family live here; she can barely imagine an escape, other than the succor she provides within the walls of her house, and now even her house is under attack. The irony is, of course, that the rest of America feels under attack too—from people just like Aida Quiles and her sons: immigrants and gangbangers invading mainstream America.

When Aida first arrived in Los Angeles from Mexico, she packaged sandwiches at a place called John's Catering, downtown on Santa Fe Avenue. She held the job for fifteen years. "I slept three hours a night," she recalls. She'd get home in the wee hours at the end of her shift and be up again at six to get the kids ready for school.

Ramiro and Daniel went through elementary school like typical kids. She was mindful of the risks of the neighborhood, but in an innocent way. "I was always calling them in off the street in the evening." She'd ask them where they'd been; their answer was always "with friends." She'd implore them not to "pick up bad habits." One day a neighbor told her that Daniel—he was twelve, maybe thirteen–was a full-fledged Marianna member. She didn't believe it. At home he was sweet as always, did what he was told. But then she saw the tattoo on his leg: "MMV," for Marianna Maravilla. Ramiro soon followed, a tattoo scrawled across his stomach. She found it harder to keep them at home. Daniel even began talking back to her. She was losing them to the street.

So she took to defending them on the street. Like the time one of the Marianna homeboys held up a restaurant a few blocks away, a foolish act—a ten-dollar stickup. The restaurant owner, gun in hand, chased the kid straight down Arizona towards Aida's house, where her sons and several other homeboys were passing the time leaning against their cars. To block the chase, the group—including one, a paraplegic in a wheelchair—formed a human chain while the robber got away.

A squad car pulled up with a screech. Several sheriff's deputies moved to take Ramiro in for the robbery. His sister María yelled, "Why don't you take him?" pointing at the gun-toting restaurateur. The deputies handcuffed her and moved in on Ramiro, guns drawn. Aida stepped in between, giving Ramiro the split second he needed to escape. One of the deputies grabbed her by the arm and as she pulled away, he lost his balance and fell, prompting laughter all around. Red-faced, he finally restrained Aida, handcuffed her, and threw her into the squad car next to María.

By this time, there was a helicopter circling above. The K-9 unit was brought in; police announced that a dog search for a dangerous criminal was underway and warned everyone to stay indoors.

Aida was beside herself. They could shoot Ramiro. The dogs could tear him to shreds. Since he was on probation, she knew that if they arrested him for suspicion of the robbery or resisting arrest, it would probably mean a prison sentence.

But the sheriffs never found Ramiro. He hid under a car in the driveway next door as the dogs sniffed and the helicopter threw its light into bushes and alleys. A neighbor finally snuck him into her house until the commotion died down. At the station, deputy after deputy tried to take Aida's fingerprints but they couldn't get a clean image; when they placed her in the holding tank, the door wouldn't stay shut. Aida and María were released without any charges.

"It was a night of miracles," she says.

But now, most days, Aida is virtually a prisoner in her own home. She won't summon the prison guards—the Sheriff's Department—for help; her experience shows they can do more harm than good. Even trying to keep the kids in school seems questionable: classrooms in East L.A. are rife with gangs. School can be as dangerous as the streets.

Why doesn't she just move to another neighborhood? She had a reason from the day she moved in—someone tossed a Molotov cocktail into a car parked in front of the house the first night she spent on Arizona Street—but she genuinely thought things would get better. Later, moving was out of the question: another neighborhood would mean the kids would have to face rival gang members. Did she overestimate what she could provide for her children at home? Did she underestimate the allure of the street?

She's scared to leave the house for even a few hours. She used to spend a lot of time away from home: she played bingo obsessively for a couple of years; her collection of little Buddhas and gold elephants sitting in the china cabinet are good-luck charms to beat the odds. But her children got into more and more trouble while she was away. Daniel started using drugs; God knows what else he and Ramiro were up to with the homeboys. Now she won't even go to parties or out dancing. And no more bingo. "Not even if I was assured of winning a million dollars."

Perhaps Aida has become a kind of gang member herself. She's barricaded in her "territory," constantly on the watch for her sons' rivals, who are no longer just other barrio children to her, but threats to the survival of her family. She even welcomes the Marianna homeboys and their weapons: better that they kill defending her family than one of her own getting killed. She sounds more guilty about playing bingo than about the automatic the sheriffs found on the roof.

Aida still believes that warmth and love at home can be the salve for the wounding world outside. It is a deeply held Mexican belief: the family is the hub of life, and the mother is at the center. But Mexicans never expected an inner-city nightmare when they crossed the border. Ill-prepared for a culture of youth violence unknown back home (gangs are exported to Mexico, not the other way around) and lacking political know-how in a system that is stacked against them, the Quileses remain trapped between an Old World memory and an unreachable American future.

Aida Quiles has a beautiful house. But it might not be enough to save her kids.

✻ Open Letter to My Friends

Richard Garcia

1993

Richard Garcia was born in 1941 in San Francisco, the son
of a Puerto Rican father and a Mexican mother. The
author of three volumes of poetry and one bilingual children's book, he has been published extensively in literary
journals and anthologies. His awards include a Pushcart
Prize and a Cohen Award from *Ploughshares.* García currently lives in California, where he has been the poet in
residence at Children's Hospital Los Angeles since 1991.

Today I learned that black smoke glowing red
at its base is a new fire. White means
the firemen are there with ropes of water.
Large flakes of ash drift by my window, dark gray
with a fringe of white, like expensive lettuce
or the edge of surf seen from an airplane.

Down below, whole families run by my front gate
carrying shopping bags full of shoes. Everything
anyone ever wanted is free. Gang members
who live across the street are more methodical,
military in their short haircuts, white T-shirts
and black baggy pants. They stride two by two
out of the alley and into their cars, returning later
with trunks full of electronic equipment.

I am becoming a connoisseur of night sounds:
the distant chatter of automatic rifles,
the popping of a .22, a car alarm.

I can tell the difference between the whoosh
of Molotov cocktails and the rip a shotgun
makes in the air. This city manufactures
its own clouds—solid, symmetrical, metallic.
They press against the sky from horizon to horizon
propped up by twirling pylons.

The streets are lined with trees bursting with purple blossoms.
But you probably don't believe me—accustomed to my lies,
you never believe me when I tell the truth.

from

✴ Puppet

*Margarita Cota-Cárdenas (translated by Barbara D. Riess,
Trino Sandoval, and Margarita Cota-Cárdenas)*

1985

Margarita Cota-Cárdenas was born in 1941 in Heber,
California, to Mexican immigrants. She currently teaches
Chicano and Mexican literature and Spanish at the
University of Arizona and is an activist on behalf of
Chicanos and women. Her semi-autobiographical book,
Puppet: A Chicano Novella (1985), uses an experimental mix
of Spanish and English to tell the story of one woman's
struggle to understand the murder of Puppet, a Mexican
American boy whose death was covered up by the police.

FÉLIX COMES OUT OF THE COUNTY JAIL EARLY IN THE MORNING, this time
he wants to get to his older brother's house by 7 am…Memo had
helped him fix everything up with the D.A., so Memo now officially
answers for his hermano…Petra's friend had done the same for several
other young men from the barrio…Now Félix's deal, this was more
complicated, since they had caught him with a bag of crude heroin in
the Chevy…They wanted for Félix to *cooperate*…The kid agreed, only
after lots of pressure from amigos y familia, 'cause these wanted Félix
to cut it off with those corrupt dopers…le propiciaban el vicio…those
suppliers just kept messin' him up…As he left the jail that crisp clean
morning, there was a red Lincoln…like blood from a deer…como la
sangre de un venado…parked but motor running, beside the curb…Félix
recognizes too late one of Samuel Longoray's lieutenants waiting for him.
Longoray, the amigo traficante that will shortly turn into his enemy the
moment that Félix…

"Testify, Petra…he was going to *testify* against those dealers…The D.A. tol' Félix he'd go free if he'd give testimony against that dirty guy…chicano sucio…They got'im, them, real young, chavalitos los agarraban…Pos, anyplace they could get'em, but in the barrio right there there's a parque…When they're eleven, twelve, they grab'em…'n' if they don'wanna, pos a juerza, well they make'em ennyway…They shoot'em up right there, injecting'em in some dark hidden corner…Everbody knows, but they're scared'a that guy…ese, es una vergüenza pa' la raza…a disgrace to us that's what he is…And one day when you don't expect it, it's your hermanito, and then he's not…Y olvídate de las esperanzas…You kin forget about any hopes…He was going to testify, Pat, y nadie nobody was s'posed to know it outside of the D.A.'s office…Sí, that's what we figure, that someone inside whistled to the *main pusher*…"

Anger got to you, the kind that enters like a hurricane and passes by, and you started to fire shots…words (in any case, palabrería, romantic words…who was going to pay attention to you? And it terrified you that…that they'd pay attention…!)
    THERE IS A CHICANO SUCIO
      WHOM NOBODY WILL NAME
    TAKES LITTLE BLACK AND BROWN CHILDREN
    AND MURDERS THE SPARKLE IN
      THEIR BEAUTIFUL BROWN EYES
      AND KILLS BLOODLESSLY
        THEIR PARENTS' LAUGHTER
    AND IN FALSE EUPHORIA
      SLOWLY DROWNS
        THE HOPES OF
      MY RAZA!
Let's see, cómo va, how does it go? Ha, ha, ha, let's see qué what of "braun ais"…ha, ha…
THEIR BEAUTIFUL BROWN EYES…there are ways to kill, without blood, and people fear those who kill…they might know their names, but they don't name them…(like as if it's for no reason, mensa, didn't you get it yet…no lo vites en las news?…)
Sí, so loving of "mi raza" here, and "mi raza" there, as if it was a samba, samba…Pero you have never done anything, I'll tell you, and you insist on keeping on, and you'll hang out all that dirty laundry you didn't want…ha, ha…

BBBBRRRRIIIINNNGGG

"Petra, it's Loreto…pues, qué te pasa what's wrong muchachona? We were hoping to see you yesterday at the meeting at the Centro de Comunidad…Pues weren't you interested in helping us with the Chicano Literature Conference? Why?…Pero we're all scared, all of us who have decided to do something, no matter what, to fight for justice…Because of the story…el relato about that kid?…Ajá…a poem you wrote against…ah caray…But no, don't believe it, muchachona…Be strong, mujer…I've seen the other Petra….in your other poems…Just so you know….No even if you were to read them in front of their faces, they wouldn't pay attention to you…Those people as full of shit as they are, they're not afraid of anyone…Look at what they do. But don't stop writing, Petra, it's too late to not say anything…Look, we're taking action so that the official investigation, no te rajes, don't back out…Sí, sí, perdón…Ah, look at you Petra… liberate yourself libérate, pues muchachona…What are you waiting for? Ajá…bueno, I'll be waiting for your call…"

DROWNED BEAUTIFUL CHOCOLATE COLORED EYES BEAUTIFUL WITHOUT BLOOD

"Cooooooolorado….coloraaaado…Like aaa deeeer's blood…" the young student from the Universidad Autónoma sings with feeling…Like a lot of those gathered at the Centro on this humid night the young student is from Sonora…Loreto, sitting by my side, gets up to congratulate the singer who has finished… "…Compañero…!" The song reminded me of something Medeiros had told me about the last Sexenio, al otro lado on the other side…of parks, of plazas, of blood….After the poetry part of the program, I imagine those distant deaths going to the parked car in a dark corner of the parking lot. Suddenly I see or I think I see that Samuel Longoray's lieutenant is waiting for me with a giant hypodermic needle that is laying out on the hood of his long shiny Lincoln, red like a deer's blood…Scared, I start to run, desperation tying me up in knots…

(EEEEEEPAAA! ha, ha, ha, ya vamos, here we go burrito, ha, ha…)

The stepmother and father used to take her own children out for dinner from time to time, but Puppet and his brothers and sisters were left home to eat "gorilla meat"…That's what they called the canned meat that las blonde ladies del welfare gave them to eat…Carne de gorila…pues, since they didn't know what animal the meat came from, they called it "gorilla"…That Puppet, pudía ser más tapaderas, he could always make a joke…Era juerte, he was strong, huh, very strong el batito…It's just that in the end, when he saw his father, in the end he couldn't any more, he just couldn't…It hurts, ya know, Pat? Aren't there things it hurts to remember…?

BRRRIIIIINNNNGGGG…BRRRIIIIIIIIINNGG, you don't want to you don't want to

"Pat? Are you coming to the wake tonight…?…No, I'm so pissed I'll explode, that woman…Yes, we just saw her at the mortuary…Ya'know what she did? All she did was bring a shirt for the chamaco, so they could bury him…Intonces, then she foun' out we was gunna bring'im some *real sharp* clothes, and, ya' know, when the vieja found out…Pues, so that we wuddn't be one up on'er, she wen and bought a jacket and a tie…But, go figure she didn't bring'im any *pants*…So, we went 'n' bought'im some…No, I don' know where his father is, he's probably all drunk somewhere…ya pa' qué, verdá?…Why bother?"

Pools of blood. There's a body inside a dark room, but you can see that it's laying in a darker pool…of blood…

"Professor Leyva? Why is it Mexican and Chicano literature…Gosh, come to think of it, that's the impression I get from all Spanish literature. How come there's so much *death*…Like it's all they think about…I don't like it, it's too heavy…Why is there, what do you call it…a *preoccupation* with death?"

(Oh, this is getting good, ha, you answer that zo mensa zozobra, that the dance with death, that *The Labyrinth of Solitude,* that the mummies in Guanajuato, you could've said something else, don't you think? But no, you say aquello otro that other stuff because you don't want to remember, you don't want to)

The body of a woman lies in a darker pool of blood…she's neither young nor old, she's got brown hair, tan skin…tangled hair…a baby cries, a newborn squirming in the woman's extended arm her legs are still curled up…the pool of blood comes from between her legs the exhausted woman who fights to breathe air, more air…Blood clots, a twisted cord, pale with dark veins, everything still warm and steaming…The woman's face and hands smeared with blood…You start to write a new objective version of Puppet's life. You start but you don't finish because you don't know where.

You could write about his death first since it was the most shocking…You throw out that idea because then it would be giving it a meaning that it didn't have, so sad and meaningless that end, making no sense…You didn't want the story in chronological order either, since that wasn't how the facts of the case had been perceived or brought to light…You look at the calendar the day you start: it is November 2…

At the University you're teaching: "Class, in the colonial city of Guanajuato, there's a really interesting cemetery…the chemical composition, or something like that, of the soil, has given the city a new addiction…forgive me, I wanted to say addition…Umhum…a basement that has mummies…No, they're contemporary mummies, not as famous as the ones in. Egypt…Qué va! Can you just see King Tut's people going 'Come and see our dead! Cinco pesos, five pesos a looksee…Just go down those stairs and you'll be really impressed with…disgust,' (although people pretend well enough, don't you think, that they're not scared shitless, ha, ha!) Five pesos…bueno, maybe it has gone up to ten, you know inflation can be contagious…"

(Oh, that professor! She got away with it again…)

And there was a woman mummy with a mummy baby in her…pues, in what were her arms…how disgusting, that notion of remembering death…But why do people do it? Qué preocupación…

"Hey, maestra, it sounds like you people sell your dead, or something, I mean, aren't you afraid of something bad happening to you? Why don't you Mexicans, I mean Chicanos, let the dead rest in peace?" (And besides, if you don't let Puppet and Félix and Medeiros's son rest in peace, y tus recuerdos, your memories, your memories…)

"And some children-guides go down with you and look at you and look at you and look at you" (don't they ever smile?…ha, ha) No, no smiling, very serious they look at you y te miran while you look tú miras (Don't they say anything after their spiel…? hee, hee) "No…they look at you, you look" (What are their eyes like? Ha, ha I caught you, te agarré guáchala, watch her now, ha, ha)

DARK EYES OF AN OLD MAN IN THE BODY OF A YOUNG KID GRANITE EYES THAT ASK YOU THEY ASK YOU SOMETHING…ARGO…

"Why do you run, Petra? What's wrong? It's like you've seen a ghost"…! Loreto is coming out of the Center as I come running down from the parking lot.

"I thought I saw a…Longoray's…his…because of what I wrote…I don't know if I'm strong enough for this crusader business, Loreto, no sé I don't know if I have the spiritual strength…I am afraid of…I don't know, te digo…" I recover, and Loreto walks me to my car. We say good-bye with a hug and he says in a low voice… "Oh, Petra, you still don't know what you can do....You don't even realize it yet...I'll call you tomorrow to see how you're holding up, eh?"

(How are you holding up? Pues cómo le va a seguir, how do you think, blind, that's how, like you've always been when you should have been afraid...you weren't, and now that there's no time left)

That night, walking to your house, you think about what you have thought about, about the scare, and when you get home you lock yourself in the apartment to write poems about how reality was and how it had been.

in Mesilla New Mexico

in the summer when I was a very little girl

"And so, every day we would go to play in the old cemetery, over on the other side of Uncle José's orchard...I used to love to run around with my cousins between the tombs, kicking up dust all over the place...When we felt like it, we would pick the fruit of the mesquite tree, yes there are still mesquites around there, and we would peel it, ajá, and we would suck it...it had both a sweet and sour-like flavor...We would see those people's tombs, boy there were a lotta dead people there...No, I was never scared of them because they were sooo quiet, they never bothered us na'a...Umhum, we used 'ta play...What?... Güeno, we would arrange our dead aunt's and uncle's dried flowers... Every once in a while, it would occur to me to stick some dead person's flower, ajá, in the back of one of my braids....Sí, yeah I would make my cousins scream...the live ones right?...But the best, lo mejor, what really gave us goose bumps out of fear...even though I liked it, I liked making them scream...was when I used to dance on a huge cement tomb...Hee, hee, it had a black skull painted on it...It was my *stage,* you know...oh, pardon me, *proscenium*...and I danced and danced and they screamed and screamed nervously...Later someone in my family told me that it was soo scandalous to insult the dead like that, that it was a sin, or who knows what but pos I say they were just *jealous,* sabe? Ahá...as if they wanted to have done it themselves, ha, ha..."

And now that they're coming to look for you, bola de miedo? And now, fearball...? Ha, ha, tú

WHY DO YOU RUN WHAT'S WRONG THE BLOOD

✸ Guerra Florida

Francisco X. Alarcón

1986

The title of this poem by Francisco X. Alarcón refers to the Flowery Wars of pre-European Mexico, in which the rulers in Tenochtitlán and several independent states (Cholula, Huexotzinco, and Tlaxcala) engaged in ritual wars in which young men of the warrior classes fought in order to prove themselves, some becoming prisoners for sacrifice.

Other poems by Alarcón that appear in this volume are "I Used to Be Much Much Darker," "Letter to America," and two poems from his *Sonnets to Madness and Other Misfortunes* (2001).

we opened
the doors
of our homes
to greet them
they came in
& evicted us
we showed them
the open green
of our valleys
the clear blue
of the sky
they cut down
the forests
for their furnaces
for their crosses

we gave them
all the fruits
of this land
they poisoned
with silvery
  mercury
   our rivers
    our veins
but we survived
the slaughter
of our days
now we face them
in this final
battle
for our lives

desert
give us
your endurance
mountains
grant us
your strength
wind
blow us
some courage
madre agua
guide us
in your flowering
& victorious
ways
brothers
& sisters
don't be afraid
the flowers
the feathers
are
on our side

COMMUNITY

✳ Sonnet XIX

Francisco X. Alarcón (translated by Francisco Aragón)

2001

The following selection by Francisco X. Alarcón is from his latest book, *Sonnets to Madness and Other Misfortunes* (2002). Another sonnet from the same book appears in this anthology, as well as the poems "I Used to Be Much Much Darker," "Letter to America," and "Guerra Florida." Mission Dolores, the subject of this poem, is the oldest building in San Francisco, built by Indians and now at the heart of San Francisco's largely Latino Mission District.

I come to your doors, Mission Dolores,
to touch your adobes with my hands,
made of the tears, the sweat, the forced
labor of a thousand natives

the whiteness of your walls shelter
the bones shattered by your cross,
how many stillborns did you christen?
how many mothers fell at your feet?

others arrived and beside you
constructed wooden buildings—
apartments for rent, and so

your barrio grew, and your roof
fastened with leather, withstood tremors,
the natives—naive—called you home

✱ The Seven Entrances to Aztlan (for Mixedbloods)

Maria Melendez

2001

Maria Melendez published her first chapbook of poetry, *Base Pairs,* in 2001, and her work has appeared in several literary magazines and the anthology *Mark My Words: Five Emerging Poets* (2001), edited by Francisco Aragón. She has been nominated for a Pushcart Prize and was awarded first place in the University of California's Poet Laureate Contest in 2000. She has taught poetry and fiction writing at the University of California, Davis, led bioregional writing workshops, and been part of California's Poets in the Schools program, for which she edited *Nest of Freedom* (2002), the organization's anthology. She is currently a writer in residence at the UC Davis Arboretum, teaching multicultural environmental poetry workshops.

Raza movement must be wrong, Aztlan can't be the Southwest,
too many giant cucarachas, there's no mention of pests
in accounts of the mythical homeland.
It could be aqui en California, except for the river
of Argentine ants on my counters, which I bait
with arsenic-laced appetizers, but in the middle of
wiping ants off the baby-food jar, I realize
      defense of territory is an entrance to Aztlan.

   Crosshairs
      mark the target range
        across this tunnel of light.

What binds us more tightly to a place than eating and excreting?
They don't call it the food chain for nothing.
Let's drink a mango smoothie and toss the islands back slick.
Unless we choose, like Gary Paul Nabhan did, not to have such a big
     mouth;
he ate only foods grown within a hundred-mile radius of his home in
     the Sonoran,
I hear he did this for a year, and I hear
he recently moved.
          Food and water are an entrance to Aztlan.

          Silvery shapes (pond weed, crawdad, pond weed, heron)
               form and reform
             as they cross this mouth.

Dead crow under a cottonwood, still clutching
the branch that broke beneath her in a windstorm, says
that last flight's really a short plummet; guards this entrance
and says Cull the alkaline emptiness
from my sockets, boil it into an indigo slag,
take a dose and be whole again
in the eye of confusion.
          No secret death's an entrance to the mythical homeland.

          Cedar branches
               leach the rain
          that falls on this trap door.

Here in poetatlan, cuervotlan, fresatlan, osotlan, the place
of poets, crows, berries and California Bears,
it must be Aztlan, because the Aztatl, white herons we call great egrets,
nest here, and they do not move to Oregon in search of scenic beauty.
Herons shock the picky home-seekers with the way they stay locked
into place (-tlan being "place of" and "tooth," as in "rooted"). I've seen
Great Blues raise twenty broods in a cottonwood rookery that's right
over a railroad;
          ("Oyen hijos, that noisy animal's more scared of you...") Which
          means the spiraling descent that started somewhere else (across the
          bridge, that border, that gap) and ends up Here, the feathered glory
          in that white rush, is an entrance to Aztlan, the mythical homeland.

Sky blue tunnel:
fall through, fall through,
the roof of this cave is on fire.

Go ask your local wise flowers, they'll tell you about the surge and curl
of landscape change. This is a long flower war, and the theater
between valley oaks is budding with goatgrass and star thistle, what's next?
It's a long flower war, and on the ground between sagebrush bushes,
cheatgrass has the present advantage, pero quien sabe lo que es proximo?
Put the toloache to your ear, it will magnify the sounds
of everything surrounding you, because
        there is a floral entrance to Aztlan.

An open corolla:
slide down a drooping pistil,
stand ankle deep in home-juice.

As my teacher said, "We are nowhere, except, maybe, here,"
with millennia rolling past Targets and Borders and Gaps,
all of it streaming by now, and the closer you look
the more it all seems like a thin, slick layer of water
on new-frozen ice, and this freaky set
of circumstances, this fake diamond
strung from the gold around our necks,
        well known as "realidad," is a way to the mythical homeland.

Bars across this entrance,
like those on a window
or a gutter with a raccoon peeking out.

Todos los viejos, and the parent rock of the Tehama formation,
they all have a place they came from before "before." By tracing origins
not just from the family tree, but from the columnar basalt
and the heron's hatchlings, this doorway gets bigger...I know my
    daughter
by the way she lifts her little chin and listens to geese...
Night herons don't even recognize their own children,
they'll feed any open nestling-shaped mouth;

so by these heron customs, nesting and caring for anyone's babies en la gran familia, anywhere the universe is becoming, is the very first entrance into the mythical homeland.

> *This circle, a black hole, converts bodies*
> *into shouting incandescence,*
> *and it can be a moss-lined bed for eggs.*

from

✻ The California I Love

Leo Carrillo

1961

Leo Carrillo is best remembered as the sidekick "Pancho" in the *Cisco Kid* television series of the 1950s. He regularly appeared in costume and on horseback in the annual Tournament of Roses Parade in Pasadena and he served as a goodwill ambassador for the New York World's Fair in 1964. Off screen he was known as a songwriter, scholar of history, and lyric poet, and in 1961 he published *The California I Love*, a memoir of his Spanish heritage and youth in Los Angeles.

SUNDAY—EL DOMINGO—WAS LIKE A PAGEANT. Into town on their palomino, sorrel, bay, and black horses each Sunday morning rode thirty or forty dapper caballeros from all the great surrounding ranches, Aguages de Centinela, Ballona, and all the others.

Heading the group was Archie Freeman of Centinela. He was more than six feet tall, sitting his horse as if he were part of the animal itself. He wore snug, blue broadcloth pantaloons with a definite bell at the bottom. Out of the bell came his small boots. Nearly all the rancheros had small feet because they were so seldom off their horses. What did they need large feet for? Certainly not for walking.

On his silver spurs was a $20 gold piece as a rosette. His jacket of blue broadcloth was decorated with black and blue buttons, and the studs on his white shirt were $2.50 gold pieces. His black hat was low crowned, tilted to one side with the barbaquejo, or chin strap, worn just below the lower lip.

Riding abreast, with full-length stirrups so all the impact of the horse was taken on the balls of the feet, the splendid phalanx would sweep into Santa Monica and up to the little church where there were hitching posts, not parking meters, for early morning Mass. The horses were tethered with mecates, or ropes, made of colored hair. The riders would loosen the cinch and throw one stirrup over the back of the horse so it could rest in comfort while they were in church.

The rumble of low, young voices would be heard then in the church in the responses to the service. Then the caballeros would emerge again en masse, tighten the cinches, remount, and dash away with whoops and yells to the old Pacific or Neptune Gardens for some refreshments. Then, even happier than ever, they would go over at noon for the big "dinner" which was served at that hour, rather than in the evening, at the restaurant of Eckert & Hoff. The full course dinner with plenty of beef, frijoles, tortillas, salsa, and all the rest was twenty-five cents but refreshments were extra. Beer was five cents, and strong drinks—whiskey, aguardiente, and brandy—were ten cents. Then after a little rest to let their meat settle, the horse games would begin.

We kids and most of the townspeople gathered around to watch these sports, which came straight out of the romantic past of California, of Mexico, and of Spain itself, dating back almost as far as that distant day when man first mounted a horse and discovered that with four legs instead of two he was one step nearer to being a demigod.

Indians and children would bring out buckets of water to wet down the unpaved street; the caballeros would come at full charge towards the long wet spot, rein up suddenly and start the horse in a long slide on all four feet, "skiing" in the mud. The object was to stop as close as possible to a line drawn across the street. Sometimes, but not often, a horse would go down as its back legs crumpled under it, and the caballero would have to leap off and take his chances of falling in the mud himself. After the winners were finally chosen, the whole troop would dash off pell-mell to the beach. There they would take the saddles off their horses, tie ropes around the horses' bellies, take off their own boots, and in their stocking feet, with their bridles off and riding the horses with loops, Indian style, they would give the animals a dousing in the sea.

Thus refreshed, the most dangerous games began.

I can well remember the playing of the game which later was barred because of its alleged cruelty, but which we all thought of as the climax to the whole proceedings. The body of a turkey or chicken would be buried in the sand up to its neck, leaving only its head sticking out above ground. Then the rider would come at full speed "colgando"—the rider hanging from the mane, with his knees under the rope around the horse's belly—and leaning over with two fingers of one hand open, try to tear off the head of the turkey or chicken. Once again the whole town would be lined up to see the riders and to decide the winner.

After all this the young men with their spirits still demanding excitement would head out for the dance halls and gambling houses in the Santa Monica Canyon area where so many knifings, shootings, and murders took place. The day that began with Mass and singing in the house of God often would end in a wild melee. It was all part of the times; it was the way the Californianos lived.

The Freeman boys, Archie and Fred, along with the Machados and the Lugos, became good friends of our family. They taught my brothers and me many tricks of riding. We had known how to ride after a fashion, as I've said, ever since we were babies, but these caballero-vaqueros were among the most skillful horsemen in the world and they imparted to us many little secrets which helped us in our endeavors to become true vaqueros ourselves.

We, too, learned to "ski" in the mud with our horses, to ride "colgando" to the consternation of our mother, who thought for sure we were going to be killed as we swept along with our heads down, hanging on to the horse's mane. It taught us self-reliance, fearlessness, and the other qualities which any good horseman must have.

During our time by the sea we learned horsemanship as well as fishing. We learned the code of the vaquero, the fact that a California caballero never showed fear under any circumstances, and that he was always ready to defend his honor, or that of any member of his family. It was a transplanting of the spirit of old Spain to the shores of the Pacific at Santa Monica.

Perhaps never again can there be such an era. We were living in the twilight of a great age. Sunset was coming for the pastoral era in California. But just as at sunset there are sudden brilliant illuminations lighting up the skies, so it was with us. We were fortunate to know the last vestiges of a magnificent time which can never return.

It was a time of horses, of quick anger, quick remorse, comradeship, and the knowledge that with the coming of civilization and progress we were to see the end of something grand on the stage of the Western world.

from

Barrio Boy

Ernesto Galarza

1971

Ernesto Galarza was born in 1905 in Mexico and as a child moved to Sacramento to work in the fields alongside his family. He held leadership positions in the Pan American Union (now the Organization of American States) and the National Farm Labor Union (now the National Agricultural Workers Union). Galarza's long list of fiction and nonfiction publications includes scores of articles and more than a dozen books, many of which, like *Barrio Boy* (1971), were inspired by his early experiences as a farmworker. In 1976 he became the first U.S. Latino to be nominated for the Nobel Prize in Literature. He died in 1984.

It was late in the afternoon after countless hours from Tucson that the conductor stopped by our seat, picked up our stubs and, pointing to us, said "Sacramento." With the greatest of ease I said "tanks yoo" and felt again the excitement of arriving somewhere. We looked out at the countryside to be sure we didn't miss the first sights of the city with the Mexican name where we were going to live. As far as I could see there were rows on rows of bushes, some standing by themselves, some leaning on wires and posts, all of them without leaves. "Vineyards," my mother said. I always wanted to know the number or quantity of things. "How many?" I asked. "A heap," she answered, not just *un montón,* but *un montonal,* which meant more than you could count, nobody really knows, sky-high, infinity, millions.

We left the vineyards behind, passing by orchards and pastures with cattle. At the crossroads, our locomotive hooted a salute to droves of cattle, automobiles, and horse-drawn buggies with school children waiting to cross.

Our train began to make a great circle, slowing down. The roadbed carried the train higher than the rooftops, giving us a panorama of the city. Track crews standing by with the familiar brown faces of Mexicans waved to us. I looked hard for Gustavo and José, for the last we had heard they were working on the Southern Pacific, making tracks or locomotives. Through the window we could see long buildings with stacks belching smoke like a dozen Casas Redondas, boxcars, flatcars, coaches, gondolas, cabooses, and locomotives dismantled or waiting for repairs.

A brakeman opened the door at the front of the coach and called, "Sack-men-ah," by which we knew he meant Sa-cra-men-to, for we had passed a large sign with the name in black and white at the entrance to the corporation yard.

Unlike the Mexicans, the Americans were not in a great hurry to leave the coach. We were the last, carrying our luggage.

We stepped down into a frightening scene, a huge barn filled with smoke and noise and the smell of burnt oil. This was the station, nearly as long as the train and with a sooty roof twice as high as the *mercado* in Mazatlán. Our locomotive was still belching black clouds from the stack. Men were hurrying along, pulling four-wheeled carts loaded with baggage, jerking hoses close to the train and thrusting the nozzles into holes here and there, washing windows with brushes on long sticks, opening the axle boxes with hammers and banging them shut.

We dashed through the confusion over the tracks and into the waiting room, myself dragging one of the shopping bags. The depot was a gloomy, dangerous place. We sat watching the crowd thin out. Our train departed, headed in the same direction, and I felt that we were being left behind.

Out of the bag my mother pulled the small envelope with the address of the Hotel Español. She handed me the paper. Holding it I watched the men in uniforms and green visors who passed by us and the clerks behind the ticket counters. Taking a chance I stopped one and thrust the paper at him. I said "plees" and waited, pinching one corner of the envelope while he read it. Like the conductor, the man guessed our problem. He smiled and held up a forefinger, crooking and straightening it while he looked at us. I had no idea what he meant, for in Mexico you signaled people to follow you by holding up your hand and closing all the fingers over the palm with a snap a few times. But Doña Henriqueta knew instantly, and he guided us under an arch and out of the station. Handing back the envelope, he pointed down the street and smiled us on.

One more stop to ask our way with another "plees" and we were at the Hotel Español.[…]

Once the routine of the family was well started, my mother and I began to take short walks to get our bearings. It was half a block in one direction to the lumberyard and the grocery store; half a block in the other to the saloon and the Japanese motion picture theater. In between were the tent and awning shop, a Chinese restaurant, a secondhand store, and several houses like our own. We noted by the numbers on the posts at the corners that we lived between 4th and 5th Streets on L.

Once we could fix a course from these signs up and down and across town we explored farther. On 6th near K there was the Lyric Theater with a sign that we easily translated into Lírico. It was next to a handsome red stone house with high turrets, like a castle. Navigating by these key points and following the rows of towering elms along L Street, one by one we found the post office on 7th and K; the cathedral, four blocks farther east; and the state capitol with its golden dome.

It wasn't long before we ventured on walks around Capitol Park, which reminded me of the charm and the serenity of the Alameda in Tepic. In some fashion Mrs. Dodson had got over to us that the capitol was the house of the government. To us it became El Capitolio or, more formally, the Palacio de Gobierno. Through the park we walked into the building itself, staring spellbound at the marble statue of Queen Isabel and Christopher Columbus. It was awesome, standing in the presence of that gigantic admiral, the one who had discovered America and Mexico and Jalcocotán, as Doña Henriqueta assured me.

After we had thoroughly learned our way around in the daytime, we found signs that did not fail us at night. From the window of the projection room of the Lyric Theater a brilliant purple light shone after dark. A snake of electric lights kept whipping round and round a sign over the Albert Elkus store. K Street on both sides was a double row of bright show windows that led up to the Land Hotel and back to Breuner's, thence down one block to the lumberyard, the grocery store, and our house. We had no fear of getting lost.

These were the boundaries of the lower part of town, for that was what everyone called the section of the city between 5th Street and the river and from the railway yards to the Y-Street levee. Nobody ever mentioned an upper part of town; at least, no one could see the difference because the whole city was built on level land. We were not lower topographically, but in other ways that distinguished between Them, the uppers, and Us, the lowers. Lower Sacramento was the quarter that people who made money moved away from. Those of us who lived in it stayed there because our problem was to make a living and not to make money. A long while back, Mr. Howard, the business agent of the union, told me there had been stores and shops, fancy residences, and smart hotels in this neighborhood. The crippled old gentleman who lived in the next room down the hall from us explained to me that our house, like the others in the neighborhood, had been the home of rich people who had stables in the backyards, with back entrances by way of the alleys. Mr. Hansen, the Dutch carpenter, had helped build such residences. When the owners moved uptown, the backyards had been fenced off and subdivided, and small rental cottages had been built in the alleys in place of the stables. Handsome private homes were turned into flophouses for men who stayed one night, hotels for working people, and rooming houses, like ours.

Among the saloons, pool halls, lunch counters, pawnshops, and poker parlors was skid row, where drunk men with black eyes and unshaven faces lay down in the alleys to sleep.

The lower quarter was not exclusively a Mexican barrio but a mix of many nationalities. Between L and N Streets two blocks from us, the Japanese had taken over. Their homes were in the alleys behind shops, which they advertised with signs covered with black scribbles. The women walked on the street in kimonos, wooden sandals, and white stockings, carrying neat black bundles on their backs and wearing their hair in puffs with long ivory needles stuck through them. When they met they bowed, walked a couple of steps, and turned and bowed again, repeating this several times. They carried babies on their backs, not in their arms, never laughed or went into the saloons. On Sundays the men sat in front of their shops, dressed in gowns, like priests.

Chinatown was on the other side of K Street, toward the Southern Pacific shops. Our houses were old, but those in which the Chinese kept stores, laundries, and restaurants were older still. In black jackets and skullcaps the older merchants smoked long pipes with a tiny brass cup on the end. In their dusty store windows there was always the same assortment of tea packages, rice bowls, saucers, and pots decorated with blue temples and dragons.

In the hotels and rooming houses scattered about the barrio the Filipino farmworkers, riverboat stewards, and houseboys made their homes. Like the Mexicans, they had their own pool halls, which they called clubs. Hindus from the rice and fruit country north of the city stayed in the rooming houses when they were in town, keeping to themselves. The Portuguese and Italian families gathered in their own neighborhoods along 4th and 5th Streets southward toward the Y-Street levee. The Poles, Yugo-Slavs, and Koreans, too few to take over any particular part of it, were scattered throughout the barrio. Black men drifted in and out of town, working the waterfront. It was a kaleidoscope of colors and languages and customs that surprised and absorbed me at every turn.

Although we, the foreigners, made up the majority of the population of that quarter of Sacramento, the Americans had by no means given it up to us. Not all of them had moved above 5th Street as the barrio became more crowded. The bartenders, the rent collectors, the insurance salesmen, the mates on the riverboats, the landladies, and most importantly, the police—these were all gringos. So were the craftsmen, like the barbers and printers, who did not move their shops uptown as the city grew. The teachers of our one public school were all Americans. On skid row we rarely saw a drunk wino who was not a gringo. The operators of the pawnshops and secondhand stores were white and mostly Jewish.

For the Mexicans the barrio was a colony of refugees. We came to know families from Chihuahua, Sonora, Jalisco, and Durango. Some had come to the United States even before the revolution, living in Texas before migrating to California. Like ourselves, our Mexican neighbors had come this far moving step by step, working and waiting, as if they were feeling their way up a ladder. They talked of relatives who had been left behind in Mexico, or in some far-off city like Los Angeles or San Diego. From whatever place they had come, and however short or long the time they had lived in the United States, together they formed the *colonia mexicana*. In the years between our arrival and the First World War, the *colonia* grew and spilled out from the lower part of town. Some families moved into the alley shacks east of the Southern Pacific tracks, close to the canneries and warehouses, and across the river among the orchards and rice mills.

The *colonia* was like a sponge that was beginning to leak along the edges, squeezed between the levee, the railroad tracks, and the riverfront. But it wasn't squeezed dry, because it kept filling with newcomers who found families who took in boarders, in basements, alleys, shanties, run-down rooming houses, and flop joints where they could live.

Crowded as it was, the *colonia* found a place for these *chicanos,* the name by which we called an unskilled worker born in Mexico and just arrived in the United States. The *chicanos* were fond of identifying themselves by saying they had just arrived from *el macizo,* by which they meant the solid Mexican homeland, the good native earth. Although they spoke of *el macizo* like homesick persons, they didn't go back. They remained, as they said of themselves, *pura raza.* So it happened that José and Gustavo would bring home for a meal and for conversation workingmen who were *chicanos* fresh from *el macizo* and like ourselves, *pura raza.* Like us, they had come straight to the barrio where they could order a meal, buy a pair of overalls, and look for work in Spanish. They brought us vague news about the revolution, in which many of them had fought as *villistas, huertistas, maderistas,* or *zapatistas.* As an old *maderista,* I imagined our *chicano* guests as battle-tested revolutionaries, like myself.

As poor refugees, their first concern was to find a place to sleep, then to eat and find work. In the barrio they were most likely to find all three, for not knowing English they needed something that was even more urgent than a room, a meal, or a job, and that was information in a language they could understand. This information had to be picked up in bits and pieces—from families like ours, from the conversation groups in the poolrooms and the saloons.

Beds and meals, if the newcomers had no money at all, were provided—in one way or another—on trust, until the new *chicano* found a job. On trust and not on credit, for trust was something between people who had plenty of nothing, and credit was between people who had something of plenty. It was not charity or social welfare but something my mother called *asistencia,* a helping given and received on trust, to be repaid because those who had given it were themselves in need of what they had given. *Chicanos* who had found work on farms or in railroad camps came back to pay us a few dollars for *asistencia* we had provided weeks or months before.

Because the barrio was a grapevine of job information, the transient *chicanos* were able to find work and repay their obligations. The password of the barrio was *trabajo* and the community was divided in two—the many who were looking for it and the few who had it to offer. Pickers, foremen, contractors, drivers, field hands, pick and shovel men on the railroad and in construction came back to the barrio when work was slack, to tell one another of the places they had been, the kind of *patrón* they had, the wages paid, the food, the living quarters, and other important details. Along 2nd Street, labor recruiters hung blackboards on their shop fronts, scrawling in chalk offers of work. The grapevine was a mesh of rumors and gossip, and men often walked long distances or paid bus fares or a contractor's fee only to find that the work was over or all the jobs were filled. Even the chalked signs could not always be relied on. Yet the search for *trabajo,* or the *chanza,* as we also called it, went on because it had to.

We in the barrio considered that there were two kinds of *trabajo.* There were the seasonal jobs, some of them a hundred miles or more from Sacramento. And there were the closer *chanzas* to which you could walk or ride on a bicycle. These were the best ones, in the railway shops, the canneries, the waterfront warehouses, the lumberyards, the produce markets, the brick kilns, and the rice mills. To be able to move from the seasonal jobs to the close-in work was a step up the ladder. Men who had made it passed the word along to their relatives or their friends when there was a *chanza* of this kind.

It was all done by word of mouth, this delicate wiring of the grapevine. The exchange points of the network were the places where men gathered in small groups, apparently to loaf and chat to no purpose. One of these points was our kitchen, where my uncles and their friends sat and talked of *el macizo* and of the revolution but above all of the *chanzas* they had heard of.

There was not only the everlasting talk about *trabajo,* but also the never-ending action of the barrio itself. If work was action the barrio was where the action was. Every morning a parade of men in oily work clothes and carrying lunch buckets went up Fourth Street toward the railroad shops, and every evening they walked back, grimy and silent. Horse-drawn drays with low platforms rumbled up and down our street carrying the goods the city traded in, from kegs of beer to sacks of grain. Within a few blocks of our house there were smithies, hand laundries, a macaroni factory, and all manner of places where wagons and buggies were repaired, horses stabled, bicycles fixed, chickens dressed, clothes washed and ironed, furniture repaired, candy mixed, tents sewed, wine grapes pressed, bottles washed, lumber sawed, suits fitted and tailored, watches and clocks taken apart and put together again, vegetables sorted, railroad cars unloaded, boxcars iced, barges freighted, ice cream cones molded, soda pop bottled, fish scaled, salami stuffed, corn ground for *masa,* and bread ovened. To those who knew where these were located in the alleys, as I did, the whole barrio was an open workshop. The people who worked there came to know you, let you look in at the door, made jokes, and occasionally gave you an odd job.

This was the business district of the barrio. Around it and through it moved a constant traffic of drays, carts, bicycles, pushcarts, trucks, and high-wheeled automobiles with black canvas tops and honking horns.

On the tailgates of drays and wagons, I nipped rides when I was going home with a gunnysack full of empty beer bottles or my gleanings around the packing sheds.

Once we had work, the next most important thing was to find a place to live we could afford. Ours was a neighborhood of leftover houses. The cheapest rents were in the back quarters of the rooming houses, the basements, and the run-down clapboard rentals in the alleys. Clammy and dank as they were, they were nevertheless one level up from the barns and tents where many of our *chicano* friends lived, or the shanties and lean-tos of the migrants who squatted in the "jungles" along the levees of the Sacramento and American Rivers.

Barrio people, when they first came to town, had no furniture of their own. They rented it with their quarters or bought a piece at a time from the secondhand stores, the *segundas,* where we traded. We cut out the ends of tin cans to make collars and plates for the pipes and floor moldings where the rats had gnawed holes. Stoops and porches that sagged we propped with bricks and fat stones. To plug the drafts around the windows in winter, we cut strips of corrugated cardboard and wedged them into the frames. With squares of cheesecloth neatly cut and sewed to screen doors, holes were covered and rents in the wire mesh mended. Such repairs, which landlords never paid any attention to, were made *por mientras,* for the time being or temporarily. It would have been a word equally suitable for the house itself, or for the barrio. We lived in run-down places furnished with seconds in a hand-me-down neighborhood, all of which were *por mientras.*

We found the Americans as strange in their customs as they probably found us. Immediately we discovered that there were no *mercados* and that when shopping you did not put the groceries in a *chiquihuite.* Instead everything was in cans or in cardboard boxes or each item was put in a brown paper bag. There were neighborhood grocery stores at the corners and some big ones uptown, but no *mercado.* The grocers did not give children a *pilón,* they did not stand at the door and coax you to come in and buy, as they did in Mazatlán. The fruits and vegetables were displayed on counters instead of being piled up on the floor. The stores smelled of fly spray and oiled floors, not of fresh pineapple and limes.

Neither was there a plaza, only parks which had no bandstands, no concerts every Thursday, no Judases exploding on Holy Week, and no promenades of boys going one way and girls the other. There were no parks in the barrio, and the ones uptown were cold and rainy in winter, and in summer there was no place to sit except on the grass. When there were celebrations nobody set off rockets in the parks, much less on the street in front of your house to announce to the neighborhood that a wedding or a baptism was taking place. Sacramento did not have a *mercado* and a plaza with the cathedral to one side and the Palacio de Gobierno on another to make it obvious that there and nowhere else was the center of the town.

It was just as puzzling that the Americans did not live in *vecindades,* like our block on Leandro Valle. Even in the alleys, where people knew one another better, the houses were fenced apart, without central courts to wash clothes, talk, and play with the other children. Like the city, the Sacramento barrio did not have a place which was the middle of things for everyone.

In more personal ways we had to get used to the Americans. They did not listen if you did not speak loudly, as they always did. In the Mexican style, people would know that you were enjoying their jokes tremendously if you merely smiled and shook a little, as if you were trying to swallow your mirth. In the American style there was little difference between a laugh and a roar, and until you got used to them you could hardly tell whether the boisterous Americans were roaring mad or roaring happy.

It was Doña Henriqueta more than Gustavo or José who talked of these oddities and classified them as agreeable or deplorable. It was she also who pointed out the pleasant surprises of the American way. When a box of rolled oats with a picture of red carnations on the side was emptied, there was a plate or a bowl or a cup with blue designs. We ate the strange stuff regularly for breakfast and we soon had a set of the beautiful dishes. Rice and beans we bought in cotton bags of colored prints. The bags were unsewed, washed, ironed, and made into gaily designed towels, napkins, and handkerchiefs. The American stores also gave small green stamps which were pasted in a book to exchange for prizes. We didn't have to run to the corner with the garbage; a collector came for it.

With remarkable fairness and never-ending wonder we kept adding to our list the pleasant and the repulsive in the ways of the Americans. It was my second acculturation.

The older people of the barrio, except in those things which they had to do like the Americans because they had no choice, remained Mexican. Their language at home was Spanish. They were continuously taking up collections to pay somebody's funeral expenses or to help someone who had had a serious accident. Cards were sent to you to attend a burial where you would throw a handful of dirt on top of the coffin and listen to tearful speeches at the graveside. At every baptism a new *compadre* and a new *comadre* joined the family circle. New Year greeting cards were exchanged, showing angels and cherubs in bright colors sprinkled with grains of mica so that they glistened like gold dust. At the family parties the huge pot of steaming tamales was still the center of attention, the *atole* served on the side with chunks of brown sugar for sucking and crunching. If the party lasted long enough, someone produced a guitar, the men took over, and the singing of *corridos* began.

In the barrio there were no individuals who had official titles or who were otherwise recognized by everybody as important people. The reason must have been that there was no place in the public business of the city of Sacramento for the Mexican immigrants. We only rented a corner of the city and as long as we paid the rent on time everything else was decided at City Hall or the county courthouse, where Mexicans went only when they were in trouble. Nobody from the barrio ever ran for mayor or city councilman. For us the most important public officials were the policemen who walked their beats, stopped fights, and hauled drunks to jail in a paddy wagon we called La Julia.

The one institution we had that gave the *colonia* some kind of image was the Comisión Honorífica, a committee picked by the Mexican consul in San Francisco to organize the celebration of the Cinco de Mayo and the Sixteenth of September, the anniversaries of the battle of Puebla and the beginning of our War of Independence. These were the two events which stirred everyone in the barrio, for what we were celebrating was not only the heroes of Mexico but also the feeling that we were still Mexicans ourselves. On these occasions there was a dance preceded by speeches and a concert. For both the Cinco and the Sixteenth, queens were elected to preside over the ceremonies.

Between celebrations neither the politicians uptown nor the Comisión Honorífica attended to the daily needs of the barrio. This was done by volunteers—the ones who knew enough English to interpret in court, on a visit to the doctor, on a call at the county hospital, and who could help make out a postal money order. By the time I had finished the third grade at the Lincoln School I was one of these volunteers. My services were not professional but they were free, except for the IOUs I accumulated from families who always thanked me with "God will pay you for it."

My clients were not *pochos*—Mexicans who had grown up in California, who probably had even been born in the United States. They had learned to speak English of sorts and could still speak Spanish, also of sorts. They knew much more about the Americans than we did, and much less about us. The *chicanos* and the *pochos* had certain feelings about one another. Concerning the *pochos,* the *chicanos* suspected that they considered themselves too good for the barrio but were not, for some reason, good enough for the Americans. Toward the *chicanos,* the *pochos* acted superior, amused at our confusions but not especially interested in explaining them to us. In our family when I forgot my manners, my mother would ask me if I was turning *pochito.*

Turning *pocho* was a half step toward turning American. And America was all around us, in and out of the barrio. Abruptly we had to forget the ways of shopping in a *mercado* and learn those of shopping in a corner grocery or in a department store. The Americans paid no attention to the Sixteenth of September, but they made a great commotion about the Fourth of July. In Mazatlán Don Salvador had told us, saluting and marching as he talked to our class, that the Cinco de Mayo was the most glorious date in human history. The Americans had not even heard about it.

 # Watts: 1932

Danny Romero

2002

Danny Romero was born in 1961 in South Los Angeles. His short stories have appeared in numerous magazines and anthologies, and he has published one novel, *Calle 10* (1996), about a young drug addict living in an Oakland barrio, and two collections of poetry, the most recent being *Land of a Thousand Barrios* (2002). "Watts: 1932" is a personal look at the Watts Towers, ninety-nine feet tall at their highest point, constructedly singlehandedly, bit by bit, by folk artist Simon Rodia over a period of thirty-four years.

My father helped build
the Watts Towers when he
was a boy no more than
10 or 11 hiding with
friends in bushes like
little brown birds waiting
for Mr. Rodia to leave home

For years already the man
had worked in that small yard
surrounded by walls on all sides
and when he was out of sight
those boys threw bottles at
that yard those walls the
spirals of cement and iron
seashells and broken plates
cups and creamers colorful
tiles both whole and chipped

all discarded pieces like
people of Nuestro Pueblo

And when he returned
the man selected the best
of those bits of glass
then added them to
the creation already rising
above this world and reaching
for the sky towards heaven

✺ Saint Aloysius

Danny Romero

1986

Danny Romero teaches in the English department at the
Community College of Philadelphia. His poem "Watts:
1932" also appears in this volume.

TWICE A YEAR THE PARISH HELD FUND-RAISING BAZAARS. They were on
weekends in October and May and were the backbone of the finances
for the grammar school and church. They were held on the blacktop of
the school yard. There were never any rides, but plenty of food, and
games of chance and amusement. It was the duty of the parents of the
schoolchildren to contribute some of their time in the organizing and
actual running of the bazaar.

My father ran the jingleboard. He carried metal rings on a metal
rod with a magnet at one end and bellowed out the prices for the rings.
They were bought, or rather rented, by the patrons of the board and
thrown at a table filled with coins and bills. When one landed clearly on
a coin or the face of a bill it became yours. He picked up the ricocheting
rings from off of the ground and table with the magnet. He was the perfect barker for a carnival somewhere out of a fifties movie, making up
little rhymes and jingles as the day went on, more and more enticing as
the evening went on. He was quite adept at the game himself, having
been running the board for ten years by the time I entered that school.

There were other games too. The goldfish pond where a person
threw Ping-Pong balls, three for a quarter, at a table filled with bowls of
the fish swimming in colored water, some of their orange tails seeming
whispery thin against the background of blue-, red-, or green-colored
water. Mrs. Tabor, whose daughter was in my first-grade class, was always
the one to run this particular booth.

There was another fish pond at those bazaars. My mother, I
remember, always worked at this one. It was a booth covered in front

with cardboard. Portholes were cut in the cardboard, and children, for the cost of a dime, were given bamboo poles with a string tied to one end and a fishhook at the end of that string. The poles were lowered into the portholes and my mother tied cheap toys onto the hook and tugged at the string. Thereupon the child would retrieve the pole, string, and hook from out of the hole and take his prize. It was the only sure winner in the entire operation.

When I first began school there at Saint Aloysius, I had a sister in the eighth grade, a brother in the sixth, another sister in the fourth, and finally my brother Felix in the second. I remember being at the bazaar with my oldest sister that first year. At that time it was still felt I needed to be with someone older, and being with my sister and her friends had its drawbacks. I had to use the girls' restroom, the boys' being far too dirty, rowdy, and violent for the six-year-old child I was. Even later when I was old enough(?), wise enough(?), dumb enough(?) to use that restroom, it remained a place of fear and uncertainty. It was a place of flooded floors and overflowing toilets, sweating Mexican men and Seconal-swallowing, zombie-eyed cholos passing the pills and cheap wine. It was the scene of the first sight of knives cutting flesh, bottles breaking skulls, and the strangeness of being fearful but curious, of being scared enough to cry but not wanting to miss a thing that tears might blind me from.

One Saturday afternoon in those first formative years I walked with my then buddy Jeffrey Leon. We bought *raspadas* from Mr. Salazar and his Boy Scout troop and crushed the confetti eggs we had spent all week preparing on the heads of our classmates. Now within the scrutiny of our parents we snuck peeks as best we could under the miniskirts of the seventh- and eighth-grade girls and the teased-hair high-school cholas. We knew there was something up under those skirts and between those long legs which everyone talked about and desired and which would be ours to partake of someday, though we didn't know at the time what it was for sure.

Bingo games were held in the Old Hall throughout the weekends. It was the only parish hall, but always referred to as the Old Hall. In the cafeteria the food prepared by the parish mothers was sold: corn dogs and buñuelos, tamales, tostadas, tortas and tacos, and burritos and menudo always for the morning after. When they were setting the booths up for the weekends, it was probably some of the best times that were ever had during the school year. During recess and lunch breaks the children of the school stood within the booths acting out what each knew or thought the weekend would be like. The yard would be filled with strange cars and trucks and the men of the parish building the booths, leaving little room for any football, basketball, or sockball.

On one such weekend while I was in the third grade, I asked my father permission to visit a friend's house who lived close by. It was the first time ever being allowed and I was getting older, more responsible perhaps. My friend Alfred and I went and looked at his older brother's *Playboy* magazines.

I used to love the mariachis who would play all decked out in their black suits and wide-brimmed sombreros, the guitarron thumping and the shrill trumpets getting louder. My father loved them too.

Sometime in the early seventies they stopped having these fund-raisers, though I have heard they have started them up again. My nephew now goes to that school. They ended because of the violence which always erupted. Cholos squaring off with each other in the crowd of people. I remember the fight that ended the show for years. The church and school lying somewhere on mutual ground, it was more than likely the bad boys from Florence against their counterparts from Watts. I stood and watched it all. It was the third night in a row. Sticks, knives, and beer bottles filled the air.

I can remember the panic and fear which engulfed me. I was alone for what was probably the first time on the streets. No brother, no sister, mother, or father within reach, just lost in a crowd more than a thousand strong. I heard the commotion starting, growling, and getting nearer. Glass broke and curses flew. People screamed and cried. Father Jose in his heavy Castilian accent stood in the middle of it, speaking in a combination of both English and Spanish, and called upon the Lord to help settle the matter.

Some of my family was there though I didn't know where at the time. I heard firecrackers which I later learned was gunfire. I saw one dark, skinny vato walk by me with the bottom of a beer bottle firmly imbedded in the side of his head. I felt sick. People ran scared. More people stuck around to see how it would turn out. The sheriffs then came to bust some heads themselves. Everyone left then, including myself, for fear of being arrested. I walked home alone at night for the first time, the sirens speeding towards where I had just left. School. Church. Someone died. The Neighborhood. Perhaps it was the vato loco with the beer-bottle bottom for a crown. I felt a fear I hoped I would never feel again.

Watts Bleeds

Luis J. Rodríguez

1991

Luis J. Rodríguez grew up in Watts and East Los Angeles. He published the literary and art magazine *Chismearte* and founded Tía Chucha Press, both organizations that support young, socially conscious poets, and he was the editor of the revolutionary *People's Tribune* in Chicago. He has taught poetry to prisoners, migrant laborers, the homeless, and gang members, and he currently works as a peacemaker with gangs in Los Angeles and Chicago. His short story "The Twenty-Ninth" also appears in this collection.

Watts bleeds
leaving stained reminders
on dusty sidewalks.

Here where I strut alone
as glass lies broken by my feet
and a blanket of darkness is slung
across the wooden shacks
of *nuestra colonia.*

Watts bleeds
dripping from carcasses of dreams:
Where despair
is old people
sitting on torn patio sofas
with empty eyes
and children running down alleys
with big sticks.

Watts bleeds
on vacant lots
and burned-out buildings—
temples desolated by a people's rage.

Where fear is a deep river.
Where hate is an overgrown weed.

Watts bleeds
even as we laugh,
recall good times,
drink and welcome daylight
through the broken windshield
of an old Impala.

Here is Watts of my youth,
where teachers threw me
from classroom to classroom,
not knowing where I could fit in.

Where I learned to fight or run,
where I zigzagged down alleys,
jumped over fences,
and raced by graffiti on crumbling
factory walls.

Where we played
between the boxcars,
bleeding from
broken limbs and torn flesh,
and where years later
we shot up *carga*
in the playground
of our childhood.

Watts bleeds
as the shadow of the damned
engulfs all the *chinga* of our lives.

In the warmth of a summer night,

gunshots echo their deadly song
through the silence of fear;
prelude to a heartbeat.

Watts bleeds
as I bled
getting laid off from work,
standing by my baby's crib,
touching his soft cheek
and fingering his small hand
as dreams shatter again,
dreams of fathers
for little men.

Watts bleeds
and the city hemorrhages,
unable to stop the flow
from this swollen and festering sore.

Oh bloom, you trampled flower!
Come alive as once
you tried to do from the ashes.

Watts, bleeding and angry,
you will be free.

from

✻ What It Takes to Get to Vegas

Yxta Maya Murray

1999

Yxta Maya Murray was born in 1970 in California. She worked as a professor of law while writing her two novels set in East Los Angeles, *Locas* (1997) and *What It Takes to Get to Vegas* (1999). She received a special mention in the 1997 Pushcart Prize anthology and won a 1999 Whiting Writers' Award for her fiction. She has been a professor of law at Loyola Law School in Los Angeles since 1995.

WE COULD HEAR THEM DOING IT DOWN THE HALL. Us and the rest of the world, it turns out, because it was a hot spring night with weather so thick that everyone in East L.A. had left their windows wide open to catch a breeze that might blow in and cut through the molasses air. The house was colored with after-midnight shadows and creeping moonlight, but Mama and Mr. Hernandez were busy whooping and praying as the springs bucked and sang under their bodies, while church-going neighborhood women lay stiff as twigs in their clean clean beds and tried to stuff a pillow inside each ear.

"I know what that is," my sister Dolores said. It was May 1986, and she was eleven then, and I'd just turned thirteen. "I know what they're doing."

I hitched up on my elbows to hear better. Mama was laughing. "No you don't. You're a liar."

"I am not." Dolores's head was under her pillow.

"Liar."

"I do too know." She peeked from under the pillow and shrieked. "They're making sex!"

I looked out the bedroom window. There was the neighborhood pretending to sleep, the black houses like humped giants, the naked trees reaching up the same as praying padres. The red sundown was hid now, nothing left up there but blue moonglow.

Mama's laugh floated into the street, making one of the houses finally flick on its electric eyes.

Señora Montoya, done up in sponge curlers, swung open her front door and threw a witch-shaped shadow on her front porch.

"Putana! Hey, Zapata la putana! Cut out your fucking so we can get some sleep!"

Her yelling made the other mujeres who'd been staring at their ceilings brave enough to switch on their lights and join in on the complaining. Pretty soon we had a row of those cat-eyed monsters staring right at us.

"Lola Zapata! Shut the hell up!"

And Mama, like to answer them, quieted her laughs down into low chuckles, then pitched a wild Siamese howl that must have perked up the ears of every tom for miles around.

Mama always was braver and louder in the nighttime, especially when she had her hands on a man. The next morning, after Mr. Hernandez had gone home to his wife, she sat at the kitchen table in a red poly-silk robe that matched her manicure and smoked her second Marlboro Light sort of moody and quiet, like a Mexican Bette Davis but without the bitchy one-liners. She was a beautiful woman. Dark, with good skin and high bones and a mouth that could go without lipstick, but not much of a talker at that hour. I ate my Lucky Charms and Dolores had her Raisin Bran out of the plastic blue bowls we'd bought at our next-door neighbor's garage sale, and we might as well have tried to figure out Mama's thoughts from the smoke signals she was making as expect her to string more than ten words together. Still, even if we threw her simple questions she was too grouchy to give us the answers we wanted: when we asked her right then to take us shoe shopping over on César Chávez Avenue, she just shook her head no.

"You know I hate that place," she said, then lit up a third cig.

Dolores looked at her. "But my sneakers are busted."

"And I need sandals for summer," I said.

"No."

"Please, okay?"

"Please, Mama?"

"No."

It took us two hours of whining to get her out the door, but as soon as we hit the streets I was happy. Back then I usually liked our town and could sometimes fool myself into thinking I fit in it; I liked walking through it, looking at it, thinking on how far it stretched and what was hid in its four corners.

My piece of east was this big: wide and deep enough to fit a mess of hoboes, boxers, nine-to-fivers, nutso church ladies, trigger-happy con men, knock-kneed Catholic-schoolers, and a handful of sexy-walking women in a space about twenty-five miles back to front. Up on top is our old street, Fisher, a nice stretch of fixer-uppers decorated with dead lawns and chained-up dogs, and to the west there's Eastern Ave, where the homeless tip back Bird in the shadow of the 710 freeway. Down south there's the number streets where the super-low-renters squeeze five or six into kitchenette studios, and then turning to the east is Divine Drive, the richest block in town, where you'll find the church ladies who stay busy barking at their maids and polishing their silverplate.

Some of the biggest action, though, was where we were walking to right then. After Mama got dressed, her, me, and Dolores headed down three blocks until we hit Chávez Ave, which is a straight black line that cuts all the way through the town like the Nile or the Styx, full of beggars and sinners dipping into the waters. César E. Chávez Avenue is that road that's named after el King César with the grapes and the marches. In L.A., there's this funny thing with naming the streets: everybody's got to see their hero up there on a sign like it means something. There's that big stretch of Martin Luther King Avenue by downtown, the Sun Mun Way in Chinatown, even the Anglos got MacArthur Place out in Oxnard. And when the Mexicans made a big enough stink we earned ourselves César Chávez Avenue, running from Dodger Stadium all the way down to Monterey Park. Orale, the day they changed it from Brooklyn to Chávez, you'd think that we'd had a Second Coming or something. I remember how there was the biggest parade with the balloons and the beautiful mariachis and the neighborhood people standing out on the corners smiling, but walking there now alongside my silent mama, my sister with her flapping sneakers, and about a hundred neighbors, I knew that the street wasn't special because it got haunted by César's ghost. The place was great because it moved, with these slow-footed viejas gliding back and forth down the sidewalk, a purse snatcher streaking through the crowd followed by three thugs and a cussing churchie, and a couple sweet young things in spikes swaying past the display window showing the leopard prints that were all the rage that season.

Chávez was the place for shopping: anything you needed you could get on the Avenue. Feeling religious? Here on the corner of Arizona was the santos shop run by that spooky Señora Gallegos who'd read your palm for free. Hungry? Right next door was Rudy's Super where you could get the city's cheapest frozen chicken, and across the street Sancho's coffee shop sold two-dollar chocolate malts. Fashionwise, farther down you'd find Carlita's Fashions for sexy-girl dresses and Diamond Jeweler's for your two-carat cubics, but since we needed sneakers and sandals we went to Payless Shoes, where you could get half off on Reeboks and my favorite jelly sandals.

"You coming in?" Mama said, holding open the door.

I went straight for the new arrivals and sniffed at the tangy plastic shoes. Dolores was already by the sportwears. She wound up spending close to an hour trying on all the size-five sneakers until she settled on some white Vans. I picked out a jelly sandal in violet. Even Mama bought this wild pair of five-inch heels in fuchsia, which the love-struck shoeman sold to her at an 80 percent discount. She was laughing when she teetered out of there, and was trying out the kind of Mae West walk that a woman can only work on that height heel, when we passed by a couple of Divine Drive churchies wearing the same poodle hairdos and eye-blinding diamonds.

"Ay, look out," one of them said when they saw Mama, "here comes the home wrecker."

That was the Widow Muñoz, a triple-chinned busybody who got the money for her pre-owned–Halston habit from her lawyer husband's estate. I guess she used to be a skinny looker with a lot of legs, but by this time she'd turned into a retired matriarch who liked to dress up in name brands and run around judging and nagging everybody to death. The more dangerous poodle was the other one, her best and closest friend in the world as well as her next-door neighbor, Señora Hernandez, who we all called La Rica Hernandez, she had so much money. La Rica was a redheaded, Dior-outlet–wearing Evita Perón wanna-be, not to mention Mama's boyfriend's wife and the unofficial mayor of East L.A. Every big decision went through this woman first—not just where to hold the church bake sales or how many turkeys each family should donate to the homeless come Christmastime, but even what to do about the wayward wife with the gambling problem (she'd cut up all of Lucy Campos's credit cards with her kitchen scissors), or how to punish a borracho ex-husband who'd stopped making his child support payments (she and six friends had gone over to old George Medina's house and carried out all his stereo equipment and his two TVs). I knew La Rica had plans for Mama, too, who hadn't just bedded down her man but didn't care who on this green earth knew about it, either, so I was relieved when she only slowed in front of us, huddled up with her crony, sucked on her teeth, and said, "Get back, putana."

"Nah, you get back, you old bulldog," Mama said.

And then those two made a big show of staring at us sideways and stepping around us like we stank.

Still, relieved or not, I did wish then that I hadn't made us come out there. Of course, I didn't feel like I fit in now, and neither did Dolores, who was pretending not to notice and was staring weird at the display window showing metallic loafers. But what was worse was watching Mama try to walk away from those churchies as though she was a fine señora, and like she didn't hear the Widow Muñoz saying bitch under her breath, because it was a real trick to step ladylike in those new fuchsia shoes. Just as she was trying to walk off without switching her behind, her heel caught in a sidewalk crack, and then there was a god-awful moment when she had to flap her arms around her head, lift up one foot, and balance on the other like a tightrope walker, just so she wouldn't go crashing to the ground. When the churchies finally passed us by she took off those shoes and slipped on her old cheapies, and didn't say one word the rest of the way home.

Mama learned that balancing act from all the times she'd got knocked flat on her behind, but when she'd first come out to L.A. from Calexico she could get tripped up pretty easy.

A few hours after we'd run into the churchies she took out some old pictures that she stored in a shoebox and looked at the one a stranger took of her when she'd been here for just two days. She did that sometimes when she got in a funk: sit on the living-room floor with a scotch and spread out the snapshots on the carpet and make me and Dolores look at them with her. We didn't mind, though. We liked it.

"Here it is," she said, picking the picture up. She was on her stomach, barefoot, flipping through the old black-and-whites and Kodachromes. "Now don't you think I could have been a Bond Girl? Couldn't you see this honey kissing Sean Connery?"

"Who's Sean Connery?" Dolores asked.

"Sean Connery was a Scottish guy who played Double-Oh-Seven," Mama said.

We just looked at her. She stared some more at the picture.

"But I don't remember ever seeing a Mexican Bond Girl," she said.

I reached out my hand. "Let me see it."

It was my favorite picture of her, and still is, but it took me until I was a grown woman myself to puzzle out the story behind her pretty face. It's a washed-color, three-by-four glossy with a white border that's dirtied up with little-girl thumbprints from all the times me and Dolores took it out to look at our red-lipped Mama standing in front of a pagoda and grinning.

She really was something. Just looking at her bubble hairdo and Peter Pan collar you could see that the girl was green. It makes you wonder: how'd a chica like that get on a Greyhound with just sixty bucks, then drive to a town where she didn't even have one tía or abuelito to call?

Well, who knows. And I guess who cares when you got a face like that? What she saw in the mirror must have asked her, Why not you, Miss Thing? Go on and take your shot in the big city, where any pretty sucker can make it, if she lives through it. City's where they got con artists in leather-interior Caddys passing for film-studio money men, and studio men hid up in their high-rises screwing the cherries they promise starring parts to. Not that Mama ever got to set foot in one of the high-rises, although she did wind up seeing her fair share of cowhide backseats. But back then she believed in it, the hands and feet pressed in concrete, the ice-cream counters where you're sure to be discovered while sipping a soda. And so there she was froze in 1967, fresh from the border town and posing outside Mann's Chinese wearing her best Barbarella bouffant and Rita Moreno smile, looking so fine you barely noticed that homemade skirt cut like a lamp shade, the clunker church-sale shoes, the Naugahyde handbag ugly as a dead dog. That takes some talent, too, because those off-the-bus Calexico clothes she was wearing must have stuck out sore in Hollywood. But Mama had what it took for Technicolor, I'd say. She had star quality.

That's what she was going to be. A movie star. Could have been one, too, in another life. She had the knockout body, the husky cigarette voice. Even yard-sale clothes hung neat and tidy off her curves, and she walked slow and swivel-hipped, like she was made of money. She'd learned how to move from watching old black-and-white movies, copied the strut-your-stuff from Grable and Crawford, the slinky-cat from la Superloca Lana Turner, the make-them-cry from Monroe, but she was born with that face pretty enough to make other ladies mad. Same as me. I loved it when people told me I was just like her; I'd run to the mirror and smile at my lashy eyes, black hair, big wide mouth. But when I got older and a little bit smarter, I saw how they didn't mean it as no compliment. Good looks and a trip to Hollywood didn't bring my mama any luck. Didn't get her name on any marquees. Just gave her high hopes and a bad reputation.

Neighborhood folks forever been saying Mama's a putana and even the God-fearing church ladies forget their love-thy-neighbor where she's concerned, but she wasn't nothing but a stripper for a couple years. Before she came to the city she'd been stuck in Calexico, California, the border armpit where all they've got is some cowboy bars, a third-run movie theater, and a fill-'er-up gas station for the blondie surfers passing through on their way to Mazatlán, and it's the kind of two-bit place where Mexican girls work a couple years behind a counter before they squeeze out a six-pack of niños and get old too damn fast. Not my mama, though. After she'd spent her early years feeding up on B-movie dreams, she ditched her folks and hopped that Greyhound all the way to Sunset and Vine, looking out for Eastwood and Brando and waiting to get discovered by a big-shot director while strolling down the street in her hand-sewn dress.

And why not? Lightning had struck brown girls before. Bet you never knew Rita Hayworth was a hot dish of Spanish rice and beans, and then there's old Dorothy L'Amour, dressed up in that sarong and as dark skinned as an Aztec. It didn't hit Mama, though, and the Boulevard gets dark and lonely if you don't get picked up by that producer right away. She got hungry, then scared, and instead of heading back home she broke down like most pretty and proud things do. Started dancing at the Cathouse, this downtown stripper club, and that's where she finally got famous for a while.

They called her the Spanish Fly and fools from all over L.A. paid good money to drink watered-down whiskeys and feed her G-string full of dollar bills. She met lots of men that way, had her pick of deep-pocket gangsters who wintered in Palm Springs and boozer CEOs with money to burn. But she wasn't a hustler, at least in the love department. She didn't choose the one who could set her up nice, with minks and penthouses, a convertible and a checking account. Mama wound up falling hard for this love-and-leave road boy, a California Mexican trucker named Eddie D who came by the Cathouse once a month with roses and poems and a busy way in bed. The man was as fertile as a field and seemed marriage-minded. He bought her a powder-blue suit and kissed her in front of a preacher before he knocked her up with us, but then one night he said he was taking a haul of eggs down to Barstow in his eighteen-wheeler and that he'd be right back in the morning. She never saw him again.

"Mr. Romance," she said now, in our living room. She was still rustling through the shoebox and she'd picked up his picture. Mr. Romance was what she always called him. Her voice when she said it makes you think of burned-black Valentines and Don Juan devils with slippery hips and toothpaste smiles, but you wouldn't know he was a playboy just to look at him. The man was, to put it plain, ugly. The picture she held up showed a guy with a crop of black curls and a face that was kind of crooked in the nose and jaw; he looked like an old boxer who'd took too many hits.

She was quiet for a minute, tapping her ash into a saucer. "Wonder where Mr. Romance is now, eh? Probably drunk. Or dead, maybe. I bet he died in that damn truck of his."

I took the picture from her and looked at my dad's busted mug. I knew Mama was wrong but I kept my mouth shut. I was sure Eddie D was still trucking through the dust bowl. I knew this because I'd once seen him alive, right on our doorstep, but I'd never told her or Dolores nothing about it.

It'd happened the year before. He'd come by the house after school, dressed up in a red tie and black pants and carrying cellophane-wrapped flowers, but I'd seen that picture of him so many times I knew who he was right away.

"Your mama home?" he'd said, then stepped back to give me the once-over. "Jesus, little Rita. Just like her. You should be proud you look so much like your mama. What about your sister, eh? Dolores? And Lola? Lola girl, you in here? Surprise, surprise. It's your old lover man come back for a visit, baby. Sweeping you off your *feet*."

The dusk was coming in through the door, but Mama had still been at work. She'd lost her Spanish Fly moves when she birthed Dolores, and had been short-order cooking at Denny's ever since. I knew she'd bust a vein if she came home and found the man who'd put her behind that stove standing on her steps like a salesman and asking nosy questions. And I didn't like him much myself, either. He was peeking past me into the house, seeing the rat-colored rug, the flower wallpaper losing its stick, and when he stepped up close to get a better view I saw how his suit was patched and he was starting to sweat. So no way. Even at my age I could tell he was a con man, and I wasn't going to let him weasel in here and try to razzle-dazzle Mama and Dolores with his slick talk and his rayon tie and his supermarket roses. Before he could push his way through, I opened up the screen, leaned over, and spit on his suede shoes, which were pinhole wing tips with rubber soles.

"Go away," I hissed, wiping my mouth. "Get out of here. We all hate you." And then I shut the door on his wide eyes, bolted up the locks, and sung the theme song to the telenovela *Maria de Nadie* until I heard him shuffling away.

from

✴ The Tattooed Soldier

Héctor Tobar

1998

Héctor Tobar was born in 1963 to Guatemalan parents. As a reporter for the *Los Angeles Times,* he was part of a writing team that won a Pulitzer Prize for coverage of the 1992 riots following the Rodney King verdict. *The Tattooed Soldier* (1998) is his first novel.

GUILLERMO LONGORIA, RETIRED SERGEANT in the Jaguar Battalion of the Guatemalan army, lived six blocks from MacArthur Park in a brick building called the Westlake Arms. He kept his one-room apartment meticulously clean, making his bed first thing in the morning and dusting his only furniture, a dresser and an old wooden chair, three times a week. Every Sunday he took a wet rag and wiped down the scratched lime green skin of the linoleum floor on his hands and knees. He worked his muscled arms hard against the scuff marks and the faint outline of dirty footprints, reaching under the bed to annihilate dust balls and loose hairs. No matter how hard he cleaned, no matter that his palms were wrinkled and white from scrubbing, the floor always seemed to be dirty again an hour later. Alone in his room, Sergeant Longoria was waging a war of attrition against the gray film of soot that infiltrated whenever he left the window open, fine particles of automobile exhaust and God knows what else that came creeping in from the streets four stories below.

This self-imposed discipline and Spartan lifestyle set him apart, he felt, from the rabble that lived around him, the Salvadorans, Mexicans, and Guatemalans who filled the Westlake Arms. He saw them in the hallways and stairways, these janitors, garment workers, and housekeepers, scrambling off to work every morning. They were on a sad minimum-wage quest, with no sense of life's greater purpose. He hated them, they were so pathetic.

Longoria considered himself a man of accomplishment. The certificates and diplomas from his military training in the Panama Canal Zone and at Fort Bragg, North Carolina, the newspaper clippings detailing his unit's exploits in Guatemala, were all carefully preserved in an album he kept in the bottom drawer of his dresser. The intellect, strategic vision, and wisdom of great military leaders had been passed down to him. A soldier did not lose those things when he quit the army; he carried them with him wherever he went, even to a city filled with criminals and drug addicts. His neighbors lived in apartments dense with people, two or even three families sharing one room. That was good enough for them, but Longoria demanded better for himself. He made enough money from his job at El Pulgarcito Express to afford living alone.

Longoria's photo album was filled mostly with snapshots of his buddies in the army, pictures of men posing with their weapons and with the company mascot, a brownish mutt named Che. One shot was a close-up of Longoria's forearm when the tattoo of the jaguar was fresh, two weeks new—yellow pelt, black spots, moist red mouth. A certificate from the School of the Americas in the Canal Zone took up an entire album page. There were several newspaper clippings, two of them from *La Prensa Libre:* an interview with Lieutenant Colonel Miguel Villagrán, commanding officer of the Jaguar Battalion, and a report of Villagrán's death in an ambush by "terrorist delinquents." Longoria loved Villagrán even more than his own father, a love that had grown stronger in the years since Villagrán was killed. The album also held a stack of battlefield photographs that Longoria rarely looked at, the last of what had once been a trunkful of war trophies, most of them given away when he left Guatemala.

In the drawer with the album, Longoria also kept his book collection, which consisted of several paperbacks, among them *Vladimir Rashnikov's Guide to Intelligent Chess* and *Fifty Chess Openings from the Grandmasters.* He had three titles by Dr. Wayne García, including *Success and Self-Fulfillment through Mind Control.*

Dr. García helped Longoria understand his inner urges. He had read all of Dr. García's books, and considered him one of the great thinkers of our time. Dr. García taught Longoria that the mind was like any machine and that he had to control the machine instead of allowing it to control him. If Longoria had read Dr. García's books when he was younger, he might have gone further in the army, might have accomplished more with his life. *Maybe I would have been an officer.* Longoria wanted to meet Dr. García one day.

Besides the dresser, the bed, and the chair, the only other objects in Longoria's apartment were a weight-lifting bench and a set of barbells, which he kept stacked like coins in a corner of his room. Although he was a small man, he could bench-press two hundred fifty pounds, almost double his weight. He bathed after each workout, in the morning before he left for work, and in the evening when he came home. Afraid of running out of shampoo, he kept extra-large bottles of silky yellow Suave in the shower. When he rinsed off, he took great pleasure in looking down to watch the dirty water drip off his body, thin black lines swirling down the drain. After just a few hours on the street, the soot was always thick and sticky on his neck and face.

He would not be swallowed by the uncleanness around him. *This place, this Los Angeles, is a cloud of filth, even the sky is muddy brown.* He found condoms and hypodermic needles on the street. There were needles everywhere: in the park, on the lawns, by the bus benches, in the gutters. All it took was one little poke, one little drop of blood to infect you. He'd seen the AIDS cases, right here in front of his building, the old *culeros* so close to death, skeleton men. *If the needle pokes me, my muscles and bones will corrode and I will die here, alone in this room. It will take them weeks to find my body. To die like that is to die without honor.*

Over the years Longoria had learned to spot the AIDS cases and the AIDS-cases-to-be: the hypes, the doomed *tecatos,* the human pincushions. The streets around MacArthur Park were thick with wan-faced heroin addicts. They were stacked in the old hotels and apartment buildings like diseased cords of wood. When they drifted toward him on the street corner, bony hands outstretched for a cigarette or a few coins, he gave them a homicidal stare.

Behind Sergeant Longoria's building was an alley where a group of these heroin addicts lived, adding another layer of scent to the putrid sweetness of the alley's dumpsters. Longoria saw the addicts and breathed in their smell every morning when he took out his trash. This was another of his rituals, something he did every day, even if there was only a single Kleenex in the red plastic waste basket he kept in his bathroom.

The addicts had been living in the alley for about two years. Their cluster of shacks pushed against the unused rear entrance to a medical clinic, under a sign reading *"Clínica Médica Familiar: Un Servicio Para la*

Comunidad." Longoria would like to see them flushed out of the alley like shit down the toilet. But there was no one to do it, because no one in Los Angeles seemed to care about trespassing, about people breaking the law.

When they first arrived in the alley the *tecatos* slept in the open air, with a piece of cardboard or a blanket thrown over them. After a few weeks they brought boxes and plastic milk crates to build snug little shelters, then some sheets of plywood to fashion a crude lean-to against the wall. Step by step they added on, and now they had this little settlement with an air of permanence about it, made from things other people had thrown away. The heroin addicts were here in the alley for the long haul.

Longoria made a point of never talking to the *tecatos*. He hardly ever looked at them anymore. Only once did he exchange words with them, on a nippy winter morning when he heard a curious noise drifting from their shacks. He was standing in the alley, raising the dumpster's table-sized lid to throw out his trash. Then this unfamiliar sound, a high-pitched tone halfway between a hum and a whistle, and the chatter of voices. When he stepped closer to investigate, the source of the noise became clear: a television set. The heroin addicts were watching television. It couldn't be, but yes, now he could make out the jovial monologue of a weatherman.

"...the forecast is for heavy snow across the Midwestern states, with icy blasts of arctic air coming down across Lake Michigan. Sorry about that, Chicago! And our hearts go out to the people of Buffalo this morning, Katie, where it's a bone-chilling fifteen below. Ouch!"

Longoria walked slowly past an opening in the wall of blankets and saw a man and a woman sitting on a mattress, bathed in the gray glow of the television screen. Inside, the space was no more than four feet wide, just enough room for two people to sleep side by side. He stepped back and saw a frayed brown wire poking out from under the rotting blankets and cardboard that were the shack's roof. The wire snaked up along the wall of the medical clinic, looped around a water pipe, and disappeared into a window in the Westlake Arms.

Intrigued, Longoria went inside and found the wire dangling from a windowsill in a second-story stairwell, attached by a crude copper braid to another wire that ran along the base of the wall. For a few seconds he stared at the wires in confusion, until he realized that the heroin addicts were using electricity from his building. It incensed him that they would do this. They sure had a lot of nerve, these hypes. This was going too far, *se estaban aprovechando*. Longoria ripped the wires apart, causing a small but fierce explosion of blue sparks that sent a quick jolt of electric current through his arms. He fell butt-first onto the floor. The television noise in the alley sputtered and died.

"Aw shit," a male voice shouted below. "We're gonna miss the rest of *The Today Show*."

"Go reconnect it, baby," a female voice said. "Hurry. I wanna watch that interview with Whitney Houston."

Longoria got to his feet and stuck his head out the window. "*Ladrones,* you were stealing our electricity! We paid for that. It's not yours, it's not free. It costs money!"

After a short silence, the male voice in the alley called back slowly, "Fuck you, buddy. Fuck you."

They came to the offices of El Pulgarcito Express clutching envelopes overflowing with Mother's Day cards, love letters, and Kodak pictures of the grandson's baptism. They carried cardboard boxes stuffed with vitamins and cold creams you couldn't find in San Salvador or Guatemala City. They took neatly folded bills from wallets and purses and bought money orders made out to relatives in Quetzaltenango, Tegucigalpa, Jutiapa, and Zacatecoluca.

They didn't trust the mail system in their native countries, painfully slow when it functioned at all, so they came to El Pulgarcito or one of its competitors: Lopez Express, Cuzcatlán Express, Quetzal Express, and a half-dozen other outfits with equally quaint Central American names, in storefronts decorated with the sky-blue and white flags of El Salvador, Guatemala, Honduras. You paid fifteen dollars and El Pulgarcito promised to deliver your letter within one week, *más o menos,* unless the destination was in one of the "zones of conflict," the euphemism of choice for guerilla-controlled territory, in which case the delivery might take a lot longer.

At the El Pulgarcito office on Pico Boulevard, branch number two, Sergeant Longoria's job was to handle complaints, to listen to the customers whine about the rates, about packages that never arrived at their destinations, about lost checks and money orders.

"My sister said she opened the letter and there was no money order, it disappeared," a corpulent Honduran woman said, waving a receipt before Longoria's face. "Two hundred dollars, gone, just like that! You know what I think? You're just a bunch of thieves, that's what."

Longoria wondered which of the five or so people who worked in this office had taken the woman's money order. Maybe it was Carlos

Avilés, the manager, who opened every letter to check for political messages, or maybe it was the owner himself, who wasn't above a little pilfering now and then. Longoria had no doubt this customer was telling the truth, but then again, she was a fool for trusting El Pulgarcito in the first place. She got what she deserved.

"We only guarantee the money order if you buy it here, with us," Longoria said for the third time. "If you put one in and don't tell us, we're not responsible. The company isn't responsible for any of that. This is what our *jefe* says. The *jefe* says those are the rules."

"Oh, so that's how it is?" the woman shot back. "I see. So that's the little racket you've got going here."

Longoria stared straight into her angry eyes. This was his practiced soldier's gaze, his *cara de matón,* the look that said he was one of the serious ones, the type to grin after he hit you over the head with his rifle butt. Anyone from Central America recognized this look. Longoria had the face of the soldier the customers remembered from back home, a Galil at his side, pants tucked into high laced boots, standing with menacing grace on a street corner in Guatemala, El Salvador. Dead dictators and demagogues lived on in these cold brown eyes. It was Longoria's great gift, his strongest personal asset. His stare always chased the complainers away, which was precisely why he had been stationed at the front counter. The Honduran woman put the receipt in her purse, turned around, and walked away.

There was a certain discipline involved in his work, and Longoria liked that. You had to be patient and resist the urge to reach over and slap the woman. Self-control. That was what he was learning from Dr. Wayne García's book, to rein in the initial impulse to strike out and solve the problem with his fists. Sometimes it took more nerve not to hit someone than to hit them.

Longoria liked working at El Pulgarcito because it was an office job. He told people he worked in "the service sector," admiring the orderly sound of this phrase. When he first came to Los Angeles, Longoria had worked in a series of factories, including eight months in a sweatshop on Washington Boulevard where his job was to tend to large vats of acid that turned regular blue jeans into "stone-washed" jeans. This was smelly work, and he felt he deserved something better than noxious fumes. Above all, he wanted a job where he could stay clean and not worry about chemicals eating into his skin.

Longoria the factory worker had begun his search for new employment on a Sunday afternoon, walking into the storefronts along Pico

Boulevard to ask the owners if they needed any help. He was turned away at a *discoteca* and a shop that sold religious articles, saints, and votive candles of all shapes and sizes. He stepped into a store called La Primerísima, which sold First Communion, wedding, and *quinceañera* dresses. Waves of lacy white fabric gushed from every corner of the cramped space, from the display windows, from hooks on the walls, from the rows and rows of racks on the floor. The young women who worked there laughed at him, asking if he wanted a job modeling the dresses.

His next stop was El Pulgarcito Express. Behind the counter stood a thirtyish pug-nosed man in a square-cut guayabera shirt, the uniform of the well-dressed Latin American businessman. The man turned quiet, his eyes narrowing, when Longoria asked if the company was hiring.

"You're a soldier, aren't you?" he said, staring at Longoria as if he were some sort of zoological curiosity. "I can tell. You're a veteran."

"Yes, *jefe. Así es.*"

"What unit were you with?"

Talking about one's military past was always risky, but Longoria already had an inkling of this man's sympathies.

"*Ejército de Guatemala,*" he answered efficiently, as if he were addressing an officer. "*Batallón Jaguar. Sargento Guillermo Longoria, para servirle.*"

The man in the guayabera broke out in a perfect white smile—a wealthy man's smile, Longoria observed—and embraced him.

"Welcome, sergeant, welcome to El Pulgarcito Express. Of course we have a job for you. You'll work the counter, you'll help with the shipments. How's six fifty an hour sound?"

This was two dollars more an hour than Longoria had ever earned before.

"Consider this your home, soldier. You're part of our family now."

 L.A. Rain

Rowena Silver

1995

Rowena Silver grew up in California's San Fernando Valley.
Her work has appeared in several journals and magazines,
and she is currently an editor of *Epicenter,* a quarterly literary
magazine published in Riverside, California.

In Torrance
where plastic flamingos
stand knee-deep in mud
a taco vendor covers his wares
and children run

splashing like New York city kids
at a hydrant
as the broken piñata sky
pours torrential sweetness enough
for everyone to take home

The soft earth is melting
opening wide
in unabashed plush opulence
streaming gutters in rivulets
of pulsing waves

An occasional Coke can
sails the street like a toy boat

but

Suddenly the sky rocks
so loudly that Angelenos
run under doorways and try
to guess the magnitude and epicenter
of the cloud

whereas

I am tucked into my stucco
house, somewhat pleased
at the taste of instant

cappuccino, content that
we are getting water and
for the moment
my roof is holding strong

Glitter

Brandy Burrows

1998

Brandy Burrows was born and raised in Corona, California, where she still lives. She is the author of three chapbooks of poetry, including *Mexican Breakfast* (1998), from which the following poem was taken.

san bernardino county

    shines

in a moving car i watch
a field of broken glass
brilliant in the sun
she wears her roadside
tight as a girl going dancing

    now i remember

the story of how corona
my crown town
got its name

a king named joker
wore a broken beer bottle
on his head
like a crown
rubies falling
into his eyes

his *novias* erected a statue
of him in memory

    places i have lived

have the luster of pretty
life

the sequin of sweat
hard work on the back
sparkle of chrome

and to all of my friends
who have moved away

we admire the stars
here
too

In December's Air

Leonard Adame

1975

Leonard Adame teaches English and multicultural studies at
Butte Community College. His poem "My Grandmother
Would Rock Quietly and Hum" also appears in this volume.

eleven-thirty:
a boy, a little girl,
the dog quiet on their laps,
waiting for Nick the attendant
near the doorstep
of Beacon Gas and Grocery

gathered like kids
in old photographs,
her nostrils frost-cracked,
their breath like steam
in december's air

i look and want
to be sorry
for the holes
in their t-shirts and shoes—
kneeling, i ask
their names,
where they live,
why they sit here;
i say nothing
of the cold

soaking through
their clothes like water...

Trinidad, Guadalupe,
Charley their dog,
waiting
to buy candy
with the fifty cents from Grandma...
        they point
to their house
three vacant lots
away: the one
with the light,
they say,
can you see
it?

✸ the rains have left and ernesto is dead

Andrés Montoya

1999

Andrés Montoya was born in 1968 and lived in Fresno until his death in 1999. A member of the Fresno School of poets, he taught creative writing in colleges in Fresno but also worked as a field hand, ditchdigger, canner, and ice plant worker, experiences that are evident in his poetry. His collection *The Iceworker Sings and Other Poems* (1999) won a 1997 Chicano/Literary Prize at UC Irvine before its publication and won an American Book Award in 2000.

for trejo

the rains have left
and the air is hot this day.
in between
the rows of vines
sparrows are feeding
on a dog and his worms.

there is no breeze
to rustle the grape leaves
or to cool the dry
pocked faces of prostitutes
around the villa motel.
there is only this season
and this night
to breed anger
in the empty stomachs of children.

a car passes on the road in front of my porch
and whips dust in swirls and again
the smell of sulfur
catches my nose by surprise.
so long, it seems, i've been
in this valley off the 99,
watching the children play in this dust,
watching mothers cry out
to God for justice for peace for death,
watching the honda civics passing by, passing through,
never stopping on this side, this scary side violent side,
this side of misspent anger.

yes, it's warm
and swamp coolers only
make me sweat more from my porch.
i can see three campesinos walking
into town, covered in dust, and i wonder
if their children will be deformed,
or maybe they will die soon,
leaving the fields to no one
but the farmers.
the sparrows have been frightened
from the dog by the three,
but they will return
to pick from his flesh
what they can.

✹ Divisadero Street, San Francisco

Pat Mora

1991

Pat Mora was born in El Paso, Texas. The author of more
than twenty nonfiction, fiction, and poetry books for adults
and children, she has also been a museum director, a consultant for U.S./Mexico youth exchanges, an English
teacher, a university administrator, and a poetry judge. Her
writing awards include an NEA fellowship, a Premio
Aztlán Literature Award, and four Southwest Book Awards.
Her latest children's books are *Maria Paints the Hills* (2002)
and the biography *A Library for Juana: The World of Sor
Juana Inés* (2002).

I watch a woman play with light,
at ease with the loud
orange of nasturtiums running
unchecked among the prim-
rose and the purple bursts of lillies of the Nile
in the cement heart of the city,
at ease with the sprawl of cats
and children wherever she kneels;
a woman who starts trees from seeds,
smells memories: the scent
of frilled rose geraniums becomes
the bubble-pop of apple jelly
she once scented with such frills. She sniffs
the pollen-heavy air for last year's bees.
Lost without dirt, she says,
so she greens this hidden square.

Light, ignored by the four straight backs
of buildings, gathers and shimmers
on the faces of daisies and poppies
open to the throat, light   dazzles
until we too shimmer.

Callas offer tall flutes of soothing cream.
I watch the woman, a tender
of possibilities, daily squeeze
one more stem into her plot.

East San José

Beverly Silva

1983

Poet Beverly Silva, a longtime resident of San Jose, teaches
English as a second language to adults. Her poem
"Wetbacks" also appears in this collection.

i love cruising down King Road
on a Sunday afternoon
watching all those shiny lowriders
hydraulics bouncing when they stop
for red lights.

i love living in East San Jo
watching all the changes
like old Story Road
being called The Boulevard now.

i love swinging the King & Story corner every afternoon
cutting through the barrio to my apartment
looking at the distinctly California ranch style houses
built in the mid-fifties
& predicted to fall apart in twenty years.

i love shopping at Tropicana Foods
buying frijoles & southern greens & ten-pound bags
of Asian rice
waiting in line with food stamps
maybe having a drink at the Red Sparks before going home.

i love looking at the cholos and cholas
guys with pompadours like old-time movie stars
girls with painted cheeks
like circus clowns.

i love being here in the middle
of this lowrider country
sharing all the energy
& feeling this pride
in what i am.

✳ Home by the Sea

José Antonio Burciaga

1995

José Antonio Burciaga was born in 1940 in El Paso, Texas, and lived his early years in the basement apartment of a synagogue, where his father was a caretaker. After serving in the U.S. Air Force, he studied fine art in college and later worked as a journalist, illustrator, and graphic designer. He published two essay collections and one book of poetry, *Undocumented Love,* which won an American Book Award in 1992, the same year he received the National Hispanic Heritage Award for Literature. He founded the publishing company Diseños Literarios, was a founding member of the comedy group Culture Clash, and, during the nine years he served as a Resident Fellow at Stanford University, painted many of the murals at the student dorm Casa Zapata, including the now-famous "The Last Supper of Chicano Heroes." He died of cancer in 1996.

FROM OUR TWO-STORY RETREAT HOME in Carmel Highlands, California, the west spans toward the vast and eternally sinking horizon of the Pacific Ocean. Most days the sky is as blue as the ocean. Below, white crests eternally ride atop the blue surf breaking and bathing the dark brown rocks of Point Lobos. Behind to the East, beautiful green cypress trees rise against the hills and a few nestled homes. To the south along the coast lies beautiful Big Sur country. To the north more beautiful coastlines, the Carmel Mission, San Carlos Borromeo del Río Carmelo.

This is California, California at its most beautiful. Less than one hundred and fifty years after this territory was claimed by Mexicanos and Indians, a pervading and almost insistent indigenous ambiance persists. It is a ghostlike charm that lingers in the Carmel Mission, its Indian cemetery, historic Mexican and Spanish adobe architecture, Casa Pacheco, Casa Vasquez, the old Mexican jail, and names like Carmelo, Monterey, Alvarado, and Big Sur.

Big Sur? As in "Big Sir" or "Big Surf?" "Big Sur" is an incomplete translation of what was once *El País Grande al Sur,* or more commonly called *la costa al sur.* Big Sur means Big South.

Carmel Highlands is an exclusive but not necessarily high-income small town with a population of just under five hundred, just south of Carmel and along California's Pacific Coast Highway, once called *El Camino Real.*

Somehow, some way or another, with savings, searching for a good deal, an honest sales agent, and after a prior investment loss, my wife, Cecilia, and I borrowed on the equity of our home to purchase a modest, comfortable home overlooking the ocean.

Our dreams of living in such a setting had never gone beyond wishful thinking. Only a fortunate few live on the California coast. A block away from our home is the late Ansel Adams' home. The area is lightly populated and serene. The clear night skies are littered with stars. The coast has been officially designated as a National Wildlife Refuge. During February, the great whale migration can be appreciated from our windows. From a sandy beach cove two blocks away, seals sunbathe on the rocks or play hide-and-seek in the water. It is beautiful beyond description. The Indians considered this area sacred.

I think of the beauty and our good fortune and remember a persistent suggestion from a dear departed friend, "Write about your new surroundings, as Chicanos." There is a tease that arouses my discomfort. A Chicano landowner! A capitalist! On prime California land! Probably the only Chicanos in Carmel Highlands or neighboring Carmel, and one of a few on the entire California coast.

Criticism or teases of Chicanos with fancy cars and homes not normally found in the barrios is prevalent. This criticism comes from Chicanos and Gringos alike who erroneously stereotype landowning Chicanos as *vendidos,* sellouts, or Marxist socialists gone wrong.

I'm reminded of two unforgettable anecdotes. First was the young Chicana Stanford graduate who became a doctor. She confided how crushed she was to see me in a coat and tie at a university function. She had the naive but prevalent assumption that all Chicanos wore nothing but working-class clothes. Second was a student who asked to borrow my siphoning hose. When I informed him that I didn't have one, he answered, "Oooohhh…What kind of a Chicano are you anyway?"

Another time, the same *bato,* may he now rest in peace, asked if he could borrow my jumper cables. Again I didn't have any, and again he responded, "Oooohhh…What kind of a Chicano are you anyway?"

Chicanos have forever been attacked for wearing a coat and tie, or for owning property, because we are breaking new ground into formerly exclusive white territory. Once a Chicano in an audience asked Luis Valdez if he could still consider himself a Chicano with probable wealth and fame. His answer: "Do I have to be poor to be a Chicano?"

Our neighbors in Carmel Highlands are most gracious and accepting. From our home in Carmel Highlands, we appreciate and relate to the regional history and can readily identify and feel that somehow the land is returning to the people that once lived here. Not only returning to *Mexicanos,* but to *indígenas,* to Chicanos, half-breeds with indigenous ancestors. Yankees have always justified stealing the land from Mexicanos because Mexicanos stole it from Indians, without realizing that Mexicanos are more Indian than Hispanic. And so in the name of our indigenous ancestors, we reclaim the land, with deed and title, once we pay off the mortgage.

But we are not the only Mexicanos in the area. The surrounding fields of Monterey County produce eighty-five percent of the artichokes consumed in this country. You need not be told who the farmworkers are.

The poorest of our new neighbors live in shacks by the expensive artichoke fields. I visited these farmworkers one day, wanting to give away a futon bed.

One dying afternoon as the orange sun was setting over the green artichoke fields and the blue ocean, I drove onto the brown dirt road by their paint-faded one-room homes and in Spanish asked a farmworker if he could use the bed tied to the top of my van.

"*¿Como sabía que necesitaba una cama?*" How did I know he needed a bed? he asked as he broke into a wide smile, throwing up his hands as if he had hit the jackpot.

"It's not very soft," I apologized after we assembled the futon on the dirt ground in front of his crowded home and an artichoke field.

"*¡Hombre!*" he answered, "*Esta noche,* I will sleep like a king!"

We talked. He was from Oaxaca. I judged him to be a good person and so I asked, "We are looking for a good, honest, and responsible person to clean and maintain our house when we are away."

"*Mi cuñada!*" he answered. Pointing north beyond a hill, he said, "My sister-in-law and her husband live over there. They would be perfect."

And perfect they were. We interviewed the young Oaxacan couple, checked their reference, agreed to their hourly fee, and gave them a key to clean our house when we were away. They were with us for a year and a half before they realized they were working too much at too many jobs and barely had time to start a family.

In fine Carmel and Monterey restaurants Mexicanos cook, wash, serve, and wait on tables. With memories of our immigrant parents ingrained, we take pride in identifying with them. We ask them what part of Mexico they are from, only to confirm that most Mexican immigrants around Monterey and Carmel come from Oaxaca. These are questions we don't ask undocumented Australian, Canadian, or European workers.

One famous Monterey resident was Robert Louis Stevenson, author of *Treasure Island,* who lived in Carmel Valley. In the late 1800s he was able to appreciate the indigenous population and lamented,

> The Monterey of last year exists no longer. A huge hotel has sprung up in the desert by the railway. Invaluable toilettes figure along the beach and between live oaks; and Monterey is advertised in the newspapers and posted in the waiting room at railway stations as a resort for wealth and fashions. Alas for the little town! It is not strong enough to resist the influence of the flaunting caravanserai, and the poor, quaint, penniless native gentlemen of Monterey must perish, like a lower race, before the millionaire vulgarians of the Big Bonanza.

But Mexicanos never did die away. Some have always lived in the shadows, in the shacks, the shanties—and worked in the sun-filled fields. Our parents were the immigrant farmworkers who pulled us away from the fields to the schools, away from hard labor and exploitation. We are not self-made; we do not owe what we have to individualistic self-made success, but to the sweat, struggle, and tears of our parents.

But somewhere, somehow, many Chicanos and non-Chicanos lost the message or became blind to the words of Emiliano Zapata, the great Mexicano hero, revolutionary, martyr, and icon. Said he: *La tierra es del que la trabaja*—The earth belongs to those who work it.

Real power begins and ends with land ownership. We don't have to be migrants in our own land. Our roots are deep in the soil and in the history of this land we are reclaiming.

To a New Friend

Francisco Aragón

2001

Francisco Aragón is the translator of numerous collections of poetry by Francisco X. Alarcón and Federico García Lorca, and he has worked as an editor of *The Berkeley Poetry Review* and as a consultant for the forthcoming second volume of *The Literature of California* anthology. As the founder of Momotombo Press, he edited the company's first book, *Mark My Words: Five Emerging Poets* (2001), and has published several limited-edition chapbooks, including *In Praise of Cities* (2002), from which the following poem was taken. His poem "Her Hair" also appears in this anthology. "To a New Friend" was written after the September 11, 2001, terrorist attack on the United States.

October, 2001
for John Chendo, George Castillo, and my mother (1932-1997)

Your need to fly east and walk
those streets, among your own
was no surprise. It was, I think,

akin to the worry and affection
I felt for a place in nineteen
eighty-nine: *NYU in Spain*'s director

caught me in the hall: *Aren't you*
from San Francisco?...told me
a section of bridge, freeway

had collapsed, the Marina
on fire and so was plunged
in speculation, completely

alone for moments at a time—
no brother, no sisters, no home…
Until she called, restoring me. Her

weekly call for years to come
a kind of ground. A voice
on the phone: a touchstone.

As when I asked you to talk
of those years so I
could picture it: your bus

from the Palisades, exiting
Lincoln Tunnel, and then
a crosstown shuttle, changing

again at Lexington to ride to Regis
for four years. On my trip
in August, I retraced your steps

down refurbished halls,
cafeteria where as a freshman
you had to eat standing. I had asked

really, to picture *you*: a new
friend—your e-mails,
your calls…since my departure

for the midwest. Years ago
—her voice on the other end—
she sees no need for me to rush

back: it's only been a week
since my return to Spain, Christmas
behind us (In between flights

all those years, I'd roam TWA's
terminal at Kennedy—a place I didn't
mind, straddling San Francisco

and Madrid all those years). From JFK
in nineteen ninety-seven, I call
from a pay phone and speak

to my sister, who says her breathing
is labored…I'm thinking now
of *your* mother: how, you said,

she grew up in that part
of Lower Manhattan, and years
later, before she died,

you stood with her
in the same plaza I sat in
last August, waiting

for my closest friend
from high school, temping
nearby, who loved

Joan Miró's green, blue
red, yellow…—tapestry
we paused at in the lobby

of tower two before
catching the subway to a
computer class. My head

slightly throbbing, I listened:
he spoke of Katie, how his real
focus now was being a good

partner: *that* I do recall,
and the wooden Art Deco walls
in the elevator—riding up

the Chrysler Building
(your city, after years
of visits, truly glows

in me), and I remarked to George
it was the first time we'd
been, together, in a space

outside California. My plane
is lifting off, flying
west, touching

down at SFO, where my sister
is waiting to take me home
to her; but my brother's

sitting beside her in the lounge
—who I wasn't expecting to see—
which means: I'm too late.

LOVE & FAMILY

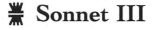 Sonnet III

Francisco X. Alarcón

2001

The following poem is from Francisco X. Alarcón's latest collection of bilingual poetry, *Sonnets to Madness and Other Misfortunes* (2001). Other poems by Alarcón in this anthology are "I Used to be Much Much Darker," "Letter to America," "Guerra Florida," and "Sonnet XIX" from *Sonnets to Madness*.

your eyes show me how to see again
like mirrors of water, understanding all,
there's no mystery they can't solve—
a single glance is more than enough

your eyes see, listen, touch, speak,
are beacons on the horizon
shedding light on shades of life
beyond the reach of words

so I start to read your body
pausing at every mole, as if
they were commas or periods

how I love to scribble on your chest,
use the muscles on your back as lines—
you and I are both page and pen

✸ If I Trust Myself

Diana García

2000

Diana García's work appears in several anthologies, and her first volume of poetry, *When Living Was a Labor Camp* (2001), won an American Book Award. Her poem "Cotton Rows, Cotton Blankets" also appears in this collection.

This time I swore I wouldn't be
like the squirrels in the park, drop
my guard to the first friendly handout.
I woke before dawn to watch day break
through designer drapes, your own savannah
of stripes, spots, horns, tusks.
I studied how light eased past beige
giraffes and cheetahs, blushed the left side
of your forehead like a large ivory
rose petal lightly veined in blue.
I listened for the way you hacked a bit
when you woke, the way you turned and smiled
when you saw me watching you.
These things take years. At times I broke,
afraid I broke a trust with self, a sense of who I was.
I followed trails to the beach, past sage and Torrey pine.
I picked selected shells at the base of cliffs,
then, pockets filled, I'd find paths back to you,
cleansed, renewed, a gift freely given.
The bond we form insinuates.
I wake these days and smell your scent on me,
the mint that overruns my garden,
a sweet fragrant planting impossible to remove.

✻ Roberto's Departure

Bernice Zamora

1976

This poem is from Bernice Zamora's *Restless Serpents* (1976). Her "Notes from a Chicana COED" also appears in this volume.

He left Saturday
heading south, South America, forever, he said.
Illness for two weeks before
wrenched objections from me.
Nonetheless, he left quietly.
It was the morning of the full moon.

Moon crazed, I resumed
routine wrestling with idols,
spent Sunday sleeping
in bitterness and rage
against moons, those full-faced
reflections tossed against
my future's window. Monday,
I concocted a draught for distraction.
Without tasting death, I drank the joke
wildly for unfrowning effect. Bam!
Like that. Just that. That that I did
pickaxed the blow gone south. Sweet sleep
offered me a pen and broke a hold on my story,
       on Roberto's chain.

 # Summer Rain

Dixie Salazar

2000

Dixie Salazar is a poet, novelist, and artist. She has written
two collections of poetry and a novel, and served as assistant
editor at the poetry review *Parnassus.* She has worked as an
art therapist, a courtroom artist, and a poetry teacher at several prisons. She currently teaches writing at California
State University, Fresno, and parenting courses at the Fresno
County jail.

for Diane Trejo

Eyes closed over despair
I can't even imagine, she listens
as I read, pause, then
skip over Lorca's Malaguena
Sabines' Black Butterflies
fan the pages
asking why there are no happy poems
except for childhood—
Machado's raindrops on windowpanes.
She likes Gloria Fuertes
leaning to see
what can be seen
from painted-on windows
her face skips over pain
for a second...blurs
to a six-year-old's sing song light
that drips from the peaches
plunks the tomatoes

sweet with sun and dirt
whole days lost, drunk on sap
and cidery winds in the orchard.

Till a dark fluttering blots
the sun…and a voice
I can't hear calls her
back, pleads with her
to eat something, anything—
instead she sleeps all day
can't be left alone
all she once gave
to culling peaches and turning compost
now turned to the quiet battle within.

I stroke her shoulder
soft and depthless
yet scaffolded with unseen bones
that now house the ground
where her own spores revolt
in a dark and fruitful mutiny.

Driving home, the road goes soft
I can't see through the window
as if raindrops stroked it
lean forward to see
what can't be seen—
imagination
my oldest friend
is failing me—whispering
like an old man giving directions
to the mad. I turn away—
I don't want to see
down the next road
I want to beg the earth
for one more summer rain
one more bumper crop of magic tomatoes
but the wind whispers through the crack
of the window like pages turning
or black butterflies scattering home.

Like the Earth

Ernesto Trejo

1990

Ernesto Trejo was born in 1950 in Fresnillo, Mexico, and grew up in Mexico City and Mexicali. While earning degrees in engineering and economics, he became associated with the Fresno School of poets and later attended the Writers Workshop at the University of Iowa. He continued to write while working as a government economist in Mexico, publishing three chapbooks in Spanish and translating many literary works into both Spanish and English. After returning to California in the 1980s, he taught English and Spanish at California State University, Fresno, and Fresno City College. He published his first full-length poetry collection written in English, *Entering a Life,* in 1990, the year before he died of cancer.

for my newborn son

My little one, you are finally
here. So much like the earth,
through a flower…
Out of the darkness, underground star,
where did you come from?
Cold space suddenly thundering
with a heartbeat.
What's in those fists?
Wrath? Happiness?
A warrior. But, where are your weapons?
Your laughter, your tears?
Like everything else in the world,

you are here flowing
like the hours.
Look at this perplexed face.
This is the face that you will wear
on the day when I become one
with the roots,
as you look over your shoulder
and see the night
swelling up in the distance,
already
a cricket
trilling in the bushes.

from

✻ Buffalo Nickel

Floyd Salas

1992

Floyd Salas was born in 1931 in Denver, of Spanish descent, and moved to Oakland when he was eight. He attended UC Berkeley on a boxing scholarship and studied writing there under the poet Josephine Miles. Salas has published several award-winning novels, a collection of poetry, and an autobiography, *Buffalo Nickel* (1992), excerpted below. He has taught writing at several California universities and was a boxing coach at UC Berkeley from 1975 to 1991. He founded and is now the president of PEN Oakland.

LARRY HAD GIVEN ME THE RIDE DOWNTOWN ON HIS BIKE. He was in the same fifth grade as me, although he was a head taller and a year older. He lived on 30th Street and Chestnut, a short block from my house on 30th and Adeline. He took me to Payless Market on 19th and Telegraph. It was a huge warehouse of a market, filled with different types of stores and stands, including a market with sundry goods. For some reason, we went in there and the next thing I knew, he was taking a pen out of a drawer, and I did, too. Then I followed him over to a side entrance, where he ducked under the turnstile.

I squatted to duck down under the turnstile and sneak out without paying, when steel fingers clamped on my shoulder and I looked up to see a woman in dress clothes pulling me back into the sundry goods section. Trapped in the pincers of her fingers, I was marched through the stalls, up some steep back stairs and into an office with wide windows that looked out over the entire store. We were right above the stand where the pens Larry and I had stolen were kept. There was a man up there who must have been watching all the time.

I was so scared, I shook. When she asked me my name, I lied and said "Floyd Sánchez," giving my mother's maiden name instead of Salas.

She pointed to the floor beneath a high counter and said, "You sit down under there!" Which I did. Then she asked me what my religion was.

When I answered Catholic, she said, "Catholics don't steal."

I just stared at the floor. She made me sit on the floor under the counter for a long time. I didn't have the slightest idea what was going to happen to me, but I knew I was in deep trouble. I knew my mother was going to spank me and that I had committed a terrible wrong, even a sin, for stealing. I was so ashamed, I couldn't look up.

Finally the woman said, "You come out of there and stand over here!" I got up and stood in front of her desk. She sat behind it and made me empty my pockets, I guess to see if I'd stolen anything else. I had ten cents in my pocket, so I wasn't penniless. But there was also a test I'd taken in grammar school with my name, Floyd Salas, written across the top of it.

"Oh, you not only steal, but you lie, too," she said, and I felt my face light up with hot shame.

"How old are you?" she asked.

"Nine," I said.

"Are you sure?" she said.

I nodded my head, afraid to insist, even though I was nine and small for my age.

"What's your phone number?" she asked. When I gave it to her, she immediately picked up the phone and dialed the number. I remember she asked over the phone, "How old is he?" She listened for a moment, then said, "Seven!" and glared at me as if I had lied to her again. Evidently the person on the phone at home was trying to help me by saying I was younger than I was. She then handed me the phone.

"Hello!" I said, and when my sister Dorothy said, "Floyd! What's the matter?" I wailed, "Oh, Dorothy!" and burst out crying.

I was sobbing so loudly, the woman took the phone from me. I don't know what else she said, but she hung up the phone and looked at me. I was still sobbing, rubbing my eyes with the back of my hand, trying to hide my face. Finally she said, "You can go home now. But don't come here and steal ever again. Do you understand?"

I nodded, still sobbing, and walked out, following her pointing finger to the swinging gate that led down the narrow steps to the ground floor.

I hurried down 20th Street to San Pablo in the warm sun, my face feeling stiff from all the dried tears. I hurried north on the east side of the boulevard, past the giant, red granite cathedral of St. Francis Catholic Church, which made me feel guilty again. I'd committed a sin and knew it, and God would punish me for it. I turned my face away towards the Greyhound Bus Depot across the street, which as usual had a lot of people moving in and out of the front door. Then I looked ahead again, up toward 30th Street, where I had to turn left to head home in a few short blocks. I was going to get my just deserts, for sure, from my mother—the second punishment, after the store detective's grilling.

When I started across 22nd Street and crossed over the streetcar tracks where the electric B Train was bound across the Bay Bridge for San Francisco, I saw a kid I knew casually from Clawsen Grammar School sitting on his shoe shine kit. He was a brown Filipino kid named Vincent. He and his sister were the only Filipino kids in school. I was so glad to see someone I knew, I stopped to talk to him. Although we weren't friends, I told him what happened to me, saying I was probably going to get a spanking when I got home. He squinted up at me, through the strands of straight black hair that fell across his eyes, and nodded.

"Do you want a donut?" I asked.

He nodded again, so I stepped into a donut shop next to the old-fashioned beer joint on the corner and bought two big, sugar-glazed donuts for a nickel. I stepped back out and gave him one. I stood next to him until we both finished. Then, my face still stiff from the dried tears, I waved good-bye and started up San Pablo towards home.

I was getting gradually more and more scared the closer I got to the house, and I was trembling when I crossed Adeline on 30th Street and saw my white house in the center of the block. It was a pretty house, solidly built, with love seats in the hallway and in the front room, wide rooms on the second story, with big walk-in closets and windows all around. It had been built in the twenties probably. But it didn't look pretty to me then. I was plain scared and could barely reach out for the front doorknob when I crossed the porch.

As soon as I stepped into the big hallway, Dorothy rushed up to me and said, "What happened, Floyd?"

"I...I..." I couldn't finish because my mother stepped into the hall and, with a worried crease between her brows, stared at me through her rimless glasses, her green eyes shimmering with pale light. I started to cry again.

"Come on," my mother said and grabbed her purse from the dining room table and crossed to the coatrack to get her coat. "I'm going to find out what's going on right now!"

I cringed and started crying even more, knowing I was going to get whatever I deserved, but really dreading having to face that woman detective again.

"You get your coat, too, Dorothy. We're going down there right now!"

"Oooooooh!" I moaned, getting a taste now of the final day when God would pass judgment on me.

Dorothy got her coat, too, and Mother turned and reached for the door, when Al came running down the stairs from the second floor. He grabbed my hand and ran up the stairs, pulling me after him, refusing to stop when my mother called, "Albert! Albert! Come down here!"

"He's already paid enough, Momma!" he called back and pulled me down the hall and into our bedroom, right at the front of the house. "It's okay, Floyd! It's okay! Just don't do it again," he said. He hugged me and rocked me back and forth. He was back with the family again after being in reform school for six months.

When my sobbing finally quieted down and my chest quit heaving, he asked, "Who took you down there?"

"Larry Andre," I said.

"It's all right for now," Al said, "but don't let anybody lead you into anything like that again."

"Okay," I said, breaking out into another sob, feeling like my chest was going to crack with wracking pain. Suddenly I heard my name being called, "Floyyyd! Floyyyyyd!" and Albert let go of me.

We both stepped to our second story window. I could see Larry out there on his bicycle, looking toward the front door below us, his brown curls falling onto his forehead.

"Did he take you downtown on his bike?" Al asked. I nodded, and he said, "Wait here," and left the room.

I saw him go out onto the porch below me and shout, "You get away from here, kid, and don't come around my little brother again." When Larry looked up at him with a pale, scared face, Al said, "You heard me! Get going!"

Larry didn't say anything. He just pushed off on his bike and quickly pumped out of sight. I felt sorry for losing a friend, but I really felt grateful to my brother, who came back up the stairs and said, "Come on downstairs now. Mom's fine. You're okay. Just learn something from it. Never steal again. You don't want to end up in a reform school like me, do you?"

"Nooooo," I said, squinting my eyes with the hot tears that rolled out again.

"Come on down, then," Al said and, taking my hand, he led me out the door and down the hall to the stairs, where I could hear my mother in the kitchen, closing the refrigerator door. When I walked into the kitchen, still scared, both Mom and my sister turned to look at me. Mom's face was pink from the heat in the kitchen, but her green eyes were gentle. Dorothy smiled, showing that one dimple in the one cheek. I looked over at my brother, who smiled at me also.

✹ La Llorona/Weeping Woman

Alma Luz Villanueva

1994

Alma Luz Villanueva was born in 1944 in Santa Barbara, of
Spanish, German, and Yaqui ancestry, and grew up in San
Francisco with her grandmother, a Yaqui Indian from
Mexico. Her experiences as a teenage mother, a battered
wife, and a welfare recipient have shaped her creative work,
which includes six books of poetry, three novels, and a col-
lection of short fiction. Her awards include a 1989 American
Book Award for *Ultraviolet Sky,* a 1994 PEN Oakland
Josephine Miles Award for *Naked Ladies,* and a 1994 Latin
American Poetry Prize for *Planet.* She currently teaches
writing at Antioch University in Los Angeles and published
two new books in 2002, *Luna's California Poppies* and *Vida.*

*All conversation between the child, Luna, and her grandmother, Isidra, is in
Spanish.*

LUNA LOOKED OUT THE RAIN-STREAKED WINDOW with sadness and boredom at the wet, gray street. "Will it ever stop raining, Mamacita? I hate
the rain." Her voice was a murmur, fogging a small patch of glass in front
of her. Luna was seven years old, and she resented being locked in with
her grandmother for the third day. Her brand new roller skates that
allowed her to skate to the end of the block stood in a dark corner by
the front door of the chilly flat. Only the kitchen was truly warm, where
her grandmother stood rolling out handmade tortillas and a huge pot of
beans simmered on the stove, sealed with fresh onions, fresh tomatoes,
ground beef, cilantro, and a whole, bright red chorizo.

"If it keeps raining this way the water will rise, Niña. It'll rise up
to the windows, maybe more." The old woman's dark face looked down
at her dark hands rolling the white flour in perfect circles without any

expression, though a faint, extremely faint, humor reflected, briefly, as a pinpoint of light in her large, dark Indian eyes that seemed to take in all light like a sponge. Like the Earth.

"Do you mean we could float away? Like a flood?" Luna's voice rose with excitement and fear.

"San Francisco is surrounded by water. The great ocean on one side, no? If it continues to rain this way, why not?" She walked over to the hot griddle and placed a perfect tortilla on it and flipped it by hand as gentle bubbles appeared on its floury surface.

"Are you scared, Mamacita?" Luna managed to ask. Where the day had been boring, watching the endless rain, now each drop was a threat, and it terrified her to think of the wild ocean getting closer. And if her grandmother was so calm, that meant there was no escape.

"If I were to hear La Llorona crying, then I'd be afraid, Niña."

Luna's eyes flew open and her small, pink mouth opened slightly, but she couldn't speak.

"All my life, in Mexico"—the child in front of her disappeared, and instead the old woman, Isidra, saw the stark desert landscape running, running to meet the wide, cool river, the cactus, the flowers, the birds, bright and plentiful, she could hear them singing—"when it rained too long, we could hear her, La Llorona, crying for her children down by the river. Crying and lamenting, with her beautiful black shawl over her head. Not for protection from the rain, no, but because she was either too beautiful, or perhaps too ugly, to behold."

A large yellow butterfly grazed her head, floating in the Sonoran heat, and Isidra remembered the tortillas. She placed the finished ones in a clean, worn towel, wrapping them tightly, and began rolling out a new white circle.

Normally, Luna would insist on a fresh, hot, buttered tortilla sprinkled with salt, but she was too absorbed by the image of a Weeping Woman who was too beautiful, or too ugly, to look at, and the rain was coming down, harder now, making the windows tremble as the wind in four loud gusts threatened the huge house, made into separate flats, with extinction. Only this kitchen is safe, Luna hoped. "Why was she crying, Mamacita?"

"For her children, Niña. When the great flood came, and the terrible men from the great ocean came, she turned her children into fish." Isidra paused to wet her dry lips. "It was the only way to save them," the old woman added, seeing the terror on her granddaughter's face.

"Were they fish forever?" Luna whispered. She imagined the house floating now out to the great ocean.

"When La Llorona cried like that, so loudly"—the old woman, Isidra, saw the river again; she longed to step in it, to touch it, to bathe— "they would come to her if her sorrow was so great. Then, she'd take the black shawl from her head, making sure no human being was near-by to witness her magic, and scooping it into the river like a net, her children would appear one by one."

The yellow butterfly, huge in the bright Sonoran sun, floated in front of her granddaughter, and Isidra thought of her three children who'd survived their infancy. The ones who'd lived long enough to hear about La Llorona. And then only one survived to adulthood: Luna's mother. May she not be like her mother, the old woman prayed for the child silently. I have no daughter, she added with her familiar sense of perpetual grief. Just the little fish the river took away, and I have no magic. No, not anymore.

The butterfly vanished into the chill San Francisco air and the child was speaking. "How many children did La Llorona have?"

"No one knows for certain, but, as far as I know, there were four like the four winds and all of them daughters. You see, Luna, she saved her daughters from the terrible men, but her sons stayed and fought and died. They were real Indians then, and the gringos just looked like plucked chickens to them." She began to laugh softly, revealing strong, square teeth. "The Indians knew they were evil when they killed even the little children for nothing, sending them to the dark side of the moon, so that the mothers couldn't even see their little ones in the Full Moon Face. Evil!" she spat.

"Why does it scare you, Mamacita, to hear her crying? Is she crying now? Can you hear her now, Mamacita?" The child drew up to her grand-mother, resting herself against that fragile strength. Her grandmother.

Isidra rarely touched the child. That's the way she'd been brought up. After infancy she was rarely touched or pampered. But this was her granddaughter and who would know, she mused, as she smoothed the thick, curling hair from the child's wondering, frightened eyes. She looks like my mother, she thought. The same eyes. The same kind of pride and something ancient like mi mamá.

"No, Niña, I don't hear her now, but if I did I'd be prepared to leave this place because if her children will not be scooped into her shawl, La Llorona kills as many people as she can. Mostly men, but one never knows." Isidra squeezed the child once with her left arm and gently pushed her away.

"I don't blame her. She has her reasons to be so angry, and she has every reason to weep." The old woman sighed deep in her belly, in her old worn-out womb. "Since coming to this country," now she spoke in a low, secretive voice, "I have yet to hear her." Her eyes watered.

Quickly, she reached up and adjusted her red headband, the one she always wore in the house, but never, ever, in the street. Then, the old woman stiffened her body and spit into the air: "Too many gringos here, mi Luna, and no room for La Llorona. No, no, she'll have nothing to do with them. Nor I."

In one swift movement she undid the towel, took a warm tortilla from the stack, buttered and salted it, and handed it to the child.

It was delicious, and the beans smelled wonderfully good now, and the rain outside seemed sad but bearable. "Do you miss La Llorona sometimes, Mamacita? She sounds awful, but I think I like her." Luna paused, glancing at the rain. "A little bit."

"What a question! Who could miss La Llorona?" Isidra laughed to herself. "Let's just hope you never hear her. But if you do, prepare yourself, Niña."

Luna's heart began to race again.

"Prepare to live or die. Yes, that's her message." As Isidra lifted the lid from the simmering beans, the brilliant yellow butterfly melted into the palm of her hand. She smiled as she scooped the beans into a bowl and placed it in front of Luna. "Now eat, Niña. Eat it all."

Thunder struck in the distance and lightning flashed, turning the kitchen window white with light, but Luna couldn't hear La Llorona. She ate without speaking, listening for the sounds of her unspeakable grief.

In the middle of the night, Luna woke to the loud voices. She froze, upright, in her bed, looking over to her grandmother's. Then she heard her grandmother's voice: "Don't treat me this way, Carmen, God will punish you. Yes, God will punish you for this." Her voice held no emphasis or threat; it was like a lament, a pleading.

"Make the bed, vieja! I feed you and put up with you. Now, make the goddamned bed, do you hear me, vieja?"

"It's a sin what you're doing. It's a sin, making me make the bed for you and that man." Then her voice changed as it rose to her old fury: "You aren't a daughter of mine! *My* children are dead!"

Luna heard her grandmother cry out, and she ran into the dimly lit front room where her mother stood over her cowering grandmother, her fist raised again. Carmen's harsh red hair shone dully in the faint light, but her eyes were bright with violence—the kind of violence that maims, or kills, the vulnerable. The kind of violence that's forgotten how to love.

"Don't touch her or I'll kill you! I'll kill you if you touch her again! I'll kill you!" Luna screamed hysterically, grabbing onto her grandmother's arm. It was as fragile and soft as a child's.

"See what you've started? I should throw you out! Out in the street! Out in the street where you belong, with this brat!" Carmen shrieked, hating the sight of the two of them together. Together against her.

There was a knock at the door and a man's voice. "Hey, Carmen, are you in there?" The voice was low pitched and impatient. He knocked again.

"Just a minute, Frank!" Instantly Carmen switched her fury to a false, feminine charm. She ran to the bathroom and hurriedly applied some bright red lipstick, checking her light-skinned makeup for streaks. She pushed back her hair in an angry gesture and ran to open the door.

"Go to bed, Niña. I'll be right there. Go to bed. Would you like some cinnamon chocolate? I'll bring you some." Isidra touched the child's shoulders, guiding her toward their bedroom, and then she went to start the milk, putting it on a low heat. It would be ready when she was finished changing the sheets.

Carmen was making the man comfortable as he handed her a bottle of wine. "Oh, I pay her room and board, some extra money, to watch the kid for me. Got to work day and night, you know," she laughed knowingly. "I found her through a friend. Just relax and I'll get some glasses, baby." Carmen bent over to kiss him, offering her breasts to him. He cupped one, hungrily, as she giggled. Then he cupped them both and squeezed them a little too hard, but she said nothing, bringing her teeth down to taste the bright red lipstick.

It was late afternoon and Luna knew her grandmother was looking for her and calling her. "LUNA!" she'd be shouting in a thin, high-pitched voice from the second-story kitchen window. "LUNA!" as though the moon would know where her granddaughter was. "LUNA!" she sang to the setting sun, but no child sang back. Some boys in the distance jeered her, laughing, "Luuunaaaa!"

Pat, Luna's older friend, had talked her into coming to the park. No one would know, she'd said. Pat swung as high as she could and leaped to the sand, screaming.

"Do you want me to get you started? Come on, I'll push you." Pat's face was flushed with excitement as she held the swing for Luna.

"What're you kids doing here so late?" a male voice said, interrupting their play. He was a teenager, but he looked like a man to the girls. They stared at him quietly.

"Don't you know it's against the law to be here this late?" He showed them a badge. "I'm a policeman and I'm going to have to take one of you in. I'm going to have to call your parents."

"She'll go!" Pat said, running down the cement path.

As the boy hurt Luna, he said, "If you scream, I'll kill you." She didn't scream or cry, but she did hear La Llorona weeping very close by.

"The hymen's intact, so he didn't rape her, and there's no trace of semen," the doctor told Luna's mother. Pat had run home, and Carmen was getting ready to go to her night job as a waitress. By the time Luna got home Carmen had called the police.

The doctor was hurting her again where the boy had put his finger, and she had to tell them about how he touched her everywhere. She looked at her mother, but she seemed only angry at the nuisance, as though Luna had staged everything to annoy her.

"So, she wasn't raped?" Carmen asked the doctor once more.

"There's no evidence of it."

"Well, nothing happened to you, Luna, so stop that trembling act. Do you hear me?"

"Excuse me," the doctor interjected, "she's been through quite an ordeal for a seven-year-old. She'll need to talk about it…"

"Well, I don't have time for all that. As it is I'm late for work." Carmen rushed Luna into her coat, pulling on her to be quick.

"Here's the number for a *free* clinic." The doctor, an older woman, handed it to her, though she knew it was useless.

As Luna and her mother settled into their seats on the bus, Carmen told her, "Keep this to yourself. Nothing happened to you anyway, crybaby." She kept her voice low in the bus, but Luna heard the hatred anyway. "The old woman makes a big deal out of nothing as it is."

"Where are we going, Mamacita?" Luna asked, looking out the bus window at the beginning darkness and the rain blurring the streets going by. They never went out at night except to go to church once a week, and then someone always picked them up in their car and brought them back home. So, Luna had no idea where they were going.

"We're going to the great ocean." Isidra had her old, dark wool coat on and a plastic scarf over her head, her going-out dress, and many pairs of stockings to keep her legs warm, but her shoes, unsuited for the rain, were wet. The umbrella rested, closed, between them, dripping a long, thin puddle towards the feet in front.

"Why?" was all Luna could say. Isidra put her hand on top of Luna's small, cold hand. Years later, Luna would remember her grandmother's touch was like dry, loose feathers. Comfort without pain. Strange, irrational—a silent comfort.

Luna had to help her grandmother off the bus because the step to the street was so high and the driver hadn't pulled close enough to the curb. There was a fast-food place a block from the beach. They entered the front door with fear and excitement. They rarely went out to eat. Luna told her grandmother the menu in Spanish and waited for her to decide. Some people came and got in front of them, but it didn't matter. Luna ordered in a shy, proud voice. No one paid the least bit of attention to them as they sat by themselves eating. And they hardly spoke as the rain came in gusts.

"Come, walk quickly, Nina," Isidra commanded, holding the umbrella up over their heads with her right hand and Luna with her left. They rushed across the street, as fast as they could go, to the roar.

It was absolutely dark now except for the flickering streetlight behind them. The immense white waves frothed at their peaks, a terrible darkness beneath them, and then, suddenly, in long, smooth lines, they'd decide to meet the earth, angrily, with their roars. Luna wanted to turn and run, she was so terrified, but her grandmother held her hand lightly. She looked up at her grandmother and her eyes looked far away as though she were straining to see something.

"There she is," Isidra hissed. "There she is!"

"Who?"

"You can't hear her because of the ocean, but there she is!" Isidra drew Luna close to her, feeling the smallness of her body. She felt the trembling stop.

There was a dark figure moving along the beach, slowly. Her shawl covered her head. She looked tall and strong as she came toward them, weeping and singing.

✳ Indulgences

Gil Cuadros

1994

Gil Cuadros grew up in Merced, California, and was part of
the Latino gay community of Los Angeles until his death at
age thirty-two. His short stories and poetry were published
in several literary magazines and anthologies, and he was
one of the first recipients of the PEN Center USA West
grant for writers living with HIV. His only book, *City of
God* (1994), is a collection of autobiographical poetry and
prose about family life, religion, the Los Angeles barrio, and
living with AIDS.

My MOTHER AND FATHER had both come from the same home town,
Merced, California. They romanticized the red checkerboard-patterned
water tower on J Street, the Purina feed store on K, the old,
semi-demolished church that looked like Mexico, rough-hewn, gritty
pink-stone L Street. Pulling off the highway, my parents would cluck
their tongues, stare out of our black Impala, disbelieving the changes.
They told my brother and me of the time when blacks kept to their own
side of town. "Now the place has gone to pot."

Dad parked at the small grocery store, El Mercado Merced, a
converted house with boarded-up windows and wrought-iron bars for
protection. The place had a little bit of everything: warped, dark,
wooden shelves carrying sodas, tortillas, lard, and eggs, things the
neighbors always seemed to run out of first. It was central to both sides
of my family. Uncle Ruben lived near the corner; Grandma Lupe,
across the street; Uncle Cosme, next to her. My great-grandfather
Tomas had lived two houses down. "Papa" would walk this street every
day, wave to my relatives as he passed by, his blanched wooden cane
steadying his balance, the handle dark where he gripped. It was Ruben

who went to try to see in the windows why Papa hadn't gone by that day. It was Cosme who called two days ago to tell us Papa was dead.

My little brother and I ached to get out of the car, the long ride had caused our legs to fall asleep. Jess had complained the whole way that I was invading his side; my father turned from his steering, "Do I have to remind you that you are fourteen years old and should just ignore your younger brother?" Dad was already irritated and said he was going to take Jess to Grandma Lupe's. I was to go with my mother. My mother wanted me to mind because someone had died.

"It's out of respect," she warned while she collected the things she needed from the glove box: a mirror, makeup, tissue. And as we walked the short distance down the street, I looked back and saw my father pull a six-pack of beer from the old cooler in front of the *mercado*. His hands dripped melted crushed ice, and the sidewalk became stained with its moisture.

My great-grandfather's house always reminded me of a ranch: the oppressive heat of the San Joaquin Valley, the large wagon wheel leaning against the standing mailbox, the way the long, tan, stucco building hugged the ground. I expected tumbleweeds to roll by, a rattlesnake to be coiled seductively in the flower bed's rocks. My mother's cousin, Evelyn, had been taking care of Papa and she met us at the door before we even knocked. My mother had just straightened herself again, licking the tips of her fingers in the driveway, touching up her hair on the porch. Evelyn and my mother fell into each other's arms as soon as they saw each other, making a show of tears, almost religiously. She was the same age as my mother, thirty, maybe a few months apart. I stood awkward on the porch, afraid to walk in unannounced. Evelyn wore a flimsy dress, a brownish print the same color as the house. Her teeth were stained, and when she smiled her long dog teeth poked out. Hair hung down her back like dry weeds.

"Well," she said, facing me, "who is this foxy young man?"

My mother laughed. "This is my oldest boy." Evelyn swung her dress like she was dancing to a *ranchero* tune, showing her kneecaps, and I stared. My mother always wore pants and it was strange, I thought, for a woman to be home in a dress. She wasn't going anywhere.

She tilted her head coyly at me. "Why don't you give me a big hug. We're family." I put my arms around her like a mechanical claw. She pulled me in tight, placing my face above her breast. I could smell her sweat, a scent of dairy products, cheese and bad milk. It felt like her breast had dampened my face and I wiped away droplets from my cheek. "He looks like your old man, Lorraine." My mother acknowledged this, standing near a cabinet filled with ceramic salt and pepper shakers, ashtrays from Vegas, Tahoe, and the biggest little city, Reno. Mom had confided to me she wanted something to remember Papa by.

My mother said, "I just came over, Evelyn, to see where it happened." She held a ceramic Siamese cat with an ear broken off and holes bored in its head.

Evelyn explained that she had come home late from work, she had found him in the bathroom, collapsed, a green mess pooled underneath him. She said, "He started having trouble, not making it in time, then I'd have to clean it up. Sometimes he'd lose it just sleeping in his chair. I told your mother, Lorraine, that he should go into a home. No one wanted to hear about it. I couldn't take care of him twenty-four hours a day."

My mother started to cry again and walked over to see the bathroom, a tissue covering her nose and mouth. I stood with Evelyn. I had heard so many stories about her, how she was dropped from the crib, how soft and impressionable the skull is at that age. My aunts would start low and sympathetic, how it wasn't Evelyn's fault for the way it was with her, but then would tell each other what a tramp, a slut Evelyn had become. They'd snicker about how she slept with black men, white men. Papa should have put her away. Evelyn's Papa's angel. Evelyn's a lesbian.

Evelyn smiled at me. I looked around the living room, touched the lamps made out of thick coiled ropes, burlap shades. Evelyn lit a cigarette, clicked shut the silver-toned Zippo lighter. "Do you have a girlfriend?"

"No, not really," I answered.

I felt embarrassed. My whole family was always asking when was I going to get a girlfriend. My mother begged me to find a girl soon, not to be so shy, said it was natural for me to like girls. She'd say she worries because she's a mother, don't you want to make your father proud, your brother should look up to you. The truth was I had a lot of friends who were girls. They would pass notes with me in class, short-lived confessions of love for some other boy. Their reasons for love were always the same: the color of eyes, the length of hair, the muscles sneaking out from the boys' short-sleeved shirts. These same boys would shove me around before the bus came. My body would grow warm and my heart would pound when they put their hands on my chest and shoulders. I would notice the color of their eyes, the strength they possessed. "Fucking sissy," they would say, and then give me one good last punch.

Evelyn seemed like she couldn't believe I wouldn't have a girlfriend. "Oh, then you like someone. What's her name?" I squirmed that

I didn't like anyone and no one liked me. She offered me a sip of her soda, it fizzed in a glass, water had ringed the wood coffee table.

"No, thank you," I said.

"Oooh, you're so polite. Why don't you sit next to me." I came over to the Afghan-covered couch where she sat. I could hear my mother's sobs, the bathroom becoming an echo chamber. Evelyn moved close to me on the couch. I bet you kiss like a stud," she said. She put her hand on my knee and I started to feel a horrible warmth between my legs, growing. She squeezed my thigh as if to make me laugh, then asked, "What do you do for fun?"

I stumbled as I stood up, fell back down. "I go to the Scouts," I offered, hoping the conversation would end and my mother would reenter the scene, grab me by the wrist, and take me away.

Evelyn looked deep in my eyes, as if to devour a creamy pastry. "Will you do me a favor?" she asked. I nodded, hoping it would involve leaving. "Will you kiss me?" I pulled back but she came forward and vise-gripped my head. Her other hand reached down and grabbed my dick, her nails digging into the khaki material of my pants. I wanted to vomit, her breath was like my father's, unclean, like a whole night of beer. I shoved her hand off my lap and got up. I licked the sleeve of my shirt, trying to get out the taste of her. She started to laugh as I unlocked the door. The brightness of outside kicked in my allergies and I started to sneeze as I ran to Grandma Lupe's house, saying out loud, "Forget my mother." My father sat on the steps drinking his Miller's. He tried to grab onto my butt as I passed him. I let the screen door slam behind me and ran for the nearest bathroom, Grandma Lupe's. I barely made it before I puked. From inside I could hear my grandma talking on the phone, saying Evelyn should have been locked up a long time ago. My head hung over the tub's edge, water rushing down the drain. The porcelain reeked of Calgon and Efferdent.

Tension and humidity hung in the old house. Relatives were arriving every moment; my grandmother was wringing her hands. My mother was still crying that she couldn't depend on anyone: my brother, too young; my father, always drinking; and me, worthless. I was too embarrassed to tell her why I had run out of Evelyn's and had decided to hide out in the backyard. I was surprised that my mother had come to get me. My brother and I were playing in the old rickety garage filled with an ancient white Chevy on blocks, wooden barrels of pecans and walnuts in the dark back corner.

My mother wanted me at the kitchen table with all my aunts and my mother's aunts. I was the only boy except for two *viejos,* my mother's uncles, both too old to decline the meeting. My mother said, "You are family. You need to hear."

My grandmother Mikala sat at the center of the long kitchen table; she mirrored the Last Supper needlepoint that hung, framed, above her head. Grandma Mickey's face was near silhouette because of the big open windows behind her. Jars of *nopales* glittered in the pantry. Cactus grew along the fence outside and guarded this secret meeting. Just as my mother would light up at the onset of a long story, Mickey smoked a Newport. She exhaled a large burst of smoke. "As you know, I went to the police. Papa had horrible bruises on his body, especially on his hand, like someone had kept on slamming the door on his wrist. I think Evelyn killed him, made him have a heart attack. The bruises on his hand were ugly."

Around the table, aunts and cousins shook their heads, each taking turns. "Evelyn has always been crazy. She was spoiled rotten by Papa. He never saw how evil she was. He always gave her dresses and toys, didn't give anything to us kids."

Grandma Mickey raised her open palms. "I will make her pay, I swear." I felt sickened that a murderess had kissed me that day and I wanted to interrupt Mickey, to tell her Evelyn had grabbed between my legs. Mom made me put my hand down, kept it hidden below the table, squeezing my fingers occasionally.

My mother's Uncle Ruben spoke. "It's all our own faults, we should have never left him alone with her. Mikala, you should have taken him instead of leaving him with that crazy prostitute. And where is Evelyn's mother? Mary is always gone, never responsible. *Hijo!* It was bad enough Papa had to take Evelyn in and raise her, just because Mary didn't want her child in an institution."

Mikala again raised her palms. "It would kill Mary to know her own girl killed Papa." There was argument all around the table about what to do, then dinner was passed, refried beans, peppered steak, homemade tortillas, Pepsi taken out dusty from the cellar. We all ate with gusto, ready to stone Evelyn. I held my secret, knowing it wasn't important. All around me people were saying, "Eat Gilberto, eat."

I had never been to a wake before, the orange and purple summer night having just started, the air extremely dry. I could make out bats flying against the sunset. My Grandma Mickey and all her sisters were behind dark netting, a special section for the immediate family. From behind the curtain, I could hear their sobbing. My mother whispered to my father that Evelyn was inside and it wasn't fair, none of the other cousins were there. My father sighed, uninterested. I pretended to be appropriately mournful since I'd never seen a dead body before. It lay in its open coffin, a spotlight illuminating his pasty face, like a stage actor, I thought. My mother huffed, "It makes me sick, you can hear her going on and on."

My father said, hot tempered, "She has a right to her grief."

My mother turned into quick anger, "You know what I mean, Danny. You heard what my mother said."

Exasperated, my father whispered sideways, "You have no proof."

"The bruises, Danny, the bruises," my mother near spat till my father said, "Shh!" In the quiet before the wake, I could easily make out Evelyn's wails. They were the kind of wails that could be mistaken for laughing, as if this were all a joke and my great-grandfather would pop up then and yell, "We pulled a fast one on all of you!"

I thumbed through the small book given to me as I had entered the mortuary, *How to Say the Rosary Apostolic and Other Indulgences.* Grandma Mickey said it was a gift for me: "The mysteries are great and powerful for the devout; the joyful, sorrowful, and glorious acts of Jesus purify our sins." It was pretty boring stuff, fifteen Our Fathers and one hundred and fifty Hail Marys. The pictures made it seem more exciting.

After the wake, uncles, aunts, grandparents, and children waited on the steps of the mortuary, leaning against the colonnades. An aunt kicked a strip of no-slip on a step with the point of her shoe, her husband held his jacket over his arm, his short-sleeved shirt exposing his various tattoos of roses and crosses. Another man with a full black mustache that covered his mouth's expression spoke with him. Aunt Mary had been hastily escorted out by her youngest daughter. Evelyn stood by the coffin long after everyone had left. "Nearly threw herself on top," an uncle said. Everyone had moved their cars so they blocked all the exits, the headlights aimed for the front door, the marble walls, the angels and muscular men along the frieze. Ruben called out, "She's coming."

When Evelyn walked outside all the car lights' high beams were turned on. The women and men stepped away from their cars, toward Evelyn. They began yelling, "Get out of here! We know you did it. You murdered Papa. Sick, sick, sick!" Evelyn had been covering her eyes, trying to see, to adjust. She wore an open black crocheted top and the headlights bore through to flesh, bounced off the black Qiana dress as if it were made of white.

She started to scream, to reason, "I didn't do it." I wondered why she didn't just run or why one of my uncles didn't put a stop to this, their barrel chests filled with breath, their shirts almost too tight, their top buttons aching to pop. But they wouldn't. She tried to block her eyes with her hands, shaking her head, "He always shitted on himself." Horns blared, hands heavy on steering wheels; my brother leaned on ours from the back seat, our father having rushed us in early. My Grandmother Mikala walked up to Evelyn and began to slap her, nails curled to puncture, looking fierce. Evelyn defended herself, thrust herself like a cat, wild and rare, on top of my grandmother; both fell dangerously down the steps, backs, spines, shoulder blades hitting the corners. People rushed in like a mob, women pulling her hair, kicking Evelyn in the stomach, the ass, her breast. The men tried, some laughing, to extract their wives from the brawl. My brother and I jumped up and down in the back seat, acted as if we could feel the blows or were giving them, vocalized the sound of each good hit, "uhh, opff." We watched as Dad returned with my mother, who was nearly scratching his eyes out, saying loudly, "That bitch."

My father hastily drove away to his mother's house, it now being fully night. My mother told me to forget what had happened, that it wasn't a good thing, that she was already feeling ashamed, her voice quiet and firm. She thought that maybe I should pray. My little brother was asleep already, his straight black hair next to my thigh. I rolled the window down slightly, letting the air rush in. I could barely hear the radio, a scatter of signals. I stared outside, wondered if my family would ever turn on me, where would I go, who would I love. The long farm roads leading back greeted my thoughts, the rows of grapevines, tomato furrows, cotton, all lined up in parallel paths ending on the horizon, designed like manifest destiny. Lit by my father's high beams, still ignited, I watched as we passed a scarecrow off the road, dry weeds for hair, a flimsy brown dress, a stake skewered up through the body, arms stretched open as if ready to embrace.

✸ The Horned Toad

Gerald Haslam

1983

Gerald Haslam was born in 1937 in Bakersfield, California, and raised in Oildale, in the Central Valley. His work comprises more than twenty fiction and nonfiction books, including the popular award-winners *Coming of Age in California* (1990), *That Constant Coyote* (1990), *The Great Central Valley* (1993), *Workin' Man Blues* (1999), and *Straight White Male* (2000). His honors include a 1990 PEN Oakland Josephine Miles Award and a 2001 Carey McWilliams Award from the California Studies Association. He is currently a professor emeritus at Sonoma State University and has written his first young-adult novel, *Manuel and the Madman* (2000), with his wife, Janice.

"¡EXPECTORAN SU SANGRE!" EXCLAIMED GREAT-GRANDMA when I showed her the small horned toad I had removed from my breast pocket. I turned toward my mother, who translated: "They spit blood."

"*De los ojos,*" Grandma added. "From their eyes," mother explained, herself uncomfortable in the presence of the small beast.

I grinned, "Awwwwww."

But my great-grandmother did not smile. "*Son muy tóxicos,*" she nodded with finality. Mother moved back an involuntary step, her hands suddenly busy at her breast. "Put that thing down," she ordered.

"His name's John," I said.

"Put John down and not in your pocket, either," my mother nearly shouted. "Those things are very poisonous. Didn't you understand what Grandma said?"

I shook my head.

"Well..." Mother looked from one of us to the other—spanning four generations of California, standing three feet apart—and said, "of course you didn't. Please take him back where you got him, and be careful. We'll all feel better when you do." The tone of her voice told me that the discussion had ended, so I released the little reptile where I'd captured him.

During those years in Oildale, the mid-1940s, I needed only to walk across the street to find a patch of virgin desert. Neighborhood kids called it simply "the vacant lot," less than an acre without houses or sidewalks. Not that we were desperate for desert then, since we could walk into its scorched skin a mere half mile west, north, and east. To the south, incongruously, flowed the icy Kern River, fresh from the Sierra and surrounded by riparian forest.

Ours was rich soil formed by that same Kern River as it ground Sierra granite and turned it into coarse sand, then carried it down into the valley and deposited it over millennia along its many changes of channels. The ants that built miniature volcanoes on the vacant lot left piles of tiny stones with telltale markings of black on white. Deeper than ants could dig were pools of petroleum that led to many fortunes and lured men like my father from Texas. The dry hills to the east and north sprouted forests of wooden derricks.

Despite the abundance of open land, plus the constant lure of the river where desolation and verdancy met, most kids relied on the vacant lot as their primary playground. Even with its bullheads and stinging insects, we played everything from football to kick-the-can on it. The lot actually resembled my father's head, bare in the middle but full of growth around the edges: weeds, stickers, cactuses, and a few bushes. We played our games on its sandy center, and conducted such sports as ant fights and lizard hunts on its brushy periphery.

That spring, when I discovered the lone horned toad near the back of the lot, had been rough on my family. Earlier, there had been quiet, unpleasant tension between Mom and Daddy. He was a silent man, little given to emotional displays. It was difficult for him to show affection and I guess the openness of Mom's family made him uneasy. Daddy had no kin in California and rarely mentioned any in Texas. He couldn't seem to understand my mother's large, intimate family, their constant noisy concern for one another, and I think he was a little jealous of the time she gave everyone, maybe even me.

I heard her talking on the phone to my various aunts and uncles, usually in Spanish. Even though I couldn't understand—Daddy had warned her not to teach me that foreign tongue because it would hurt me in school, and she'd complied—I could sense the stress. I had been afraid they were going to divorce, since she only used Spanish to hide things from me. I'd confronted her with my suspicion, but she comforted me, saying, no, that was not the problem. They were merely deciding when it would be our turn to care for Grandma. I didn't really understand, although I was relieved.

I later learned that my great-grandmother—whom we simply called "Grandma"—had been moving from house to house within the family, trying to find a place she'd accept. She hated the city, and most of the aunts and uncles lived in Los Angeles. Our house in Oildale was much closer to the open country where she'd dwelled all her life. She had wanted to come to our place right away because she had raised my mother from a baby when my own grandmother died. But the old lady seemed unimpressed with Daddy, whom she called *"ese gringo."*

In truth, we had more room, and my dad made more money in the oil patch than almost anyone else in the family. Since my mother was the closest to Grandma, our place was the logical one for her, but Ese Gringo didn't see it that way, I guess, at least not at first. Finally, after much debate, he relented.

In any case, one windy afternoon, my Uncle Manuel and Aunt Toni drove up and deposited four and a half feet of bewigged, bejeweled Spanish spitfire: a square, pale face topped by a tightly curled black wig that hid a bald head—her hair having been lost to typhoid nearly sixty years before—her small white hands veined with rivers of blue. She walked with a prancing bounce that made her appear half her age, and she barked orders in Spanish from the moment she emerged from Manuel and Toni's car. Later, just before they left, I heard Uncle Manuel tell my dad, "Good luck, Charlie. That old lady's dynamite." Daddy only grunted.

She had been with us only two days when I tried to impress her with my horned toad. In fact, nothing I did seemed to impress her, and she referred to me as *el malcriado,* causing my mother to shake her head. Mom explained to me that Grandma was just old and lonely for Grandpa and uncomfortable in town. Mom told me that Grandma had lived over half a century in the country, away from the noise, away from clutter, away from people. She refused to accompany my mother on shopping trips, or anywhere else. She even refused to climb into a car, and I wondered how Uncle Manuel had managed to load her up in order to bring her to us.

She disliked sidewalks and roads, dancing across them when she had to, then appearing to wipe her feet on earth or grass. Things too civilized simply did not please her. A brother of hers had been killed in the great San Francisco earthquake and that had been the end of her tolerance of cities. Until my great-grandfather died, they lived on a small rancho near Arroyo Cantua, north of Coalinga. Grandpa, who had come north from Sonora as a youth to work as a vaquero, had bred horses and cattle and cowboyed for other ranchers, scraping together enough of a living to raise eleven children.

He had been, until the time of his death, a lean, dark-skinned man with wide shoulders, a large nose, and a sweeping handlebar mustache that was white when I knew him. His Indian blood darkened all his progeny so that not even I was as fair skinned as my great-grandmother, Ese Gringo for a father or not.

As it turned out, I didn't really understand very much about Grandma at all. She was old, of course, yet in many ways my parents treated her as though she were younger than me, walking her to the bathroom at night and bringing her presents from the store. In other ways—drinking wine at dinner, for example—she was granted adult privileges. Even Daddy didn't drink wine except on special occasions. After Grandma moved in, though, he began to occasionally join her for a glass, sometimes even sitting with her on the porch for a premeal sip.

She held court on our front porch, often gazing toward the desert hills east of us or across the street at kids playing on the lot. Occasionally, she would rise, cross the yard and sidewalk and street, skip over them, sometimes stumbling on the curb, and wipe her feet on the lot's sandy soil, then she would slowly circle the boundary between the open middle and the brushy sides, searching for something, it appeared. I never figured out what.

One afternoon I returned from school and saw Grandma perched on the porch as usual, so I started to walk around the house to avoid her sharp, mostly incomprehensible, tongue. She had already spotted me. *"¡Venga aquí!"* she ordered, and I understood.

I approached the porch and noticed that Grandma was vigorously chewing something. She held a small white bag in one hand. Saying *"¿Qué deseas tomar?"* she withdrew a large orange gumdrop from the bag and began slowly chewing it in her toothless mouth, smacking loudly as she did so. I stood below her for a moment trying to remember the word for candy. Then it came to me: *"Dulce,"* I said.

Still chewing, Grandma replied, *"¿Mande?"*

Knowing she wanted a complete sentence, I again struggled, then came up with *"Deseo dulce."*

She measured me for a moment, before answering in nearly perfect English, "Oh, so you wan' some candy. Go to the store an' buy some."

I don't know if it was the shock of hearing her speak English for the first time, or the way she had denied me a piece of candy, but I suddenly felt tears warm my checks and I sprinted into the house and found Mom, who stood at the kitchen sink. "Grandma just talked English," I burst between light sobs.

"What's wrong?" she asked as she reached out to stroke my head.

"Grandma can talk English," I repeated.

"Of course she can," Mom answered. "What's wrong?"

I wasn't sure what was wrong, but after considering, I told Mom that Grandma had teased me. No sooner had I said that than the old woman appeared at the door and hiked her skirt. Attached to one of her petticoats by safety pins were several small tobacco sacks, the white cloth kind that closed with yellow drawstrings. She carefully unhooked one and opened it, withdrawing a dollar, then handed the money to me. *"Para su dulce,"* she said. Then, to my mother, she asked, "Why does he bawl like a motherless calf?"

"It's nothing," Mother replied.

"Do not weep, little one," the old lady comforted me. "Jesus and the Virgin love you." She smiled and patted my head. To my mother she said as though just realizing it, "Your baby?"

Somehow that day changed everything. I wasn't afraid of my great-grandmother any longer and, once I began spending time with her on the porch, I realized that my father had also begun directing increased attention to the old woman. Almost every evening Ese Gringo was sharing wine with Grandma. They talked out there, but I never did hear a real two-way conversation between them. Usually Grandma rattled on and Daddy nodded. She'd chuckle and pat his hand and he might grin, even grunt a word or two, before she'd begin talking again. Once I saw my mother standing by the front window watching them together, a smile playing across her face.

No more did I sneak around the house to avoid Grandma after school. Instead, she waited for me and discussed my efforts in class gravely, telling mother that I was a bright boy, *"muy inteligente,"* and that I should be sent to the nuns who would train me. I would make a fine priest. When Ese Gringo heard that, he smiled and said, "He'd make a fair-to-middlin' Holy Roller preacher, too." Even Mom had to chuckle, and my great-grandmother shook her finger at Ese Gringo. "Oh you debil, Sharlie!" she cackled.

Frequently, I would accompany Grandma to the lot where she would explain that no fodder could grow there. Poor pasture or not, the lot was at least unpaved, and Grandma greeted even the tiniest new cactus or flowering weed with joy. "Look how beautiful," she would croon. "In all this ugliness, it lives." Oildale was my home and it didn't look especially ugly to me, so I could only grin and wonder.

Because she liked the lot and things that grew there, I showed her the horned toad when I captured it a second time. I was determined to keep it, although I did not discuss my plans with anyone. I also wanted to hear more about the bloody eyes, so I thrust the small animal nearly into her face one afternoon. She did not flinch. *"Hola señor sangre de ojos,"* she said with a mischievous grin. *"¿Qué tal?"* It took me a moment to catch on.

"You were kidding before," I accused.

"Of course," she acknowledged, still grinning.

"But why?"

"Because the little beast belongs with his own kind in his own place, not in your pocket. Give him his freedom, my son."

I had other plans for the horned toad, but I was clever enough not to cross Grandma. "Yes, Ma'am," I replied. That night I placed the reptile in a flower bed cornered by a brick wall Ese Gringo had built the previous summer. It was a spot rich with insects for the toad to eat, and the little wall, only a foot high, must have seemed massive to so squat an animal.

Nonetheless, the next morning when I searched for the horned toad it was gone. I had no time to explore the yard for it, so I trudged off to school, my belly troubled. How could it have escaped? Classes meant little to me that day. I thought only of my lost pet—I had changed his name to Juan, the same as my great-grandfather—and where I might find him.

I shortened my conversation with Grandma that afternoon so I could search for Juan. "What do you seek?" the old woman asked me as I poked through flower beds beneath the porch. "Praying mantises," I improvised, and she merely nodded, surveying me. But I had eyes only for my lost pet, and I continued pushing through branches and brushing aside leaves. No luck.

Finally, I gave in and turned toward the lot. I found my horned toad nearly across the street, crushed. It had been heading for the miniature desert and had almost made it when an automobile's tire had run over it. One notion immediately swept me: if I had left it on its lot, it would still be alive. I stood rooted there in the street, tears slicking my cheeks, and a car honked its horn as it passed, the driver shouting at me.

Grandma joined me and stroked my back. "The poor little beast," was all she said, then she bent slowly and scooped up what remained of the horned toad and led me out of the street. "We must return him to his own place," she explained, and we trooped, my eyes still clouded, toward the back of the vacant lot. Carefully, I dug a hole with a piece of wood. Grandma placed Juan in it and covered him. We said an Our Father and a Hail Mary, then Grandma walked me back to the house. "Your little Juan is safe with God, my son," she comforted. We kept the horned toad's death a secret, and we visited his small grave frequently.

Grandma fell just before school ended and summer vacation began. As was her habit, she had walked alone to the vacant lot but this time, on her way back, she tripped over the curb and broke her hip. That following week, when Daddy brought her home from the hospital, she seemed to have shrunken. She sat hunched in a wheelchair on the porch, gazing with faded eyes toward the hills or at the lot, speaking rarely. She still sipped wine every evening with Daddy and even I could tell how concerned he was about her. It got to where he'd look in on her before leaving for work every morning and again at night before turning in. And if Daddy was home, Grandma always wanted him to push her chair when she needed moving, calling, "Sharlie!" until he arrived.

I was tugged from sleep on the night she died by voices drumming through the walls into darkness. I couldn't understand them, but was immediately frightened by the uncommon sounds of words in the night. I struggled from bed and walked into the living room just as Daddy closed the front door and a car pulled away.

Mom was sobbing softly on the couch and Daddy walked to her, stroked her head, then noticed me. "Come here, son," he gently ordered.

I walked to him and, uncharacteristically, he put an arm around me. "What's wrong?" I asked, near tears myself. Mom looked up, but before she could speak, Daddy said, "Grandma died." Then he sighed heavily and stood there with his arms around his weeping wife and son.

The next day my Uncle Manuel and Uncle Arnulfo, plus Aunt Chintia, arrived, and over food they discussed with my mother where Grandma should be interred. They argued that it would be too expensive to transport her body home and, besides, they could more easily visit her grave if she was buried in Bakersfield. "They have such nice, manicured grounds at Greenlawn," Aunt Chintia pointed out. Just when it seemed they had agreed, I could remain silent no longer. "But

Grandma has to go home," I burst. "She has to! It's the only thing she really wanted. We can't leave her in the city."

Uncle Arnulfo, who was on the edge, snapped to Mother that I belonged with the other children, not interrupting adult conversation. Mom quietly agreed, but I refused. My father walked into the room then. "What's wrong?" he asked.

"They're going to bury Grandma in Bakersfield, Daddy. Don't let 'em, please."

"Well, son…"

"When my horny toad got killed and she helped me to bury it, she said we had to return him to his place."

"Your horny toad?" Mother asked.

"He got squished and me and Grandma buried him in the lot. She said we had to take him back to his place. Honest she did."

No one spoke for a moment, then my father, Ese Gringo, who stood against the sink, responded: "That's right…" he paused, then added, "We'll bury her." I saw a weary smile cross my mother's face. "If she wanted to go back to the ranch then that's where we have to take her," Daddy said.

I hugged him and he, right in front of everyone, hugged back.

No one argued. It seemed, suddenly, as though they had all wanted to do exactly what I had begged for. Grown-ups baffled me. Late that week the entire family, hundreds it seemed, gathered at the little Catholic church in Coalinga for mass, then drove out to Arroyo Cantua and buried Grandma next to Grandpa. She rests there today.

My mother, father, and I drove back to Oildale that afternoon across the scorching west-side desert, through sand and tumbleweeds and heat shivers. Quiet and sad, we knew we had done our best. Mom, who usually sat near to the door in the front seat, snuggled close to Daddy, and I heard her whisper to him, "Thank you, Charlie," as she kissed his cheek.

Daddy squeezed her, hesitated as if to clear his throat, then answered, "When you're family, you take care of your own."

from

✹ Esperanza's Box of Saints

María Amparo Escandón

1999

María Amparo Escandón was born and raised in Mexico City, where she began writing and publishing short stories in magazines and anthologies. After moving to Los Angeles, where she currently teaches writing at UCLA Extension, she started writing short stories in English, eventually expanding one of those stories into the novel *Esperanza's Box of Saints* (1999), which has been translated into thirteen languages and distributed in more than forty countries. Instead of directly translating the book into Spanish, Escandón rewrote the entire novel in her native language, making culturally significant changes to the plot. She also adapted the story into a Spanish-language screenplay that has won several international film awards. The following excerpt describes the title character's journey across the U.S./Mexico border in search of her twelve-year-old daughter, whose death during a tonsillectomy Esperanza denies after experiencing a holy vision.

JUDGE HAYNES PARKED HIS CAR ON AN EMPTY TIJUANA STREET. He and Esperanza got out. He opened the trunk. Neither of them spoke. She took off her shoes and jumped in, squeezing herself between a brand-new suitcase and her box of saints. He shut the trunk gently, got back in, and drove to the line. He turned the music up. Oldies. He liked to listen to rock bands from the sixties. They reminded him of his marijuana days when college was, most of all, an excuse to be far away from his father, who had never left Wilmington, Delaware. Scott was certain that the near-military style in which his father had educated him had determined his choice of career. But another aspect of his personality overshadowed his passion for the law. And he didn't share it with his father. Out of respect. Out of fear. He liked freedom. And he found it on the border.

He loved the contrast between Mexico and California. An exuberant San Diego filled with impeccable golf courses, right next to a barren Tijuana where dust devils never gave local housekeepers a minute of rest. Scott felt comfortable in a place where the confusion of identity created hybrid town names, like Mexicali and Calexico. Where Chinese ate their chili dogs with green tea. Where someone had the sauciness to print "Juan López—Smuggler" on his business card. Where a dental technician brought up in Faribault, Minnesota, could find her Latin lover in an illegal immigrant who came from a tiny ranch somewhere in Jalisco. In Tijuana, Scott had screamed through the fanciest residential neighborhoods at three in the morning. He had picked several fights at El Reventón, always knocking someone unconscious. He had mingled from table to table, kissing other men's women. He had drunk himself beyond self-respect on countless occasions. And he had gotten away with it all.

The United States wasn't the ultimate free country after all. Mexico wasn't either. Instead, it was that piece of land where one met the other in an unavoidable frontal collision. But what he really loved about the border was that he could be a respectable, law-abiding, and law-enforcing San Diego judge and, in a matter of minutes, become an unidentifiable being sleeping in the arms of a prostitute, in a place where no one cared if what he did was right or wrong. And now that he was bringing Esperanza across the line with him, the parallel sides of his life were about to merge. He had found Esperanza after years of visiting Mexican whorehouses three times a week in search of a woman, other than Gladys, to share his life with. He was in love. He was willing to take the risk. And his father would never know.

His hands slid on the steering wheel. He noticed they were sweating. Things like this didn't happen to him. Not even in court. Not even when his father had caught him smoking a cigarette at age sixteen. Not even the day before, when he finally told Gladys that he had never really cared for her. Of course, he didn't tell her he was leaving her to pursue the love of a Mexican whore. In fact, he couldn't remember any time in his life when his hands had sweated. Then again, he had never helped a prostitute enter the United States illegally.

He lined up behind fifty or so cars, all waiting to cross the border. Peddlers sold miniature plaster replicas of Michelangelo's *David,* stone-carved birdbaths, magazines, newspapers, toys with a very short life span, car stereos, pirated cassettes of hit norteña bands, watches, rearview mirrors, bumper stickers, both in Spanish and English.

Everyone in Mexico knew the unwritten rule when it came to street peddlers. If you weren't interested in the merchandise, you should avoid all possible eye contact. At the slightest flicker of interest, at least three people would be shoving their wares through the window, and it didn't matter if the car was in motion or not. They were good runners, even though some had had their feet fractured by passing car tires. They must think the pain beats paying taxes, Scott thought. Since he was experienced at crossing the border, he knew the drill. He was even familiar with some of those hucksters, although their eyes had never met.

While he waited, he thought of Esperanza, snuggled among her saints in the trunk of his car. He still hadn't determined exactly what attracted him so much to that woman. She was beautiful, but he had slept with many beautiful women before. She was candid. Tender. All the mother anyone could desire. She was a mother-and-a-half. There was enough motherhood in her to keep plenty for oneself and still have some left over to give away. Best of all, he loved the taste of her skin. Spicy, pungent, tangy, like tamarind candy, especially so around her left nipple. He couldn't stop licking it. His tongue burned so much that every night after he left the Pink Palace, he had to stop at a little restaurant he knew was open twenty-four hours to drink six glasses of *horchata* with cinnamon sprinkled on it and lots of ice before heading back to San Diego.

He knew she wasn't really a prostitute. He knew she was looking for her daughter. During the nights they spent together, she had told him all about her search. The apparitions. The hospital. The doctor. The cemetery. The authorities' suspicious reactions.

How could she be looking for her dead daughter among the living? That was the one thing he did not understand. It didn't matter that her English wasn't good or that his Spanish was broken beyond repair. They had reached a state of communication that was greater than just two people understanding each other. A communion of the souls. And because he could read her soul, it was clear to him she did not love him. But if she stayed with him, he would certainly take what little she had to offer.

Inside the trunk, Esperanza prayed to Juan Soldado, holding his statue in one hand and touching the scapulary fastened to her dress, right above her heart, with the other. "Dear Juanito, I know the man driving this car is not a Mexican, but he could well be. Please help him cross the border. I haven't known you for long, but I understand you've helped thousands of immigrants reach a better life. I'm not an immigrant, but I do want a better life with my daughter back in my own town. Maybe San Judas Tadeo has already filled you in on this. I'm just going to look for her up north. If I find her, I'll come back with her. If she's not there, I'll look for her elsewhere. So, don't count me as an immigrant, but help me as one."

"American citizen?"

"Yes, sir."

"Do you have anything to declare?"

"No, sir."

Bored with his job, the young immigration officer motioned Scott to move along. Scott was uncontrollably nervous. With a jerky motion, he managed to put the car in forward gear, but suddenly the immigration officer stopped him.

"Hey! Hold it!"

Scott slammed on the brakes, causing the tires to screech. He could hear Esperanza banging around in the trunk.

"Is there a problem, sir?"

The immigration officer looked inside Scott's car. He inspected his face very closely. He looked him in the eye like he would never look at a street peddler.

"Aren't you Judge Haynes?"

"Yes. I'm Judge Haynes."

"Of course! I know you! You let my brother go off on parole last year! He was accused of smuggling pot in a plastic action figure, remember?"

Scott pretended to remember. He had to give his best performance. His career was at stake. If he was caught, he'd go to jail. Esperanza would be deported.

"That's right! I remember your brother."

"Nice to see you again! I'll tell him I saw you."

"Well, give him my regards, please."

"Sure will, when I visit him on Thursday. He's back in the joint. Only this time he smuggled some illegal aliens."

"He did?" Scott couldn't breathe.

"Yeah, can you believe it?"

"What isn't there to believe?"

The immigration officer shook his sweaty hand. Judge Haynes gave him an exaggerated grin and sped off.

Scott drove faster than he should. Esperanza had gotten out of the trunk right after San Onofre and by Las Pulgas Road was still stretching her arms and legs. She entertained herself reading the freeway signs indicating the different towns between San Diego and Los Angeles: Del Mar, Escondido, Encinitas, San Clemente, San Juan Capistrano, Santa Ana.

"Looks like it's going to be easy to get around here. Everything's in Spanish." Esperanza was amused.

"Supposing your daughter is in fact alive, why are you looking for her in a brothel?"

"Because San Judas Tadeo said she was there. I've told you already."

"When he said it, did he call it a brothel, a whorehouse, a one-night-stand motel, or what?"

"Well, now that you bring it up, I don't remember what he called it."

"Did you hear it in his own voice?"

Esperanza felt uncomfortable. Had she actually heard her saint say it, or had she reached that conclusion on her own? She was confused by the intricacies of her own explanations. She wished she had San Judas Tadeo himself sitting in the backseat, leaning forward as far as his seat belt would allow and whispering in her ear the answers to Scott's questions.

The whole conversation disturbed her. Unlike Soledad, who ruled out the apparition without a doubt, Scott wanted to believe, but he needed hard facts. Esperanza knew that in matters of faith, there are no hard facts. How could she come up with them?

"There you go again, the judge interrogating the accused," she teased, hoping he'd change the subject.

"Maybe you just imagined he said it."

"Blanca is not dead, Scott."

"If she's in the States, I can find her. There are lots of help lines dedicated to finding missing children. You are not alone. Just stay with me and we'll look for her. We'll organize a search party. We'll have her picture on every milk carton in the nation. We'll distribute millions of flyers. We'll get the media's attention. I'll offer a reward to anyone providing information leading to her whereabouts."

"I'm so sorry, Scott. You have been very good to me, but I must look for her by myself. I already tried to involve my *comadre* Soledad, and now she doesn't believe anything I say. My priest has asked me to keep all this to myself and not involve anyone. There's a reason for it. Or has San Judas Tadeo appeared before you, too?"

"Unfortunately not."

"Well. There you have it. But you know I am thankful anyway."

Scott wondered why Esperanza was turning down such valuable help. Her chances of finding the girl, if she was alive, were better if Esperanza stayed with him. Maybe her priest was right. Only a powerful, otherworldly reason could keep her from accepting his help. A reason his mind, so accustomed to making decisions resulting from hard proof, could not comprehend. The bottom line was that this was Esperanza's private quest.

Scott checked his map a few times before they arrived at the corner of Pico and Union in downtown Los Angeles. A theater built in the twenties occupied the northeast corner. The Fiesta Theater. The marquee displayed a misspelled sign in Spanish: HOY FUNSIÓN: OJO POR OJO.

As soon as Scott parked, a young African American man approached him with a small paper bag in his hand. Without a second thought, Scott rolled down the window, gave the man a twenty-dollar bill, and took the bag, stashing it under his seat. He hadn't smoked marijuana in at least two years. His crisis with Esperanza was enough to make him start again. He had no intentions of running for office anyway.

Esperanza thought that the young man might be San Martín de Porres, the black saint she loved so much. Perhaps he had materialized to point her in the direction of the Fiesta Theater. All the storefront signs were at least partly in Spanish. González Bakery. El León Market. Rosita Records and Tickets. The street was almost empty. She saw a wall with more graffiti than it could display, with signs that read: NO A LA 187.

"Scott, really, I have to go." The number on the side door of the Fiesta Theater corresponded to the one scribbled on the piece of paper in her hand.

"We'll rent an apartment. We can live together."

"I will not do to you what you did to Gladys. I'm sorry."

Scott realized then that he had not lost Esperanza. How could he lose someone he never really had? He began inventing reasons why she should stay with him until he had made up so many they bumped against one another in his mind, like people in a crowded elevator all trying to get out at once. He loved her. He was rich. He had resources. Confusion prevailed. Why would she want to get out of his plush new car that smelled of vanilla extract and leather and leave him, disappearing for good in such a sad-looking neighborhood? He felt the urge to hold her back. He just did not understand. He had so much to give her. How could she not love him?

Esperanza knew he did not understand. His eyes said so. The tiny tear clinging to his eyelash said so. He was a defeated bull about to lose his life in the bullring. He was a thousand men crying all at once, the last handful of dirt thrown into a grave.

Before Esperanza opened the car door, Scott scribbled a name and a phone number on the back of his business card, and gave it to her with six hundred dollars that he took from his wallet.

"The owner of this travel agency owes me a favor. Call her. Maybe she'll give you a job." He pointed at the card.

Esperanza took the card and returned the money.

"I'll be all right."

"You don't have to be so proud, Esperanza. I don't need this money."

"Okay, just so you don't worry."

She made the sign of the cross on his forehead with the money rolled up in her hand and got out of the car. He put her suitcase and her box of saints on the sidewalk and, before leaving, gave her one last long look.

✶ Beneath the Shadow of the Freeway

Lorna Dee Cervantes

1994

Two other poems by Lorna Dee Cervantes, "Cannery Town in August" and "Poem for the Young White Man Who Asked Me How I, an Intelligent, Well-Read Person, Could Believe in the War Between Races," appear in this anthology.

1

Across the street—the freeway,
blind worm, wrapping the valley up
from Los Altos to Sal Si Puedes
I watched it from my porch
unwinding. Every day at dusk
as Grandma watered geraniums
the shadow of the freeway lengthened.

2

We were a woman family:
Grandma, our innocent Queen;
Mama, the Swift Knight, Fearless Warrior.
Mama wanted to be a Princess instead.
I know that. Even now she dreams of taffeta
and foot-high tiaras.

Myself: I could never decide.
So I turned to books, those staunch, upright men.
I became Scribe: Translator of Foreign Mail,
interpreting letters from the government, notices

of dissolved marriages and Welfare stipulations.
I paid the bills, did light man-work, fixed faucets,
insured everything
against all leaks.

3

Before rain I notice seagulls.
They walk in flocks,
cautious across lawns: splayed toes,
indecisive beaks. Grandma says
seagulls mean storm.

In California in the summer,
mockingbirds sing all night.
Grandma says they are singing for their nesting wives.
"They don't leave their families
borrachando."

She likes the way of birds,
respects how they show themselves
for toast and a whistle.

She believes in myths and birds.
She trusts only what she builds
with her own hands.

4

She built her house,
cocky, disheveled carpentry,
after living twenty-five years
with a man who tried to kill her.

Grandma, from the hills of Santa Barbara,
I would open my eyes to see her stir mush
in the morning, her hair in loose braids,
tucked loose around her head
with a yellow scarf.

Mama said, "It's her own fault,
getting screwed by a man for that long.

Sure as shit wasn't hard."
soft   she was   soft

                5
in the night I would hear it
glass bottles shattering the street
words cracked into shrill screams
inside my throat   a cold fear
as it entered the house in hard
unsteady steps   stopping at my door
my name   bathrobe   slippers
outside a 3 a.m. mist heavy
as a breath full of whiskey
stop it   go home   come inside
mama if he comes here again
I'll call the police

inside
a gray kitten   a touchstone
purring beneath the quilts
grandma stitched
from his suits
the patchwork singing
of mockingbirds

                6
"You're too soft…always were.
You'll get nothing but shit.
Baby, don't count on nobody."

—a mother's wisdom.
Soft. I haven't changed,
maybe grown more silent, cynical
on the outside.

"O Mama, with what's inside of me
I could wash that all away. I could."
"But Mama, if you're good to them
they'll be good to you back."

Back. The freeway is across the street.
It's summer now. Every night I sleep with a gentle man
to the hymn of mockingbirds,

and in time I plant geraniums.
I tie up my hair into loose braids,
and trust only what I have built
with my own hands.

from

✳ The Miraculous Day
of Amalia Gómez

John Rechy

1991

John Rechy was born in 1934 in El Paso, Texas, to a Scottish
father and a mother descended from Mexican aristocracy.
He has written twelve books, including the national and
international bestsellers *City of Night* (1963) and *Numbers*
(1967). His first nonfiction book, *The Sexual Outlaw: A
Documentary* (1977), was named one of the one hundred best
nonfiction books of the century by the *San Francisco
Chronicle Book Review*. Rechy's work has been translated into
more than twenty languages, his articles and essays have
appeared in major magazines including the *Los Angeles Times*
and *New York Times* book reviews, and his plays have been
performed on American and European stages. He received a
lifetime achievement award from The Publishing Triangle
and is the first novelist to receive PEN USA West's Lifetime
Achievement Award. He currently teaches literature and film
for writers at the University of Southern California, and his
most recent novel is *Bodies and Souls* (2001).

WHEN AMALIA GÓMEZ WOKE UP, a half hour later than on other Saturdays
because last night she had had three beers instead of her usual weekend
two, she looked out, startled by God knows what, past the screenless iron-
barred window of her stucco bungalow unit in one of the many decaying
neighborhoods that sprout off the shabbiest part of Hollywood Boulevard,
and she saw a large silver cross in the otherwise clear sky.

Amalia closed her eyes. When she opened them again, would there
be a dazzling white radiance within which the Blessed Mother would

bask?—a holy sign *always* preceded such apparitions. What would *she* do first? Kneel, of course. She might try to get quickly to the heart of the matter—in movies it took at least two more visitations; *she* would ask for a tangible sign on this initial encounter, proof for the inevitable skeptics. She would ask that the sign be…a flower, yes, a white rose. Then there would follow a hidden message—messages from Our Lady were always mysterious—and an exhortation that the rose and the message, exactly as given, be taken to a priest, who would—What language would the Virgin Mother speak? "Blessed Mother, please, I *do* speak English—but with an accent, and I speak Spanish much better. So would you kindly—?"

What strange thoughts! Amalia opened her eyes. The cross was gone.

She *had* seen it, knew she had seen it, thought she had. No, Amalia was a logical Mexican American woman in her mid-forties. There had been no real cross. No miraculous sign would appear to a twice-divorced woman with grown, rebellious children and living with a man who wasn't her husband, although God *was* forgiving, wasn't He? The "cross" had been an illusion created by a filmy cloud—or streaks of smoke, perhaps from a sky-writing airplane.

Amalia sat up in her bed. The artificial flowers she had located everywhere to camouflage worn second-hand furniture were losing their brightness, looked old and drab. She heard the growl of cars always on the busy streets in this neighborhood that was rapidly becoming a barrio like others she had fled. Looking dreamily toward the window, she sighed.

It was too hot for May! It's usually by late August that heat clenches these bungalows and doesn't let go until rain thrusts it off as steam. Amalia glanced beside her. Raynaldo hadn't come back after last night's quarrel at El Bar & Grill. Other times, he'd stayed away only a few hours after a spat; usually he was proud of the attention she drew, liked to show off his woman.

And Amalia was a good-looking woman, with thick, lustrous, wavy black hair that retained all its vibrant shininess and color. No one could accuse her of being "slender," but for a woman with firm, ample breasts and sensual round hips, her waist was small; any smaller might look ridiculous on a lush woman, she often assured herself. "Lush" was a word she liked. An Anglo man who had wandered into El Bar & Grill once had directed it at her, and that very night Raynaldo had called her "my lush brown-eyed woman, my lush Amalia."

Daily she moistened her thick eyelashes with saliva, to preserve their curl. She disliked downward-slanting eyelashes—but not, as some people of her mother's generation disdained them, because they were supposed to signal a predominance of "Indian blood." Unlike her mother, who repeatedly claimed "some Spanish blood," Amalia did not welcome it when people she did housework for referred to her—carefully—as "Spanish." She was proud to be Mexican American.

She did not like the word "Chicano"—which, in her youth, in El Paso, Texas, had been a term of disapproval among Mexicans; and she did not refer to Los Angeles as "Ellay." "The city of angels!" she had said in awe when she arrived here from Texas with her two children—on an eerie day when Sant' Ana winds blew in from the hot desert and fire blazed along the horizon.

Raynaldo was not her husband, although—of course—she had told her children he was. Gloria was fifteen, and Juan seventeen. They slept in what would have been a small living room, Juan in a roll-out cot, Gloria on the pull-out sofa. When Teresa, Amalia's mother, was alive, she occupied the small other "bedroom," a porch converted by Raynaldo. The last time he was out of jail, Manny, Amalia's oldest son, shared it, sleeping on the floor next to his grandmother's cot. Now the improvised room was vacant, surrendered to two deaths.

On a small table in Amalia's room were a large framed picture of Our Lord and one of his Blessed Mother, next to a small statue of the Virgin of Guadalupe on a bed of plastic flowers. There, too, was a photograph of President John F. Kennedy. When he was murdered in her home state, Amalia and her mother—her father was on a binge and cried belatedly— went to several masses and wept through the televised funeral, the only time Teresa did not resent "Queen for a Day" being pushed off the black-and-white television.

Amalia made her slow, reverential morning sign of the cross toward the picture of Christ, hands outstretched, his bright red Sacred Heart enclosed in an aura of gold; and she extended her gesture to the Blessed Mother, resplendent in her blue-starred robe. *They* would certainly understand why it was necessary that she tell her children Raynaldo was her husband: to set a moral example, why else?

Almost beefy and with a nest of graying hairs on his chest nearly as thick as on his head, Raynaldo was not the kind of handsome man Amalia preferred, but he was a good man who had a steady job with a freight-loading company, and he helped generously with rent and groceries. He had been faithfully with her for five years, the only one of her men who had never hit her. Once he had paid a mariachi—who had wandered into El Bar & Grill from East Los Angeles in his black, silver-lined *charro* outfit—to sing a sad, romantic favorite of hers, "A Punto de Llorar"; and he led her in a dance. God would forgive her a small sin, that she pretended he was a handsome groom dancing with her one more time before their grand church wedding.

Amalia pulled her eyes away from the picture of Christ and the Holy Mother because she had located the place on the wall where the plaster had cracked during a recent earthquake. She had felt a sudden trembling in the house and then a violent jolt. As she always did at the prospect of violence, she had crouched in a corner and seen the crack splitting the wall. Now every time the house quivered from an idling truck, she thought of rushing out—although she had heard repeated warnings that that was the worst thing to do. But what if the house was falling on you? She wished the talk of earthquakes would stop, but it seemed to her that constant predictions of a "Big One" were made with increasing delight by television "authorities."

My God! It was eight-thirty and she was still in bed. On weekdays she might already be at one of the pretty houses—and she chose only pretty ones—that she cleaned. She preferred to work at different homes in order to get paid daily, and for variety. Too, the hours provided her more time with her children, although now they were seldom around. She was well liked and got along with the people she worked for, though she felt mostly indifferent toward them. She always dressed her best, always wore shimmery earrings; one woman often greeted her with, "You look like you've come to visit, not work." Amalia was not sure how the remark was intended, but she *did* know the woman was *not* "lush." Lately Amalia had begun to feel some anxiety about her regular workdays because "new illegals"—Guatemalans, Salvadorans, Nicaraguans without papers—were willing to work for hardly anything, and one of her employers had laughingly suggested lowering her wage.

Amalia sat on the edge of her bed. A strap of her thin slip fell off her brown shoulder. Had it really happened, in the restaurant-bar, after Raynaldo left and that young man came over? Amalia pushed away the mortifying memory.

She walked to the window. One side of her bungalow bordered the street. At the window she did not look at the sky.

Daily, the neighborhood decayed. Lawns surrendered to weeds and dirt. Cars were left mounted on bricks. Everywhere were iron bars on windows. Some houses were boarded up. At night, shadows of homeless men and women, carrying rags, moved in and left at dawn. And there was the hated graffiti, no longer even words, just tangled scrawls like curses.

When she had first moved here, the court looked better than now. The three bungalows sharing a wall in common and facing three more units were graying; and in the small patches of "garden" before each, only yellowish grass survived. At the far end of the court, near the garage area taken over by skeletons of cars that no longer ran, there remained an incongruous rosebush that had managed only a few feeble buds this year, without opening. Amalia continued to water it, though, hating to see anything pretty die.

Still, she was glad to live in Hollywood. After all, that *was* impressive, wasn't it? Even the poorest sections retained a flashy prettiness, flowers pasted against cracking walls draped by splashes of bougainvillea. Even weeds had tiny buds. And sometimes, out of the gathering rubble on the streets, there would be the sudden sweetness of flowers.

There were far worse places inhabited by Mexicans and the new aliens—blackened tenements in downtown and central Los Angeles, where families sometimes lived in shifts in one always-dark room, tenements as terrible as the one Amalia had been born in—at times she thought she remembered being born within the stench of garbage....Still other people lived in old cars, on the streets, in the shadows of parks.

As she stood by the window of her stucco bungalow, Amalia did not think of any of that. She was allowing her eyes to slide casually across the street to a vacant lot enclosed by wire—and then her eyes roamed to its far edge, past a row of white oleanders above which rose jacaranda trees with ghostly lavender blossoms. Even more slowly, her eyes glided toward the tall pines bordering the giant Fox Television Studio that extended incongruously from the end of the weedy lot to Sunset Boulevard; and then her gaze floated over the huge HOLLYWOOD sign amid distant hills smeared with flowers, crowned with beautiful homes. Finally, she looked up into the sky.

The cross was not there!

Of course not—and it had never been there. And yet—

Yet the impression of the silver cross she had wakened to had altered the morning. Amalia was startled to realize that for the first time in her recent memory she had not awakened into the limb of despondence that contained all the worries that cluttered her life, worries that would require a miracle to solve.

Trying not to feel betrayed, she turned away from the sky. She heard the sound of tangling traffic on the nearby Hollywood Freeway, heard the cacophony of radios, stereos, televisions that rampaged the bungalow court each weekend.

Amalia touched her lips with her tongue. Last night's extra beer had left a bitter taste. No, it was the memory of it, of that man she allowed to sit with her last night at El Bar & Grill. Released with a sigh, that thought broke the lingering spell of the morning's awakening, and her worries swarmed her.

Worries about Juan!—handsomer each day and each day more secretive, no longer a happy young man, but a moody one. He'd been looking for work but what kind of job would he keep—proud as he was? He had made terrible grades that last year of Manny's imprisonment. Was *he* in a gang? She had fled one barrio in East Los Angeles to keep him and Gloria from drugs and killings and the gangs that had claimed her Manny. Now, students carried weapons in school and gangs terrorized whole neighborhoods. Yesterday she thought she had seen bold new graffiti on a wall. The *placa* of a new gang? That is how *cholo* gangs claim their turf. And Juan was coming home later and later—recently with a gash over one eye. He had money. Was he selling *roca*—street crack?

And who wouldn't worry about Gloria? So very pretty, and wearing more and more makeup, using words even men would blush to hear. What had Gloria wanted to tell her the other morning when she hadn't been able to listen because she was on her way to work and came back too late to ask her? Gloria had turned surly toward Raynaldo, who loved her like a father all these years. Did she suspect they weren't really married?... Amalia was sure God knew why she had to live with Raynaldo, but she wasn't certain He would extend His compassion, infinite though it was, to a sullen girl.... *What had she wanted to tell her that morning?*

Something about her involvement with that Mick?—that strange young man who rode a motorcycle and wore a single earring that glistened against his jet-black long hair? Although he was Mexican American, he had a drawly voice like those Anglos from the San Fernando Valley, and he wore metallic belts and wristbands. *What had Gloria wanted to tell her?*

And Raynaldo! If he didn't come back—but he would—there would be mounting bills again, constant threats to disconnect this and that. There was still the unpaid mortuary bill—Teresa had demanded that there be lots of flowers at her funeral. Amalia could afford this bungalow, small and tired as it was, only because of Raynaldo. Had his jealousy really been aroused last night so quickly because the man staring at her at El Bar & Grill was young and good-looking? Or had he used that as an excuse for anger already there, tension about Gloria's—and, increasingly, Juan's—abrupt resentment of him?

Of course, *of course,* Amalia missed Teresa—who wouldn't miss her own mother?—dead from old age and coughing at night and probably all her meanness, thrusting those cruel judgments at her own daughter. Who would blame her for having slapped her just that once? Certainly God would have *wanted* her to stop the vile accusations she was making before Gloria and Juan during those black, terrible days after Manny's death. And who could blame her for having waited only until after the funeral to pack away the old woman's foot-tall statue of La Dolorosa, the Mother of Sorrows?...Of course, however you referred to her, she was *always* the Virgin Mary, whether you called her Blessed Mother, the Immaculate Conception, Our Lady, the Madonna, Mother of God, Holy Mother—or Our Lady of Guadalupe, the name she assumed for her miraculous appearance in Mexico to the peasant Juan Diego, long ago. Still, Teresa's La Dolorosa, draped in black, wrenched in grief, hands clasped in anguish, tiny pieces of glass embedded under agonized eyes to testify to endless tears, had always disturbed Amalia, had seemed to her— God would forgive her this if she was wrong—not exactly the Virgin Mary whom she revered, so beautiful, so pure, so kind in her under-standing—and so miraculous!

Yes, and now there wasn't even her trusted friend, Rosario, to turn to for advice, crazy as her talk sometimes was when they both worked in the "sewing sweatshop" in downtown Los Angeles. That tiny, incom-prehensible, strong woman was gone, fled—*where?*—had just disappeared among all those rumors that she was in trouble with the hated *migra,* the Immigration, for helping the illegals who tore her heart.

And Manny—

Manny.

Her beloved firstborn. His angel face haunted her. A year after the blackest day of her life, she still awoke at night into a stark awareness of his absence. Did he hear the guards approaching along the desolate cor-ridor toward his isolated cell? Did he recognize them in the gray dark-ness as the two he had broken away from earlier, the one he had hit across the face with handcuffs? Did he know immediately what they were going to do to him?

The horror of it all would push into Amalia's mind. She saw the guards tightening the shirt around his neck. Did he cry out to her as he had each time he was arrested?...What were his last thoughts?—that he would never see her again, about his love for her, of course.

No, she would not even open the letter that had arrived yesterday from the public attorney. She knew what it would say. More investigations!

She could not go through any more pain, listen to any more filthy cop lies. Let her son rest!

And then last night—

She cursed the extra beer that allowed last night to happen. She had said yes when the young man offered it to her, but only in defiance—the Blessed Mother would attest to that—because Amalia was a moral woman who had never been unfaithful to any of her husbands, nor to a steady "boyfriend." She spat angrily now. The hot humiliation of last night grasped her—Raynaldo stalking out of the bar, accusing *her* of flirting with that young man, who had kept staring at her. And so—

"Yes, I will have that beer," she had told him. He joined her in the "family" section of the restaurant-bar. He brought his own beer and a fresh one for her. Yes, he was good-looking—why deny what everyone could see? He had dreamy dark eyes, smooth brown skin, and he wore a sacred cross on a tiny golden chain on his chest. He was from Nicaragua, his family displaced; where?...Like her he spoke English and lapsed into Spanish. She was sure he thought she was younger than she was. She attracted all types of men, after all, and she was wearing one of her prettiest dresses, watery blue, with ruffles—and her shiniest earrings, with golden fringe.

"*Bonita* Amalia," he had said.

"How do you know my name?" She was not flirting, just asserting that it was *he* who was interested in her.

"I heard the man you were with." Then he told her his name: "Angel."

Angel! Amalia had a weakness for handsome men with holy names. Her first husband's name was Salvador, savior; her second was named Gabriel. She hated it when "Angel" was mispronounced by Anglos as "Ain-jel." It was "Ahn-hel"...The holy cross on his chest, the sadness about his family, his beautiful name, and his eyes—and Raynaldo's unfair accusation—that's what had goaded her...

Amalia drank the extra beer with him, and then—

In her bedroom now, Amalia's eyes drifted toward the window. It would be a beautiful summer-tinged spring day, she told herself. Yet a sadness had swept away the exhilaration of this day's beginning.

She stood up to face the day. She could hear Gloria and Juan talking in their "bedroom." They were so close she sometimes felt left out of their lives....And why shouldn't they sleep in the same room? After all, they were brother and sister, weren't they?—and of the same father. Soon one of them would be moving into Teresa's room, where Manny had slept—and they had adored their reckless half brother. They were avoiding moving into that room, Amalia knew, but there was just so long that you could avoid things, and that's what she must tell them.

She dressed quickly. Now she would leave this room with its aroused worries. She would allow no more, none, not about Juan— Hiding what, with his new moodiness? Was he using drugs? Who was that Salvadoran boy he had let sleep in the garage; hiding from what?...No more worries! Not about Gloria. She had thrown up recently. Was she pregnant by that odd Mick with his colorless eyes and dark, dark eyebrows? *What had she wanted to tell her that morning?*...No more worries! Not about Raynaldo, either—What was really bothering him? Would he come back? *No more worries!*

And she was not going to give one more thought to the white cross—no, it had been silver!—that she had seen—thought she had seen this morning...although it had been *so* beautiful.

from

✡ Under the Feet of Jesus

Helena María Viramontes

1995

Helena María Viramontes was born in 1954 in East Los
Angeles. Her work includes a collection of short stories, the
novel *Under the Feet of Jesus* (1995), and two anthologies she
co-edited, *Chicana Creativity and Criticism: Charting New
Frontiers in American Literature* (1988) and *Chicana (W)Rites:
On Word and Film* (1995). Her award-winning work has
appeared in many anthologies and magazines, and she currently teaches English at Cornell University.

WHAT ESTRELLA REMEMBERED MOST OF HER REAL FATHER was an orange.
He had peeled a huge orange for her in an orchard where they stopped
to pee. They were traveling north where the raisin grapes were ready for
sun drying and the work was said to be plentiful. The twins wore diapers then, babies whose fists punched the air with hysteria. The boys
managed to relieve themselves without ceremony by the side of the
pickup, while Estrella and the mother had to walk to the middle of the
orchard for privacy.

They squatted within a circle of trees and the oranges hung like
big ornaments above their heads. The mother didn't consider it thievery
when she plucked a few, so many were already rotting on the ground.
The two were alone with no foreman to tell them the fruit they picked
wasn't free, no one to stop her from giving Estrella an orange so big
Estrella had to carry it to her father with two hands. Her father's boot
rested on the insect-splattered bumper of their pickup. What impressed
her most was the way his thumbnail plowed the peel off the orange in
one long spiral, as if her father plowed the sun, as if it meant something

to him to peel the orange from stem to navel without breaking the circle. Sometimes she remembered him with a mustache, sometimes smoking a Bugler tobacco cigarette, but always peeling an orange.

The women in the camps had advised the mother, *To run away from your husband would be a mistake.* He would stalk her and the children, not because he wanted them back, they proposed, but because it was a slap in the face, and he would swear over the seventh beer that he would find her and kill them all. Estrella's godmother said the same thing and more. *You'll be a forever alone woman,* she said to Estrella's mother, *nobody wants a woman with a bunch of orphans, nobody. You don't know what hunger is until your huercos tell you to your face, then what you gonna do?*

Instead, it was her father who'd run away, gone to Mexico, the mother said at first, to bury an uncle just as they settled in a city apartment with the hope of never seeing another labor camp again. Estrella hadn't remembered a lot of those years, except that the twins started calling her mama. What she remembered most was the mother kneeling in prayer or the pacing, door slamming, locked bathroom, the mother rummaging through shoe boxes of papers, bills, addressed correspondence, documents, loose dollars hidden for occasions like this; the late-night calls, money sent for his return, screaming arguments long-distance, bad connections, trouble at the border, more money sent, a sickness somewhere in between. Each call was connected by a longer silence, each request for money more painful. She remembered every job was not enough wage, every uncertainty rested on one certainty: food.

The phone was disconnected. She remembered the moving, all-night packing with trash bags left behind, to a cheaper rent they couldn't afford, to Estrella's godmother's apartment, to some friends, finally to the labor camps again. Always leaving things behind that they couldn't fit, couldn't pack, couldn't take, like a trail of bread crumbs for her father. The mother didn't know about change-of-address cards or forwarding mail, and for a while Estrella thought the absence of his letters was due to their own ignorance.

Estrella would never know of the father's repentance. Never know if he thought of them as the mother did of him. She could see it in the wet stone of the mother's eyes. "Is he eating an egg at this moment like I am eating an egg? Is he watching the moon like I am watching the moon, is he staring at a red car like I am, is he waiting like I am?"

It didn't happen so fast, the realization that he was not coming back. Estrella didn't wake up one day knowing what she knew now. It came upon her as it did her mother. Like morning light passing, the absence of night, just there, his not returning.

"You have no business in the barn," Perfecto wheezed in a voice like a whisper. His chest stretched as if his lungs were about to snap. The crying twins clung to Perfecto's belt, each pawing for his attention. He bent his head, clamped his hands on his knees to catch his breath, and his hat tumbled onto the ground. The boys ran to the barn to hear him scold Estrella.

"Are you blind? Can't you see the walls are ready to collapse? You could've hurt the girls."

Perfecto sucked in air, his nostrils flaring. He wanted to say something else, but licked the dryness of his splintered lips instead.

"Go help your mother. Get going. NOW!" Arnulfo and Ricky ran off laughing, but Estrella was stunned by the force of his words. Her chest breathed and crackled like kindling. Most of her braid had unraveled, and her loose long hair bent lazily around her chin. She flipped a few strands over her ear and stared at him and bit her lower lip. Finally, her cheeks as red as hot embers, Estrella stomped away. Perla picked up Perfecto's straw hat and handed it to him while Cookie wiped her runny nose with the back of her hand.

Estrella caught up with her brothers. She grabbed Ricky's striped green and brown T-shirt and shoved him forward, then jerked him back. He swung at the air with fists tight as walnuts. After a few jerks, she was satisfied with her revenge and let go. She heaved herself over the side board of the corral fence, flipped a leg and straddled it, then jumped down while her brothers ducked between two boards. Estrella led the way to the bungalow. Their heads bobbed over the shimmering of tall grasses.

"Ay come on, Star," Ricky called after her. "Don't be mad."

"He's not my papa," Estrella said.

"So?" asked Arnulfo, trying to keep up with her.

"Sew your pants, they're torn," she snapped, and she ran, her hair bouncing like a black tassel. Her brothers followed suit, and the twins scrambled after. Perfecto walked behind them all, fanning himself with his hat.

A car wreck waiting to happen, Petra had said. Estrella's real father looked up at her as he pulled out the old shoelaces. The freeway interchange right above their apartment looped like knots of asphalt and cement and the cars swerved into unexpected steep turns with squeals of braking tires. Sunlight glistened off the bending steel guardrails of the ramps. Just you wait and see, Petra said in a puff of breath on the window glass, a car will flip over the edge.

His new laces were too long and so he cut them with his single-blade razor, the one he had brought with him all the way from Jerez, Zacatecas. He had pinched spit on the loose ends to rethread the laces carefully through the eyes of his shoe, then bent his chin to his knees as one foot vanished into a thick leathered shoe, then the other. His back curved like a sickle against the window and her garlic-scented fingers ran up and down the beads of his spine. He was a man with lashes thick as pine needles, a man who never whispered; his words clanked like loose empty cans in a bag and she had to hush him in the presence of the sleeping children. Her fingers purred on his backbone until he stood up and walked out.

The traffic swelled and cars lined up on the curving on-ramp of the freeway until the cars yanked loose like a broken necklace and the beads scattered across the asphalt rolling, rolling, and she waited, her breath gone until the rubber treads of the tires connected with the pavement again.

He had the nerve, damn him, the spine to do it. She was almost jealous. The stories of his whereabouts stacked up like the bills she kept in a shoe box. Was it really him with a business in Ensenada selling bags of peanuts and ceramics? Was it him crossing Whittier Boulevard in Los Angeles with a woman who wore pumps so high she was almost as tall as him? Could it be? Petra lied to Estrella because she shouldn't know her father evicted all of them from the vacancy of his heart and so she lied right to her daughter's face, right through the cage of her very teeth, and then she realized that truth was only a lesser degree of lies. Was it he who had the nerve to disappear as if his life belonged to no one but him?

She rolled the beads of the rosary between her fingers, made the sign of the cross, stopped his promises from flooding into her head and her mouth desperate, desperate for air. She was falling, toppling over a freeway bridge, her eyes shut to the swamp-colored trash bags squatting full of the family's belongings scattered about the room. Only noises hinted at another life: a neighbor dragged a trash can out to the curb (morning); a toilet flushed (someone is home from work); the twins crying (mealtime); cars screeching with murderous brakes, long piercing dial tone of horns (the first of the month speeding faster than any car); the siren ring of the phone stilling her heart like spears of a broken clock.

Estrella had carried the fussing twins in the hoop of her arms and sat them in front of an overturned zinc bucket and handed them wooden spoons. Petra could hear them right through the bathroom door. She had bitten the muscle of her thumb, tore flesh, then reeled herself back and ran cold water in the tub to vanish the blood drops like pomegranate seeds. The babies clanked the zinc bucket until the tin echos clamored and clinked like loud smashing car wrecks and Petra burst the door wide open. She clapped her hands against her ears and screamed Stop it, Stop it, Stop it! and the boys, terrified of her wailing, hid under the box spring bellyache down, until finally Estrella, with specks of green in her brown eyes, stood between her and the children, near the open cabinet where dead cockroaches brittled in the corner of the shelf and hollered You, *you* stop it, Mama! Stop this now!

Nothing in the cabinet except the thick smell of Raid and dead roaches and sprinkled salt on withered sunflower contact paper and the box of Quaker Oats oatmeal. Estrella grabbed the chubby-pink-cheeks Quaker man, the red and white and blue cylinder package, and shook it violently and its music was empty. The twins started to cry, and for a moment Estrella's eyes narrowed until Petra saw her headlock the Quaker man's paperboard head like a hollow drum and the twins sniffed their runny noses. One foot up, one foot down, her dress twirling like water loose in a drain, Estrella drummed the top of his low-crown hat, slapped the round puffy man's double chins, beat his wavy long hair the silky color of creamy hot oats, and the boys slid out from under the box spring. Estrella danced like a loca around the room around the bulging bags around Petra and in and out of the kitchenette and up and down the box spring, her loud hammering tom-tom beats the only noise in the room.

Petra broke, her mouth a cut jagged line. She bolted out of the apartment, pounded down the plaster stairs through the parking lot and out into the street and ran some more. She stalled on the boulevard intersection divide and waited for the cars to stop, waited for him, for anyone, to guide her across the wide pavement; but the beads rolled on, fast howling shrieks of sharp silver pins just inches away from her.

Petra inspected her hands, remembering how their bodies were once like two fingers crisscrossing for good luck. Blood was crusting on the dots of her self-inflicted bite. The endless swift wind slapped against her face. The twins so hungry and her feet too heavy, too heavy to lift. Echos of voices, shouts of anger, threats of some kind she could barely hear over the blasting horns. Then, she remembered her father who worked carrying sixty pounds of cement, the way he flung the sacks over his hunching shoulders for their daily meal, the weight bending his back like a mangled nail; and then she remembered her eldest daughter Estrella trying to feed the children with noise, pounding her feet drumming her hand and dancing loca to no music at all, dancing loca with the full of empty Quaker man. One foot up, one foot down, Petra finally pulled herself across the lanes of the wide fierce boulevard and car brakes screeched and bumpers crushed, and headlights exploded like furious tempers. One foot up, one foot down no more dancing with the full of empty Quaker man.[…]

Not even a few drops of menstrual blood in his coffee would keep him from leaving. Estrella's father tore the last stick of gum in two, giving Petra one half. He unwrapped his piece and placed it in his mouth and chewed, tossing the tinsel wrapper onto the floor. Then he said he had to go and promised to return by the end of the week. But it was something Estrella said about his shoes with the new laces that made Petra realize he might not come back.

"Estrella, mi'ja," Petra had said, "Papi's leaving. Say good-bye for now."

"Mama, hide his shoes so he won't go," Estrella pleaded. And it was too late, too late because the door slammed shut and Petra cupped the cry in her mouth, damming the pure white anger from spilling onto her daughter.

So what is this?

When Estrella first came upon Perfecto's red tool chest like a suitcase near the door, she became very angry. So what is this about? She had opened the tool chest and all that jumbled steel inside the box, the iron bars and things with handles, the funny-shaped objects, seemed as confusing and foreign as the alphabet she could not decipher. The tool chest stood guard by the door and she slammed the lid closed on the secret. For days she was silent with rage. The mother believed her a victim of the evil eye.

Estrella hated when things were kept from her. The teachers in the schools did the same, never giving her the information she wanted. Estrella would ask over and over, So what is this, and point to the diagonal lines written in chalk on the blackboard with a dirty fingernail. The script A's had the curlicue of a pry bar, a hammerhead split like a V. The small i's resembled nails. So tell me. But some of the teachers were more concerned about the dirt under her fingernails. They inspected her head for lice, parting her long hair with ice cream sticks. They scrubbed her fingers with a toothbrush until they were so sore she couldn't hold a pencil properly. They said good luck to her when the pisca was over, reserving the desks in the back of the classroom for the next batch of migrant children. Estrella often wondered what happened to all the things they boxed away in tool chests and kept to themselves.

She remembered how one teacher, Mrs. Horn, who had the face of a crumpled Kleenex and a nose like a hook—she did not imagine this—asked how come her mama never gave her a bath. Until then, it had never occurred to Estrella that she was dirty, that the wet towel wiped on her resistant face each morning, the vigorous brushing and tight braids her mother neatly weaved were not enough for Mrs. Horn. And for the first time, Estrella realized words could become as excruciating as rusted nails piercing the heels of her bare feet.

The curves and tails of the tools made no sense and the shapes were as foreign and meaningless to her as chalky lines on the blackboard. But Perfecto Flores was a man who came with his tool chest and stayed, a man who had no record of his own birth except for the year 1917, which appeared to him in a dream. He had a history that was unspoken, memories that only surfaced in nightmares. No one remembered knowing him before his arrival, but everyone used his name to describe a job well done.

He opened up the tool chest, as if bartering for her voice, lifted a chisel and hammer; aquí, pegarle aquí, to take the hinge pins out of the hinge joints when you want to remove a door, start with the lowest hinge, tap the pin here, from the top, tap upwards. When there's too many layers of paint on the hinges, tap straight in with the screwdriver at the base, here, where the pins widen. If that doesn't work, because your manitas aren't strong yet, fasten the vise pliers, these, then twist the pliers with your hammer.

Perfecto Flores taught her the names that went with the tools: a claw hammer, he said with authority, miming its function; screwdrivers, see, holding up various heads and pointing to them; crescent wrenches; looped pliers like scissors for cutting chicken or barbed wire; old wood saw, new hacksaw, a sledgehammer, pry bar, chisel, axe—names that gave meaning to the tools. Tools to build, bury, tear down, rearrange, and repair, a box of reasons his hands took pride in. She lifted the pry bar in her hand, felt the coolness of iron and power of function, weighed the significance it awarded her, and soon she came to understand how essential it was to know these things. That was when she began to read.

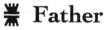 # Father

Leroy V. Quintana

1996

Leroy V. Quintana was raised by his Mexican grandparents, and much of his work reflects the folklore and Mexican culture he learned as a boy. His writing also shows the influence of his service in Vietnam, college studies in anthropology, brief work as an alcohol counselor, and a writing apprenticeship under the Native American author N. Scott Momaday. Quintana has been teaching film, creative writing, and composition at San Diego Mesa College since 1976. Quintana's poem "187" also appears in this collection.

There were always whispers about my mother.
The rest of the family knows
more about her failed marriage.
She sent her son to live with her parents.
Scandalous.
He still wonders about his father.
There are 500 years of me back home,
of blood.
However, I am here in California,
and my father is here in California,
yet we are only others' whispers
of each other.

❈ My Father Is a Simple Man

Luis Omar Salinas

1987

Luis Omar Salinas has been honored by the Library of
Congress and received a General Electric Foundation
Literary Award and a Stanley Kunitz Award from Columbia
University. He currently lives in Sanger, California. His
poem "Aztec Angel" also appears in this collection.

I walk to town with my father
to buy a newspaper. He walks slower
then I do so I must slow up.
The street is filled with children.
We argue about the price
of pomegranates, I convince
him it is the fruit of scholars.
He has taken me on this journey
and it's been lifelong.
He's sure I'll be healthy
so long as I eat more oranges,
and tells me the orange
has seeds and so is perpetual;
and we too will come back
like the orange trees.
I ask him what he thinks
about death and he says
he will gladly face it when
it comes but won't jump
out in front of a car.
I'd gladly give my life
for this man with a sixth
grade education, whose kindness

and patience are true...
The truth of it is, he's the scholar,
and when the bitter-hard reality
comes at me like a punishing
evil stranger, I can always
remember that here was a man
who was a worker and provider,
who learned the simple facts
in life and lived by them,
who held no pretense.
And when he leaves without
benefit of fanfare or applause
I shall have learned what little
there is about greatness.

The Fights

Gary Soto

1992

Gary Soto is one of the most recognized names in Latino
literature. His many awards include a 1975 Discovery-
Nation Prize, a 1975 Academy of American Poets Award, a
1985 American Book Award, a 1999 PEN Center West
Award, and a United States Award from the International
Poetry Forum. He currently lives in Berkeley. His poem "A
Red Palm" is also included in this anthology.

WHENEVER ANY AUNT OR UNCLE BROUGHT OUT A BROWNIE CAMERA, my
brother and I began fighting. We grunted and wrestled, the hot snot of
anger shining our upper lips. We growled, teeth bared, and karate chopped
with one eye on the camera. When we fell, our bony elbows ripped holes
into their lawns, and worms squirmed to get out of the way. We breathed
hard and cussed when a button came loose. We smiled at our relatives
fumbling for coins in their pockets. We thought people liked to watch
fights, and even better, liked snapshots of front-yard fights.

I visited my Aunt Jesse on a Saturday and sat on her long flowery
couch, which was sealed in a clear plastic, and looked through her album
of ancient snapshots also sealed in plastic. I drank from a ceramic coffee
cup, laughed, and spilled four ugly drops of chocolate on the couch. I
moved over and let my jeans absorb the drops.

My aunt, chicken-print dish towel in hand, pulled a chair up next
to me, careful not to rake the legs across her shag carpet. She wiped the
couch and sat down. We pressed our heads together and looked at the
photo album. In one black-and-white snapshot, I'm on the ground,
balled up like a potato bug. In another, Rick's face is slurred from a right
cross, and in the next Rick has me in a headlock but both of us are smiling into the camera. In still another, only my legs are showing, and the

shadow of my sister with a pinwheel. The pinwheel, I remember, was later ripped from her hand when she hung it outside the car window. I liked the snapshot of Brother and me baring our new, grown-up teeth to the tops of the gums. Our fists are held high and Rick's cowlick is standing up like a feather. And there was one in which Rick has me pinned to the ground while blood wiggled from his nose to his cheek. I remember that well. He was mad because an elbow caught him in the face, and he had to go to our cousin's wedding with a bloody shirt.

"You kids were really something," my aunt said. She picked up my cup from the end table and wiped the ring of water. When she offered me a cookie, I smiled but refused because a grain or two of crumbled cookie might fall on her rug.

In the same photo album there were nice snapshots of beaches and new cars and houses. Grandfather is standing in front of his avocado tree. Grandmother is pinching aphids from a rose bush. Mexico is a still-water fountain splashing forever in the dusty light of Mexico. My aunt pointed to a distant uncle with a *guitarrón* in his arm, and tapped a long red fingernail on the face of the Raisin queen of a 1940s parade. "This is a friend of mine," she said, and then said, "she didn't last long like that," meaning her flat tummy and pointed breasts, meaning her hair piled up and the flashy beauty of straight teeth. She followed my aunt to the cannery and a dull marriage of stewing diapers on the stove.

When I turned the page, we returned once again to brotherly snapshots, this time in color. Rick and I are leaping high from a playground swing, our arms crossed and our faces stern as mad genies. In a creased snapshot, we are flinging down a handful of popcorn to a gray sea of pigeons. Sister's shadow is flat on the ground, minus her pinwheel, and there's the start of another shadow which may well be our mother's.

I bit into one of my aunt's cookies. Three crumbs fell on the rug and immediately she dropped to one arthritic knee. I turned the page of the album. There were photographs of my cousin's wedding in San Jose. No one looks happy or young, except Rick and me. We had discovered the laundry chute and two wet mops that we used as lances as we ran down the hall. We had discovered that we could eat and drink as much as we pleased.

My brother and I loved fighting at family get-togethers. We were lucky not to lose teeth. We didn't bruise easily or break arms when we fell. Neither of us liked the sparks of pain, but neither of us could quite stop windmilling our tiny arms at each other. It was too much fun.

Now at Christmas, we stand next to each other talking about money made and money lost. We open expensive presents and make funny faces into the Polaroid camera when we've drunk too much. Rick likes to bare his teeth, and I like to lower my head slightly so that my eyes roll up like a doll's peering through its frontal lobe. My sister's shadow falls on the wall. I look and catch her licking sweets from one long, red fingernail. She likes to eat, and likes to bring in money. I wonder if she remembers her pinwheel and the time when she stomped a black shoe in a little dance. Back when our uncles stood around fumbling for coins in their pockets. When the days were black-and-white, and Brownie cameras sucked in a part of our lives through round, smudged lenses.

Permissions

Oscar Zeta Acosta. From *The Revolt of the Cockroach People* by Oscar Zeta Acosta, copyright © 1989 by Oscar Zeta Acosta. Used by permission of Alfred A. Knopf, a division of Random House, Inc.

Leonard Adame. "My Grandmother Would Rock Quietly and Hum" and "December's Air" by Leonard Adame. Copyright © 1975 by Leonard Adame. Reprinted by permission of the author.

Francisco X. Alarcón. "I Used To Be Much Much Darker" and "Letter to America" from *Body in Flames* by Francisco X. Alarcón, trans. by Francisco Aragón. Copyright © 1990 by Francisco X. Alarcón. Reprinted by permission of the author. "Guerra Florida" by Francisco X. Alarcón from *Best New Chicano Literature 1989,* ed. Julian Palley. Copyright © 1989 by Francisco X. Alarcón. Used by permission of Bilingual Press/Editorial Bilingüe, Arizona State University, Tempe, AZ. "XIX" and "III" from *Sonnets to Madness and Other Misfortunes* by Francisco X. Alarcón, with a selection of translations by Francisco Aragón. Copyright © 2001 by Francisco X. Alarcón. Reprinted by permission of the author.

Fernando Alegría. Excerpt from *My Horse Gonzalez* by Fernando Alegría, translated by Carlos Lozano. Copyright © 1964. (New York: Las Americas Pub. Co.)

Isabel Allende. Pages 213–227 & 229 from *Paula* by Isabel Allende and trans. by Margaret Sayers Peden. Copyright © 1994 by Isabel Allende. Translation copyright © 1995 by HarperCollins Publishers. For additional rights/territory contact Agencia Literaria Carmen Balcells, Diagonal 580, 08021 Barcelona, Spain. Pages 337–343 from *Daughter of Fortune* by Isabel Allende. Copyright ©1999 by Isabel Allende. Reprinted by permission of HarperCollins Publishers Inc.

alurista. Reprinted with permission of The Regents of the University of California from "we've played cowboys" from *Floricanto en Aztlán* Creative Series, no. 1 (1971), UCLA Chicano Studies Research Center. Not for further reproduction.

Octavio Paz. From *The Labyrinth of Solitude* by Octavio Paz, translated by Lysander Kemp. Copyright © 1962 by Grove Press, Inc. Used by permission of Grove/Atlantic, Inc.

Vicente Pérez Rosales. Excerpt from *Diario de un viaje a California* by Vicente Pérez Rosales from *We Were 49ers!*, trans. and ed. by Edwin A. Beilharz and Carlos U. López. Copyright © 1976 by Ward Ritchie Press.

Mary Helen Ponce. Excerpt from *Hoyt Street* by Mary Helen Ponce. Copyright © 1993 by Mary Helen Ponce. Reprinted with permission of the University of New Mexico Press.

Nellie Quinn, with Anthony Quinn. Excerpt from *The Original Sin* by Anthony Quinn. Copyright © 1972 by Anthony Quinn. Published by Little, Brown.

Naomi Quiñonez. "No Shelter" by Naomi Quiñonez from *In Other Words: Literature by Latinas of the United States,* ed. Roberta Fernandez. Copyright © 1994 by Naomi Quiñonez. Reprinted by permission of the author.

Leroy V. Quintana. "187" from *The Great Whirl of Exile* by Leroy V. Quintana (Curbstone Press, 1999). "Father" from *My Hair Turning Gray Among Strangers* by Leroy V. Quintana. Copyright © 1996 by Bilingual Press/Editorial Bilingüe, Arizona State University, Tempe, AZ. Used by permission of the publisher.

John Rechy. *The Miraculous Day of Amalia Gomez,* by John Rechy. Copyright © 1991 by John Rechy. Reprinted by permission of George Borchardt, Inc.

Margarita Luna Robles. "It's About Class, Ese" by Margarita Luna Robles. Copyright © 1990 by Margarita Luna Robles. Reprinted by permission of the author.

Garcí Rodríguez Ordóñez de Montalvo. Excerpt from *Las sergas de Esplandián* by Garcí Rodríguez Ordóñez de Montalvo, trans. by Edward Everett Hale.

Luis J. Rodríguez. "The Twenty-Ninth" and "Watts Bleeds" from *The Concrete River* by Luis J. Rodríguez (Curbstone Press, 1991) reprinted with the permission of Curbstone Press. Distributed by Consortium.

Richard Rodriguez. From *Days of Obligation* by Richard Rodriguez, copyright © 1992 by Richard Rodriguez. Used by permission of Viking Penguin, a division of Penguin Putnam Inc.

Index of Authors

Rick Heide has a degree in Latin American studies from the University of California, Berkeley, and he attended the Institute of Latin American Studies in London. He has been a member of the San Francisco Bay Area publishing community since 1968, working twenty years as a typesetter, for clients including the North American Congress on Latin America, *Nicaraguan Perspectives,* and numerous small presses, magazines, and journals with a multicultural focus. He is currently a freelance typesetter, editor, and co-publisher.

Juan Velasco received a Ph.D. from the Universidad Complutense de Madrid, Spain, and a second Ph.D. from the University of California, Los Angeles. He is currently a professor in the English department at Santa Clara University, where his research and teaching fields include Latino literature, border studies, film, auto-biography, and creative writing. He has written many scholarly articles on ethnicity, race, and nationalism in Mexican American texts, and he published his first novel, *Enamorado*, in Spain in 2000.

Other California Legacy Books

ONE DAY ON BEETLE ROCK
By Sally Carrighar, foreword by David Rains Wallace,
illustrations by Carl Dennis Buell
Written with exquisite detail, Carrighar brings readers to an exhilarating consciousness of the skills, intelligence, and adaptations of Sierra wildlife.

DEATH VALLEY IN '49
By William Lewis Manly, edited by LeRoy and Jean Johnson,
introduction by Patricia Nelson Limerick
This California classic provides a rare and personal glimpse into westward migration and the struggle to survive the desert crossing.

ELDORADO: ADVENTURES IN THE PATH OF EMPIRE
By Bayard Taylor, introduction by James D. Houston, afterword by Roger Kahn
A quintessential recounting of the California gold rush, as seen through the eyes of a New York reporter.

FOOL'S PARADISE: A CAREY MCWILLIAMS READER
Foreword by Wilson Carey McWilliams, introduction by Gray Brechin
Examines some of historian/journalist Carey McWilliams's most incisive writing on California and Los Angeles.

NOVEMBER GRASS
By Judy Van der Veer, foreword by Ursula K. Le Guin
This novel transports readers to the coastal hills of San Diego County and brings clarity to questions of birth, death, and love.

LANDS OF PROMISE AND DESPAIR:
CHRONICLES OF EARLY CALIFORNIA, 1535–1846
Edited by Rose Marie Beebe and Robert M. Senkewicz
This groundbreaking collection presents an insider's view of Spanish and Mexican California from the writings of early explorers and residents.

THE SHIRLEY LETTERS:
FROM THE CALIFORNIA MINES, 1851–1852
By Louise Amelia Knapp Smith Clappe,
introduction by Marlene Smith-Baranzini
With the grandeur of the Sierra Nevada as background, this collection presents an engaging, humorous, and empathetic picture of the gold rush.

UNFINISHED MESSAGE: SELECTED WORKS OF TOSHIO MORI
Introduction by Lawson Fusao Inada
This collection features short stories, a never-before-published novella, and letters from a pioneer Japanese American author.

UNFOLDING BEAUTY: CELEBRATING CALIFORNIA'S LANDSCAPES
Edited by Terry Beers
The beauty of California is reflected in this collection of pieces by John Muir, John Steinbeck, Wallace Stegner, Jack Kerouac, Joan Didion, and sixty-four other writers.

If you would like to be added to the California Legacy mailing list, please send your name, address, phone number, and email address to:

California Legacy Project
English Department
Santa Clara University
Santa Clara, CA 95053

For more on California Legacy titles, events, or other information, please visit www.californialegacy.org.